VIOLENT FRATERNITY

Violent Fraternity

INDIAN POLITICAL THOUGHT
IN THE GLOBAL AGE

SHRUTI KAPILA

PRINCETON UNIVERSITY PRESS
PRINCETON & OXFORD

Requests for permission to reproduce material from this work should be sent to permissions@press.princeton.edu

Published by Princeton University Press
41 William Street, Princeton, New Jersey 08540
99 Banbury Road, Oxford OX2 6JX

press.princeton.edu

Library of Congress Control Number 2021940610
First paperback printing, 2024
Paper ISBN 978-0-691-22106-9
Cloth ISBN 978-0-691-19522-3
ISBN (e-book) 978-0-691-21575-4

British Library Cataloging-in-Publication Data is available

Editorial: Ben Tate and Josh Drake
Production Editorial: Jill Harris
Jacket/Cover Design: Jess Massabrook
Production: Danielle Amatucci
Publicity: Kate Hensley and Kathryn Stevens

This book has been composed in Arno

Printed in the United States of America

For my father, Ramesh Kapila

CONTENTS

VIOLENT FRATERNITY

Introduction

BURIED IN A FOOTNOTE in Sigmund Freud's masterful study of mass psychology is a fable that captures the central concern of this book. 'A family of hedgehogs', the fable goes, 'massed very close together one cold winter's day, hoping to use one another's warmth to protect themselves against the cold. However, they soon felt one another's prickles, which made them draw apart. When the need for warmth brought them closer together once again, this second evil was repeated, with the result that they were bounced back and forth between the two ills until they established a moderate degree of distance from one another in which they could best endure their condition.'[1]

The famous fable was deployed by Freud to illustrate the relationship between the work of preservation and unity, or love, and the drive to kill and destroy, or death drive, and their mutual potency for humanity. Freud's point was a simple one, even though it is hard fully to comprehend and accept: it is love objects alone that can incite hatred. Published in the wake of the First World War, and with Nazism looming ahead, Freud's study remains powerful and insightful. The ambivalent but ultimately reversible play between love and hatred, as Freud would elaborate, causes war but also offers the potential for peace. In the terms of the fable, it was only proximity that made it possible for the prickly creatures to shield themselves, yet the collision of their sharp points in close intimacy forced them apart. Freud was thus fixated by the play of opposing sentiments in forging human life as he founded psychoanalysis as a discipline devoted to the workings of the psyche and sentiments.

1. The fable was taken from Arthur Schopenhauer's *Parerga and Paralipoena*, Part 2, 'Gleichnisse und Parabeln' (Allegories and fables), quoted in Sigmund Freud, *Mass Psychology and Other Writings*, trans. J. A. Underwood (London: Penguin Books, 2014), 55–56.

India's founding fathers—and the figure of the father is consciously invoked here—were above all animated by the forging of life with others in a context that was shot through with an intimacy that incited hatred and violence. As the fable instructs, however, proximity and intimacy also carried the potential for peace and fellowship. Eschewing the psychological to focus upon the political, this book reconstructs and interprets the significance of intimacy and enmity in the thought of essential, even everlasting, figures and texts that laid the political foundations of modern India.

It is a historical conundrum, and a provocation, that while in 1857 the 'Mutiny'—the greatest anti-imperial rebellion of the nineteenth century—witnessed mass violence against the British, a mere ninety years later, Indian freedom was, by contrast, founded on a deadly fratricide that singularly spared the outgoing masters. A profound transformation of the twinned question of the violence and the enmity or antagonism that frame the political took place in the short but decisive opening decades of the twentieth century. That transformation in the understanding of political violence, this book contends, was crucial. The intimacy of enmity and the making of a violent fraternity relate not only to this question, but significantly also to the nature of political foundations of modern India. As some of the most insightful and classic writings tell us, new orders are preceded by violence; that awareness informs the perspective here, as it rejects the interpretation of violence as simply being functional or causal in relation to historical change.[2]

By focusing on the political thought of well-known figures such as M. K. Gandhi, Muhammad Iqbal, B. R. Ambedkar and Vinayak Savarkar, the book converts these all-too-influential political actors into political thinkers. It furthermore brings into focus significant but now obscure figures such as B. G. Tilak, considered by none other than Lenin as the 'fountainhead of revolution in Asia', Har Dayal, the leader of a violent global insurrection against the British Empire, and Sardar Patel, India's original 'strongman' and first home minister, as the authors of a new and essential canon of political thought. It detaches these figures from their instantly recognisable, if debatable, partisan moorings. In doing so, it seeks to restore and explain the reflective and conceptual capacities that oriented and defined a new political horizon. Their

2. Hannah Arendt, *On Violence* (Orlando: Harcourt Publishing Co., 1970) is particularly insightful especially in discussion of revolutionary change and Karl Marx's work, 11–21; see too Étienne Balibar, *Violence and Civility: On the Limits of Political Philosophy*, trans. G. M. Goshgarian (New York: Columbia University Press, 2015).

presentation here as thinkers renders them somewhat unfamiliar figures, as it replaces the mechanistic role of 'self-interest' or even realpolitik, with the power of ideas as the ruling principle of political life.

The book addresses violence as the essential political question, and is bounded by the end of the first, if failed, 'mass moment' of modern Indian politics—namely, the *Swadeshi* or Home Rule movement of 1905–8 that was triggered by the proposed but soon aborted partition of Bengal—and by the independence and partition of India in 1947. The aim is not to apportion blame or adjudicate responsibility, nor is the approach here to accept violence as a means to gain a political end. Although the fact goes largely unnoticed, India's most influential political actors expended considerable reflective energy on this question of political violence, and not merely to decry it or deny its occurrence, albeit they also often did so.

As the book elaborates, the question of violence was posited in relation to life with others and the possibility of fraternity under sovereign conditions. This became an inescapable and even urgent issue in the context of the hectic anticolonial mobilisation and periodic imperial constitutional consultations that unfolded in this dramatic and decisive period. Taking the focus away from the history of events and movements that have been extensively covered and constantly reinterpreted elsewhere, the book centrally positions instead the *power of ideas* in instituting the political foundations of modern India.

It is often remarked, with equal measures of celebration and exasperation, that India is arguably the most political place in the world. As the first country to be decolonised from the British Empire since America, the joint history of its independence and the formation of Pakistan have been understood primarily in the received languages of nationalism and imperialism, in which political machinations of its leaders, the mobilisation of people and the intentions of outgoing rulers have held sway. India, and its historical transformations that produced both the world's largest democratic republic and the first avowedly Muslim nation-state in world history, can no longer be reduced to and understood in terms of a sum of social, economic and cultural approaches and processes.

The power of ideas, and their reconstruction here, enables us to address fundamental questions regarding the nature of the political and its domination in India, the remaking of modern political languages and the generative potential of place in relation to ideas considered in this book. India's struggle for freedom has by and large been received and understood in terms of the nonviolence that made Gandhi not only its global icon but crucially the antithesis of the muscular militarism of Hitler and Stalin that epitomised the catastrophic violence of the mid-twentieth century. Whether mythic or historical, this powerful narrative of nonviolent transformation has at the very least marked out India's transition to independence as exceptional.

Yet, as this book reconstructs their political ideas, all the major political actors presented here as 'ideological innovators' were in fact fixated by the fundamental political question of violence, not excluding the apostle of non-violence, Mahatma Gandhi.[3] 'Violence' is a capacious category that includes its visible and invisible forms, whether structural or embedded, symbolic or cultural, economic or epistemic, and so on. The focus of the book remains strictly in the political domain, as it takes a minimal, if exacting, view of violence. This is to say that sovereign power is understood here in relation to its ultimate import; that is, its association with the question of killing and dying, as opposed to 'freedom' in any simple sense.[4]

The book foregrounds the question of killing and dying as articulated and understood by modern India's canonical—even 'father'—figures. Although in itself a pointed one, the question of violence was implicated in the larger issues of the political subject, from the individual to the republican ideal of 'the people', of sacrifice, and of the Indian social as the historic source of sovereign power, all of which receive attention here. Violence and sovereignty were inextricable from the central question of life with others, or fraternity. Violence, fraternity and sovereignty thus made up an intimate, deadly and highly consequential triangle of concepts that produced what has been termed here 'the Indian Age'.

India, the book argues, is instructive and definitive of the twentieth century, as it remade modern political languages through an ideological revolution that defied fidelity to any given ideology, whether it be liberalism, Marxism or communism. Opening with the high moment of anti-imperial politics in the early years of the twentieth century and closing with the civil war of 1947 and

3. I take the term 'ideological innovators' from Quentin Skinner, *Visions of Politics*, vol. 1: *Regarding Method* (Cambridge: Cambridge University Press, 2002).

4. There is a robust and detailed literature on the sociology of violence or 'riots' and even subaltern political action of the late colonial period. Equally, more recent historical works are uncovering the British Empire as a deeply violent polity both in its brutality and also its ostensibly civil forms such as education institutions, railway infrastructure and public welfare endeavours. The role of the postcolonial Indian state in terms of violence, meanwhile, has now gained the attention of scholars, primarily anthropologists, generating a considerable number of studies and insights.

the establishment of the world's largest democratic republic, the book foregrounds the power of political ideas in directing historical transformation. 'The Indian Age' produced a highly consequential set of political ideas that have not only endured to the present but continue to provide critical insights into the global condition.

India's dizzying diversity of languages and of religions, and, above all, its scale offer a miniature of the global form itself. Most significantly, foundational questions of modern politics, namely sovereignty and republicanism, were there discovered, posited and deployed in a context of both imperialism and nationalism that compelled ideological innovators to discover the lineaments and potential of the political horizon in a situation rife with distinctions and conflict. Thus, the displacement of the West and a departure from its ideological and political vocabularies allowed for their remaking, to produce the world's largest and most diverse democaracy. The most profound and consequential transformation that was undertaken was in the concept of fraternity, or fellowship and life with distinct others.

The transformative and destructive potential of violence, the promise of peace and fellowship: these centre the entirely innovative and powerful interventions that this book historically contextualises within theoretical perspectives on the global political order. Focused on the formation of fraternity and its relationship to violence, new ideas of sovereignty and republicanism underlay the foundation of independent India and the world's first avowedly Muslim nation, Pakistan.

Indian political thought, especially as it emerged in and through its 'nationalist' canon of the twentieth century, was primarily the domain of political actors and practitioners, and they were all—whether a B. R. Ambedkar or a Jawaharlal Nehru—preoccupied with, to invoke Karl Marx's famous dictum, changing the world, rather than only interpreting it. Yet the book not only 'denationalises' these figures, as it decolonises political thought and places the Indian Age in the global field of interlocution on fundamental questions of violence, sovereignty and fraternity. It also casts the all-too-familiar reception of these figures in a radically new light in relation to the fully ackowledged political thinkers of the twentieth century ranging from Carl Schmitt, through to Hannah Arendt, and Alain Badiou.

Rather than being an 'exception', political thought of the Indian Age instead marked a defining departure from the West, as it radically reconstituted the place and potential of violence. The central norm of modern politics as experienced and theorised from the West is that of the 'state'. Whether it is in the work of the foundational thinker of modern sovereignty, Thomas Hobbes, who wrote in the era of civil wars in seventeenth-century England, or of the founder of sociology in the twentieth century, Max Weber, the state has come to be seen as violence's natural and rightful home. The state became the legitimate holder of the monopoly on violence, as the vast and vibrant canon of modern politics and theory testifies. Above all, the state became the natural destination of modern politics. This has much to do with liberalism as a creed of individual rights and the architecture of power and division in the organs of government. It is, therefore, not surprising that liberalism, including in its imperial form, has animated recent scholarly works, making it the principal focus of political thought.[5]

The primacy of the political in India was initially forged through the rewriting, if not the rejection, of liberalism in the opening years of the twentieth century.[6] As they became icons of an ideological revolution, Gandhi and his ideological predecessor, Tilak, forged a new vocabulary that broke with liberal considerations as they critiqued and circumvented dominant ideas of contract and self-interest as the basis of political life. This consideration of the domain of the political was posited in relation to its ethical boundaries. Such a positioning of politics and ethics allowed for the circumvention of the 'state' and powerfully instituted an anti-statist political subject. In creating a subject-oriented horizon of the political, Tilak and Gandhi subtracted violence from the state and posited it as an individual capacity. The political, in short, was discovered at the limits and ends of the law. To be sure, 'the political' here refers to the consideration and the domain of power, conflict and antagonism, rather than to either the institutional management or representation of 'interests' commonly understood as 'politics', or even to the domain of deliberation and freedom associated with a wide range of traditions, from classical liberalism to the thought of Hannah Arendt.[7]

The notion of an anti-statist subject with a commitment to the precepts of 'sacrifice' nourished a wide range of the political thinking that is historically

5. Uday Singh Mehta, *Liberalism and Empire: A Study in Nineteenth-Century British Liberal Thought* (Chicago: University of Chicago Press, 1999), and Jennifer Pitts, *A Turn to Empire: The Rise of Imperial Liberalism in Britain and France* (Princeton, NJ: Princeton University Press, 2005).

6. But see notably C. A. Bayly, *Recovering Liberties: Indian Thought in the Age of Liberalism and Empire* (Cambridge: Cambridge University Press, 2011).

7. Chantal Mouffe, *On the Political (Thinking in Action)* (Abingdon: Routledge, 2005).

reconstructed and analysed here. From Tilak to Gandhi and the *Ghadar* (global insurgency) that became integrated with Pan-Islamism during the First World War, and beyond into the founding of Hindutva by its ideologue Vinayak Savarkar, anti-statism remained potent. Eschewing any recuperative temptations to fold the Ghadar into anarchism, communism or nationalism, this book instead deepens the history of the new, anti-statist political subject as militant, mobile, partisan and taking the planet as its horizon. In doing so, this anti-statist political subject promoted globally a new and powerful vocabulary of sovereignty that was premised on secrecy, death, sacrifice and martyrdom. Predicated on the visibility of spectacular violence as communication, it not only caused a breach in normative languages of sovereign power and order, notably those of empire and nation, but created a potent irregularity and interruption. Meanwhile, in direct contrast to its highly visible violent acts, secrecy was in fact the premise of the individualised but fraternal bonds of the global Ghadar. Hindutva then transformed secrecy and fraternity into an anonymous and institutionalised bond.

The twentieth century specifically positioned fraternity, as opposed to liberty or equality, as the 'real manifestation' of the political order.[8] Marked by an appraisal and even the overcoming of the past, the century posited combat, confrontation, war and scission regardless of scale—from the private to the planetary—as its subjective identity. Questions of violence, enmity, civil war and sacrifice, but equally the promise of peace and the ambitions of agonism or struggle, are reconstructed in this book through the political thought of significant but also obscured political actors who founded and instituted the political foundations of India, with enduring ramifications for both contemporary India and the global order.

In a foundational departure from Western political thinking, violence and enmity were understood for the Indian Age only as an aspect of intimacy.[9] Neither the fabricated foreigner nor the invented internal enemy was salient; instead, the foe or enemy was discovered to be the intimate brother and kinsman with a potential for destruction. The conversion of kinsmen into enemies became the central concern of the founding of the political and its potential for antagonism in an entrenched context of deep colonialism. Sovereignty was thus detached from its mooring in the state and deposited in the political subject, including in the latter's profound potential for violence.

8. Alain Badiou, *The Century*, trans. Alberto Toscano (Cambridge: Polity Press, 2007).
9. Shruti Kapila, 'A History of Violence', *Modern Intellectual History* 7:2 (2010), 437–57.

The year 1908 was a turning point and point of departure for Indian political thinking. The 'failure' of the mass anticolonial movement of the Swadeshi (Home Rule) era incited deep reflection. Three major and foundational texts were written within a few short years of this watershed point: Tilak's monumental commentary on the *Bhagavad Gita*, Gandhi's aphoristic *Hind Swaraj* and Savarkar's historical account of the Indian Mutiny and Rebellions of 1857, that in drawing out the above-mentioned themes reconsidered the nature of politics and its horizons. In reconstructing these texts, together with related texts such as Savarkar's political writings, and speeches and essays by Tilak, Gandhi and the global *ghadris* (insurgents), this book investigates the role of time or temporality in relation to political action. It further develops the work of intimacy and enmity in relation to a new historical outlook. History and its writing became the template to consider and convey political ideas. The book further recovers the salience of secrecy and secret societies and publicity for the creation of a new but violent fraternity that was amplified in Hindutva, and particularly in the highly influential historical writings of Savarkar. Crucially, Hindutva here is reconstructed as a theory and creed of violence, rather than as a history of identity.

In the now classic intervention by Ashis Nandy, India's relationship with the West, and particularly the Enlightenment, was uncovered as one of intimate enmity, with an estrangement that marked Indian selfhood.[10] This book, by contrast, posits the opening of the twentieth century as the time that saw a forceful and powerful positioning of a new subject-oriented horizon of the political, and at which enmity was delineated instead in relation to the proximate. Whether it was the commentaries on the *Bhagavad Gita* that became ascendant, or other related texts, the emphasis of politics, this book shows, was to think beyond and after imperialism. Yet the political was not conceived as a set of idealised interactions predicated upon some normative vision of national or international order; rather it was expressed in terms of the most disruptive violence.

Directed to a future beyond the colonial state, debates on subjective and fraternal horizons represent the coming into being of a world in which everything was possible. Precisely because hostility was understood to stem from identification and intimacy, its power was all the more significant, as it offered potential for its reversibility. Such an intimate enmity thus entailed the dual

---

10. Ashis Nandy, *The Intimate Enemy: Loss and Recovery of Self under Colonialism* (Oxford: Oxford University Press, 1983).

logics of murder and affinity, that led to wars, but was ultimately equally significant in the creation of fellowship. A violent fraternity was thus born at the
limits and ends of colonial covenants, that circumvented, if it did not destroy,
liberal ideas of contract, positing instead the ambivalence of intimacy and hostility centred on the anti-statist political subject. The first half of the book
elaborates on this in relation to Tilak, Gandhi, the global insurrection of the
Ghadar and the making of Hindutva.

The absence of a liberal contract and the making of this new form of fraternity as a basis of political life was, however, notably critiqued and successfully
revised by the Dalit leader B. R. Ambedkar, in steering discussions towards and
uncovering the violent basis of caste, and in unmasking what I have termed the
'dispersed monarchy of the Brahmin'. Taking the Brahmin as the historic basis
of sovereignty in India, Ambedkar's redirecting of fraternity was concerned
with the conversion of violent antagonism into nonviolent competition between adversaries. In a departure from prevalent receptions of Ambedkar that
have portrayed him as a caste leader and a theorist of liberal constitutionalism,
equality or justice, this book revises our understanding of him and places him
centrally as the arch-thinker of modern sovereignty. Ambedkar was not squeamish on the question of violence, nor did the theme of 'separation' cause him
anxiety. The book thus interprets his writings on the founding of Pakistan
within the same analytical frame as his writings on caste and his debates with
several contemporaries, notably Gandhi. Ambedkar's agonism and struggle
thus marked both the triumph of fraternity and the recognition of a new
nation—namely Pakistan.

Unlike all the nation-based historical accounts that have obscured the mutually constitutive worlds of divergent views and actors that made the Indian
Age, this book centrally reconstructs Muslim political thinking, rather than
treating it as discrete. It elaborates on the work of the twentieth century's arguably most influential Muslim thinker, namely Muhammad Iqbal, identifying
him as a thinker of republican sovereignty who eschewed the global and long-
distance thrust of political Islam for, instead, a proximate and sovereign fraternity. Republican Turkey as opposed to Arabia incited a new, and potent, political vocabulary of Muslim republicanism. Such potency was not simply
related to the individual subject for which Iqbal, as a philosopher, is primarily
known. Instead, Iqbal articulated a new political meaning and purpose for
modern Islam. Like his contemporaries of the Indian Age, he made the intimate and the fraternal the focus of exclusionary impulses. Crucially and tellingly, for Iqbal, such intimate hostilities turned towards his co-religionists.

The book concludes with the fratricide of 1947, approached as a 'civil war'. The work of intimate violence for the historical transformation of fraternity and the making of brothers into neighbours is centred in this account. The catastrophic violence is here interpreted as political. In creating an internal sovereign order with the demarcation of new borders, the event of violence occasioned the discovery of 'the people' as the basis of the new republic, displacing the political subject of fraternity in favour of the singularity of unitary popular sovereignty. Through a reconstruction of the speeches of Sardar Patel, the symbolic remaking of this violence as republican peace is here seen as pointing to the convertibility of violence into order for the start of a new history.[11] Patel's political ideas also refer to the transformation of fraternity into republican sovereignty, or a search for 'brotherhood' into the rule of 'the people'. This is in sharp contrast to dominant receptions that have approached 'partition violence' as 'memory portraits' located purely in the subjective terrain of the individual or family.

In revising 'partition violence' as civil war, the concern with fraternity, fellowship and life with others was transfigured into the domination of the language and pursuit of sovereignty. This transfiguration was founded in the violence of civil war. The language of brotherhood and fellowship, however fraught, was replaced with the discovery and the demarcation of 'the people' that found its repeated utterance in powerful pronouncements. The arrival of the people as the proper subject of the political in independent India was founded in violence. As the new but dominant political category, the people not only inaugurated and went on to become the basis of the Indian constitution soon after this civil war, but also, crucially, became the foundational principle of the new sovereign power of India.

The second half of this book, in short, addresses the enduring legacy of anti-statist political subjectivity that marked out a violent fraternity for the making of a republican sovereignty. As opposed to the French revolutionary discovery of republican ideals and popular will, there was no automatic replacement of a displaced monarch by 'the people'. In contrast to the French or the American republican revolutions, the immanent and intimate nature of violence, as uncovered in chapters here preceding discussion of this point, led instead to the integration of the 'social' as the basis of republican sovereignty. Further and in this context, the retention of 'sedition' laws in the Indian constitution, that have been resurrected and weaponised in our own times, point

11. Balibar, *Violence and Civility*.

to the legal suspicion of the political that independent India has enshrined in a bid to curtail the hostile powers of a violent fraternity.

The study of political thought has by and large confined itself to a highly particular canon of thinkers, primarily if not exclusively Western. Their work is zealously and finely attended to with regard to their intentions, the context of their writings, the range of their influences and the nature of the reception of their works. The modern canon of political ideas is dominated by the figure of the scholar-philosopher. By contrast, almost all the figures considered here were prime political actors. The notable exception is Iqbal; yet he too delved, if fitfully, into concrete politics. In transfiguring these figures' role into that of thinkers here, an eclectic set of sources, from letters and pamphlets to speeches, has undergone examination alongside the interpretation of books and texts that they wrote. The book is necessarily 'pointillistic', rather than being an exhaustive or comprehensive synthesis. In relation to the established canon of modern political thought, the book is neither comparative nor derivative. In integrating certain canonical and contemporary insights into the political, it places the Indian Age at the centre of a reworking of the political foundations of the twentieth century.

The focus on some of the most powerful figures of the last century is deliberate. The recent thrust of popular biographies of India's founding figures seeks to amplify or multiply the official canon of national heroes. The concern has been primarily to 'balance', to revise or to reposition the partisan matrix of this period. In particular, two figures from opposite ends of the ideological spectrum have come to the fore. On the one hand, Ambedkar and his foundational role have been receiving hitherto unprecedented attention, and he is increasingly positioned as the antithesis to Gandhi. Patel, on the other hand, has recently received much revisionist attention, not only from political parties but also from writers who increasingly argue for his foundational role to be seen as certainly equal to that of Nehru, if not overwhelming him, and others too.

The book is not especially focused on any one particular figure. Unlike most of those considered here, Gandhi's stature as a philosopher has become increasingly secure, thanks to the recent spate of excellent works that have revised and repositioned him as a thinker.[12] If his reputation as a philosopher has acquired near canonical status, however, his reputation and reception as an icon of justice is today certainly deeply contested. Gandhi's reception as a

---

12. Faisal Devji, *The Impossible Indian: Gandhi and the Temptations of Violence* (London: Hurst and Co., 2012); Ajay Skaria, *Unconditional Equality: Gandhi's Religion of Resistance* (Minneapolis: University of Minnesota Press, 2016).

philosopher is inversely related today to his reputation as a political actor.[13] Significantly, Ambedkar is meanwhile gaining attention, especially in his role as a thinker of mid-twentieth-century justice and law.

The profound, deep and foundational legacy of political thinking is widely and popularly apprehended in what can thus be termed 'father figurations'. The founding political actors of India remain figures of visceral identification. In contemporary India, it is hard to escape the partisan polemics, political rhetoric and dispositions that now fill opinion pages and are the stuff of popular best-seller accounts, and particularly biographies of political figures of this age. Far from being dead, or even dated, these father figures of the era termed here 'the Indian Age', whether it be Patel or Ambedkar, have returned (that is, if they ever left), haunting and animating a new political landscape. Their returning, re-made figurations serve as landmarks in tracing new lineaments of hostility and violence as they are redrawn in India's competitive democracy in unexpected ways. The political thought of the Indian Age can be presented here, therefore, as instructive in regard both to the last century and to the contemporary political order.

The Indian Age thus refers as shorthand to an orientation of thinking and a horizon of thought on the fundamental question of violence. To be sure, it does not rehearse the now worn-out but viscerally alive cliché of the 'idea of India' penned by Nehru. For Nehru, India's history was a testament to a new theory of nationality that could be based on her much-vaunted and celebrated diversity. India was more than a place: it was also a vision.[14] By contrast, Perry Anderson has sought to replace Nehru's pithily conveyed celebration with 'The Indian Ideology'—an equally pithy term that excoriates the 'idea of India' as supreme and self-serving nationalist myth-making. Essentially, Anderson's highly influential intervention resurrects the old chestnut of the malevolent intentions of India's political elites, coming alive yet again through the thickets of realpolitik.[15] Ideas, and especially nationalism—whether self-serving or magical myth-making—for Anderson only reflect and testify to the bad faith of India's political elites, and, above all, of Gandhi.

In circumventing the registers both of calculating realpolitik and of ready-made if internal histories of an 'ism' or ideology—notably nationalism, or even

13. Pankaj Mishra, 'Gandhi for the Post-Truth Age', *The New Yorker*, 22 October 2018.

14. Jawaharlal Nehru, *The Discovery of India* (New Delhi: Asia Publishing House, 1961 [1945]).

15. Perry Anderson, *The Indian Ideology* (Delhi: Three Essays Collective, 2012).

the state as the naturalised modern pre-eminent actor—this book is instead concerned with the paradigm of the political. It demonstrates the constitution of the political through the remaking of concepts over and above fidelity to any received ideology. This remaking of foundational concepts from the inside out can only be ignored at our peril.

India, indeed, conjures an idea, and is thus both a place and horizon of vision. The Indian Age here refers not to the civilisational grandeur envisioned by Nehru, but rather to the historical epoch of a new political thinking. Its ambitions were concerned with the creation of political norms that repeatedly returned to the essential question of violence. The Indian Age points to the historical, and to the importance of India as generative of political ideas that were instructive for the global twentieth century. As a historical time, orientation and field of thinking, this era was highly consequential for the political foundations of what was to become the world's largest democratic republic. In capturing the innovations of this era as it presents India as the generative site of political ideas, this book resists the temptation to offer a manifesto or an instruction manual for scholarship.[16] In a related way, it also resists the urge to referee the ongoing partisan rise and fall of fatherly reputations in current Indian political polemics.

Is India potentially the new Europe? To ask this is to ask whether the political ideas and innovations of the Indian Age do not contain a new, if unacknowledged, universal grammar. Although Europe, as a place but above all as a name conveying a set of norms, has remained the (contested) habitus for modern conceptual political vocabularies, is it not rather India that signals the political conditions of our own global age? Does the political thinking of the Indian Age offer insights, or even a historical precedent? This book is an open invitation and provocation to consider the possibility. The power of intimacy as a condition of enmity and the resurrection of sovereignty have become compelling in our new century. The book above all presents India as generative of political ideas—even if, or perhaps precisely because, this world-transforming era was made not by self-identified philosophers, but by some of the most influential of political actors.

---

16. But see Shruti Kapila, 'Global Intellectual History and the Indian Political', in Darrin McMahon and Samuel Moyn (eds.), *Rethinking Modern European Intellectual History* (New York: Oxford University Press, 2014), 253–74.

1

Political Theology of Sedition

The Extremists of to-day will be Moderates tomorrow, just as the Moderates of to-day were Extremists yesterday.

—B. G. TILAK[1]

ON 29 JANUARY 1919, at the High Court in London, a defamation case opened to a packed gallery.[2] Two formidable foes came to court for a decision on the true nature of politics in India. One was Balgangadhar Tilak, famed if feared. Though superseded by Mahatma Gandhi as the icon of Indian freedom, Tilak had been anointed as *Lokmanya* or the 'Will of the People' in India and declared by none other than Vladimir Lenin to be the revolutionary figurehead of Asia.[3] Tilak had sued Sir Valentine Chirol for defamation. Chirol was the former editor of the London *Times*, a public figure and a writer with friends in the imperial bureaucracy and the British establishment. At the time of the trial, Chirol was a 'diplomat without portfolio' and an emissary to the Paris Peace Conference convened at the end of the First World War.

Tilak came to London at the very end of his life, ostensibly to clear his name. As the presiding judge, Mr Justice Darling, reminded the court before the verdict, the law of libel regards the wrong that is committed in the

1. B. G. Tilak, 'Tenets of the New Party', speech at Calcutta, 2 January 1907, in B. G. Tilak, *Bal Gangadhar Tilak: His Writings and Speeches* [with] *Appreciation by Babu Aurobindo Ghose*, 3rd edn (Madras: Ganesh & Co., 1922), 55–67, at 55.

2. V. D. Divekar (ed.), *Lokmanya Tilak in England, 1918–19: Diary and Documents* (Pune: Tilak Samarak Trust, 1997).

3. V. I. Lenin, *The National Liberation Movement in the East*, trans. M. Levin (Moscow: Foreign Languages Publishing House, 1962), 14–15.

defamation of character; and 'the character of a person is something which, although it is incorporeal—you cannot see it or touch it—is a possession, and a person's character is that which he has created for himself during the time which he has lived'.[4] Mr Justice Darling could well have added that, much like character, ideas too are incorporeal and, as the trial itself had testified, moreover carried an enormous power to effect historical change. The trial was in effect a battle of political ideas, some of which had been authored by Tilak personally, and an assessment of their effects as these had been represented by Chirol's pen. It would be no exaggeration to say that what was above all at stake in the defamation suit was how to 'name' Indian politics.

Undoubtedly, Tilak was the author of a new form of politics in India. A couple of years prior to his arrival in London, he had spent six years in solitary confinement in a prison in Rangoon. Indicted and punished for sedition in a high-profile case in 1908, he had spent a part of his prison sentence writing a monumental commentary on the *Bhagavad Gita*. His commentary, as will be elaborated below, identified a new horizon of the political, premised on the circumvention and denial of the state as the bearer of sovereignty. In articulating the anti-statist subject as the basis of sovereign power, through a reinterpretation of the *Gita*, and especially with regard to killing and violence, Tilak profoundly rooted the notion of political enmity in the internal and intimate.[5]

Tilak's *Gita* was a conceptual articulation of the anti-statist subject that identified and delineated the political realm and action in relation to ethical questions of life and death, enmity and kinship, duty and sacrifice. Before his imprisonment in Rangoon, and prior to writing his most famous book, Tilak was already a public figure and had led a life punctuated by confrontations with the colonial state. These controversies included publicity-generating episodes of litigation and an insistent polemic conducted through two newspapers that he owned and edited: the *Mahratta* in English and the *Kesari* in Marathi. They encompassed a wide range of debates, whether as to the social question on the age of consent for women in India, the delimitation of law in relation to religion, or even the rights of princely rulers.[6]

---

4. Summing-up of libel trial, 21 February 1919, in Divekar (ed.), *Lokmanya*, 551.

5. Shruti Kapila, 'A History of Violence', *Modern Intellectual History* 7:2 (2010), 437–57.

6. Dhananjay Keer, *Lokmanya Tilak: Father of Our Freedom Struggle* (Bombay: S. B. Kangutkar, 1959), one of the earliest and most detailed biographies.

Often cast, including by Chirol, as a Hindu revivalist who introduced religion into the political domain, or as an extremist in contrast to his liberal and moderate contemporaries, Tilak nevertheless inaugurated the political in India in a very precise sense, elaborated in this chapter, initially surpassing, through popular mobilization, the polite politics of dissent of the Indian National Congress, of which he was also a member. From converting religious congregations and festivals into occasions for declaring political and nationalist agendas to organising mill workers in western India, Tilak had earned both his sobriquet as 'the Will of the People' and his status as revolutionary figurehead: even though his brand of revolution—despite Lenin's optimism—while radical indeed, was decidedly conservative.[7]

Tilak created what can be termed a new 'political theology'. What is meant here is not simply the public life of religion. More specifically, political theology refers to the fact that foundational concepts of modern political life are undergirded by theology.[8] In Western historical experience, theology, though potently associated even with political modernity, has more often than not been obscured behind modernity's proclaimed universalisation, dominated by a particular form of rationalism commonly labelled 'secularism'.[9] However, as the controversial legal and political theorist Carl Schmitt famously stated, all modern political ideas, and ideas of the state in particular, are in effect 'secularized theological concepts'.[10] The work of theology and its persistence in politics is now being rigorously exposed, if not to radicalise political vocabularies then certainly to critique dominant and liberal accounts of religion, in approaches ranging from the French communist philosopher Alain Badiou's

7. Stanley Wolpert, *Tilak and Gokhale: Revolution and Reform in the Making of Modern India* (Berkeley: University of California Press, 1962), Richard I. Cashman, *The Myth of Lokmanya: Tilak and Mass Politics in Maharashtra* (Berkeley: University of California Press, 1975) and Jim Masselos, 'Social Segregation and Crowd Cohesion: Reflections around Some Preliminary Data from 19thCentury Bombay City', *Contributions to Indian Sociology* 13:2 (1979), 145–67 remain the most comprehensive studies on Tilak's forging of 'mass' politics and the segregation of Hindus and Muslims that it wrought.

8. Carl Schmitt, *Political Theology: Four Chapters on the Concept of Sovereignty*, trans. George Schwab (Cambridge, MA: MIT Press, 1986).

9. Hent de Vries and Lawrence E. Sullivan (eds.), *Political Theologies: Public Religions in a Post-Secular World* (New York: Fordham University Press, 2006) offers new perspectives; also see the magisterial study by Charles Taylor, *A Secular Age* (Cambridge, MA: Harvard University Press, 2007).

10. Schmitt, *Political Theology*, 36.

theorisation of revolution to the American critical liberal-legal theorist Paul Kahn's arguments on contemporary global warfare.[11]

By contrast, in the Indian context, religion is all too visible, especially in its relationship to a political domain that arguably lacks a proper veil. Religion is thus often depicted, in contemporary scholarship and commentary on India, as a difficulty either vitiating relations between communities and neighbours or comprising a set of uncontainable public practices that the supposedly transcendent authority of the state seeks in vain to manage or restrict to the private sphere. The failure of the postcolonial state to distance religion from the political, and the heightened visibility of religion in general, are both widely perceived as problems to be overcome, especially in the wake of the recent electoral successes of Hindu nationalism.[12] Secularism in India has been understood at best, by those who oppose Hindu nationalism, as stillborn; or at worst, as argued by Hindu nationalists, as a malevolent form of hypocrisy. More than secularism, as the discussion of Tilak below will clarify, it is political theology, or the mutual re-articulation of religion and modern political concepts, that, brooking no boundaries, has instead clothed religion with new political concepts. Such a political theology, it is argued here, realised new and potent forms of sovereign power that could not be contained within the law.

Political theology, as Schmitt noted, is fundamental to sovereignty. Tilak is not only iconic in terms of the debate on sedition in India—his 1908 sedition trial becoming a cause célèbre—but at a more foundational level, as discussed below, he redirected and broke the imperial hold upon and legal regulation of Indian politics. Equally, Tilak represents the initial, foundational and open interplay between a religion and a politics that the imperial state not only sought to separate, but whose separation it zealously policed.[13] Yet it was precisely because the realm of religion offered a relatively autonomous domain under colonial conditions that it became productive of a political theology that discovered sovereignty beyond the bars of its powerful statist cage. Tilak's

11. Paul W. Kahn, *Sacred Violence: Torture, Terror and Sovereignty* (Ann Arbor: University of Michigan Press, 2008); Alain Badiou, *Saint Paul: The Foundation of Universalism*, trans. Ray Brassier (Stanford, CA: Stanford University Press, 2003).

12. Rajeev Bhargava (ed.), *Secularism and Its Critics* (Delhi: Oxford University Press, 1998) and Ashis Nandy, 'An Anti-Secularist Manifesto', *India International Centre Quarterly* 22:1 (1995), 35–64; on Hindu nationalism and secularism, Swapan Dasgupta, *Awakening Bharat Mata: The Political Beliefs of the Indian Right* (New Delhi: Penguin Books, 2019).

13. Sandra B. Freitag, *Collective Action and Community: Public Arenas and the Emergence of Communalism in North India* (Berkeley: University of California Press, 1989).

political theology, in short, established a crucial gap between sovereign power and the legal order, with consequences that persist to this day.

Sedition is the negation or the breaching of sovereign power and order. Even as sovereignty remains a 'borderline' concept entailing both preservation and the disruption of order, it is most palpable in its exception that reveals state authority making visible the normally invisible sovereign power. Yet, as Schmitt alerts us, sovereign power is neither quantifiable nor easily absorbed entirely into institutions or even the legal order. Lying inside but crucially also above the law, its own rules of exception allow for the visibility of sovereign power.[14] Further, fundamental challenges to it render the otherwise opaque nature of sovereign power visible. As with Tilak's case, the question of violence is salient to sedition. Sedition is the exemplary legal instrument and a point of ascription that pushes antagonism into an intense legibility defining not only the stakes of sovereignty, but also the limits of law. Sedition is thus essentially related to sovereignty.

The initial problem the colonial law of sedition in 1908 had to address in the face of a new anti-statist political theology of Tilak was how to name and label his political action and incendiary prose. In coming to London to clear his name a decade later through a libel suit against Chirol—even though he lost that trial too—Tilak aimed to curtail the endlessly expansive horizons of imperial sovereignty. The scholarship on imperial sovereignty has highlighted its 'lumpy' nature in its expansive hold over distinct territories that forced either its concentration or dilution, or negotiation with the people that it ruled over.[15] Equally, the uncovering of the role of cultural mores, especially of race and custom, has gained attention insofar as it helps to explain the longevity of British imperial rule and its legal instruments.[16] While cognisant of this robust and insightful scholarship, however, the emphasis here is not on the creation or preservation of British imperial authority.

In focusing on Tilak's iconic confrontation with sedition, it is argued here instead that the law—and by extension the state—became the legible limit and visible point of departure for the inauguration of a new and potent measure of the political. Striking against the fundamental idea of the state as the

14. Schmitt, *Political Theology*, 5–24.

15. Lauren Benton, *A Search for Sovereignty: Law and Geography in European Empires* (Cambridge: Cambridge University Press, 2010).

16. Anthony Anghie, *Imperialism, Sovereignty and the Making of International Law* (Cambridge: Cambridge University Press, 2007).

monopolist of violence, Tilak's rendition of the political decoupled law from violence. In related writings that brought Tilak to the zealous attention of imperial courts, violence was increasingly posited as a human and individual capacity that not only challenged imperial rule but also, significantly, created a new political subject. Such an anti-statist political subject was not defined by mere negation of the state or law. Rather, discovered and endowed with the capacity to kill and die, and with sacrifice and duty as its ethical precepts, the individual subject, crucially, became the repository of sovereignty. The anti-statist subject was fundamental and consequential for the Indian remaking of political enmity and fraternity.

Defaming Sedition

Tilak had taken Chirol and his publisher Macmillan to court over Chirol's book *Indian Unrest*. Published in 1910, this was a best-selling account of the events of 1905–8 commonly known as the Swadeshi (Home Rule) movement in India and had previously appeared as a series of articles in *The Times*. As Sir Alfred Lyall, an old India hand, rightly put it in his preface to the book, 'In the first years of the present century came events which materially altered the attitude of Asiatic nations towards European predominance.'[17] Fifty years after the Indian Mutiny that had constituted the most violent and extensive uprising against the British Empire in the nineteenth century, widespread 'unrest' and violence had once more erupted in the subcontinent. The Swadeshi period of 1905–8 is often presented as the inaugural 'mass moment' of Indian nationalism.[18]

Yet the events of 1905–8 became a global conjuncture. While it was specifically the proposed partition of Bengal that had sparked the Swadeshi movement in India, from an imperial perspective like that of Chirol, it was part of an anxiety-provoking new pattern. The opening years of the twentieth century had witnessed protests, violent mobilisations, a 'dress-rehearsal' for an imminent revolution and a full-scale conventional war between Russia and Japan, not to mention the rise of the Young Turks in the Ottoman Empire—all

17. Valentine Chirol, *Indian Unrest* (London: Macmillan & Co., 1910), ix.

18. Sumit Sarkar, *The Swadeshi Movement in Bengal, 1903–1908* (New Delhi: People's Publishing House, 1973); Bipan Chandra, *The Rise and Growth of Economic Nationalism in India* (New Delhi: People's Publishing House, 1966).

pointing away from the power of the West.[19] In diverse locations, a new global geography sought to undo European expansionism, consisting as much in new ideologies, from Pan-Islamism to Bolshevism, as in the proliferation of violence in forms ranging from conventional warfare to anarchist assassinations and bombings.

Tilak's 1919 libel case in London was a replay of the words, acts and events that had instigated the charge of sedition against him in Bombay in 1908. It featured what was in essence a roll call of British political celebrities. It involved men, much like Tilak in India, who moved easily between the world of the law and that of politics and public life. At issue in the trials in both London and Bombay were the effects of words on events and the power of language to incite murderous acts. The words of Tilak, a man already convicted of sedition, were deemed to be dangerous and deserving of harsh punishment. Beyond this, however, it was the problem of naming and identifying the nature of Indian politics that vexed the trial judges both in London and in Bombay, and continued to impede any consensus between the warring parties. As it turned out, Tilak lost both cases. Thus, the libel case did not concern Tilak's reputation, so much as being a contest over the name and nature of the Indian politics that he had authored.

In turning to the law of libel and defamation, Tilak was not seeking to salvage his 'seditious' name. Rather, this move pointed to a radicalisation of origins, since the law of sedition in British law was genealogically and historically linked to the law of libel. The law of libel in early modern England had made the monarch immune from it, while the subsequent law of sedition and treason (an offshoot of libel law) became increasingly defined in terms of the sovereign and rebellion against the ruler. Both libel and sedition laws, however, shared the principle of 'the public peace' as the crucial criterion that brought regulation and surveillance of the written word within their purview. Historically, thus, the policing of words and ideas has been moored in laws and powers related to sovereignty, and in particular if those words opposed the figure of the monarch.[20] Significantly, Indian nationalist leaders approached the

---

19. Cemil Aydin, *The Politics of Anti-Westernism in Asia: Visions of World Order in Pan-Islamic and Pan-Asian Thought* (New York: Columbia University Press, 2007); C. A. Bayly, *Remaking the Modern World 1900–2015: Global Connections and Comparisons* (Hoboken, NJ: Wiley Blackwell, 2018), 12–29.

20. David Ibbetson, 'Edward Coke, Roman Law and the Law of Libel', and Martin Dzelzainis, 'Managing the Later Stuart Press 1662–1696', both in Lorna Hutson (ed.), *The Oxford*

British monarch as the 'enunciative supreme' or ultimate arbiter, in a bid to undermine both the colonial government and the universality of law; as nationalists, they sought to appeal to the monarch's 'personal conscience'.[21] In both his sedition and his libel trials, Tilak's defence was primarily addressed to the sovereign—the British monarch—in an attempt to circumvent and challenge British colonial policy and officials. The law of libel was intentionally deployed to invert the logic of sedition, blurring the line of personal injury between the sovereign and the subject.

To move to a different purview and jurisdiction—from sedition to defamation and from Bombay to London—was, if not to jeopardise, then at least to mark the limits of British and imperial sovereignty. Detached from British India, the operative spatial and territorial context of sedition was held in suspended animation, not least because Tilak could not be punished for the same crime twice. This was a recursive move on Tilak's part, and by reversing the historical sequence of law, that is, from sedition to defamation, the themes of sovereignty and territoriality became salient. Consequently, the trial in London centred primarily upon the global dimension and historical reconfiguration of the new Indian political imagination.[22] The problem for law was not merely the worldwide effects of the words of political leaders. More significantly, what proved intractable was the nature of a language laden with metaphors being deployed in making political arguments.

Chirol's *Indian Unrest* singled out Tilak as the author of anti-imperial action and noted the common colonial anxiety and difficulty in defining Indian politics given the 'vagueness that generally characterizes the pronouncements of Indian politicians'.[23] Swiftly scouring Indian vernacular press clippings, however, his book went on to identify an 'incendiary' prose of myths and allegories that amounted to religious 'revivalism' and was laden with political intent and meaning. Chirol, in other words, rehearsed the colonial problem of getting a 'fix' on Indian political discourse that was encountered not as opaque in nature, but as mired in a cognitive arena of signs and symbols that were only comprehensible to their target audience. Myths and metaphors from epics and

---

Handbook of English Law and Literature (Oxford: Oxford University Press, 2017), 487–506 and 530–45.

21. Mithi Mukherjee, *India in the Shadows of Empire: A Legal and Political History, 1774–1950* (Oxford: Oxford University Press, 2010), 123.

22. Divekar (ed.), *Lokmanaya*, 210–325.

23. Chirol, *Indian Unrest*, 8.

legends smuggled in political ideas that were disseminated through the press, popular images and orations. It was precisely this problem that the law of sedition in late colonial India tried to regulate and resolve.

Though it did not figure in the defamation suit, Chirol's *Indian Unrest* had noted the repeated circulation and performance of the Marathi play *Kichaka-Vadd*, or *The Killing of Kichak*, throughout western India and beyond. It also became one of the earliest Marathi films, produced in 1918. The play had been banned, and one of its later interpreters, Khadlikar, an associate of Tilak's Marathi newspaper *Kesari*, was prosecuted for sedition in the same year as Tilak (1908); but not before it had disseminated its message.

Deriving from the *Mahabharata*, the play *Kichak-Vadd* is extracted and reinterpreted from Book IV of the *Book of Virata*. This part of the epic relates to the final year of exile of the five Pandavas and their shared wife Draupadi who, having had their kingdom taken away, are exiled for thirteen years after losing a game of dice to their ambitious and envious cousins the Kauravas. The conditions of exile for the Pandavas stipulate their living in a forest for the first twelve years and a final but testing year incognito in a city distant from the imperial capital of Hastinapur. Disguised as court servants in this last year of exile, the five brothers along with Draupadi are in Viratnagar, the capital of the minor kingdom of Virata. Kichak, the commander-in-chief of the kingdom of Virata and an ally and friend of the eldest Kaurava, Duryodhana, encounters Draupadi at the court and is instantly enchanted by her beauty. In the hearing of the eldest Pandava, before the virtuous and truthful but now disguised husband Yudhishthira, Kichak asks for Draupadi to be sent to his harem. This poses a dilemma for Yudhishthira: either to suffer his wife's dishonour or to reveal his true identity and thus sacrifice the right to reclaim his empire from his cousins. It falls to the younger but mighty third Pandava, Bhima, to protect Draupadi. Bhima kills Kichak, posing as a statue of a god just at the moment when Kichak is set to rape Draupadi at a temple.

Chirol decoded the play as an allegory suffused with political meaning and explained its matrix:

These things are an allegory. Although his name is nowhere on the stage or mentioned in the printed play, everyone in the theatre knows that Kichaka is really intended to be Lord Curzon [Viceroy and the architect of the Bengal Partition that occasioned the Swadeshi movement], that Draupadi is India, and that Yudhishthira is the Moderate and Bhima the Extremist Party. . . . since the play first appeared in 1907 the whole Deccan has been

POLITICAL THEOLOGY OF SEDITION 23

blazoning forth the identity of the characters. Once they have been recognized, the inner meaning of the play becomes clear. A weak Government at home, represented by King Virata, has given the Viceroy a free hand. He has made use of it to insult and humiliate India. Of her two champions, the Moderates advocate gentle—that is, constitutional—measures. The Extremists, out of deference to the older party, agree, although satisfied of the ineffectiveness of this course. Waiting until this has been demonstrated, they adopt violent methods, and everything becomes easy. The oppresser is disposed of without difficulty. His followers—namely the Anglo-Indians are as it is prophesied in the play and as narrated in the *Mahabharata*, massacred with equal ease. And the Extremists boast that, having freed their country, they will be able to defend it against all invaders.[24]

Like quicksilver, plays such as *Kichak* could not be contained or regulated; indeed, their spread, as Christopher Pinney convincingly demonstrates, was the inevitable, and even productive, outcome of zealous colonial proscription and censorship.[25]

In explaining the proliferation of myths and metaphors through words or images in late colonial India, Pinney argues that 'iatrogenesis'—literally, the causation of disease by the intervention of the doctor—had found its perfect exemplar in colonial censorship. Colonial-official policy had designated the social and the religious as 'apolitical', but Pinney suggests that 'because of the practice of colonial censorship and proscription, an "authorized" religion increasingly became the vehicle for a fugitive politics'.[26] While the censor and the magistrate were eagle-eyed in suppressing political discourse, the realm of religion proved potent to articulate all that could not be said under what was officially deemed political. Thus, the triangulation of religion, censorship or sedition law and the political produced, in Pinney's term, a deadly 'cosmological politics'. In my view, this relationship between law and religion was constitutive of a political theology. A cosmological register of politics had existed

24. Ibid., 338–39.

25. Christopher Pinney, *Photos of the Gods: The Printed Image and Political Struggle in India* (London: Reaktion Books, 2004); and idem, 'Iatrogenic Religion and Politics', in Raminder Kaur and William Mazzeralla (eds.), *Censorship in South Asia: Cultural Regulation from Sedition to Seduction* (Bloomington: Indiana University Press, 2009).

26. Pinney, 'Iatrogenic Religion', 30; and on censorship, N. G. Barrier, *Banned: Controversial Literature and Political Control in British India, 1907–1947* (Columbia: University of Missouri Press, 1974).

since at least the late eighteenth century, and throughout the colonial period temples and mosques and other congregations had been the locus for the dissemination of 'subversive' messages in which the lay and the ecumenical orders together participated, alongside the expanding realm of the printed word.[27]

What was novel in the early twentieth century, however, was the emergence of a precise grammar of signs and meanings through religious epics, and particularly *The Mahabharata* with its countless parables and fables, that became a template for political rhetoric and ideas. Political theology, then, was the opposite of a fugitive politics. It created a normative vocabulary of politics whose allusions were rooted in specific figures, religious myths and metaphors that were all too recognisable: it was only from the point of view of the law, that is to say, that this form of politics appeared as veiled, conspiratorial or metaphorical. It was entirely visible to its audience. Such a vocabulary as constituted a new political theology remained immune to the stricture that political ideas ought to be conducted and articulated in the standard language of law, rights and representation. Centrally focused on violence and action, Tilak's political theology, having become implicated with sedition, created a breach between law, religion and politics as it created a new political horizon premised on the individual subject.

The libel case in London rehearsed evidence from Tilak's sensational sedition trial in Bombay a decade earlier, affirming his culpability and reiterating faith in Chirol's colourful depiction of Indian politics as riven with secret intent and metaphorical messages. In mobilising the law in London, Tilak was perversely seeking ownership of the very ideas that named and categorised him as seditious.

Seductions of Sedition

In the summer evening of 24 June 1908, Tilak was arrested in Bombay. On the same evening, his house and newspaper offices in distant Pune were ransacked and locked by the imperial police.[28] The next day, Tilak was brought before the Bombay Magistrate, who summarily dismissed his application for bail, whereupon he was sent back to the local jail in Dongri and given a week to

27. C. A. Bayly, *Empire and Information: Intelligence Gathering and Social Communication in India* (Cambridge: Cambridge University Press, 1996), 180–211.

28. N. C. Kelkar, *Trial of Tilak* (New Delhi: Publications Division, Ministry of Information and Broadcasting, Government of India, 1986 [1908]), 17.

prepare for trial. Thus began arguably the most famous sedition trial in Indian history.

This was not the first time that Tilak had been arrested for sedition. A decade earlier, in 1897, he had been charged with the same offence for a speech that he had given at a celebration of the eighteenth-century Maratha ruler Shivaji. Entitled and reported as 'Shivaji's Utterances' and smattered with mythic allusions and metaphors while extolling the virtues of the *Gita*, Tilak's speech outlined an ethics of just rule and violence, in the course of which he furthermore invoked the killing of a Muslim general by the Hindu Shivaji. Within a week of the address, the two Chapekar brothers assassinated a senior British official, Walter Charles Rand, and his military escort Lt Ayerst, in Pune. Rand was the chief prosecutor of the Plague Commission set up to quell the epidemic that had engulfed western India in the symbolically significant diamond jubilee year of the Queen Victoria's coronation. The commission and its policies were not only widely criticised for a brutal pursuit of control, but also occasioned open protest and defiance, not least by Tilak, who by then was already a leading public figure of the region and beyond.[29]

The law of sedition was part of the colonial legal apparatus codifying rules of political engagement between ruler and ruled and was included in the draft penal code penned in 1835 by Thomas Macaulay. Invested with greater clarity of meaning by James Fitzjames Stephen in 1870, 'sedition' as defined under section 124A of the Indian Penal Code (IPC) was introduced to manage publicity and press, to counteract the spread of Wahabism specifically and anti-imperial propaganda more generally.[30] The initial legislative import of the notion of sedition in colonial India was closely identified with the idea of 'disaffection', which remained vague but unchanged till the closing years of the nineteenth century. In the initial version of the colonial law, 'disaffection' was primarily interpreted by the imperial power in relation to the maintenance of public order between communities and its regulation by the colonial state.

29. Rajnarayan Chandavarkar, *Imperial Power and Popular Politics: Class, Resistance and the State in India, 1880–1950* (Cambridge: Cambridge University Press, 1998), 234–65, and Ian Catanach, 'Plague and the Tensions of Empire: India, 1896–1918', in David Arnold (ed.), *Imperial Medicine and Indigenous Societies* (Manchester: Manchester University Press, 1995), 149–71.

30. G. K. Roy, *Law Relating to Press and Sedition* (Simla, 1915); Walter Russell Donogh, *A Treatise on the Law of Sedition and Cognate Offences in British India, Penal and Preventive, with an Excerpt of the Acts in Force Relating to the Press, the Stage, and Public Meetings* (Calcutta: Thacker and Spink, 1911).

Crucially, a seditious act was not necessarily equated with an act of disloyalty. It is striking that for the relatively long period of twenty years between 1870 and 1890, no individual or group was prosecuted for sedition; whereas, against the backdrop of polemics in the press and rising protest, the closing decade of the nineteenth century by contrast witnessed a surge in sedition trials.[31] It was Tilak's confrontational cases in 1897 and 1908, however, that forced a 'rearmament' of the law of sedition.

Tilak was convicted in 1897 for his speech on Shivaji, as his words were deemed to be seditious in that they had incited 'disaffection'; but the trial failed to establish a direct relationship between the assassination of Rand and Tilak's speech and writings. It thus occasioned the further clarification and amplification of the law, as it had revealed 'disaffection' to be a vulnerable and vague category when it came to the identification of sedition.[32] 'Disaffection', in short, was silent on the question of 'enmity' against the sovereign. The then prevailing law of sedition was relatively relaxed regarding criticism of the government, and the related legal term 'disapprobation' was also not necessarily equated with sedition.[33] The court, having failed to establish a direct relationship between Tilak's speech—critical though it may have been of colonial policies and government—and the murder of British officials by the Chapekar brothers, convicted Tilak of sedition, but he was sentenced to a short, albeit rigorous, prison term of eighteen months. His trial had revealed the urgent need for the law to create and define a boundary between criticism of the government and enmity against the sovereign.

In the revision of the law, the sovereign was deemed to not care for 'affection', such that sedition could no longer be defined as 'disaffection' alone. In rearming the law, the more appropriate dimension to the subject's relationship with the sovereign was clarified, and was specified instead in terms of 'loyalty'. The law of sedition was amended and amplified with 'disaffection' specifically understood as 'disloyalty and all feelings of enmity'. The 1898 Act thus augmented and amplified the meaning of sedition. It retained the original idea of 'disaffection', and of incitement to 'hatred or contempt' via 'words, either spoken or written, or by signs, or by visible representation' as punishable. What was striking was that 'disaffection' was for the first time explicitly classified as 'disloyalty' towards the sovereign.[34]

31. Donogh, *Treatise*, 10–40.

32. Ibid., 50.

33. Ibid., 40–45.

34. Roy, *Law*, 104; Barrier, *Banned*, 3–66.

In explaining the amended law, James Strachey singled out Tilak's 1897 trial that had set him free after eighteen months, and stated unequivocally that it was 'loyalty, not affection' that is 'looked for'. Sedition was now categorically defined as an 'offence against the State'.[35] In his defence, in 1897, and even under the rearmed law of 1908, Tilak had excoriated the colonial government while remaining silent, if not pliant, towards the British monarch, who was the ultimate if distant sovereign. The amended law in 1898 further clarified that 'Government' was the 'abstract conception of British rule in India', and an attack on even its individual representatives with 'seditious intent' was categorised as an offence under Section 124A. The new law, in short, narrowed the distance between the monarch, or the ultimate bearer of sovereign power, and even its most lowly administrator, creating equivalence between government, its officials and administrators and the British queen or king, with the stated aim of preservation of the public peace.[36] Tilak, by his words and confrontations, disrupted precisely this abstract if pervasive sovereign power with the concrete specificity of individual action and violence. While the individuated work of violence repeatedly formed his defence in trials, it was meanwhile given a potent philosophical and ethical meaning in his commentary on the *Gita*.

While Tilak's utterances on Shivaji in 1897 were deemed seditious but worthy only of a short prison sentence, thereby requiring that the law of sedition be newly spelt out explicitly in terms of disloyalty to the sovereign, his prosecution in 1908 exposed this rearmed law as incapable of combating effectively a new form of political thought and action. In his confrontation with sedition in 1908, Tilak re-drew the political horizon, making the law its outer boundary. This new horizon of the political became impervious to the policing logic of imperial law.

Words, Weapons and World History

Clerk of the Crown: On the charges [of sedition] do you plead guilty or not guilty?

—TILAK: I CLAIM TO BE TRIED.[37]

With his newspaper offices in Pune raided, Tilak in Bombay was charged and imprisoned on charges of sedition under Section 124A, and of incitement of hostility under Section 153A, of the IPC, for the publication of articles in

---

35. Donogh, *Treatise*, 70–73.
36. Ibid., 83.
37. Kelkar, *Trial*, 51.

June 1908. The clutch of seditious articles originally published in Marathi in his newspaper *Kesari*, entitled in translation 'The Country's Misfortune', 'These Remedies Are Not Lasting' and 'The Secret of the Bomb', formed the main evidence for the prosecution. These were placed alongside a battery of other references to Tilak's career, writings and their dissemination in India and across the world.

In an echo of his 1897 trial, a failed assassination set the context for the charge of sedition. The year 1908 too had seen an attempt to kill a British official, in distant Bengal; it had missed its target, but Khudiram Bose's bomb instead had claimed the lives of two English women, with a direct impact upon Tilak's trial in Bombay. The 'Muzafarpore outrage', as it came to be known, transformed the eighteen-year-old Khudiram into the stuff of legend, as he was immediately hanged for the bombing and the deaths of the two women. Tilak's published articles commenting on this event, regarded as incriminating evidence of sedition, had been neither squeamish nor contrite, as he sought to uncover Khudiram Bose's motives and explain the meaning of political violence in stark terms.

Initially, Tilak appointed Muhammad Ali Jinnah, the future founder of Pakistan and at that time a very successful lawyer in Bombay courts, as his counsel. After the initial hearings, however, he decided to mount his own defence, and thus took direct ownership of his words and their effects. This is especially significant as regards the manner in which an Indian political theology, as rendered by Tilak, became intractable and irregular, especially in its relationship to the colonial state and law more generally. Tilak spoke for a marathon thirty-six hours, broken only by a short 'tiffin' break and the overnight adjournment of the court. Sedition became the matrix through which the anti-statist political subject, or partisan, initially came into view, while exposing the impossibility of legally regulating its politics.[38]

Tilak's political theology of violence was premised on three inter-related principles that vexed the law but could not be contained by it, even as that law was successful in punishing Tilak himself. Tilak's defence articulated, firstly, the power of the individual subject that derived from his ability not only to kill others through assassinations and bombings, but also significantly from being able to sacrifice his own life. Secondly, a sovereignty detached from legally sanctioned rules of living, killing and dying was posited: the

38. Carl Schmitt, *Theory of the Partisan: Intermediate Commentary on the Concept of the Political*, trans. G. L. Ulmen (New York: Telos Press, 2007), 35–36.

abstract power of sovereignty was redirected and deposited with the individual subject. Thirdly and finally, acts of violence committed by individuals in such a context were neither random nor a replication of acts committed in the wider world. While Tilak recognised the bomb as a weapon with global ramifications, its use in India coinciding with its visibility elsewhere, especially Russia, its role and purpose in India, he argued, was distinct. The simultaneity of bombings across the world, in short, should not be construed as implying similarity of political purpose or meaning. Such a distinction enabled Tilak to forge 'India' as a distinct political entity, rather than as a mere example of a global pattern.

In a series of articles by Tilak in 1908, the bomb and its users' agility were juxtaposed against the regular and systematic force of the state, ushering in a language of death and sacrifice in direct opposition to that of the organised killing of conventional wars between states. In one such essay in *Kesari* that encapsulated his ideas (becoming damning evidence in both his trial in Bombay and his libel suit in London), Tilak expounded the thesis that

> Death is ordained at the very time of birth. Birth is first seen; the veil over death subsequently begins to be removed. God Himself creates this Universe (and) God Himself is the Governor of the Universe; it was the Westerners' science itself that created new guns, new muskets and new ammunition; and it was the Westerners' science that created the bomb. . . . The duty of taking away pride of worldly life is assigned to death (and) therefore death makes care not to allow life to become impure. The military strength of no Government is destroyed by the bomb; the bomb has not the power of crippling (the power of) an army but the owing to the bomb the attention of Government is rivetted to (a) the disorder which prevails owing to the pride of military strength.[39]

The agency of death and sacrifice that for Tilak in his initial writings constituted the new political subject was framed around the techniques of the bomb. Though Tilak was writing in the specific context of the killing by explosives of two European women in Muzaffarpur, the use of the bomb nevertheless tied this event to contemporary events in Tsarist Russia, where anarchists and other revolutionary groups had shaken the country through assassinations and bomb-throwing. While the bomb connected the local to the global, Tilak's articles were focused on its explosive power. The bomb was

39. B. G. Tilak, 'The Secret of the Bomb' (translation from Marathi of 'Bambgolyaa chaa Kharaa Anth'), *Kesari*, 26 May 1908, in Kelkar, *Trial*, 351.

seductive, and Tilak infamously termed its powers a form of 'witchcraft' or 'charm', even calling it a 'secret amulet', as it was mobile, easy to assemble and, above all, hidden: but highly effective.[40] Pinney compares bomb technology with that of the printing press, attractive and, as Tilak argued, pregnant with 'democratic' possibilities. At the same time, the simplicity of this weapon, Pinney argues, relayed a 'mythic structure', effectively updating the iconic sword of Shivaji that had previously been central to Tilak's propaganda.[41]

Bomb-throwing created a level playing field, connecting the powerful and the oppressed through a 'common suffering'.[42] Tilak wrote that the bomb caused a sense of 'outrage' and offence to the 'aggrieved', or its victim, and equally to its cultic following of 'righteous revolutionaries'. The bomb made visible, like connective tissue, the hidden ties between the powerful who were its targets and the 'misguided' but desperately powerless who had been seduced by its secret charms. Previously, if the powerful had become 'irresponsible', the so-called 'revolutionary' had been rendered 'helpless'. The bomb had broken this impasse, as it allowed for the suffering of the powerful and of the dispossessed to be shared.[43] In seeking to dignify death, the bomb-thrower such as Khudiram Bose, according to Tilak, was stripped of any self-interest and could in no way be categorised as an 'ordinary criminal'. Writing in his English newspaper *The Mahratta*, Tilak stated that 'the touch of humanity is bound to be equally deep', placing Bose and the colonial official within the same horizon of human action made finite by death. Such a political actor as Bose, he argued, though 'misguided', had no 'gross constituent of character'. Lacking any deformity, such an agent betrayed no sign of 'private grudge' or 'mean spite', but demonstrated instead the 'futility of ordinary methods of political agitation'.[44] This was as true of Russia as it was of India; and thus, finally, the mobile logic of the bomb revealed the global dimension of the political order. Crucially, however India was not Russia.

The bomb exploded (literally) the global configuration of the organised political unity of empire and its hidden mechanisms of control and power. Furtive

40. B. G. Tilak, 'These Remedies Are Not Lasting' (translation from Marathi of 'Ha Upaay Tikau Naahint'), *Kesari*, 9 June 1908, in Kelkar, *Trial*, 319–24.

41. Pinney, *Photos*, 121.

42. B. G. Tilak, 'The Bomb Outrage and Its Lessons', *The Mahratta*, 10 May 1908.

43. This theme is developed in the next chapter, on international anti-imperial violence and the figure of the partisan.

44. Tilak, 'Bomb Outrage'.

in its operation and dramatically visible in its consequences, it disrupted the neat armed territories of the planet. An underlying connected geography of superficially distinct locales, hitherto contained and defined by their organised powers, was brought to the surface, as it were, through explosions; yet the forces acting within the component parts of this connected geography could not, according to Tilak, be subsumed under any single political label or invested with a unified meaning:

> There is a wide difference between the bombs in Europe desiring to destroy society and the bombs in Bengal as between the earth and heaven . . . The Bengalis are not anarchists, but they have brought into use the weapon of the anarchists; that is all. That the bombs came to a stop in Portugal, or, that the series of bombs in Russia did not lengthen will not be set down by anyone to the credit of the policy of repression. New desires and new ambitions have risen among the people and are gathering strength everyday.[45]

Historical and geopolitical analogies formed the polemical thrusts of Tilak's writings and were reiterated during his sedition trial and libel suit. In rehearsing these world connections and analogies, Tilak located and marked the place of India within an external and global-historical logic. By contrast, questions of political theology were primarily introverted. Imperial geography and the imperialists' hold on distant lands were among the central preoccupations of Chirol's book as he articulated a global pattern of imperial anxiety. In imperial perceptions, the comparison of India with Russia was radical, and part of a new and dangerous pattern. For Tilak, however, while the bomb was indeed common to anarchists or nihilists and the militant politics of young 'revolutionary' Indians, the comparison with Russia only highlighted the distinction of India. He was categorical in stating that the 'bombs in Europe were a product of the hatred for millionaires', as opposed to the 'patriotism' displayed by their use in India.

Tilak fixed India in contemporary and comparative world history through the common denominator of the bomb. 'Outrages' such as in Muzaffarpur only highlighted the depth of 'repression', and Tilak singled out the British Empire for de-politicising India for the first time through the total disarmament of its people.[46] In the long history of successive empires in India, Britain's dispensation as the 'tyranny' of 'tenants' was worse than even that of his hero

45. Ibid.
46. Kelkar, *Trial*, 321–22.

Shivaji's rival, and the last great Mughal, Aurangzeb. Individual acts of violence such as bomb-throwing and assassinations, Tilak opined, were a critical if desperate form of 'self-injury'. This form of self-injury denoted a deformity of the subject, and one that was caused by the tyranny of the sovereign. Such self-injury (*triage* in Marathi), Tilak conceded, carried the dual risk of also causing harm to the sovereign.[47] The bomb that tied the subject and sovereign in mutual destruction had in his view exploded belief in the permanence of the empire.[48]

In his lengthy defence, Tilak had recourse to linguistic arguments and cited the impossibility of translation of certain concepts. In the sedition trial in Bombay in 1908, he had taken it upon himself to authenticate words and meanings when legal categories were employed to decode metaphors and fix meaning and causality. Though Jinnah, who represented Tilak in the lower courts, was not familiar with Marathi, he too opened Tilak's defence on the basis that translations from the vernacular to English could not be valid evidence, since the very act of translation added new meaning.[49] Tilak pursued this line at the High Court in Bombay where he represented himself, arguing:

> We have to write upon current political topics; on political science, on political events, on historical events, and so on. The old Marathi language was not certainly capacious for the purpose. We have words, for instance, for "monarchy" but none for "democracy". The very idea of constitutional monarchy has to be expressed in a roundabout manner. We cannot find words for it either in Molesworth's or in Candy's Dictionary. As to the words "Killing, murder, and assassination", there is a word for 'murder' and for 'killing' but not one word for assassination. This is the peculiarity of the language. The western ideas are new ideas and every writer in Marathi has a very peculiar difficulty to perform. He has not only to express his ideas in popular language but to coin words.[50]

'Assassination' and its translation from the vernacular had proven to be the touchstone of the trial. Whether it was *rastravadh*, translated by the court as 'assassination', or *zulm*, rendered as 'tyranny', Tilak disputed each translation produced by colonial officials. Linguistic specifics were buttressed, however,

47. Ibid., 55.
48. Tilak, 'These Remedies'.
49. Kelkar, *Trial*, 40–4.
50. Ibid., 127.

by contextual claims. Tilak's central claim remained that it was impossible to demonstrate authorial intent.

A charge of sedition rested upon the notion of intent, and in this connection the court was steered through a litany of examples of words and their translations to demonstrate these as neither merely transparent nor necessarily expressive of any single or stable meaning.[51] It would be erroneous to infer that in deploying the issue of linguistic plurality and translation, Tilak was merely mobilising 'cultural difference' as a defence against the language of political mastery. Rather he aimed to occlude and obfuscate the meaning and freight of concepts and not just their linguistic register. In this vein, he sought to query the idea of assassination itself by arguing that 'mere killing is not murder and merely taking away a purse is not theft',[52] and dismissed any easy conclusion with regard to intent by asking whether, 'If I were to declare I want to be a millionaire, [will you] infer from it that I want immediately to commit a dacoity?'[53]

Tilak's argument, in short, was that it was impossible to fix any given intention to a concept, as context was supreme in the operation of ideas. The primary criterion of 'disaffection' in relation to sedition had to be put to the test, above all, he argued, in relation to the 'society to which that particular writing was addressed'.[54] Though he rarely used the category of popular sovereignty, he surmised that 'disaffection' was a political and not simply a legal category, that could only be demonstrated in relation to the wider milieu in which political ideas operated. Tilak in his trial thus sought to undermine the category 'sedition' that resided only in the content of words whose meanings the law might aim to fix, but could not monopolise.

As soon as Tilak was bundled off in secrecy to prison, the mill workers went on strike and Bombay erupted into violence, killing scores in the city despite the clamping down of martial law. Prosecuted and imprisoned in Rangoon, for what he said was the 'thankless task' of representing 'public opinion' on Khudiram Bose, Tilak's political theology had nevertheless escaped the logic of law. His popularity soared, such that he was soon declared to be 'Lokmanya' or the 'Will of the People'.[55] A new political language had, as Tilak concluded it would, indeed defined the new anticolonial atmosphere.

51. Ibid., 60–74.
52. Ibid., 84.
53. Ibid., 81.
54. Ibid., 81–82.
55. Ibid., 102.

The sedition trial, instructively, did not focus on the question of freedom or its expression. This was not only because India and its subjects were marked by unfreedom. Rather, and as Tilak recognised, both disloyalty and disaffection were part of the conceptual matrix of sovereign power. In both his writings and his legal defence, Tilak created an opening for a political subject that was defined at the limits of the law. Such a political subject—announced by Tilak through his writings on Khudiram Bose—either through self-injury or sacrifice broke the compact between law as the preservation of peace and order and law as the holder of norms. In these 'seditious' articles, Tilak was not aiming to create a legend, or even a martyr, out of an assassin. Instead he gave a glimpse of a new political subject that would breach the abstract nature of sovereign violence and its legal edifice. In becoming the iconic seditious subject, Tilak weaponised the disruptive potential of law. In related writings, he elaborated the potential of a political subject that produced a gap between law and violence, and abstract principles and concrete contexts. A new political subject was armed with ethical precepts for political action and was consequential for the framing of political enmity and fraternity. Tilak's confrontation with the formidable architecture of imperial law proved to be a defining departure; above all, sedition delineated law as the limit against which there emerged a new and powerful political subject.

Descent of the Divine and the Invisible Sovereign

We have the grand and eternal promise Shri Krishna has given in the Gita that whenever there is decay of Dharma, He comes down to restore it.

—TILAK, 1906[56]

Tilak's political theology was centred not on liberty, but on the pursuit of sovereignty and fraternity. He may have rightly earned his reputation as a 'Hindu revivalist', but the point for emphasis here is the manner in which he sought to dismantle the established liberal political language of rights, interests, contract and representation to erect a new political theology replete with duty and sacrifice as its principal precepts. Although Tilak's repeated invocation of the Maratha ruler Shivaji has been construed as a reification of a Hindu past that has certainly aided his reputation as a nativist-chauvinist, the

---

56. B. G. Tilak, 'The Bharata Dharma Mahamandala', speech at Benares, 3 January 1906, in Tilak, *Bal Gangadhar Tilak*, 35–41, at 37.

following discussion, in reconstructing his political ideas, highlights his new individual-focused theology of violence and sovereign power, one that also redirected the power and place of the king or sovereign.

Prior to his sedition trial, in a speech in the city of Benares, Tilak invoked the capacious (and notoriously difficult to define) concept of *dharma*.[57] Without delving into its myriad and metaphysical meanings, ranging from law to moral order to religion, Tilak spelt out his version clearly: 'The word Dharma', he stated, 'means a tie and comes from the root *dhri* to bear or hold. What is there to hold together? To connect the soul with God, and man with man. Dharma means our duties towards God and duty towards man.'[58]

Annexing *dharma* as an aspect of a tie and union, Tilak directed attention to the relational aspects of the concept: to fraternity and sovereignty. Both 'unity' and 'union' he stated to be absent in India. The invocation of Krishna, as extracted in the epigraph above from his Benares speech, was as much a call to a 'leader' as it was a foregrounding of the imperatives of ties. It was only in times of 'chaos' that a new order, Tilak surmised, could be forged, through a leader. While in this speech Tilak invoked the eighth-century Hindu scholar Shankaracharya, who he claimed had warded off the 'chaos of Buddhism', in another speech a few months later he extolled, yet again, the leadership of the eighteenth-century ruler Shivaji. The speech cryptically concluded that 'a future leader may be born in India and who knows, [he] may even be a Mahomedan.'[59] The question of leadership was directly related to Tilak's conception of the king and the challenges of producing and sustaining a sovereign order.

Tilak summarily dismissed the liberal language of contract as in the Queen's proclamation in India, in the aftermath of the rebellions in 1858, instituting a new relationship between the sovereign and her subjects. Indian liberals were mistaken, Tilak stated in a speech in 1907, in comparing the foundational document or the proclamation to 'the theory of social contract of Rousseau', or even in seeing it as a contract at all. 'For my part', he went on, 'I think the word "contract" cannot be made applicable to relations existing between unequals, and it is dangerous for us to be deluded into a belief that the Proclamation is anything like a contract.' While not disputing its 'solemn' intentions, Tilak clarified that

---

57. P. V. Kane, *History of the Dharmashastra*, vol. 1 (Poona: Bhandarkar Oriental Research Institute, 1930), 1; Bimal Krishna Matilal, *The Collected Essays of Bimal Krishna Matilal*, ed. Jonardon Ganeri, vol. 2: *Ethics and Epics* (Delhi: Oxford University Press, 2017), 37.

58. Tilak, 'Bharata Dharama', 13.

59. B. G. Tilak, 'Is Shivaji not a National Hero', in Tilak, *Bal Gangadhar Tilak*, 48–51, at 51.

the proclamation was 'primarily calculated to make peace'.[60] It thus amounted to a declaration of India's subject status, and complete depoliticisation, as the British monarch became the keeper of her order and peace.

Pursued in the immediate aftermath of the infamous split of the Congress Party of 1906 that had fissured it into its liberal or moderate and 'extremist' or non-liberal elements, Tilak's fundamental dispute with Indian liberals was not simply about methods of political action. Though predominantly understood as a division between advocates of constitutional and of violent methods, the defining fissure went deeper than any simple question of means in the pursuit of ends, or even regarding the primacy of the 'representation' that liberals took as their main political aspiration, as opposed to the notion of religion as the 'spirit' and 'soul' of India that the extremists led by Tilak held to.[61]

The fundamental difference, and the most significant for our purpose here, was between the language and pursuit of liberty, and that of sovereignty. For Tilak as for his liberal counterparts, detachment from empire remained the ultimate end. But for the former, the emphasis remained on violence—its application and effects—rather than upon how rights or interests, whether of the individual or of groups, may be secured and represented in institutions of government.[62] For this reason it was the figure of the sovereign, either through historic illustration or allusion, that animated Tilak's thoughts and pronouncements.

Recognising that the king or sovereign was part of the Godhead and derived his power from divinity, Tilak steered the discussion to the attributes of such a sovereign. The British sovereign, he stated, was marked by categorically distinctive features. In the first place, as a representative of the divine, the sovereign was deemed infallible. Since the king could 'do no wrong', loyalty had become the salient aspect of the subject's relationship to the sovereign. While this was undoubtedly significant in terms of the notion of sedition that he

60. B. G. Tilak, 'The Shivaji Festival', speech in Pune, 25 June 1907, in Anon, *Bal Gangadhar Tilak*, 60–61. On the Queen's proclamation and the grafting of colonial sovereignty, see Alastair McClure, 'Violence, Sovereignty and the Making of Colonial Criminal Law in India, 1857–1914' (unpublished doctoral dissertation, University of Cambridge, 2017).

61. For instance, Tilak's ally in Bengal, Bipin Chandra Pal, *The Soul of India: A Constructive Study of Indian Thoughts and Ideals* (Calcutta: Choudhury & Choudhury, 1911).

62. See Bayly, *Recovering Liberties*, 245–342, on the communitarian and group emphasis of a reconstituted Indian late liberalism; and on the shifting meaning of kingship in particular, see Milinda Banerjee, *The Mortal God: Imagining the Sovereign in Colonial India* (Cambridge: Cambridge University Press, 2017).

mocked in his speeches, a more fundamental attribute of the British sovereign that Tilak posited was that of being abstract, 'invisible' and above all 'alien'. The sovereign, though universal, was 'invisible'; and as such only became 'visible', or, more precisely, the sovereign order only acquired potency, through its representatives, deputies and administrators. Mediated by its representatives, such an order gained expression through a 'contract', whereby the 'interest' of the king's deputies and representatives acquired visibility as these became the executive force of the sovereign order.[63]

In critiquing the contractual arrangements of the sovereign order of interest and liberalism more generally, Tilak clarified that the Hindu king was neither infallible nor the ultimate holder of sovereign power. The divinity of the king in the Hindu order of things was only guaranteed by just rule. The unjust ruler lost his status, as he became a demon (*asura*). Indeed, Hindu divinity was transient, since when moral and political turpitude beset kings, they not only became demons, but their lines also died out. Such an order, making kings into godheads, but if they failed, turning these gods into demons, operated under the eternal supervision of a divine justice that weighed them in its scales.[64] Tilak cited by way of illustration the dying out of Shivaji's successors or the Peshwas: dynastic devolution of power without moral vigilance would also decay and die. Likewise, he extracted from epics accounts of the falls of several godheads to demonstrate the synonymity of the order of justice with the sovereign order. That it was so, Tilak contended, was obvious.

He also cited Shivaji, who, he claimed, was not concerned with scripture, but also 'surely did not know what Hobbes or Locke thought about the principles of political government much less Rousseau or the Encyclopeadists who were all anxious to replace the religious theory of kingship by the secular one of contract. He knew his Vedanta all right and knew how to put it to practical use'.[65] This invocation of Vedanta (the essence of the Hindu scriptures or four *Veda*s) was intended to stress the joint nature of subject, sovereign and the divine, rather than the exceptional powers of a heroic king.

Divinity, Tilak argued, was immanent to, present in and a part of every subject. He invoked the related precept of Vedanta and a resurgent monism that had re-inscribed the 'unity' of the human with the ultimate or the divine to negate the power of mediation and interest. Though Hindu kingship too

63. Tilak, 'Shivaji', 62–64.
64. Ibid., 60–63.
65. Ibid., 65.

marshalled intermediaries, he conceded, their role was limited to 'legislation' that was, moreover, sanctioned only by 'disinterestedness'. Without a doubt, such a rendition is open to critique, and as our chapter below on Ambedkar elaborates, the historic and sovereign order of caste was sustained, if not by interest alone, certainly too by violence.[66]

Tilak's understanding of sovereignty and political enmity had two related implications: firstly, that kingly orders were neither permanent nor necessarily always divine; and secondly, that divinity was part of both the subject and sovereign, as an immanent force. Crucially, it was only the sovereign or king who was vulnerable to loss of his divinity if he failed in his duty to justice. In one of his earlier 'seditious' articles, 'What is the Meaning of Raj [rule] and Rajya [realm]', Tilak had baldly stated that a raja or a king could only be considered a sovereign if he 'drives his car of sovereignty with true justice'.[67] This was neither a direct call for the end of British sovereign power nor indeed for anarchy. Tilak reminded his audience that order was essential to the conduct and flourishing of human life: illustrating from the *Mahabharata* once more, he made it plain that any idea of a country without order, king or 'supervising body' should be abandoned.[68]

Given that order was essential, Tilak recognised that sovereign authority was divided between its ultimate holder and its devolved and constituent elements, mediators and representatives. Such a division was articulated as one between the 'invisibility' and 'visibility' of sovereign power. The sovereign in its 'invisible' form could indeed command sentiment. Without openly dismissing the British imperial monarch, Tilak highlighted the invisible, abstract and alien nature of ultimate sovereign power in British India. By contrast, the subject shot through with immanent divinity was exhorted to recognise the potential of his own governance, or *Swaraj* (self-rule).[69] The centrality of the invisible monarch was thus replaced by that of the immanent subject of sovereign power. Such a characterisation of sovereign power as invisible and alien further suggested that it had little to no significance for any existential identity of the immanent subject of Swaraj. Distant, removed and invisible, the

66. Shruti Kapila, 'Ambedkar's Agonism: Sovereign Violence and Pakistan as Peace', *Comparative Studies in Study of South Asia, Africa and the Middle East* 39:1 (2019), 183–95.

67. Donogh, *Treatise*, 136.

68. B. G. Tilak, 'Home Rule Speech at Belgaum', 1 May 1916, in Tilak, *Bal Gangadhar Tilak*, 104–37, at 106–7.

69. Ibid., 104ff.

purposive logic of the subject was to recognise the potential of its own visible and immediate horizon of action.

It was not simply that the king's body was 'divided' between metaphysical and the representational roles (Tilak was deeply conversant with Western political ideas and their functioning).[70] A similar notion applied to kingship in India, as Vedanta too made a distinction between the manifest and the latent, characterising the distinction in terms of permanence (*brahma*) and change (*maya*), whilst the Western notion of kingship was vested in infallible or permanent divinity.[71] Crucially, Tilak mounted the argument that British sovereign power was so 'universal' and abstract as to make urgent the potential visibility of the divinity of the subject. Moreover, the sovereign's 'alien' nature, when it became visible, only took the form of repression. Tilak understood 'alien-ness' not as a function of race or religion, but as an outcome of 'interests'; and it was interest alone that had rendered the British crown foreign and distant. In contrast to the Mughals and the Peshwas, he clarified, who 'understood the duty to the nation', the British sovereign was in effect exceptional, in being neither loyal nor duty-bound—just radically alien.[72]

Devoid of ethical and moral precepts, the invisible sovereign power of the British rendered even antagonism, hostility and enmity meaningless in relation to it. As Tilak spelt it out, 'I want to have the key to my house and not merely one stranger turned out of it'.[73] Even in his sedition and defamation trials, Tilak remained steadfast in his 'loyalty' to the British crown, not because it was supreme or one that commanded sentiment, but rather because so distant and alien a sovereign evoked little to no existential hostility. It was instead colonial officials whom he excoriated, as these not only visibly

---

70. Ernst Kantorowicz, *The King's Two Bodies: A Study of Medieval Theology* (Princeton, NJ: Princeton University Press, 1957); Carl Schmitt, *Roman Catholicism and Political Form*, trans. G. L. Ulmen (Westport, CT: Greenwood Press, 1996); and, for insightful critiques, Jennifer Rust, 'Political Theologies of the *Corpus Mysticum*: Schmitt, Kantorowicz and de Lubac', in Graham Hammill and Julia Reinhard Lupton (eds.), *Political Theology and Early Modernity* (Chicago: University of Chicago Press, 2012), 102–23; Martin A. Ruehl, '"In This Time of No Emperors": The Politics of Ernst Kantorowicz's *Kaiser Friedrich der Zweite* Reconsidered', *Journal of the Warburg and Courtauld Institutes* 63 (2000), 187–242. All these have informed the above discussion.

71. Tilak, 'Speech at Belgaum', 107ff.

72. B. G. Tilak, 'Home Rule Speech at Ahmednagar', 31 May1916, in Tilak, *Bal Gangadhar Tilak*, 138–62, at 142–43.

73. Tilak, 'Tenets', 64.

represented repression or tyranny, but were singularly bereft of the morality and ethics upon which true sovereign power was founded. Displacing rights with duty and 'suffering' as the conditions 'of a revolution in the "theory" of Government', Tilak declared both the possibility and the necessity of such a revolution.[74]

The fate of the Swadeshi movement and seditious confrontations with the law made visible the limits of possibility and the inadequacy of existing technologies of the political, particularly the subject and its potential for action. The Swadeshi era marked a closure in the public lives of many of its leaders, whether Aurobindo Ghosh or Rabindranath Tagore. The movement's failure made the nature of the colonial state and its repressive capacities all too evident.[75]

As regards Tilak, far from being exiled from public life, the failure of the Swadeshi movement and his own imprisonment in Rangoon forced him to reconfigure the relations between agent and action. Swadeshi failure pointed to the limits of the idea of transformation as a dialectical outcome of preparation and confrontation, commonly associated with Hegelian approaches. In such historicist approaches, an event—revolutionary or liberationist—is primarily expressive of all that was understood as suppressed; confrontation is an outcome of antinomies that are interpreted as concluding a historical sequence. In the monumental commentary upon and translation of the *Bhagavad Gita* that Tilak undertook in solitary confinement in Rangoon, in the aftermath of the Swadeshi, he radically altered the focus on the event, to see it not as conclusive but instead as the radical opening of a new historical sequence.

Swadeshi politics, especially of the 'extremist' or Tilak's brand, had made anti-statism its main doctrinal plank. More recent rethinking, notably by Alain Badiou, has persuasively argued that the event, by definition, lies, or happens, beyond the boundaries of the state. This is because through law, policing and the army, the modern state categorically defines the limits of political ruptures. Furthermore, while claiming a monopoly on violence, it pushes violence to its own boundaries—quite literally, through the deployment of armies at its frontiers.[76]

74. Tilak, 'Shivaji', 64

75. Arjun Appadurai, 'Introduction', special issue on 'Failure', *Social Research* 83:3 (2016), xix–xxv.

76. Paul W. Kahn, *Putting Liberalism in Its Place* (Princeton, NJ: Princeton University Press, 2008).

It is striking that Tilak's commentary on the *Gita* treated the event as a rupture. His commentary, while engaging with nineteenth-century preoccupations, including that of historicism, ultimately constituted a break from such forms of thinking. Instead, the theme of the subject as contingent on the event became the focus of his project. His commentary on the *Gita* focused on the subject as the bearer of sovereign power and violence. As the subject was shot through with divinity, a theory of action could be mounted that turned to the immediate, and the intimate, the fraternal as opposed to the external, and forged anew the primacy of the political.

Detached Action

From among the sacrifices,
I am the sacrifice in the shape of a prayer.

—*BHAGAVAD GITA*[77]

At the centre of the epic *Mahabharata* is the *Bhagavad Gita*, or 'Song of the Lord', that remains one of the most influential, translated and commented upon philosophical texts.[78] Telling of the fratricidal war that ushered in the black age of our present, the *Bhagavad Gita* takes the form of a dialogue between its hero, Arjuna, and his divine charioteer, Krishna. Set just before the apocalyptic battle that will mark the passing of an age, this conversation occurs in the no-man's-land between opposing armies, where Arjuna has halted his chariot to wonder at the senselessness of a war that requires the killing of his relatives, friends and preceptors. Krishna's role in the dialogue that follows is to rouse Arjuna to action by preaching to him the doctrine of acting out of duty alone, without the desire for any particular result. It is the sacrifice of such desire, says the Lord, which can liberate not only warriors but also men and women of all classes from the chain of cause and effect, allowing action to escape its own consequences and thus remain inviolate. Tilak in his commentary expounded on the theme of sacrifice and detached action as foundational to the subject.

Categorically, Tilak claimed, renunciation was mistaken for, and overlapped with, freedom. Equally, detachment was upheld as a virtue and a matter

77. B. G. Tilak, *Gita Rahasya or Karma Yoga Sastra*, trans. Bhalachandra Sitaram Suthankar (Poona [Pune]: Vaibhav Press, 1935 [1915]), 407.

78. Shruti Kapila and Faisal Devji, 'The *Bhagavad Gita* and Modern Thought: Introduction', *Modern Intellectual History* 7:2 (2010), 269–73.

of disposition. Thus, the agent or subject seeking freedom, whether individually or collectively, was idealised because it stood apart from the worldly. Clarifying the overlapping categories, Tilak in his commentary on the *Gita* asserted that the fundamental problem in the Indian context was with the available understandings of the subject and of freedom itself. Tilak intervened within these existing concepts by specifying detachment not as an ideal disposition, but as one that was salient for action. This detached form of action, then, was neither endless nor everyday, but was to be summoned as sacrifice, and that above all was what marked out, as the *Gita* taught, the event as rupture from the everyday unfolding of time.[79]

Alain Badiou's interpretation in *The Century* strikingly captures the situation Tilak faced. According to Badiou, this fundamental delineation of the event as neither historical nor quotidian resonates with the twentieth century more generally, in that the century itself is seen to be in a confrontation with history. The twentieth century was, indeed, the Nietzschean century, in which the past had to be confronted and annihilated, for a new beginning. The radical commencement of the future by necessity had to be discontinuous from the inherited past. The subject in the twentieth century has been constituted through a confrontation between necessity and will, predicated on the event thus causing a rupture in the nature of historical time itself. This has been explained further in terms of the salience and significance of war for the century.[80] On this view, rather than providing a historical conclusion, the event is the opening up of new possibilities. It is this perspective on the event, and the radical nature of violence that was premised upon a non-historicist subject, that must be borne in mind in the discussion of Tilak's *Gita* which follows.

Following the rules of argumentation laid down in the Mimansa tradition, Tilak departed from other commentaries by focusing on the event. Making it explicit that all commentators had neglected the beginning (*upkrama*) and conclusion (*phala*) of the *Gita*, Tilak argued that this neglect had allowed for a multiplicity of interpretations and had therefore led to their 'cultic' and doctrinal effects and readings. Stringently and stridently, Tilak was opposed to all existing understandings of the *Gita* that posited knowledge (*gyan*) or devotion (*bhakti*) as ideal paths to self-realisation and freedom. As part of this conceptual clearing exercise, Tilak argued that knowledge and devotion were ultimately

79. Tilak, *Gita Rahasya*, 510–65.
80. Badiou, *Century*.

similar, in that both these rival and dominant schools involved a privileging of the idea of renunciation as the ultimate goal of self-realisation. Shankaracharya's method of knowledge and Ramanuja's devotional practices took the idea of desireless action (*nishkaam-karma*) as a technique towards freedom (*moksha*), rather than as an end in itself. To be sure, Tilak took issue with every given doctrinal interpretation of, and philosophical argument derived from, the *Gita*, from those of monists to those of qualified monists, dualists, Vedantists and Mimansa philosophers. At the outset, he accepted that there was a fundamental difficulty, given the multiplicity of interpretations; but he cautions that, nevertheless, 'the Gita is not such a pot of jugglery, that anyone can extract any meaning he likes out of it'.[81]

Existing commentaries had then focused on the notion of love for union with God as a form of detachment from material and conjugal attachment. Equally, the pursuit of knowledge (*gyan*) had focused on the rigours of discipline as a form of self-emancipation. This focus on the technologies of love and knowledge in the pursuit of ultimate freedom in the form of detachment from the material realm of the world had made 'desireless action' or *nishkaam-karma* a powerful but an unexplained moral injunction. In short, pursuing desireless action as an ethical end would amount to, as he put it, 'treating the owner [self] of the house as a guest'.[82] According to Tilak, then, the earnest pursuits of love/devotion and discipline/yoga, while worthwhile in themselves, left the central dilemma of the *Gita* unresolved.[83]

The dilemma that appeared in the context of the event, or beginning of war, was that of Arjuna on the battlefield: whether or not to kill one's kinsmen. It is striking that the entire commentary of a thousand-odd pages was focused on this event alone and the dilemma that it posed. By focusing on action, Tilak construed the self as neither natural nor historical, but requiring a decision to become a subject through action in an event. To put it in terms of the *Gita*, as Krishna exhorts Arjuna to war, he foretells the event and outcome of that war. The conundrum did not regard whether the war would take place, but rather whether Arjuna (the warrior) would remain Arjuna (the subject) if he did not go to war. In short, the subject Arjuna was made by the event itself. By making

81. Tilak, *Gita Rahasya*, 28.

82. Ibid., 37.

83. This position is in direct contrast to that analogously theorised by Foucault, which posits labour (*oekesis*) and love (*eros*) as techniques for the will-to-selfhood: Michel Foucault, *Hermeneutics of the Subject*, trans. Graham Burchell (New York: Picador, 2005).

the event central, Tilak's comprehensive commentary brought together the epistemological and metaphysical approaches in both Western and Indic traditions.[84]

Tilak's foundational aim and intervention amounted, in the end, to a critique of the ethical and its subordination to the political. He elaborated by marking out 'exceptions' that closed off the ethical and the everyday to permit the eruption of the event establishing new conditions. At the outset, Tilak accepted that all religious and ethical ideas were about the categorical imperative of *ahimsa*, or nonviolence. The *Mahabharata* epic that had placed the *Gita* in the context of war had nevertheless enshrined the doctrine of *ahimsa paramo dharma*—'nonviolence is the highest religion'—as much as the foundational Jewish and Christian commandment had privileged 'thou shalt not kill'. Nonviolence was further recognised as the condition of truth. In other words, truth and nonviolence were universal pillars of ethics and religion. Tilak, however, and significantly, detailed exceptions to this rule of truth, citing illustrations from both the *Mahabharata* and ordinary life that allowed for subtle distinctions between truth and falsehood.[85] Having conceded the virtue of truth, Tilak constantly reminds the reader that the central actor of the *Gita* is Arjuna, the warrior hero, rather than Yudhishthira, the ideal and truth-seeking king.

Intimate Enmity

Forgiveness in all cases or war-likeness in all cases is not the proper thing.

—TILAK[86]

Antagonism, hostility or enmity has in short defined the dimensions of the political in the twentieth century. In its most influential but controversial rendition by Carl Schmitt, the political has been identified as the distinction between friend and foe, with the possibility of the real and existential destruction of the enemy as its primary condition. For Schmitt, such an enmity is both spectral and permanent, but is above all related to the law. Tilak too took

---

84. German and British idealism, evolutionary theories, utilitarianism and principles of sovereignty, especially as rendered by Hobbes, were cited and integrated into an imposing synthesis in Tilak's commentary, which endorses only Nietzsche, however.

85. Kapila, 'History of Violence', 447–49.

86. Tilak, *Gita Rahasya*, 45.

antagonism and hostility as central to the identity of the political. But in contrast to Schmitt, for him the political was foundationally related to the ethical—as opposed to the legal—order. Enmity, as Tilak insisted via his commentary in the *Gita*, was neither spectral nor permanent; instead, it emanated from and was strictly limited to the question of fraternity or brotherhood.[87]

Although inherently natural, the fraternal was not pre-eminent because it was permanent. The crucial feature of the fraternal for Tilak was rather that it was the only relationship open to the real possibility of conversion and mutation into enmity. The *Gita* was instructive, in that it focused on this precise paradox of intimacy and enmity that the figure of the brother posed. For Tilak, then, the political referred strictly to the conversion of kinsmen into enemies and the existential destruction of the brother. Neither the 'stranger' nor the 'friend', the central categories that have informed writings on political ethics in the twentieth century, figure in his commentary. Moreover, enmity did not inhere in difference; rather, the brother acquired the dimension of enmity in the event of conflict between brothers. This was because relationships such as those with preceptors, parents and kinsmen marked the paradigm of ordinary circumstance—the ordinary, according to Tilak, was an ethical state (*dharma*). It was only the mutation of kinship on the eve of war that had the capacity to disrupt the ethical and the ordinary. For Tilak, the indeterminacy of the fraternal—natural yet not permanent—is what demands ethical clarity. But it was only in the state of exception or in the context of the extraordinary that these relations were strained to their very limits, open to mutation, and that the ethical was put to the test and potentially into jeopardy.

A comparison with Gandhi makes the radicalism of Tilak's conception plain. Gandhi's ideas are elaborated in Chapter 4 below, but a brief illustration here can clarify the distinction between the two thinkers regarding political violence and its fraternal ends. This is all the more significant as Gandhi too wrote his manifesto or *Hind Swaraj* in the immediate aftermath of the Swadeshi movement, as Tilak did his commentary on the *Gita*, and both were primarily concerned with the question of violence. For Gandhi, the arch-theorist and practitioner of sacrifice and nonviolence, these were tested to the extreme under conditions of violence.[88] Fraternity for him was not so much a relationship of virtue, whether of equality or love, but acquired salience through

87. Carl Schmitt, *The Concept of the Political*, trans. George Schwab (Chicago: University of Chicago Press, 1996).

88. Devji, *Impossible Indian*.

self-sacrifice. In a passage on cow protection in *Hind Swaraj* that antagonised both Hindus and Muslims, Gandhi writes,

> A man is just as useful as a cow, no matter whether he be a Mahomedan or a Hindu. Am I, then, to fight with or kill a Mahomedan in order to save a cow? In doing so I would become an enemy of the Mahomedan as well as of the cow. . . . If I were overfull of pity for the cow, I should sacrifice my life to save her, but not take my brother's.[89]

The point for emphasis here is that for Gandhi, sacrifice made fraternity possible, and is not open to exception; whereas for Tilak, the nature of the antagonist of the brother was not central; rather, sacrifice as detached action, or *karma*, was tested at the extremities of 'misfortune'.[90] Strikingly, in contrast to Gandhi's concrete naming of communities, Tilak elaborated his political ideas through metaphors. Regarding the fraternal, Gandhi refers candidly to Hindus, Muslims and the totemic cow, and this naming sharpens the distinction between Gandhi the ethical philosopher and Tilak the political philosopher. The question arises as to why Tilak chooses not to 'name' his politics or indeed identify Hindus, Muslims or others in his extensive elaboration of the *Gita*.[91] This was, after all, the stuff with which his ordinary political life was replete. It is his insistence on the event, however, that explains his preference for deploying metaphors rather than names in this context. If Tilak took the event as being a break from the historical and the everyday unfolding of time, and the event was indeed the central lesson of the *Gita*, does it not follow that this deliberate namelessness was simply fidelity to the exceptionality of the event? The event demanded and was dependent on judgement, or the ability to discriminate between everyday or ethical time and the exceptionality of its interruption. Even so, the killing of the brother or the fraternal, Tilak decreed via the *Gita*, should only be undertaken for the protection of life. Such killing or sacrifice was in consonance with the restoration of *dharma* (moral order). The intimate hostility of brotherhood alone conferred meaning upon the principle that life must be protected. Detached action and sacrifice and killing understood as duty could therefore only apply to the exceptional event. Such

89. M. K. Gandhi, *Hind Swaraj*, ed. Anthony J. Parel (Cambridge: Cambridge University Press, 2005 [1909]; hereafter *HS*), 54.

90. Tilak, *Gita Rahasya*, 65.

91. The not-naming by Tilak of actors, groups and even enemies is specific to the translation and his commentary on the *Gita*.

an event or opening of violent hostilities was neither permanent nor random, but entirely dependent on the principle of discrimination and judgement of time and sacrifice.

The Event as Exception

[A]s occasion arises, it becomes necessary to consider which of the two actions of 'remaining alive' or 'dying' is to be chosen. When this consideration arises, the word Karma (Action) can also be understood [as] Duty.

—TILAK[92]

Arjuna is the central character of the Gita, but Tilak devoted significant attention too to the negative example—not, as one would expect, the brother-to-be-killed, Duryodhana, but instead Prahlada. A virtuous figure in the epic tradition, Prahlada was also a follower of desireless action, who had conquered all spheres and had been involved in parricide. As in the story of Abraham, sacrifice of kin was central as proof of loyalty to the gods, as well as for the preservation of the kingdom. For Tilak, though, the example of Prahlada highlighted the central issue of judgement, or the ability to recognise the moment of sacrifice. Although Prahlada had been dutiful and had sacrificed kin, he had misrecognised the moment or the event of sacrifice. In a dream-state, Prahlada was asked to sacrifice his father, and (so the story goes) carried out in his wakeful state this sacrifice that had only been demanded in a dream. In the case of Prahlada, this parricide resulted in dejection and renunciation of the worldly. Abundant in virtue, but lacking in discrimination, Prahlada had only one option: that is, to renounce. Thus, for Tilak instructively, Prahlada's failure was a failure to judge the moment of sacrifice. This was important, as for Tilak the event of violence or war occasioned the suspension of ethical norms. Thus the ability to judge the nature of the time, as everyday or exceptional, demanding either restraint or sacrifice, was crucial. On the few occasions that Tilak mentions the anti-hero Duryodhana, it is to signify his abject failure to sacrifice his self-interest, which had then made war possible. Sacrifice and judgement were indeed central to Tilak's conceptual repertoire.

Singling out the key distinction between Western political theory and Indian thought—that desirelessness rather than happiness sustains the possibility of life in the collective—it follows that sacrifice rather than self-interest is

92. Tilak, *Gita Rahasya*, 75.

paramount. As Tilak argued, 'for protecting a family, one person may be abandoned; for protecting a town, a family may be abandoned, and for the protection of the Atman [soul], even the earth may be abandoned'.[93] Theorists in
the West, Tilak contended, had erroneously focused on happiness rather than
on duty as the principle of life (collective and individual). Their insights into
the political thus could refer only to the role of interest and reason, to the exclusion of will. While he did in fact recognise that sacrifice had been central
to Western political thought, the problem in his view was that the sacrifice was
conceptualised according to a calculus of interest, and, just as significantly, in
Western political thought sacrifice was premised on the notion of historical
time. Pursuing this argument, Tilak criticised Hobbes, arguing that for the
English philosopher sacrifice for the sake of another person's interest was
merely a 'long-sighted variety of selfishness'.[94]

Yet as he saw it, Indic traditions offered only the alternative of renunciation,
the creation of a subject prone to inaction, as the highest form of virtue. It was
this connection above all that he aimed to disrupt.[95] For example, killing in
anger would not constitute a just act of war, and would therefore automatically
preclude the possibility of an opening or event. Disassociating action from its
'fruits' or detached action (*nishkaam-karma*) therefore became the central
aspect of Tilak's project. In elaborating a new political subject, he ensured that
it would not be predicated on utilitarianism, vitalism or intentionalism.

The idealised subject was the warrior, or Arjuna, and was imbued with detached action, the capacity for violence and for killing. Neither a superman nor
a slave to violence, this subject was based in forms of action. To this end, Tilak
categorised action as sacrifice (*yagya*), as duty (*kartavya*) and as desirelessness
(*karma*).[96] Finally, Tilak expounded on the key attributes of the ideal (warrior)
subject who was identified by his ability to act without desire. This subject, in
Tilak's influential term *stithiprajna*, would be constituted via desireless action,
a type of action isolated from its own consequences and therefore immutable
through historical motion. A detached subject that is immutable thanks to its
immunity to attachment, or *stithiprajna*, thus comes to the fore in Tilak's commentary on the *Gita*. Yet the *stithiprajna* was not the celibate monk, but like

93. Ibid., 558.
94. Ibid., 113.
95. Ibid., 49–101.
96. Ibid., 70–85.

Arjuna the warrior was instead the householder who was surrounded by plea-
sures. Detachment for Tilak was strictly understood in terms of a break between
cause and effect or action and its fruits, but was nevertheless a form of engagement with the world. In short, debunking renunciation, which had long been
idealised in Indic traditions, Tilak instead sought to equip the subject for detached action, even killing.

In this context, judgement of time was crucial, as it identified the nature of
action in knowing what is do-able and what is not: being able to distinguish
the normal time of ethics from the moment of the exception. While the former
called for a submission to the prevalent ethics—the normative framework—of
everyday life, the latter entailed the suspension of these norms in the context
of macro-disruptive events, such as famine or war. If ethical times were times
of duty or *kartavya*, then exceptional events demanded sacrifice.

The ethical in everyday life consists in the perpetuation of life; during crises, such as famine, however, duty becomes the protection of the good life
(*bios* or valuable life), for the sake of which action that violates quotidian and
ethical principles is justified by its feasibility. Tilak's repeated example in this
context is the breaking of taboos and of the Brahmin eating rotting flesh during times of famine. He makes a related claim about the taking of life. We know
that for Gandhi the 'true warrior' befriends or domesticates death rather than
taking possession or control of the killing of the Other. For Tilak, however, the
stithiprajna (desireless subject) is exhorted, through the example of the ideal
warrior-subject Arjuna, to kill in order to restore the moral order; that is, in
order to protect the perpetuation of good life from the irruption of evil.

To be sure, the question remained of how to understand the exact nature of
evil. One answer that is suggested by Tilak is that nature itself is unnatural, inasmuch as it is sustained by killing. Evil, for Tilak, suffused the natural world,
and he expended considerable effort in summarising prevalent debates and
commentaries on natural law. For all that, Tilak was however advancing a different argument. Focused again on the theme of temporality, he contextualised
evil as being the spirit of the age. He identified the contemporary or modern era
as not only immoral but imperatively as an end-time (*kaliyuga*). This means
that nonviolence (*ahimsa*)—recognised as the highest form of religion—is
suspended. Does this imply that *kaliyuga* is the perpetual state of exception?
Tilak clarified that not all killing partakes of the realm of the political. Rather
he consistently located killing in its connection to the event, and especially to
war. War (*yudh*), as the exception within the exception of *kaliyuga* (that is, the

contemporary era), became the focus of attention.[97] This is precisely why Tilak's *Gita* was an exhortation to recognise and declare a state of exception.[98] His idealised warrior-subject, in that light, was equipped with the will to act on his judgement, which entailed, essentially, the lucidity to be able to identify one's brother as the enemy. In short, for Tilak, the quintessential political act involved the capacity to discriminate between the brother as kin to whom was owed ethical duty in normal times and the brother as the enemy whose sacrifice of death was demanded in exceptional times.

Tilak's proposed insight remained that the political was indeed the antithesis of the ethical, or that the political was to be found, at least, at the margins of the ethical.[99] If 'life is the life of life', killing and life were considered co-constitutive.[100] It followed that duty was an *act* of discrimination and protection of this principle, especially as 'discontent' created dynamism.[101] Harmlessness (*ahimsa*) was suborned to the 'necessity of discrimination of duty and non-duty'. And the reinterpretation of the *Gita* by Tilak triangulated violence, the subject and intimate enmity. A new political theology thus gave birth to the warrior as its ideal subject. Even prior to the writing of his commentary, Tilak had in a speech explicitly declared that 'political questions are all Kshatriya [warrior] questions'.[102]

Unlike Schmitt's idea of the enemy, Tilak's emphasis on the transformation of kinsman into enemy was a matter of judgement and existed only in and during the event. In light of this, Tilak's commentary on the end of the *Gita*, on the *shanti parva*, or festival of peace, discussed the salience of closure, when precisely those who had killed their kinsmen had to then perform the death duties of their elders, brothers and preceptors. The declaration of the end of the event was marked by the resumption of the ordinary course of *dharma*, the moral order, as enemies were reconverted back into kinsmen. The fratricide of

97. On the horizons of time as everyday in relation to the epochal and the event, see Shruti Kapila, 'The Time of Global Politics', in John Robertson (ed.), *Political Thought, Time and History* (Cambridge: Cambridge University Press, forthcoming).

98. See Tilak, *Gita Rahasya*, 66–69, for a pointed discussion on the do-able and the exceptional.

99. Alain Badiou, *Metapolitics*, trans. Jason Barker (London: Verso, 2011), and its insights are integrated here.

100. Tilak, *Gita Rahasya*, 41–49, quotation at 44.

101. Ibid., 147–48.

102. B. G. Tilak, 'Our Gain at the Congress', speech in Calcutta, 2 January 1907, in *Tilak's Speeches* published by Raghunath Bhagvat (Poona: Sharda Press, 1908), 19.

the *Mahabharata* had rendered even the virtuous morally tainted. Neither side was absolved nor atoned for, but both were re-inserted into the everyday time of ethical obligations.

The political, which dwells in the event, was therefore neither the culmination nor the expression of suppressed desires. Instead, since the event is by definition exogenous, no preparation was possible in facing it. Thus, for Tilak, the political was mainly about the opening up of the possibility of war. Tilak's *Gita* was crucially concerned with the awakening or recognition of the political, rather than with any naming of it as 'national', 'anti-imperial', 'free' or even 'Hindu'. The political, for Tilak, in ordinary, quotidian or normal times, was understood to be passive. For Tilak and his times, the everyday or the quotidian belonged to the British. The mundane world of employment, education, food, clothing—all that latterly came to be identified with colonialism—were in effect deeply British conditions in India.

Rejection, which had become the hallmark of Tilak's political actions, was not really a boycott of the state. Instead, it was a suspension, rejection and boycott of the quotidian. While the empire read his polemics as 'conspiratorial' and allegorical, his commentary on the *Gita* escaped censorship, becoming a best-seller and running to several reprintings, translations and even a pocket-book summary version within months of its publication.[103] This was not only, as argued above, due to the policing of politics as opposed to religion that had initially opened up the seditious arena of a new political theology. In his trial defence, Tilak had pointed out the difficulty of writing and its reception that defied an easy or causal relationship between the text and its reception. He wrote,

> What appears horrible today may appear quite different 10 years hence. It is a threefold question. The question of writing is one factor, the state of the society to which that particular writing was addressed at that particular point is the third factor. . . . it [involves] three unknown qualities.[104]

Tilak's *Gita* belonged, properly speaking, to the pursuit of philosophy that is widely acknowledged as essential to political life. Preoccupation with the ancient or the classical, in Tilak's case the epic, in relation to the present assumed the form of an esoterics. As a text, its range of meanings and consequences was

---

103. First published in Marathi in 1915, other vernacular editions in Hindi, Gujarati, Bengali, Telugu and Tamil soon followed. By 1925, the Hindi and Marathi editions were in their sixth print runs, in the tens of thousands.

104. Kelkar, *Trial*, 99.

expressed neither openly nor entirely clearly. Esotericism, as a form of conceal-ment, as Leo Strauss explained, gains force as a result of the gap between pre-vailing public opinion and philosophical truth.[105] Strauss alerted us to the persistence and power especially of an esotericism that is deployed under conditions of persecution, and this perspective is relevant to the present case. Tilak's *Gita* was written neither for the past nor for the present, but for a time in the future. This is to say, fratricide indeed became the condition of Indian freedom in 1947, but Tilak's *Gita* was neither a prophecy of that fratricide nor a call for it, or even a contributory cause. Instead, the philosophical effects of his commentary became visible as a direct consequence of partition violence. The final chapter of this book elaborates the historical nature of the Indian civil war that converted brothers into hostile neighbours and enemies.

As the author of the dominant slogan of the era, that endured—'Swaraj is my birth-right and I shall have it'—Tilak through polemics, propaganda and philosophy installed a new political subject. Anti-statist, it discovered and po-sitioned itself in the gap between violence and law, as Tilak's own seditious confrontations clarified. The British sovereign having been depleted by being rendered invisible, the Empire's potential for hostility was not merely exter-nalised, but evacuated. In the form of Arjuna, the new political subject idealised as a warrior was recognised and amplified as a holder of sovereign violence who pointed to the enmity as a form of fraternal intimacy. Tilak's political theology surpassed sedition, as it became potent, paradigmatic and even, for a brief mo-ment, global. The virtues of the bomb that Tilak extolled gained worldwide dimensions, and the salience of the battlefield as the political horizon of frater-nity, resurrected through his rendition of the *Bhagavad Gita*, became essential to the new and potent idea of Hindutva.

105. Leo Strauss, *Persecution and the Art of Writing* (Chicago: University of Chicago Press, 1988 [1952]); Michael L. Frazer, 'Esotericism Ancient and Modern: Strauss Contra Straussian-ism on the Art of Political-Philosophical Writing', *Political Theory* 34:1 (2006), 33–61.

2

Ghadar!

VIOLENCE AND THE POLITICAL
POTENTIAL OF THE PLANET

SOME TIME IN 1920, Vladimir Lenin met Pandurang Khankhoje in Moscow.[1] Lenin had admired, and even invested Asian revolutionary hopes in Khankhoje's mentor, the Maratha leader Balgangadhar Tilak. A mutual admiration for Tilak was not, however, the main reason for this encounter between the newly installed leader of a successful revolution in Russia and the middle-aged Khankhoje. For Khankhoje, the unrealised revolutionary aspirations of his past retained their potency. The meeting was thus fraught with possibilities. It had been engineered by a Bengali, also in middle age, named Chatto, who had also appeared in Moscow, via Berlin, at the end of the First World War.[2] The secret spirit behind the meeting, though absent, was a third man, from Punjab: Lala Har Dayal. Har Dayal was a public intellectual and leader of a global insurrection, or *Ghadar*, that had coalesced dramatically if equally ephemerally in the theatres of the Great War. At the time of this meeting, Har

1. Savitri Sawhney, *I Shall Never Ask for Pardon: A Memoir of Pandurang Khankhoje* (Delhi: Penguin Books, 2008), 217–19. Tilak had sponsored and eased the passage of several young Indian men who were involved in anti-imperial activities, including Khankhoje: B. G. Tilak, *Selected Documents of Lokmanya Tilak, 1880–1920*, ed. Ravindra Kumar, vol. 1 (New Delhi: Anmol Publications, 1992). The names of student radicals have been redacted from the record.

2. 'Chatto', as he was called, was short for Virendranath Chattopadhyaya, brother of the Indian nationalist leader Sarojini Naidu: Nirode K. Barooah, *Chatto: The Life and Times of an Indian Anti-Imperialist in Europe* (Delhi: Oxford University Press, 2004); and his record at 1947 including efforts to find details of his death, British Library, London, India Office Records (hereafter IOR/) L/PJ/7/12100, and an earlier account, IOR/L/PJ/12/280.

Dayal was in the safe and secluded political haven of Switzerland. This trinity of Indian men had been central to the Ghadar, which, involving several thousand others, was one of the largest armed movements against the British Empire.

Nearly twenty years after this meeting, on the eve of the Second World War, both Chatto and Har Dayal were dead. Chatto was shot on Stalin's orders in Leningrad (now St Petersburg) in 1937. Har Dayal, who had made a final journey to America, the erstwhile nodal headquarters of the Ghadar, was discovered dead in a hotel in Philadelphia in 1938.[3] Khankhoje meanwhile had escaped, with considerable difficulty, from the far-reaching holds of Communist Russia, imperial Britain, India and continental Europe.

During the tumultuous and destructive years of the Second World War, Khankhoje was leading a settled life, cultivating corn and fulfilling his familial duties to his Belgian émigré wife and children in Mexico. He was no ordinary farmer, but a celebrated agrarian experimentalist, appointed by the Mexican government to help meet the demands of food sufficiency through the development of plant seeds and technologies. He was memorialised by Diego Rivera in a large mural, and this portrait of Khankhoje distributing bread to the poorer nations hangs today in the Secretariat of Education in Mexico City. On the eve of the centenary year of the Indian Rebellions or Mutiny of 1857, and nearly fifty years after leaving on his very own revolutionary road across the planet, Khankhoje returned to independent India, to Pune, in 1956.[4]

To the historian, this chronology of lives and events might appear in retrospect as pregnant with significance, at once portending both world-historical transformations and Indian trajectories of political change. At first glance, the near simultaneous deaths of Har Dayal in America and Chatto in the Soviet Union might seem to prefigure the global division that the Cold War wrought over the second half of the twentieth century; while Khankhoje's life in Mexico, in the middle decades of the last century, experimenting with plant seeds and corn, points to the contest with hunger that the 'third world' of poor but newly independent nations was to seek to overcome through the promises of science. Yet this would be to view the lives of these men, and to 'slice' the last century chronologically, solely from the vantage point of its exhausting

3. Emily C. Brown, *Har Dayal, Hindu Revolutionary and Rationalist* (Tucson: University of Arizona Press, 1975).

4. Pandurang Khankhoje Papers, Nehru Memorial Museum and Library, New Delhi (hereafter NMML), and Sawhney, *I Shall Never*.

end; whilst lurking behind this chronology of world history is in fact the landmark event of modern Indian history: the Mutiny/Rebellions. While its naming still defies consensus, its import can be conveyed entirely simply by citing the year: '1857'.

In a direct and deliberate echo of 1857, 'Ghadar'—approximately translating both as 'rebellion and chaos' and as 'sedition' or 'treason', was the name given to a series of violent acts and events that occurred from Shiraz to Shanghai to Singapore, from Kabul to Kanpur via California, from London to Lahore to Laos, from Bushire to Berlin to Benares, spanning the first three decades of the twentieth century. Indeed, many more towns, cities and ports could be added to this tri-continental geography of violence across Asia, Europe and America.[5] The prime movers behind these actions were Har Dayal and Khankhoje, with the support of several thousand students, labourers, peasants and soldiers. These *ghadris* (insurgents) were shadowed by imperial spies, and their actions resulted in a slew of 'conspiracy' trials, memorably associated with particular cities and towns and coming to be known simply as the Lahore conspiracy trials, the Delhi conspiracy trials, and so on.[6]

What were officially referred to as 'conspiracies', and otherwise as 'revolutionary activities', the flimsy organisational structures of the ghadris, deemed 'secret societies', and their capacity for violence were subsumed into a comprehensive imperial narrative. With a view to the control of anticolonial politics and the enactment of ever more stringent sedition laws, the report of the infamous Rowlatt Committee of 1918 is the first account in which the Ghadar is presented as a series of connected insurgent events across India and the world.[7] A systematic account of imperial fear, the report scripted a coherent imperial narrative out of a series of disjointed events spanning the decade from 1908 to 1918. This arc of imperial fear induced by radical violence began with Tilak's activities and the murder of Rand by the Chapekar brothers in Pune

5. Harish K. Puri, *Ghadar Movement: Ideology, Organisation and Strategy* (Amritsar: Guru Nanak Dev University Press, 1983); J. S. Grewal, Harish K. Puri and Indu Banga (eds.), *The Ghadar Movement: Background, Ideology, Actions and Legacies* (Patiala: Patiala University Publication Bureau, 2013).

6. Richard J. Poplewell, *Intelligence and Imperial Defence: British Intelligence and the Defence of the Indian Empire* (London: Routledge, 1995); Malwinder Singh Waraich and Harinder Singh (eds.), *Ghadar Movement Original Documents*, vol. 1: *Lahore Conspiracy Cases I and II* (Chandigarh: Unistar, 2008).

7. S.A.T. Rowlatt (committee president), *Sedition Committee Report, 1918* (Calcutta: New Age Publishers, 1973 [1918]).

and continued through Bengal, Punjab, Madras and beyond, including the so-called Muhammadan current, but was above all concerned with the Ghadar movement, which defied any provincial location, within India or elsewhere.

The Rowlatt Committee viewed these men and their actions as violent but shrouded in secrecy that the imperial bureaucracy and espionage had proceeded to uncover. Undoubtedly, the insistence upon these activities being 'secret 'or 'conspiratorial' became the backdrop for, and furnished evidence to justify, ever greater imperial surveillance. The Ghadar and other anticolonial activities gave rise to draconian strategies of control that recast the Empire towards the end of the First World War.[8] The Rowlatt Report, having begun by citing 'revolutionary activities', switched its points of reference to conclude, in what are to us eerily familiar terms, that the Ghadar and related acts amounted in fact to 'terrorism', demanding in response special 'emergency' laws.[9] Sedition laws requiring loyalty to the sovereign and his realm or territory, as discussed in the last chapter, were now deemed inadequate.

As is well known, it was a public protest against the Rowlatt Committee Report by peasants and relatives of Punjabi soldiers who had gathered in Jallianwala Bagh that became the flashpoint igniting the infamous Amritsar Massacre. A historical amnesia, however, pervades the connections of this imperial massacre with the Ghadar movement. Often rendered as a popular protest against the Empire's rearmament by means of laws and oppressive taxation at the end of the Great War, the now iconic protest meeting was in fact organised in part by the relatives of various ghadris. On 13 April 1919, or Baisakhi (north-Indian harvest festival) Day, at Jallianwala Bagh, relatives of ghadris gathered to protest against the harsh sentences it was feared were to be meted out to those who had participated in the movement. The fear of harsh punishment was not misplaced: immediately prior to the Jallianwala Bagh meeting and in a short period of two years between 1913 and 1915, 279 ghadris from Punjab alone were tried, forty-nine men were hanged, and the majority of the rest sentenced to transportation for life.[10]

8. Poplewell, *Intelligence*; John Gallagher, *The Decline, Revival and Fall of the British Empire: The Ford Lectures and Other Essays* (Cambridge: Cambridge University Press, 1982).

9. Joseph McQuade, 'Terrorism, Law and Sovereignty in India and the League of Nations, 1897–1945' (unpublished doctoral dissertation, University of Cambridge, 2017).

10. F. C. Isemonger and J. Slattery, *An Account of the Ghadar Conspiracy 1913–1915*, reprinted with a foreword by Ved Prakash Vatuk (Meerut: Archana Publications, 2007 [Lahore, 1919]), Appendix T, xlviii.

A few days after the new emergency laws were enacted, and with martial law declared in Punjab, over a thousand men and women were killed at the Baisakhi Day protest meeting against the Rowlatt Report in Amritsar, as a result of orders of General Reginald Dyer. The spectre of the Ghadar had convinced authorities such as Dyer and the governor of Punjab Michael O'Dwyer that they faced the single greatest 'imperial peril' yet.[11] Punjab was, if not the epicentre of the Ghadar network, a critical nodal point. Thus, this episode of imperial violence and its occurrence in Amritsar were not incidental, but rather communicated the imperial urge to pin the Ghadar to a specific provincial location. In the event, however, it shattered the supposed loyalism and quiescence associated with Punjab ever since the original Indian Mutiny/Rebellions of 1857.

Nationalist accounts tend to portray the decade between 1908 and 1918 as a silent period in Indian politics, by and large perceived as a hiatus between the whimpering end of the Swadeshi movement, with the internment of various leaders, and the dramatic arrival of Mohandas Gandhi. The dominant nationalist narrative asserts that the Amritsar Massacre and the rise of Gandhi in the nationalist arena alone shattered this political silence.

Nevertheless, as part of what Tim Harper recently termed the 'Asian underground', the Ghadar erupted forcefully across the planet during this supposedly quiet decade. Nor was it merely a shadowy replica of imperial globalisation, connecting disparate locales and societies through aggression and modern technology. Even though imperial anxiety and surveillance sought connections, synchronicity and coherence, the welter of underground violent activities of this 'underground', though decidedly anticolonial, was rarely 'vocalised as a systemic creed but left its residue in others': from revolutionary communism and anarchism to internationalism and, above all, nationalism.[12] It was the Rowlatt Committee, as recounted above, that first sought to provide a systematic account of the movement, framed by ideas of imperial fear, violence and control. Subsequent historical accounts, meanwhile, have sought to fold the Ghadar into the pre-history of communism, or

11. Michael O'Dwyer, *India as I Knew It: 1885–1925* (London: Constable & Co., 1926); and for an excellent historical account, Kim A. Wagner, *Jallianwala Bagh: An Empire of Fear and the Making of the Amritsar Massacre* (Delhi: Penguin Random House India, 2019).

12. Tim Harper, 'Singapore, 1915 and the Birth of the Asian Underground', *Modern Asian Studies* 47:6 (2013), 1782–1811.

to present it as an instantiation of anarchism and peasant radicalism, or as a radical chapter in the history of modern migration and diaspora.[13]

Punctuated by a series of spectacular violent acts, whether the attempted assassination of Viceroy Hardinge, or the raiding of imperial ammunition stores in far-flung Indian hinterlands, or the disrupting and cutting of imperial telegraph lines, this Asian underground operated most visibly in the years of the First World War. The Singapore Mutiny of 1915 made visible a momentary coalition of labouring men, young students and deserting soldiers, generating a shock wave that further distilled the imperial fear that the Empire was a vulnerable block of the distinct entities that have been referred to collectively as the 'Euro-Islamic condominium'.[14] Indeed, the simultaneous events of what came to be known as the 'Silk Letter Movement', or *Tehreek-e-Reshmi Rumaal*, and the declaration of a provisional government of India in Kabul in 1915, further discussed below, made Pan-Islamism a manifest and mobile expression of anti-imperialism. Crucially, it is argued here, the effect of Pan-Islamism was to make India the pivot of a new political Islam. These events were to generate a new chapter in the story of the 'Great Game' of empire: what came to be called the 'German Hindu Conspiracy', as the German Kaiser and his counsellors courted the ghadris and intermittently supported or funded their activities. Several Indian insurgents, including Har Dayal, made their way to Berlin on the eve of the First World War.[15]

There was nothing conspiratorial, however, about the Ghadar, spanning the period from roughly 1910 to 1925, and its activities were anything but silent. This chapter reconstructs the activities of the Ghadar and its ideological lineaments as being foundational to a rethinking of violence and its relationship to territorial nationalism and extra-territorial anticolonialism. The Ghadar, it is argued, ruptures the Indian nationalist account of nonviolent emancipation, inasmuch as it expresses an anti-imperial radicalism that is necessarily global in both form and content. Equally, the chapter eschews any invocation of the

13. Maia Ramnath, *Haj to Utopia: How the Ghadar Movement Charted Global Radicalism and Attempted to Overthrow the British Empire* (Berkeley: University of California Press, 2011).

14. Harper, 'Singapore', 1788, and see R.W.E. Harper and Henry Miller, *Singapore Mutiny* (Singapore: Oxford University Press, 1984).

15. Lala Har Dayal, *Forty-Four Months in Germany and Turkey, February 1915 to October 1918: A Record of Personal Impressions* (London: P. S. King & Sons, 1920); Nirode K. Barooah, *India and the Official Germany, 1886–1914* (Frankfurt: Peter Lang, 1977); Kris Manjapra, *Age of Entanglement: German and Indian Intellectuals across Empire* (Cambridge, MA: Harvard University Press, 2014), 88–110.

global as a category transcendent of the nation-state. The global here is understood as a totality and as an abstraction that finds its specification in a new subjectivity that appears on the horizon of the twentieth century. Contra recent historical approaches that posit the nation-state as antithetical to the global, and privilege connections and networks, the emphasis here is on a new political subject and the particular politics that it generated, which was writ large across the world in this period. A new subject, marked by its capacity for sacrifice, rendered the planet as a whole, by a deliberate and militant mobility, the open horizon of politics. Such a potentiality, it is argued here, was predicated on the subjective and the individual rather than upon any institutionalised form of politics, whether romantic, revolutionary or realist.

This chapter resists the temptation to fold and collate the events, acts and words that came under the insignia of the Ghadar into a systematic synthesis expressive of any particular ideology. Instead, in reconstructing the ideas, acts and biographies of the Ghadar as a disjointed bricolage, it acknowledges the primacy of secrecy that lent credence to and provided the crucial context for a new and subject-oriented horizon of a political fraternity. With sacrifice and martyrdom as the professed goal of its self-fashioning, such a heightened and even exaggerated politics of the self, as the chapter elaborates, was directly related to the very character of the twentieth century, as this new subject deliberately sought to confront history. With violence as its preferred and visible language of communication, the Ghadar spectacularly posited an opening and a rupture between the settled forms of nation and empire. The global, in other words, did not amount to an extension of physical scale, but through the militant subject became a site of potentiality, a space that pointed to an irreducible gap between nation and empire and, above all, between the possible and the actual.

Egotopia: Secrecy and Subjectivity

On 5 June 1913, the Ghadar was declared from the west coast of America as a message of chaos and insurrection.[16] The message was broadcast worldwide, traveling from New York to continental Europe, Persia, Japan and India—as the message's pre-eminent site—and back to Canada, Argentina and Mexico.

---

16. I take the word 'egotopia' in the heading to this section, as expressing a conjunction of utopia and self-making, from John Miller, *Egotopia: Narcissism and the New American Landscape* (Tuscaloosa: University of Alabama Press, 1997).

In packed auditoriums in Astoria and Berkeley, Har Dayal, its architect and author, announced the Ghadar not as a political party, and still less as a movement, but as a pledge, an oath to become a ghadri or insurgent. A large number of agrarian labouring men on the US west coast, primarily from Punjab, and a handful of young Indian men studying in colleges, technical institutions and universities were in attendance. The oath proclaimed and solemnised the ghadri as an outcome of negations: vowing not to earn money, not to become a parent and to break with all social bonds.[17] A year later, a war within the First World War was declared eponymously in the *Ailan-e-Jang* (Declaration of War) that became the Ghadar credo, typified by this oath taken by the 'self-sacrificing warriors':

Salary: Death
Reward: Martyrdom
Pension: Freedom
Field of Battle: Hindustan[18]

Har Dayal's reputation preceded his arrival, in 1912, in America, where he was hosted by the 'loose' and 'dangerous' Emma Goldman, today resurrected as a figurehead of twentieth- century anarchism. Although shrouded in secrecy, his prior activities in England had nevertheless attracted publicity that had resulted in what was to be lifelong surveillance by imperial spies.

Har Dayal's vision of the Ghadar as a political formation, intensely secretive, small and intimate, was in contrast to the workings of a political party. A few days after his public lecture that had ended with the ritual of the oath, in a letter to his friend, the American literary critic Van Wyck Brooks, he referred to his 'great pleasure to stand out boldly for my ideas. I hate [the] hole and corner of hypocrisy and silence.' However, this profession of relief at being able to express his thoughts and claim them publicly was swiftly followed by the insistence that 'you must not think that I attach too much importance to public lectures. A lecture is only a kind of drum to get people together. The real work begins with the slow interpenetration of personalities'.[19]

17. Dharamvir, *Lala Har Dayal: Prassidh Deshbkta* . . . (Delhi: Rajpal & Sons, 1970), 185.

18. *Ailan-e-Jang*, British Library, London, India Office Records (IOR), Proscribed Publications Microfilms; also cited in Ramnath, *Haj*, 1; Sawhney, *I Shall Never*, 118–19.

19. Har Dayal to Van Wyck Brooks, 14 August 1912, Van Wyck Brooks Collection, University of Pennsylvania.

In this spirit, Har Dayal had set up the Bakunin Institute, combining peda-gogical facilities, a hostel and a commune and ashram where young men lived together, in Oakland, California. Their work, evidently, was to publish and distribute across the world a new kind of propaganda that resembled neither the considered prose of a newspaper editorial nor a letter from a distant friend or relative. *Ghadar di Goonj* (Echo of [the 1857] rebellion) was fashioned more like a mobile billboard, pithy and declaratory in style. Written in the colloquial parlance of North India that was an amalgamation of Hindustani, Urdu, Pun-jabi and English, both the form and content rendered the pamphlet easy to convert into any number of Indian vernaculars and other languages, including Persian.

Whether the activities that took place within what was variously known as the Bakunin Institute or the Yugantar Ashram took the form of ascetic practice or of individual labour, what the community operating therein amounted to, in the end, was a form of secret society, as opposed to a party, commune or ashram. Har Dayal had spent two years, in the Swadeshi era, in the foremost secret society set up at the India House in London by its revolutionary and wealthy patron, Shyamji Krishnavarma.[20] As is well known, several Indian nationalists, including Gandhi and the Hindutva ideologue Vinayak Savarkar, at one time or another were housed in or had visited this seemingly innocuous Hampstead mansion.[21] Its form was replicated by other India Houses, notably in two disparate corners of the world, New York and Tokyo, by Barkatullah, to whom we will return below.

In specific contrast to an organised party and its principle of 'the people' to be represented, the Yugantar Ashram became the Ghadar headquarters and the nodal point in a militant global mobile entity based on the individual who be-longed to a secret fraternity. Such a flimsy organisation of men meeting and living in secret in fact came closer, ironically, to the etymological root of the term 'party' to the extent that it refers to division, side-taking or separation—a theme to be developed further below. This was indeed the world of the partisan, who is a part of or partner in a (guerrilla) fight.[22] To this extent, a separation

20. Indulal Yagnik, *Shyamji Krishnavarma: Life and Times of an Indian Revolutionary* (Bom-bay: Lakshmi Publications, 1950).

21. Shruti Kapila, 'Self, Spencer and Swaraj: Nationalist Thought and Critiques of Liberal-ism, 1890–1920', *Modern Intellectual History* 4:1 (2007), 109–27; Harald Fischer-Tiné, *Shyamji Krishnavarma: Sanskrit, Sociology and Anti-Imperialism* (Delhi: Routledge India, 2014).

22. See https://www.etymonline.com/search?q=partisan.

was forged by the complete rejection of social norms such as marriage, but also of the public arena, of associations and of parties as conventionally understood. The intimacy of the ashram as a secret society held up a mirror to the alienating and abstract nature of the planet, and the Ghadar sought to mobilise these two opposing aspects via a militant engagement against the Empire.

The rejection of social ties and the pledge to remain unmarried consecrated a bond that implied the purity of male work. In seeking to reconstitute political subjectivity, the purpose of the Yugantar Ashram was to shore up a form of agency in which discrete elements of work and social relationships were to be coalesced into a commitment to the secret fraternity. What Har Dayal had aimed for was not a large-scale movement, but a select band of young men, preferably sons of 'moneylenders and landlords', who could live and work in close proximity but would die apart, yet bound in the intimacy of their common cause.[23] 'Let us form a secret society of those who prefer death' became the watchword of its ever increasing number of members as the Ghadar's cellular formation also multiplied. Within a few months its membership had reached five thousand, with several such societies in America alone.[24] Aspiring members were inducted into the ashram by two existing members and had to undergo six months of probationary work before political tasks or trust more generally could be shared.

Epitomising the key principle of a secret society, that of offering potential invisibility, through the ashram, the Ghadar was a radical formation. While individual members were connected by a secret, the group or collective thus forged was concealed. It is therefore hard to describe the Ghadar as a party, or even as a movement, in any conventional sense, as it is individual biographies of martyrdom and betrayal that give it any, or nominal, collective identity. The Ghadar could thus only be conceived of as a 'conspiracy' by its opponent: the imperial state. Decentralised, as a secret cell, and subsumed in the anonymity of an American suburb, the Yugantar Ashram induced imperial fear precisely because its concealment defied control. Yet the oath taken by its members

23. British intelligence reports on Indian activity in Persia, Baluchistan, Java, Jakarta and the Andaman Islands, German and Turkish correspondence, and lists of Indians imprisoned: IOR/L/PS/103 (1916). The potential of youth for political action was recognised and publicised as a national duty by Har Dayal's mentor, Lala Lajpat Rai: *Young India* (Lahore: Servants of the People Society, 1927).

24. Ramnath, *Haj*, 36–37; A. C. Bose, *Indian Revolutionaries Abroad* (Delhi: Northern Book Centre, 2002); G. F. MacMunn, *The Underworld of India* (London: Jarrolds, 1933).

served to conjure an alliance, political and tacit, that was ultimately defined by a commitment to combat a political adversary. The individual member, the ghadri, founded a politics that was secret in origin, with no point of return or settlement in any 'home', characterised instead by a constant movement or mobility whose effects, however, were to become only too visible, indeed spectacular.

It was a secret society par excellence, dependent on the individual who was part of a concealed collective. Har Dayal described its members as 'social dynamite'. Explosive in nature, much like their bomb-making activities and the poetic propaganda that detonated across and through the imperial and global postal system, the individual that prefigured this politics was an outcome of a deliberate disruption. The Ashram's life is often portrayed as a romantic utopia, an egalitarian microcosm of India's diversity, with Sikhs, Muslims and Hindus united in their work against an oppressive empire. Often presented as the metonym for the ideal nation, or even a repressed but imagined revolutionary party, the Ghadar and its cellular fraternity was in fact the opposite.

Secret societies, whether the Masonic lodges of the Victorian age or those common to traditional societies, or even those indulged in by various men of letters, have always been popular, but feared. Marked by the privatisation of trust, the secret society, as classically understood by George Simmel, above all 'offers a possibility of a second world alongside the manifest world'.[25] This second world of alterity and fraternal secrecy is based on reciprocity of information and behaviour. The secret itself is the basis of the bond, infusing it with mystical powers and intense intimacy. It is in this sense that the cause of the nation, however nebulous, acquired a mystical power. This was because it was precisely in her name that the oath to die was taken: so that the nation could come alive.

The celebrated ghadri, and a key poet of the fraternity, Kartar Singh Sarabha had travelled from Ludhiana in Punjab to Berkeley in California to study chemistry, and he attended the inaugural Ghadar meeting in 1913. Considered a leading combatant in the Ashram's division into 'intellectual' and 'activist' wings, Sarabha returned to India for his appointed Ghadar tryst with history in 1915. Betrayed by one of his own fraternity, he was hanged in Lahore the

25. George Simmel, 'The Sociology of Secrecy and of Secret Societies', *American Journal of Sociology* 11:4 (1906), 441–98; and, for an especially insightful discussion, Gilbert Herdt, *Secrecy and Cultural Reality: Utopian Ideologies of the New Guinea Men's House* (Ann Arbor: University of Michigan Press, 2003).

same year, before he was twenty years old.[26] His poem below articulates a subject both driven by death and detached from the nation, but whose sacrifice wills the very source of mystical power into being:

> I am a particle of the ravaged India's ruins
> This is the only name I have
> The only hallmark, the only address
> Oh, Mother India this was not to be my fate
> My good fortune
> That with every moment of mine
> I could have worshipped your feet
> O Mother India
> If my head is offered
> My life is sacrificed
> In your service
> Then, I would understand
> Even in my death
> I will attain
> A life of eternity[27]

Death or sacrifice became the promissory note of life itself. Yet between these absolute poles of death and eternity lay the work of disruption, individual and mobile, that traversed the planet and left a landscape of potentiality, unmoored from any theological base, even though martyrdom is a virtue and cornerstone of both Sikhism and Islam. The sacrifice or the reckoning of death, runs the argument here, emanated from a profound understanding of a lack of constitutive deficiency. The lack was understood as being, and signified, that of the nation, as several such poems confessed. This point of lack and a consciousness marked by a profound absence founded the subject of the Ghadar. Death, sacrifice and violence then founded a politics of subtraction with the potentiality of the double negative: a dual lack, that of the nation and the absence of life or death itself; and their coming together was sought in order, potentially, to convert this into a positive, or the real. Entirely aware of the highly individualistic potential of death, the Ghadar's politics was defined by the individual

26. Waraich and Singh, *Ghadar Movement*, 126–36; Kirat Singh Inqalabi (ed.), *Gadhri Yodha Shaheed Kartar Singh Sarabha* (Delhi: Delhi Book Shop, 2014); Guracharan Singh, *Vir Nayak Kartar Singh Sarabha* (Patiala: Punjabi University, Publications Bureau, 1994).

27. Isemonger and Slattery, *Account*, xiv.

subject who could be sacrificed for a cause greater than himself. The act of taking an oath to die dissolved the individual into the historical project that exceeded him: namely, the Indian nation.[28] It is therefore not surprising that Sarabha invoked his own subjectivity as a particle of the ruin called India, individual yet dissolved in its fabric. Though he 'served' and 'worshipped' the ruin, as he called India, a living relationship with her was confirmed only by its denial and impossibility. Thus, the public enacting of the oath, or the poetics of death and the secret society, all pointed to a subject as an outcome of a profound deficiency and lack. It was such a subject, his own death pledged on oath, who became the cause, effect and conclusion of a new politics, sacrificial yet spectral. In short, for the politics of the Ghadar, the sacrificial subject, with death and violence as spectacular events, remained pre-eminent.

This new sacrificial subjectivity as the basis of a new form of politics was premised on a break from established norms, whether of employment or marriage, and formed the common motif of individual biographies and the bricolage of activities of the Ghadar. A series of general formative conditions from which such a disruptive political subject emerged can nevertheless be identified. Whether it was Har Dayal, Sarabha, Khankhoje, V. G. Pingle or V.V.S. Aiyar, all had departed from the seemingly destined path of a settled existence, whether of regular employment or an education that improved prospects. Har Dayal's rejection of a scholarship and first-class Oxford degree during the Swadeshi period, in 1905–6 on the eve of his graduation, incited both imperial fear and publicity in India.[29] Exhilaration and hope, but also dejection and despair, marked such decisions that affected individual lives; but these were imbued with and recognised a potentially greater import than that of the singular existence. Har Dayal wrote approvingly to the Tamil firebrand V.V.S. Aiyar when the latter resigned from the bar in London in 1910, and sought him out to edit his paper, *Bande Mataram*.[30] Aiyyar's trajectory was similar to that of other ghadris. Moving from Madras and arriving in London from Min in 1906 via a legal position in Rangoon, he became a member of the London India House, and soon rejected the strictures of law in favour of a fiery pen and

---

28. On India as mother, see Sumathi Ramaswamy, *The Goddess and the Nation: Mapping Mother India* (Durham, NC: Duke University Press, 2010), and Mrinalani Sinha (ed.), *Selections from 'Mother India' by Katherine Mayo* (New Delhi: Kali for Women, 1998).

29. Kapila, 'Self, Spencer and Swaraj'.

30. Har Dayal to Sardar Rana from Algiers, 1910: Dharmavira (ed.), *Letters of Lala Har Dayal* (Ambala: Indian Book Agency, 1970), 89.

deadly weapons. By 1910 he was a certified enemy of the law. Returning to India the same year, Aiyyar was exiled in Pondicherry and reappeared only in 1914 when a German ship landed and bombarded the southern Indian shores.[31] Whether or not this was a coordinated act of the Ghadar, emanating from its headquarters in California, or the work of a decentralised cell in the global vectors of the First World War, such acts highlighted an individual secrecy that only became visible 'above ground' in theatrical confrontations.

The event or moment of confrontation was, however, more often than not an outcome of willpower and despair. In the letter that congratulated Aiyyar for his act of dissent, Har Dayal also expressed the desolation of, yet necessity for, such self-consciousness. Marooned in Algiers at that point, Har Dayal was unable to return to India because of heightened imperial surveillance triggered by the assassination in London of a high imperial official, Curzon Wyllie, by Madanlal Dhingra, an India House compatriot. With the swift de-campment of the India House and increased surveillance, Har Dayal had escaped to Algiers via Paris. Penniless and battling for physical and mental stability, he once again underscored the need to reject any life of predictable comfort. Writing to one confidant, an Indian prince, Sardar Rana, Har Dayal confessed,

> I don't go away from anger, caprice or anything of the kind, but from fore-sight and deliberation. Much is at stake! All earnest youths of Northern India are watching me . . . I was horribly tempted to fall and become a mer-cenary in occupation for the sake of living in Paris and regaining my strength by a quiet regular life. I was inclined to do it. But as I thought and thought, I discovered that it was not necessary to fall at all, if I could only give myself the trouble of journeying and leading an irregular life of some hardship and uncertainty.[32]

Expressing this burden of choice on the eve of his departure westward to Cali-fornia, Har Dayal could derive no comfort from faith in the coming nation, or a 'windbag bluffy kind of "patriotism"', as he put it, and had done previously too, when he rejected his Oxford degree. He continued,

> The natural order is Morality first, then Politics and Patriotism. For mo-rality comprises everything—patriotism is only a derived virtue and

---

31. V.V.S. Aiyar, Diary 1916–20: V.V.S. Aiyar Papers, NMML.
32. Har Dayal to Sardar Rana, *Letters*, 89–90, 93.

applies to affairs relating to the State as against the States. If we only had one State in all the world . . . patriotism (as understood now) will not be a virtue at all.[33]

Such a repositioning of ethics over politics as the founding of a new subject of transformation was to become central to the Gandhian project. Even as Har Dayal sailed to unknown shores, the nation or patriotism was only a contingent condition, rather than the professed goal of everyday and ultimate sacrifice. Much as for other militant nationalists—Tilak before, and later Gandhi—anti-statism was the first principle of this new politics of the subject.

The planet, or the global, would emerge, however, through a militant mobility, as the horizon of a new political subject. Such a political subject—the ghadri—lay below and above the nation, but never quite settled into a living relationship with it, even as an armed agility, as we shall see, unsettled the fixed geography of empire. The despair, hope and terror that formed the subjective terrain of the Ghadar were not merely counterpoints to the given patterns of life, whether of employment or the totality of empire, but formed the basis of the new project of politics. Necessity and will, along with a combination of discipline and preparedness, formed a subject who would appear as a combatant, and a partisan in dispersed localities. A deliberate set of irregularities then was forged, in which a dislocated subject and de-territorialised idea of India became pre-eminent.

Significantly, the novelty of the twentieth century became the context for a radical apprehension of time that grounded the species of subjectivity which coalesced under the banner of the Ghadar. In an essay on 'India and the World Movement', Har Dayal posited considerable power in the novelty of the century itself. As he predicted, 'The twentieth century will witness a mighty revolution in India and the world. The time-spirit will ring out the old and ring in the new. . . . The nineteenth century has been the period of destruction, criticism and preparation . . . the twentieth century will be the era . . . of fulfillment.'[34]

To be sure, this era of fulfilment was a confrontation with history itself. The twentieth century was indeed the Nietzschean century, in which the past had to be confronted and annihilated in order to create a wholly new beginning.

---

33. Ibid., 93–94.

34. Lala Har Dayal, 'India and the World Movement', in Lala Har Dayal, *Writings of Har Dayal* (Benares: Swaraj Publishing House, 1922), 155.

This radical commencement of the future had, by necessity in such a reckoning, to be taken as discontinuous with the inherited past. The twentieth century, as recent philosophical interpretations remind us, 'has borne a combative conception of existence. . . . Whatever its scale, private or planetary, every real situation is a scission, a confrontation, a war.'[35] It is in this context, the reclaiming of 1857—the original Ghadar—in the twentieth century reflects, in a new political formation, the disconnected genealogy of history.

Time's Arrow: Echoing 1857

In naming itself after the year 1857, the act of Ghadar was an echo and a search for deliberate repetition. On 1 November 1913, the Yugantar Ashram bombarded the Indian and imperial postal network with cyclostyled handbills entitled *Ghadar di Goonj* (The echo of rebellion).[36] The Ashram's name—'Yugantar', signifying the 'new age', or more precisely the 'transition of an epoch'—was chosen to resonate with Bengali radical and militant politics.[37] Words and acts, both fiery and deadly, announced a new political formation that sought to repeat 1857, the greatest armed rebellion against the British Empire in the nineteenth century. The name 'Ghadar' thus tied the new and secret fraternity and its declared activity to another moment in history. The choice of this name for their politics betrayed a deep yearning for redemption, given that '1857' connoted rebellion as much as it did a profound failure. Despite, or because of, the fact that the Ghadar's predominantly Punjabi cadre associated 1857 with the region's quiescence in that historic uprising, this designation then was intended to create an opening with history by confronting it.

In a pamphlet named for the date of the 1857 rebellion—simply *The 10th of May*—Har Dayal declared that there was an 'interval . . . between each sunrise and the next'. Such an interval, puncturing the ordinary unfolding of time, created, in his view, 'memorable events'.[38] Most such memories and intervals, he wrote, had to do with a welter of historical experiences, 'of some splendid victory or some sad defeat', or 'the making of fortunes, of slaves

---

35. Badiou, *Century*, 37.
36. Isemonger and Slattery, *Account*, 17.
37. On Bengal, see Durba Ghosh, *Gentlemanly Terrorists: Political Violence and the Colonial State in India, 1919–1947* (Cambridge: Cambridge University Press, 2017).
38. Lala Har Dayal, *The 10th of May* (n.p, n.d.), IOR Proscribed Publications Microfilms.

becoming kings, and kings becoming slaves, of the building up of empires or the crumbling to dust of thrones'.[39] The recall or echo of 1857 was unlike any moment, however, in that the incitement to memory was a call to repeat and redeem history itself. 'But in our present inglorious downfall,' the pamphlet continued, 'in our ignominious slavery and degradation, we have most need to bring back to memory the places where our sires fought and bled and died . . . who rose by ardent self-sacrifice . . . who gave all that they could give.' Such 'magical inspiration', or the 'worship before immortal memories', was an act that he urged was to be repeated from 'city to city' and 'battlefield to battlefield'. This repetition in the interval of time, in short, had to apprehend the future and a 'rising out of the blood and ashes of their [1857] failures'.[40]

The invocation or the echo of a failed past thus expressed a yearning for redemption that contained a dimension of the future.[41] To this extent, the Ghadar was literally 'revolutionary', in that it explicitly sought, through enactment, a repetition of a past that could be redeemed retroactively. In isolating 1857, however, the aim was to arrest or immobilise the historical time of empire itself. This compulsion to repeat reflected, in other words, the need to create an immediacy, or a short-circuit, between the past and the present.

This differed from the approach of the Swadeshi-era nationalists, who had invoked the same moment for inspiration. For them, 1857 was a source of their politics because the Rebellions had been repressed. Whether by Tilak or his arch-enemy *The Times* journalist Valentine Chirol, the fiftieth anniversary of 1857 was perceived as a return of the repressed, offering hope and fear in equal measure.[42] '1857', for Swadeshi politics, was, in short, a leap into the past and a search for support in tradition. In claiming and naming itself after 1857 as a politics of insurrection, what the Ghadar declared was the opposite. It was an open measure of the future. Failure and its redemption fuelled the poetic propaganda that declared the past as 'false' and the assumption of a new future as authentic. Take, for instance, a poem entitled *10th May 1911*:

39. Ibid.
40. Ibid.
41. The ghadri Gobind Behari Lal, 'Detailed Account of the Ghadr Movement', in T. R. Sareen (ed.), *Select Documents of the Ghadr Party* (Delhi: Mountbo Publishing House, 1994), 56, testifies to the attempt at deliberate repetition of 1857.
42. Chirol, *Indian Unrest*.

Is it so, that the sword is broken,
Our sword, that was halfway drawn?
Is it so, that the light was a spark,
That the bird we hailed as the lark
Sang in her sleep in the dark,
And the song we took for a token
Bore false witness of dawn?[43]

The question of time, its reckoning as either authentic or false, provided the Ghadar with conceptual ammunition, which sought an intervention in the present and the immediate.[44] If this new political subject, or ghadri/insurgent, was an outcome of the deliberate disruption of individual destiny, then the neat progression of time too was broken by an interruption. The Ghadar that was declared on 13 June 1912 was, in effect, a declaration of the end of the past. More to the point, this date was taken as the chosen moment when the account book of history was to be closed, and scores settled. It is striking that one of the most widely circulated pamphlets of the Ghadar, *Aankhon ki Gawaahi* (An eyewitness account), is simply a handbill in two columns, in which figures on one side of the page recorded the Indian population and the number of Indian soldiers, while the other column detailed taxation figures and the numbers of Indians who had died in imperial wars.[45] At a superficial level, this amounted to a politico-economic critique of empire, in bald statistics for maximum impact. From another point of view, it could be argued that such a stark accounting also reflected a particular disposition towards history itself—history seen as an account sheet of death, taxes and blood that could only be measured from the perspective of Judgement Day, when time itself had been halted.[46]

The naming of this politics as 'Ghadar', an echo of 1857, should not be understood, however, as indicating a progressive unfolding of time, but with a slight shift in perspective. The aim here is not to construe it as revolutionary in the sense of being a repetition of the past, though this time from the point of view of the oppressed. The Ghadar and its politics was no mere search for inversion or reversal of the failed history of 1857. On the contrary, and despite

43. Anon., *10th May 1911* (n.p., n.d.), IOR Proscribed Publications Microfilms.
44. Christopher Clark, *Time and Power: Visions of History in German Politics from the Thirty Years' War to the Third Reich* (Princeton, NJ: Princeton University Press, 2019).
45. IOR Proscribed Publications Microfilms.
46. Slavoj Žižek, *The Sublime Object of Ideology* (London: Verso Books, 1989), 138–44.

its vaunted politics of mobility, the Ghadar instituted a moment of pause, or even stasis, when all that had previously failed was to be summoned, so that the future could redeem it.

Predating the revolutionary year of 1917, Har Dayal's own concern lay more with the agency of the self than with any awakening of a repressed but collective capacity. Dismissed by later Indian communists as a 'drop out' from the revolution, he had published in 1912—the year of the proclamation of the Ghadar—a scathing critique of Marxism.[47] In his much publicised and translated article 'Marx a Modern Rishi', he rejected the materialist conception of history describing it as 'vicious and misleading', albeit Marx's insights, in his view, displayed a 'moral grandeur', and Marx had in fact 'helped the art of ethics'. But the Marxist 'fanaticism for economics', with class struggle as the principle of history, was altogether dismissed and damned. In consonance with Har Dayal's politics of disruption, history displayed no grand theme of redemption. 'History', he argued, 'reveals no law discernible. . . . The rest is chaos, which great men try to turn into cosmos.'[48] Such a view would be instructive, as the Ghadar embraced chaos and took the totality of the planet as the horizon or the cosmos of action that defied any singular thematic thread or principle.

Deadly Politics

Disruption was anything but erratic, however, or simply expressive of individual zeal. The bomb armed the agile ghadri as the preferred ammunition that created a specific set of irregularities and ruptures against the regular order of the imperial state. This came to a momentous if momentary and spectral confrontation in the First World War. Yet the potency of the bomb was affirmed before the war. None other than the governor-general of India became the initial target of the Ghadar's deadly politics. Following the declaration of Delhi as the new imperial capital, and one year to the month after the Delhi Durbar of 1911 that saw the British sovereign on the subcontinent's soil, a bomb was detonated: on 23 December 1912, while passing through the historic imperial boulevards in Delhi in a procession to mark his entry as governor-general to

47. P. C. Joshi and K. Damodaran (eds.), *Marx Comes to India: Earliest Indian Biographies* (Delhi: Manohar Book Service, 1975), 35.

48. Lala Har Dayal, 'Marx a Modern Rishi', in Joshi and Damodaran (eds.), *Marx Comes to India*, at 66, 72, 67.

the new capital, Lord Hardinge's cavalcade was bombed in Chandni Chowk. Though Hardinge was only injured, this attack nevertheless announced a new politics, shrouded in subterfuge. The conspiracy was uncovered only three years later, and by that time the main protagonist, Rash Behari Bose, was in Tokyo. An attack of such audacity was enabled by an underground network that connected western and eastern India via the north Indian heartlands and beyond, to America and ultimately to Japan.[49]

This event occasioned the issuing of the infamous *Yugantar Circular*, the closest that the Ghadar ever came to offering a political manifesto, hailing the bomb as 'epoch making' and 'thought provoking'.[50] 'The bomb', it declared, 'has come as a fitting conclusion of the "Durbar" . . . May Durbars and bombs go together.' As a manifesto of enmity, it declared a war, as it 'welcomed the world to a storm' that could only be articulated by dispersal by the dynamite itself. Similarly to Tilak, who a few years earlier had deemed the bomb a weapon of democratic and sublime possibilities, the Circular affirmed the bomb as lightning that became visible only in the pitch darkness of human history. A manifesto of the bomb, it extolled new connections:

> Where the tyrant is, there am I also . . . and the bomb is the tongue of fire, that utter [s] my word. . . . When 'Caesar' calls himself the 'Son of God' the bomb answers that he is but the 'Son of man'. The bomb thus enters the service of democracy, as indispensable instrument. . . . It breaks the spell [of power]. It is the voice of the millions speaking a tongue that all can understand. It is the Esperanto of Revolution. . . . [The bomb has] spoken.[51]

Destruction and violence served as a form of communication in which the bomb became pre-eminent. Spectacular destruction and individual martyrdom were thus acts of communication. The time had come, the Circular declared, for 'service and sacrifice'. Even though martyrdom, as several poems declared, was the ultimate goal, this sacrificial subjectivity was not limited to the individual. From assassinations to the theatres of the First World War, this violence was appropriated and given meaning by others, which more often

---

49. Dharamvira, *I Threw the Bomb: The Revolutionary Life of Rash Behari Bose* (Delhi: Orient Paperbacks, 1979).

50. Lala Har Dayal, *The Yugantar Circular*, IOR Proscribed Publications Microfilms.

51. Ibid. For a comparative discussion, see Benedict Anderson, *Under Three Flags: Anarchism and the Anti-Colonial Imagination* (London: Verso, 2005).

than not took the form of claiming such sacrificial acts for the nation or revolution. Yet, and in effect, violence conveyed a profound intimacy between subjects and the large-scale processes of history; this is to say, the death drive of martyrdom revealed the inherent but abstract and anonymous violence of empire and the economy.

Through spectacular events involving bombings and subsequent hangings, the aim of such a politics was in the end to give subjectivity to the abstraction of violence itself. This politics thus began and ended with the individual subject, seeking to square a circle by deifying death through the work of chaos, mobility and insurrection. Its theatrical moment of confrontation came, however, through a third-party war, in the global theatre of the First World War. In that world-historical moment of total destruction, the Ghadar's productivity lay in making violence subjective, and through that it unfixed, albeit spectrally, the fixity of the global territory of empire.

Militant Mobility, or, a Partisan's World War

The ghadri was the quintessential partisan who broke away and waged war behind enemy lines like a guerrilla, with a surface commitment to a fraternity. The political world order, Carl Schmitt in his controversial but insightful writings argues, is constituted by what he termed 'the partisan'. Emerging from and belonging to a party, and with 'intense political character', the partisan for Schmitt is above all an 'irregular fighter' whose horizon is shaped by and is dependent on the 'regularity he challenges'. Schmitt clarifies that although the partisan is a metaphor, he or she is nevertheless equipped with concrete attributes, ranging from an attachment to an autochthonous space—what Schmitt terms his or her 'telluric' nature—and a technical agility and mobility that are related to, but confound, the normative organisation of the political order. Crucially, the irregularity of the partisan is made possible by the legitimacy that is conferred on this politics by the dominant or regular power.[52] To this extent, rearmament of the imperial state in the wake of the Ghadar, whether in the form of the Rowlatt Act or the battery of martial laws, perversely but surely made evident the formidable nature of its enemy. Schmitt focuses, however, on those partisan politics that subsequently converted their irregularity to form a new regularity, notably the revolutionary states of Castro's Cuba and Mao's China. Here, our argument

52. Schmitt, *Theory of the Partisan*, 14–61.

is rather that the extra-territoriality of India represented by the Ghadar created a counter-geography to the British Empire that was borne by an individualised militant mobility worldwide.

If Har Dayal conceived the ghadri philosophically as a partisan and a sacrificial subject, then the arch-combatant as partisan was Pandurang Khankhoje. Khankhoje had moved from Nagpur to Tokyo after the assassination of the plague commissioners Rand and Ayerst and that had led to Tilak's famous sedition trial. Tilak himself had connected the two men when Har Dayal visited him in Pune a year before his internment in 1908.[53] By that time Khankhoje was in California, having made his way there via Japan, but had failed in his intention to get into a military academy there. Studying agriculture and the workings of weaponry, he founded the Yugantar Ashram with Har Dayal. Establishing an armed partnership with Mexican revolutionaries, and keen to militarise 'several fronts' of the British Empire, in particular Baluchistan, Khankhoje became the principal 'striker' or combatant (*praharak*), complementing Har Dayal's role as propagandist-missionary (*prachark*). This dual division gave a nominal semblance of structure to the Ghadar.

Underground and secretive, Khankhoje evaded all surveillance, as he 'despised publicity', donning several disguises and taking names as such Pir Khan and Muhammad Khan. His life story is scattered with associations with twentieth-century revolutionaries, be it Sun Yat Sen in Tokyo, Booker T. Washington in America, Agnes Smedley in Berlin or Lenin in Moscow. He had founded his own small secret fraternity, called Azad-e-Hind, which was absorbed into the Ghadar in San Francisco. Khankhoje openly disputed the naming of the Ghadar, as he preferred the trope of war to that of mutiny or rebellion. Har Dayal prevailed, however, in the naming of their politics as 'Ghadar'.

The First World War redistributed the individuated and cellular structures of the Ghadar. Though Khankhoje was hostile to dealing with the Germans, preferring open alliances along the Empire's West Asian frontier, he, together with Har Dayal, nevertheless apprehended the war as a ready-made theatre of combat in which the ghadri could appear as a combatant behind the overt and conventional confrontation between declared enemies. The war was recognised as the partisan's historic opportunity to redraw the boundaries between friend and foe.

---

53. Sawhney, *I Shall Never*, 97–101, and Khankhoje Papers, NMML.

In keeping with the Ghadar's enthusiasm for proclamations and dates, 19 February 1915 saw the declaration of a war within the war, the initiation of coordinated insurrections from Dacca to Lahore, and Persia to south-east Asia.[54] This date was communicated once more via a postal campaign. On this occasion, the letter-campaign was primarily directed at the Indian soldiers stationed across the war's various theatres; but 19 February was also declared the date for insurrection by ghadris, such as Sarabha, who had returned to India. As a secret fraternity, the Ghadar announced itself as an insurrection of 'unlimited membership'.

In Singapore, Sepoy Ismail Khan of the 5th Light Infantry fired the first shot; the subsequent releasing of German prisoners-of-war from a camp and the killing of several soldiers alerted the British imperial state to a global 'conspiracy'.[55] In Punjab, the United Provinces and Bengal, and across Indian hinterlands through small scale ambushes, ammunition depots were ransacked. Railways were attacked and telegraph wires cut or bombed. The armed and connected network of the Empire became the target of disruption.

At this point, armed and mobile, Khankhoje left San Francisco with the help of Mexican revolutionaries and appeared in Berlin, where Har Dayal, Barkatullah of Bhopal and Tokyo and an Indian prince from what is today Haryana, Mahendra Pratap, had set up the India–Berlin Committee, negotiating arms and support with German and Ottoman consuls. Khankhoje left Berlin for Constantinople. The Ghadar was in fact waging third-party warfare. Enver Pasha, Kadri Bey, the Ottoman minister of defence and Wilhelm Wassmuss—often called 'the German Lawrence'—met Khankhoje. The Germans were explicit in their aim to rouse the 'Muslim World';[56] the ghadris, and particularly Khankhoje, were clear, however, that this was not an ideological coalition, but a contingent formation. The tight, cellular and secret fraternity that had formed the Ghadar remained in its mobilised state a decentralised structure, as it was entirely dependent on individual action.

54. British Intelligence Reports, IOR/L/PS/103 (1916).

55. Sho Kuwajima, *Mutiny in Singapore: War, Anti-War and the War for India's Independence* (Delhi: Rainbow Publishers, 2006).

56. Lal, 'Detailed Account', 39; for background, see Sean McMeeken, *The Berlin–Baghdad Express: The Ottoman Empire and Germany's Bid for World Power, 1898–1918* (London: Allen Lane, 2010); David Motadel (ed.), *Islam in European Empires* (Oxford: Oxford University Press, 2014).

Khankhoje went from Constantinople to the war zone of Aleppo, from Aleppo to Bushire in Iraq, and from Bushire to Shiraz in Persia. In the span of less than a year, he had fought on all these fronts.[57] Disconnected from any centralised communication, and combating British forces but not fighting alongside the Germans, he recalled,

> There was no way of knowing what had elapsed since we left other Ghadrites. Communications were still very primitive, particularly in these remote areas. We depended mainly on the Germans to pass on information to us but were busy with their own concerns. We received no confirmation from our friends, we had received no news from America, and we had no idea what had happened to our friends after they arrived in India. . . . [W]e [only] knew that there were many patriots working ceaselessly on this front.[58]

Unbeknownst to the ceaselessly mobile Khankhoje, another date, in May 1915, was announced for another ambush, under the direction of M. N. Roy, with its epicentre in Batavia (Jakarta), towards the opposite end of the frontier from Bengal.[59] Entirely disconnected from these activities, Khankhoje was meanwhile in Shiraz, along with a man of many reputations and disguises known as Sufi Amba Prasad.

Amba Prasad was a typical ghadri. Born in Punjab, he converted from Hinduism to Islam as a young man. Tried for sedition in India in 1897, he escaped from prison to Persia, where he continued to publish pamphlets that included translations of Tilak's speeches.[60] He is revered today as a seer, both in the Indian Punjab and in Shiraz, though his life in fact ended in rather prosaic circumstances. For a few years before the First World War, he edited the multilingual Pan-Islamist newspaper-pamphlet by the name of *Intiqaam* (Revenge).[61] Moving from Afghanistan to Persia, and recruiting local chieftains' forces along the way, he moved into Shiraz where he held a British consul hostage and killed the British resident. An eight-month siege finally ended the

57. IOR/L/PJ/71438, and Sawhney, *I Shall Never*. Khankhoje's memoirs detail various battles: Khankoje Papers, NMML.
58. Sawhney, *I Shall Never*, 165, and Khankhoje Papers, NMML.
59. M. N. Roy, *Memoirs* (Delhi: Ajanta Press, 1984), 290–485.
60. Donogh, *Treatise*, 55; Tilak, *Selected Documents*, 12–16.
61. British Intelligence Reports, IOR/L/PS/10/683 and IOR/L/PS/103.

Sufi's career in the closing years of the First World War. Captured by Percy Sykes, leader of the British campaign in Persia, Amba Prasad committed suicide in captivity.[62]

Khankhoje decamped from Persia and moved to Bam in Baluchistan, with the aim of slowly inching his way towards confrontation in Punjab. 'This [Baluchistan] portion of the country', as he wrote later, 'was wild and untamed, almost inaccessible for others. Its people were fiercely independent. All these were ideal for our purposes.'[63] Although he too was captured by Sykes, unlike Prasad he disguised himself as a Baluchi tribesman and escaped with the help of locals. His combatant credentials gained him a Persian patron, and by means of a circuitous and dangerous journey, this time in Persian garb, he turned up in India in 1919. His main aim was to meet his mentor Tilak, which he succeeded in doing in Girgaon in Bombay. Tilak, as his memoir states, was 'annoyed' at Khankhoje's dare-devilry in risking his life by returning to his mentor and India. Categorically instructed by Tilak to leave India, as it was 'too dangerous [. . . and] had no place for him', Khankhoje immediately retraced his steps out back to Persia, then went on to Moscow, and eventually settled in Mexico.[64] Whereas Prasad, Khankhoje and several others established a productive coalition with Muslim tribesmen, Har Dayal, in the very midst of the war, gave up on the partisan combat of the ghadri and took refuge in Switzerland, dismissing Ottoman collaboration as shot through with 'nationalism' and declaring that there was 'no such thing as Pan-Islamism'.[65] Scorning his own efforts, Har Dayal now applied his pen to the topics of 'race' warfare and the future of small states. More generally, partisans' individual lives as well as their theatres of combat, however, remained too dispersed to easily be assembled piece by piece into any narrative or ideological cohesion.

62. Prasad was dubbed an 'anarchist', and his newspaper *Intiqam*, regarded as Pan-Islamist propaganda: IOR/L/PS/10/683; on the campaign, Percy Sykes, *A History of Persia* (Oxford: Oxford University Press, 1922).Various such groups or cells connected or imputed to be connected to the Ghadar were intercepted in the territories from Baghdad to Afghanistan between 1915 and 1918: see 'History of the Revolutionary Party in Baghdad', 'Baghdad Conspiracy Case' and 'Punishment of Indian Revolutionaries' in IOR/L/MIL/7/18504.

63. Sawhney, *I Shall Never*, 178.

64. Ibid., 208, 209–25.

65. Har Dayal, *Forty-Four Months*, 2–35, and see, for instance, his 'Some Aspects of Zionism', *The People*, 28 March 1926.

A Finite Declaration, or, India in Kabul

The Ghadar came to a climax on 1 December 1915, with the declaration of a Provisional Government of India in Kabul. This Provisional Government was hosted by Amir Amanullah, one of the sons of the Afghan ruler and the future leader of Afghanistan. It brought together the cellular fraternities of the Deoband cleric Ubaidullah Sindhi and of Barkatullah Bhopali, an ally of Har Dayal and the editor of *Islamic Fraternity*, under the leadership of Mahendra Pratap, a princely bon vivant who was declared president.

The formation of this government not only created a counterpoint to the Turkish Caliphate as it rallied to the cause of free India, but also gave a brief glimpse into the combination of intrigue and violence that sought to remake the ideological map of the world. Much like the partisans' war discussed above, the conventional warfare and mass destruction of the First World War fuelled but also obscured what were nevertheless undeniably audacious endeavours such as the Provisional Government of India in Kabul.

Mahendra Pratap was a princely overlord, married into Punjab's Sikh royalty, who had dined and banqueted his way around the world twice before the war and in the course of his travels had befriended the patron of insurgents, Krishnavarma. Idealistic and restless, Pratap had donated a part of his considerable estate in north India to a technical educational institute named 'Prem' (Love) and gone into self-imposed exile from India in 1914. Princely entitlement gained him an audience with the Kaiser when he arrived in Berlin, via Turkey, soon after the war broke out, and in 1915, the German diplomatic and military establishment directed him to Kabul, where he was greeted as a royal personage. This was a bold bid to synergise a 'Great Game' in the tribal outback of Persia, Central Asia and Afghanistan, and to declare a German presence on the British Empire's prized Indian frontier. Pratap appears as a high-level fixer, a rugged traveller and a man with a penchant for risky intrigue. His main role was to connect and triangulate three anti-imperial vectors—the Ghadar as represented by Barkatullah, the radical Pan-Islamic cells that predated the Ghadar and the key figure Ubaidullah Sindhi—with political masters in Kabul, accompanied by German cash and arms in abundance.[66]

Although it is disputed, Sindhi was considered by many to be the author of the fantasy-driven 'silken letters' that had declared war on British India. He

---

66. Raja Mahendra Pratap, *My Life Story*, expanded edn, ed. Vir Singh (Delhi: Originals Publishers, 2004 [1943]), 36–74, and *Reflections of an Exile* (Lahore: Indian Book Company, 1946).

was born to a Sikh family in Sialkot, had converted to Islam at a young age, became a travelling religious teacher and missionary and was associated with the Deoband seminary and its famous leader, Hasan Madani.[67] In the shadow of the Balkan Wars and prior to the First World War, an intricate web of associations, bodies and individual voluntarism from the north Indian heartlands had dispatched men and money across the Muslim world.[68] A mixture of Pan-Islamism, anti-imperialism and humanitarianism had inspired a variety of men, some of whom would later become well known as nationalist Muslims, such as Maulana Azad and M. A. Ansari, together with Abdul Bari and several young labouring men and students. Azad had both assisted men such as Sindhi in their travels and, through his Urdu newspaper *Al-Hilal*, expounded on the themes of *jihad*, civilisation, empire and the fate and future of Islam in the face of its constriction by an aggressive European expansionism.[69]

Moving from north and western India to Mecca and Medina, or the Hejaz and Kabul, Sindhi traversed this older Muslim landscape in a bid to galvanise Muslims to wage war. The three letters written on pieces of yellow silk cloth cryptically detailed entreaties to key officials in the Muslim world and plans for a large-scale movement of Indian Muslims to Kabul with fantastic plans for a violent confrontation. This was to be achieved through a new coalition that included the Muslim leaders mentioned above, Mahendra Pratap, the Germans, the Russians and the Afghans.[70] But before that could happen, Sindhi was captured. Intercepted by British intelligence in late 1916 and considered to be a participant in another potent 'conspiracy' of the Junood-e-Rabbaniyah (Muslim Salvation Army), Sindhi was indicted and arrested in Mecca. Several hundred other Muslims (much like the ghadris) were also arrested in a sweeping crackdown on madrasas, mofussils and cities across India

---

67. Muhammad Hajjan Shaikh, *Maulana Ubaid Allah Sindhi: A Revolutionary Scholar* (Islamabad: National Institute of Historical and Cultural Research, 1986); Barbara D. Metcalf, *Islamic Revival in British India: Deoband, 1860–1900* (Princeton, NJ: Princeton University Press, 1982).

68. Aydin, *Politics of Anti-Westernism in Asia*; Adrian P. Ruprecht, 'De-Centering Humanitarianism: The Red Cross and India, c. 1877–1939' (unpublished doctoral dissertation, University of Cambridge, 2017); and on the instability of the archival record and narrative, Faridah Zaman, 'Revolutionary History and the Post-Colonial Muslim: Re-Writing the "Silk Letters Conspiracy" of 1916', *Journal of Asian Studies* 39:3 (2016), 626–43.

69. Ayesha Jalal, 'Striking a Just Balance: Maulana Azad as a Theorist of Trans-National *Jihad*', *Modern Intellectual History* 4:1 (2007), 95–107.

70. On Russia and Indian 'revolutionaries', see G. Dmitriev, *Indian Revolutionaries in Central Asia* (Gurgaon: Hope India Publications, 2002).

before any confrontation could place.[71] The *Tehreek-e-Reshmi Rumaal*, or Silk Letter Conspiracy, became for the imperial authorities evidence of a crucial 'Muhammaden current' that flowed through the Ghadar and was a critical factor in the declaration of a provisional government of India in Kabul. Several thousand Indian Muslims who had appeared in Kabul in response to a call for *hijrat* (migration or exodus) by their leaders were left spectacularly stranded and deported back to India to face imperial wrath and punishment.[72]

Soon after this imperial intervention, Kabul, which had primarily played the role of a host, asked its guests such as Mahendra Pratap, Barakatullah and several other Indians to leave Afghanistan.[73] Pratap reappeared in Moscow and spent another two decades outside India, circumnavigating the world twice more, either flying the red flag or advertising the cause of Pan-Asianism in Japan, continuing to live the good life and meeting leading figures such as Marcus Garvey in New York.[74] Returning to India in late 1946, he devoted the rest of his long life to education. Eschewing both the Congress and the Communist parties, he ran as an independent candidate for Parliament and is above all remembered today for defeating, in the general elections of 1957, the leader of Hindu nationalism, and later prime minister of India, Atal Bihari Vajpayee.

Sindhi for his part moved, in the interwar period, between Moscow and Turkey and eventually back to the Hejaz, spending the majority of his time teaching and researching in madrasas in Mecca. After spending a quarter of a century away, he returned to India, joined the Congress and, like other leaders of the Deoband seminary, remained opposed to separatism and partition.[75] He fitfully sought to update Islamism with Bolshevism;[76] his clearest ideological

---

71. 'Silken Letters Conspiracy Case: A Brief Report of the Case': official documents published in Muhammad Miyan Deobandi, *Silken Letters Movement: Accounts of 'Silken Handkerchief Letters Conspiracy Case' from British Records*, trans. Muhammadullah Qasmi (New Delhi: Shaikhul Hind Academy/Manak Publications, 2013), 98–312.

72. Rowlatt, *Sedition Committee Report*.

73. Shaikh, *Maulana Ubaid*, 30–119.

74. Pratap, *My Life Story*.

75. Shaikh, *Maulana Ubaid*, 260. Sindhi wrote first-person accounts including *Dhati Diary* (Lahore, 1946) and *Kabul Mein Sat Sal* (Lahore, 1955) and a political text entitled *The Constitution of the Federated Republics of India* (Istanbul, 1926), trans. Zafar Hasan, and several discourses on the Quran, including *Khulasat al-Quran* (Hyderabad, n.d.), on revolutionary Islam (*Qurani Jang-e-Inqlab*), and on the figure who inspired him most, *Shah Walli Allah aur Unki Siyasi Tahrik* (Lahore, 1952).

76. On Sindhi's Bolshevism, see Ammar Ali Jan, 'A Study of Communist Thought in India, 1919–1951' (unpublished doctoral dissertation, University of Cambridge, 2017).

inspiration, however, was and arguably remained the nineteenth-century Wahabi thinker Shah Wali Ullah. In his traversing of Muslim lands, Sindhi was retracing the lines of an older geography to radicalise the origins of Islam, rather than being foundationally novel or even profoundly disruptive.

Barkatullah, on the other hand, eventually returned to California via a brief stop in the newly formed Soviet Union where, as noted at the start of this chapter, he met Lenin. Like Khankhoje, however, he remained unconvinced enough to avoid becoming a fully paid-up communist. Making the Yugantar Ashram his perch, he died there in 1927 shortly after delivering a lecture to a packed auditorium of the students and immigrant labourers who continued to converge upon the salubrious surroundings of Sacramento, but by then mainly to converse rather than conspire.[77]

After the stillborn declaration of the Provisional Government of India in Kabul, Barkatullah tossed between the different ideological currents of Europe for several years without anchor. In Rome in 1924, he sought alignment with Mussolini's Fascist Party for an 'Indo–Italian Commercial Syndicate' that never came into effect, while aiding Ansari and others associated with the Khilafat (Caliphate) movement at the same time. The end of the war and the fall of the Ottoman Caliphate had concentrated the efforts and attention of several Muslims in India and, as is well known, Gandhi allied the Indian National Congress to the Muslim movement for the Caliphate's restoration. Barkatullah wrote pamphlets urging this, as it represented for him the true constitutional spirit and form of Islam.[78] But he remained restless. His attempt to become the Comintern's representative for India was declined in favour of M. N. Roy, and he worked only fitfully in the Bolshevik cause. He returned once more to Kabul, only to head back definitively to Sacramento.[79] Interestingly, he did not join Pratap, after the war, in Tokyo — a city that had been hospitable to him in the opening years of the century.

Primarily a ghadri, Barkatullah remained on the move: his militant mobility indeed predated many of the world-historical events that collided with his own life and defined the course of the last century. One of his biographers, from

77. Shyam Sundar Saxena, *Barkatullah Bhopali* (Bhopal: Swaraj Sansathan Sanchalya, Government of Madhya Pradesh, 2004), 54–55.

78. Mohammad Barkatullah, *The Khilafat* (reprinted; Dacca: Society for Pakistan Studies, 1970). I am grateful to Cemil Aydin who alerted me to this and for a copy of the book.

79. Supplementary History Sheet of Maulvi Barkatullah, IOR/R/15/5/62, IOR/L/PJ/12/213 and IOR/L/PS/11/173; also, summaries of pamphlets and lists of the scores of Muslims sentenced to either prison or death in this campaign, IOR/R/15/5/62 and IOR/L/MIL/7/18504.

his hometown of Bhopal in central India, claims that it was soon after hearing a lecture by the late nineteenth-century radical anti-imperialist thinker Jalaludin Al-Afghani that Barkatullah first left India.[80] Like several other Indian students, he received Krishnaverma's patronage in England, first in London and then in Liverpool, and with the decampment of India House then left for Tokyo. In 1909 Barkatullah was appointed as a language teacher at Tokyo University, a position that was bankrolled by Krishnaverma's friend Madame Cama and her circle of Parsi benefactors, including the famed business family of the Tatas.[81] In the absence of a coherent ideology and committed fidelity to it—whether it might be Pan-Islamism, Pan-Asianism, Bolshevism or even fascism—Barkatullah's trajectory points to an individual life as both weapon and object of a new kind of politics that the Ghadar signified.

Creating the partisan as a deliberate outcome of confrontation, the Ghadar's inchoate and short-lived coalition with the historical if itinerant politics of Islam through the Provisional Government in Kabul was neither purely contingent nor entirely instrumental. For one thing, Islam had always been characterised by a genuinely global outlook and horizon that has historically been dependent on the mobility of its co-religionists, as Islam transcended territories.[82] The radicalisation by the Ghadar of a militant mobility and its involvement with Pan-Islamism came to imbue the latter with the opposite sense, however: one of territoriality. *Ghadri-Mujahideen*, or the amalgamation of the Ghadar with Pan-Islamism, centred Islam upon a specific location, as it placed India centre-stage.

Secondly, with the movement of the centre of Islam from Constantinople—however fleetingly—four years before the fall of the Caliphate, Kabul emerged as the seat of a second Caliphate. The Afghan ruler Habibullah, considered at this moment a Caliph, although largely neutral with regard to the British Empire, was soon assassinated: a point that was not missed by his rivals.[83] Yet, the

80. Saxena, *Barkatullah*, 11–13; also M. Irfan, *Maulana Barkatullah Bhopali* (Bhopal: n.p., 1969), and Humayun Ansari, 'Maulana Barkatullah Bhopali's Transnationalism: Pan-Islamism, Colonialism and Radical Politics', in Gotz Nordbruch and Umar Ryad (eds.), *Transnational Islam in Interwar Europe* (New York: Palgrave Macmillan, 2014), 181–209.

81. Bose, *Indian Revolutionaries*, 111–12.

82. Pankaj Mishra, *From the Ruins of Empire: The Intellectuals Who Remade Asia* (London: Allen Lane, 2012), ch. 2; Nikki R. Keddie, *An Islamic Response to Imperialism: Political and Religious Writings of Sayyid Jamal al Din 'al-Afghani'* (Berkeley: University of California Press, 1968).

83. This event triggered the third Anglo–Afghan War: Willem Vogelsang, *The Afghans* (Oxford: Blackwell, 2002); on the Great Game involving Russia, Germany and Turkey, see F. M. Bailey and Peter Hopkirk, *Mission to Tashkent* (Oxford: Oxford University Press, 2002).

declaration of the Provisional Government of India and its associated actions decentralised Muslim authority even as it briefly established a new territorial centrality. Ostensibly and arguably, this ushered in the division of a global Muslim brotherhood along territorial boundaries. Kabul thus appeared as the frontier between South Asian and Ottoman- or Arab-centred Islam. Such a division, between an Arab or Turkic Islam on the one hand and on the other an Islam with its political pivot in India that sought to detach itself from Arabian influence, not to say imperialism, was philosophically elaborated and strengthened by none other than Muhammad Iqbal. As a subsequent chapter of this book describes, Iqbal's critique and rejection of Pan-Islamism not only brought him into direct confrontation with the *ulema* (clerics), but also, critically, enabled him to develop a new and consequential language of political Islam that envisaged the rejection of Arabia and the Caliphate in favour of a republican sovereignty.

Finally, these events in Kabul helped to dismantle the idea of unitary global *ummah* (brotherhood). India became politically pre-eminent in the global life of twentieth-century Islam. Such a flipping between the de-territorialised India invoked and staged by the Ghadar, that sought to redistribute Islam's territory ephemerally and spectrally even through the Provisional Government, and the sensational story of the Silk Letter controversy, endowed Kabul with the potential to repeat a historical sequence: the Ghadar having identified itself with the memory of 1857, it is striking that Kabul has resurfaced in the twenty-first century as the pivot of new militant Islam.[84]

The Ghadar's commitment to violence as communication, militancy as mobility and the disruption of institutionalised politics, premised on the death drive of sacrifice, remains instructive. In its aftermath, the imperial state re-armed itself against such insurrections through law and violence and influenced the establishment of international jurisdictions. The subjective element of this politics, on the other hand, has left interruptions, or traces and residues, in other ideologies too. Unique in its form and content, the Ghadar cannot be understood in terms of fidelity to any specific ideology, or even as a set of formal propositions.

Yet, and primarily, it was the global that emerged as an abstract totality mirroring the subjectivity that lay at the foundation of the Ghadar's politics. That

84. See Faisal Devji, *Landscapes of the Jihad: Militancy, Morality, Modernity* (London: Hurst & Co., 2005) for an insightful discussion of the dispersal of militant Islam, its capture of Kabul and the place of India in its imagination in the twenty-first century.

is to say, the subjectivity of the ghadri derived its existential dimension from the abstraction of 'the planet'. The intermediation of militant mobility momentarily unfixed territorial demarcations, thus opening the possibility of the global as a political landscape or horizon. It was precisely in its inchoateness that the Ghadar aimed to subvert the settled imperial connectivity of the globe, whether in the form of the postal system or the telegraph. This was achieved by taking violence as a means of strategic communication, with the individual as the mobile and sacrificial subject that summoned the whole world as its stage. There is an almost fictional quality to the episodes and lives sketched above: the quality that made *Greenmantle* a best-selling novel of the twentieth century; viewed from the other side, indeed, the successful foiling of these so-called conspiracies has formed the evidence and basis for the writing of triumphal stories of the institutionalisation of secret services in that century.[85] The cellular and decentralised formations of the partisan, meanwhile, can be interpreted as having had another, profound and potent, effect.

The Planet as Potential

The Ghadar, through individualised insurrection, created a global geography of interruptions. Territory is one of the central and most powerful ways of imagining and focusing the twentieth century's norm of politics and has been constituent of modern empires and nations. It was, however, through the subjectivisation of violence that the objective territory of empire was made visible. The ghadri, as a subjective form of violence, was ultimately narcissistic. But the Ghadar, which powerfully and visibly made of extra-territoriality a militant practice, was neither an extension nor the circumvention of the national. This geography, conducted through the politics of radical violence, whereby territory was neither simply imagined nor measured but was instead traversed and travelled, from one locale to another, had no final refuge or telos. The Ghadar's geography, in short, was neither territorial nor global in a spatial sense, but was profoundly phantasmic, in that it was visionary but also illusory. Such a geography became visible through single acts of violence, and then disappeared.

The Ghadar was, in short, a landscape of potential. Never actualised as state power, whether in India or elsewhere, this subjective violence and the figure

85. John Buchan, *Greenmantle* (London: Penguin Books, 2008 [1910]).

of partisan were concerned above all with an opening. As a set of practices, it had no determinate or unified content and meaning; but as an opening it portended elements of the future. The impossibility of its becoming institutionalised, or rather its steadfast anti-statism, mark the Ghadar as a series of effects that can be glimpsed in other political projects but cannot be simply incorporated into, or circumscribed by the limits of, such historical formations. It has been considered either as a failure of revolution or as a precursor to it—whether for the Kirti Kisan Sabha in Punjab or Indian communism, or even the sacrificial politics of the iconic Bhagat Singh, all of which claim a genealogy or inspiration from it. In short, transcending its own specifics, the Ghadar has become a trope, even a symbol.

In its ultimate import, the Ghadar attached itself to the determining and dominant predicates of empire and nation, both sources of privation and denial, even as it created potential in relation to them. Disavowal defined its relations with empire, and the nation became a source of mystical power for the sacrificial subject. This opening, or potentiality, called into question the strongest principles of both nation and empire. As a force-field of effects, a related potential lay in the possibility that it forged between the actual and the not-actual: an indeterminacy that allowed this historical opening to be a fusion between the active and the dormant, and thus vulnerable to appropriation. Today it nourishes the histories both of Sikh and of Indian nationalism, of Indian communism, of global anarchism and even, as interpreted from the imperial perspective, an account of the success of surveillance and the suppression of revolution. It is the potentiality of the Ghadar—an opening or rupture in the continuum of settled histories of empire and nation, with its anti-statist and subjective thrust, secrecy as its mode of operation and violence as its visible expression—that has rendered it amenable to exposure and appropriation. Several, even contradictory, ideological projects, from anarchism to nationalism, incorporate the events of the Ghadar and the individual life-narratives of ghadris, which are often thus redistributed along those registers. The Ghadar remains, however, an unassimilable phenomenon, its uses, much like its actions, inexhaustible, but ultimately irregular and resistant to capture by any one ideology.

With the self as the founding and conclusion of a politics, life trajectories and biography were ruled by disruption that sought to unsettle the fixity of empire. Prior to his death in an American hotel, Har Dayal had seemingly settled into the life of a cosmopolitan emigré and public intellectual in

London, inhabiting libraries and giving lectures, and was an active member of The Open Conspiracy, the literary-activist society set up to promote the ideas of H. G. Wells.[86] He had ostensibly lost his former zeal for armed action and had penned an excoriating critique of German–Turkish exploits with Indian radicals and his own experience, in which racial discrimination loomed large.[87]

In the interwar era, lecturing and writing articles on the future of the state in the world, Har Dayal nevertheless kept a watchful eye on international affairs, and his attention was repeatedly drawn to what he deemed the insuperable but misplaced division of the world into 'east' and 'west'.[88] If a productive despair had marked Har Dayal's initial itinerary, then his last and major work, *Hints for Self-Culture*, published, in a deliberately philosophical vein, in 1934, didactically (as opposed to politically) repositioned the primacy of the individual subject.[89] Though lacking the aphoristic and arresting insights of a Nietzsche, Har Dayal's *Self-Culture* was nevertheless a call for the re-evaluation of philosophical inheritances. Elsewhere he had announced that 'I have never been able to discover what Hinduism is',[90] and in this spirit his book eschewed the metaphysical encasing and obsessions that had previously dominated Indian insights into self-realisation. But Har Dayal remained steadfast in his belief in the potential of the young, and the book in fact constituted a long sermon directed at the uninitiated but energetic curiosities of the adolescent. As such, while it exhorted the re-assessment of history by the individual, it is suffused by injunctions typical of a parent or teacher. Har Dayal's cosmopolitan pieties and instructions in *Hints for Self-Culture* were in direct contrast to his earlier writings, in which he had singled out education and its English incarnation as both the sign and weapon of an undesirable pacification,[91]

---

86. British Library, London, Add MS 71235: Peter Wells Papers, vol. 1, 1–68, Correspondence and lectures of Dr Har Dayal (1934–36).

87. Har Dayal, *Forty-Four Months*.

88. Lala Har Dayal, 'The Union of East and West: Some Difficulties and Problems', lecture delivered 26 July 1934, London (British Library, Add MS 71235: Peter Wells Papers).

89. Lala Har Dayal, *Hints for Self-Culture* (London: Watts & Co., 1934).

90. Lala Har Dayal, 'Some Phases of Contemporary Thought in India', in Har Dayal, *Writings*, 184.

91. Lala Har Dayal, *Amrit mein Vish* ... (Calcutta: Vanik Press, 1922) and the same in English, *Our Educational Problem* (Madras: Tata Printing Works, 1922); both works were re-publications of essays written in the opening decade of the twentieth century and appeared through the support of Lala Lajpat Rai.

breaking away from which, and indeed from the life of the intellectual, had been constitutive of the partisan ghadri.

Curiously, then, Har Dayal had moved away from the creed of violence, admonishing that 'Imperialism provokes murder and then retaliates by murder . . . But do ye vow to have no part in murder of any kind. All can take life, but no one can restore it.'[92] Notwithstanding calls for reform ranging from dietary habits to a new kind of conjugality, and condemnation of nationalism in favour of a notion of the free subject of a future 'World State', the book lacked any potent radical thrust.[93] In the end, the primacy of an ethics of self-hood that Har Dayal expounded in *Hints for Self-Culture* appeared at best well intentioned, and at worst unexemplary. It neither exploited nor synthesised the spectacular itineraries of the self that he had, above all, personally forged or traversed.[94]

The Ghadar had deliberately sought a collision with epochal events of the last century that had highlighted the potency of the self in its global horizons. The highly individualised subject of the Ghadar had made visible the possibilities of a restless and sacrificial self. The ghadri was, by definition, devoid of the cosmopolitan sanctimony that characterised Har Dayal's later reflections upon the self. It would seem, nevertheless, that till the end, a discontinuity with the past marked Har Dayal's life, words and actions. In his later strategic silence regarding the audacious project of the self that the Ghadar had announced, he left entirely open the question of whether it had been a failure, or a mistake, or remained a potentiality.

The emphasis of its exegesis in this chapter has been upon the Ghadar as potentiality alone, in that it created the possibility of something that could happen, but does not appear to have been actualised. As a chimerical actuality, then, the Ghadar was without predicates. The sacrificial subject defined by the Ghadar sought to unsettle violently the deep sediments of history. In doing so, it made manifest the condition of a new political possibility. The Ghadar's focus upon the force of the self and the death drive of sacrifice was not, in the

92. Har Dayal, *Hints*, 234–35.

93. Ibid., 270–363; for a counter-interpretation of this book, see Daniel J. Elam, 'The Anti-colonial Ethics of Lala Har Dayal's *Hints for Self-Culture*', NMML Occasional Paper 9 (New Delhi: Nehru Memorial Museum and Library, 2013).

94. One possible explanation could be that he finally ceased to be 'stateless', having acquired a passport via the British government. At any rate, his last book's emphasis on a new kind of cosmopolitan piety was at odds with the project of the Ghadar.

event, simply depleted or destroyed; by redirecting the death drive of a sacrificial politics with the individual as its pre-eminent subject, Gandhi, as Chapter 4 describes, surmounted the powerful truth of violence to arrive at a new
and visible fraternity. While the ghadri's militant mobility globalised India by
leaving her shores, it was, conversely, in his return to India from South Africa
that Gandhi expounded most clearly and consequentially a politics of the self.
Gandhi's nemesis, Savarkar, a leading occupant of the India House in Hampstead in 1910, was however forced to return to India a few years earlier than the
Mahatma. Savarkar, as the next chapter elaborates, discerned and discovered
anew the seductions of secrecy for the summoning of a violent fraternity.

3

Hindutva's War and the Battlefield of India

In the name of God

In the name of Bharat Mata

In the name of all the Martyrs that have shed their blood for Bharat Mata

By the love, innate in all men and women, that I bear to the land of my birth,
wherein lies the sacred ashes of my forefathers, and which is the cradle of my
children,

By the tears of Hindi Mothers for their children whom the Foreigner has
enslaved, imprisoned, tortured and killed,

I, ...

Convinced that without Absolute Political Independence or Swarajya my
country can never rise to that exalted position among the nations of the earth
which is Her due,

And convinced also that Swarajya can never be attained except by the waging
of a bloody and relentless war against the Foreigner,

Solemnly and sincerely Swear that I shall from this moment do everything in
my power to fight for Independence and place the Lotus Crown of Swaraj
on the head of my Mother;

And with this object, I join the Abhinav Bharat, the Revolutionary Society of
all Hindusthan, and swear that I shall ever be true and faithful to this solemn
Oath, and I shall obey the orders of this body;

If I betray the whole or any part of this solemn Oath, or if I betray this body
or any other body working with a similar object,

May I be doomed to the fate of the perjurer!

—*BANDE MATARAM*, THE OATH OF
ABHINAV BHARAT (YOUNG INDIA)[1]

1. Vinayak D. Savarkar, *Oath of Abhinav Bharat* (n.p., n.d.), IOR Proscribed Publications
Microfilms 11599/6. (NB: 'Hindutva' here refers to the ideology developed by Savarkar, while
italicised *Hindutva* refers to the specific work that he authored and published.)

VINAYAK D. SAVARKAR, known today as the author of Hindutva, wrote the above oath a few years before his arrest at Victoria Station in London on 13 March 1910. He was arrested for, among other things, writing incendiary prose, including this oath, which eventually led to his transportation for life and a long prison sentence in the penal colony of the Andaman Islands. Though no direct connection was established, Savarkar was believed to have inspired Madanlal Dhingra, who had assassinated Curzon Wyllie, a British army official and aide-de-camp to Lord Morley, the secretary of state for India, in 1909 at a public meeting in London. Head of India House, the secret society based in London, at the time of his arrest, Savarkar's four-year sojourn in London had been eventful. He had also set up another secret cell, Abhinav Bharat, or Young India; it is its oath declaring the necessity of war that opens this chapter.

Curzon Wyllie's assassination and Dhingra's swift hanging in Pentonville prison in 1909 ensured the dispersal of the India House group, taking its insurrectionist denizens in different global and ideological directions. The charismatic Har Dayal went underground in Algiers and reappeared only a few years later in America, becoming the elusive and short-lived figurehead of the Ghadar, as discussed in the previous chapter. Dhingra, who was from Amritsar in the Punjab, had been a member of Savarkar's Abhinav Bharat and resident of the India House while ostensibly studying engineering in London. Savarkar was suspected of having provided firearms training to Dhingra.[2] In a short statement at his trial, Dhingra echoed the oath, citing his duty to his Motherland, so as to 'prove the justice of my deed'.[3] His final words on the gallows were somewhat incoherent, but restated the sentiment and message of the oath penned by Savarkar:

> I believe that a nation unwillingly held down by foreign bayonets is in a perpetual state of war. Since open battle is rendered impossible, I attacked by surprise . . . since cannon could not be had I drew forth and fired a revolver . . . Neither rich nor able, a poor son like myself can offer nothing but his blood . . . The only lesson required in India at present is to learn how to die, and the only way to teach it is by dying alone.[4]

2. Malwinder Jit Singh Waraich and Kuldip Puri, *Tryst with Martyrdom: Trial of Madan Lal Dhingra* (Chandigarh: Unistar, 2003).

3. Madan Lal Dhingra, Assassination and Killing, criminal record ref. no.: T19090719-55, Old Bailey online, https://www.oldbaileyonline.org/browse.jsp?id=t19090719-55-offence-1&div=t19090719-55#highlight.

4. Waraich and Puri, *Tryst*, 52.

The powerful idea conveyed by the oath of Abhinav Bharat of sacrifice understood specifically as 'learning how to die', as Dhingra recapitulated it at his
hanging, was foundational to the political ideas and practices of the Ghadar,
and later, even for Gandhi.

Since at least 1908, and as discussed in earlier chapters, the language of
sacrifice suffused emergent and powerful political languages, which turned on
the question of fraternity. For Tilak, sacrifice was equated with a theory of
political action that enabled the rupture of ordinary relations and historical
time, and that allowed for violence. Emanating from and centred on the subject, political action as a form of sacrifice was for Tilak marked by its exceptional nature, distinctive and not to be confused or equated with ordinary
duties or times. For the Ghadar, the language of sacrifice was formalised
through oath-taking and poetry recitation and as a commitment to die for a
historical cause greater than the subject. Gandhi, as will be discussed in the
next chapter, intervened in this deathscape by making central a form of sacrifice that was oriented especially towards the Other, whether hostile or intimate, but that was once again premised and focused on the individual as the
subject of political and ethical transformation.[5] The deployment of sacrifice
wherein was invoked the language of life and death *in extremis*, whether by
Tilak, Gandhi or the ghadri, created and activated a subject-centred idea of
sovereignty. The emphasis on war, with India as its principal theatre, however,
was specific to Savarkar's political ideas; and it should be noted that in 1948,
just short of forty years after Dhingra was hanged, Savarkar was to be implicated once more, though not convicted, for his role in Gandhi's assassination.
Once again, it was his follower who fired the shot, and Savarkar can be identified as the shadow behind the deed, though without direct guilt or
responsibility.[6]

War, as this chapter elaborates and argues, was the foundation-stone of
the political ideas of Hindutva, whose authorship is indelibly associated
with Savarkar. However, the conception of war and its necessity as expounded by Hindutva was not to be construed or elaborated within an ethical
or even a theological context, as it was by Savarkar's mentor Tilak, through a
resurgence and reinterpretation of the *Bhagavad Gita* that became foundational

---

5. Devji, *Impossible Indian.*

6. J. L. Kapur, *Report of the Commission of Enquiry into the Conspiracy to Murder Mahatma
Gandhi* (New Delhi: Government of India, 1970), 1–6; A. G. Noorani, *Savarkar and Hindutva:
The Godse Connection* (New Delhi: Leftworld Books, 2002), 12–25.

for twentieth-century political thought.[7] Nor was it to be understood as a deliberate confrontation with history within the context of global warfare, as predicated by the partisan politics of the Ghadar. Instead, the salience of India as a battlefield would emerge as the most significant theme for Hindutva.

Gandhi's Shadow

Savarkar's political life spanned the first six decades of the twentieth century. Prior to Dhingra's assassination of Curzon Wyllie—the deadly shot that marked the opening sequence of a global militant politics—Savarkar was already acknowledged as a political figure of some importance, although as yet not associated with the idea of Hindutva. In 1908, within months of each other, Tilak and Gandhi published their foundational political texts, on the *Gita* and *Hind Swaraj* respectively; and it is notable that in 1909 Savarkar too published his first large-scale study, but in the historical tradition. Written in London, his *The Indian War of Independence*—now regarded as a 'totemic' record of the events of 1857—was immediately banned upon publication. It was Gandhi's *Hind Swaraj*—although this too was banned, in 1910—that attracted a wide audience, whether in appreciation or denigration of the idiosyncratic text.

Widely considered to be his political manifesto, Gandhi's short but provocative book was among other things a response to the idea of violence as sacrifice for political transformation that he had encountered amongst the young Indian men in India House. Savarkar appears for the first time as a shadow in Gandhi's text. It is debatable, or rather it remains unproven, whether Savarkar was indeed the unnamed adversarial interlocutor in Gandhi's book, which was written in the form of a dialogue. *Hind Swaraj* was nevertheless addressed to precisely such a figure: one who espoused a new political language of violence.[8] Gandhi had even considered Dhingra to be 'innocent', on account of his being in a 'state of intoxication' due to 'ill-digested reading of worthless writing' and having been 'egged on' by the truly guilty. The Mahatma dismissed Dhingra's passionate defence in terms of India as the

---

7. Shruti Kapila and Faisal Devji (eds.), *Political Thought in Action: The Bhagavad Gita and Modern India* (Cambridge: Cambridge University Press, 2013).

8. Anthony J. Parel's 'Introduction' to Gandhi, *HS*, xviii–xix.

mother as having been 'learnt by rote'.[9] Four decades later, Savarkar was to be perceived once more as a shadow: this time behind the plot to kill the 'Father of the Nation' himself.

The use of the metaphor of the shadow for Savarkar is deliberate. Evoking the idea of duplication, the shadow is a source of identification inasmuch as it has been construed as a figuration of the death drive. Since the writings of Freud, and through the twentieth century, the shadow has been understood as having both destructive and creative potential. Above all, in Freudian terms, as an unconscious element, its existence, expression or personification is denied by the subject precisely because it has the capacity to overwhelm that subject. In the interwar period Freud elaborated, in numerous writings, upon the equal significance of hatred and antagonism and of love and desire in human history. The ambivalent interplay of desire and death, as he famously wrote to Albert Einstein on the eve of the Second World War, was crucial to understanding the endurance of violence and war. At the behest of the League of Nations, Einstein had asked Freud to address not only the persistence of war, but also the ease with which hatred and war could impassion and captivate individuals and collectivities alike.

In his response, Freud restated that desire and death were equally essential, concurrent with and constitutive of humanity, and that this duality manifested itself as what he termed 'identification'.[10] In related writings, he singled out identification as one of the principal phenomena of political life, encompassing emulation and admiration, but equally hatred. Identification, he argued, manifests particularly potently in intimate bonds and relations: the hostility and hatred that stemmed from identification and intimacy is powerful precisely because aversion between intimates is reversible or bridgeable. Such intimate enmity, entailing the dual logics of murder and affinity, led to wars, but was equally significant for creating fellowship.[11]

One of the central arguments of this book is that hostility and enmity in India gained significance and salience from intimacy. Thus far psychoanalytic

9. M. K. Gandhi, 'Curzon Wyllie's Assassination', after 16 July 1909, *Collected Works of Mahatma Gandhi*, www.gandhiserve.net/about-mahatma-gandhi/collected-works-of-mahatma-gandhi (hereafter *CWMG*) 9, 302–3, at 302.

10. Sigmund Freud, 'Why War?', in Sigmund Freud, *On Murder, Mourning and Melancholia*, trans. Shaun Whiteside (The New Penguin Freud, ed. Adam Phillips) and (London: Penguin Books, 2005), 219–32.

11. Freud, *Mass Psychology*, 17–106.

approaches have remained undeclared; their overt invocation here is in part informed by the need to understand the emotive charge that underlies the defining duality represented by Gandhi and Savarkar, one that remains intact to date; *à propos*, this is perhaps the only political antagonism in India that has occasioned any, albeit sporadic, psychoanalytic discussion, due to the psychic burden that overwhelms the issue of parricide.[12]

Recent scholarship and political commentary have posited Gandhi's antagonism with regard to the Dalit leader B. R. Ambedkar as fundamental to the political unfolding of modern India;[13] subsequent chapters in this book elaborate upon the nature of fraternity and hostility in relation to caste, and especially Ambedkar's divergence from Gandhi and from anti-statist, individuated languages of sovereignty. From the outset, however, Gandhi and Savarkar were twinned as antagonists, and as this chapter and the next will argue, their antagonism was borne of an intimate 'identification' in the Freudian sense. Not only did their antagonism predate Ambedkar; it did not acquire the form of denial, denunciation and debate that marked Gandhi's and Ambedkar's political differences. The antagonism between Gandhi and Savarkar remained unspoken, if entirely understood. The stakes and objects of identification that formed their intimate enmity amounted to a rivalry over Hinduism, particularly its potential for fraternity; in short, its political relationship to India. A known atheist, Savarkar coined 'Hindutva' as a new political vocabulary, while Gandhi famously embraced religion openly, to court friendship and fraternity.

Savarkar, although implicated, would not be convicted for the assassination of Gandhi; but it was his Hindutva ideology that formed the Mahatma's shadow, and and was eventually to kill him. In the forty-year period between the publication of *Hind Swaraj* in 1908 and Gandhi's murder in January 1948, the Indian political landscape was irrevocably transformed. Eventful and highly mobilised, the realisation of the nation-state on the subcontinent, along with its contested narratives, has formed the basis of historical scholarship. Equally, in the context of the electoral success of political parties

12. Ashis Nandy, 'Final Encounter: The Politics of Assassination of Gandhi', in Ashis Nandy, *At the Edge of Psychology: Essays in Politics and Culture* (Delhi: Oxford University Press, 1999), 7–98.

13. Arundhati Roy (ed.), *The Annihilation of Caste: The Doctor and the Saint* (London: Verso, 2014) and Aishwary Kumar, *Radical Equality: Ambedkar, Gandhi and the Risk of Democracy* (Stanford, CA: Stanford University Press, 2015).

associated with what has been termed 'Hindu nationalism' in the last decade of the twentieth century, a 'reverse teleological' move has claimed this nationalism's 'origins' in Savarkar's ideology.[14] These approaches have overwhelmed and obscured the historical context within which Hindutva was actually articulated and elaborated. Arguably neither a variant upon nor a religious specification of it, Hindutva was rather pitted against the dominant form of Indian nationalism.

Hindutva was, I argue, a theory of violence in search of its history. It emerged strictly in the context of Gandhi and his political ideas and practices. Savarkar's militant ideas and historical writings were forged primarily in relation to Gandhi, in relation to whose visible politics he functioned as at best a hidden and at worst a secretive parallel. Although their mutual hostility would remain largely unexpressed, albeit widely assumed, Savarkar's shadow confers a figuration upon Gandhi. Minimally, this constitutive and mutual figuration of Savarkar and Gandhi has been received and symbolised as one of violence versus nonviolence.

Strikingly, Savarkar and Gandhi met only twice. Their first set of meetings took place in London, and they met for the final time after a gap of nearly two decades, in 1927, in Ratnagiri. For most of that period Savarkar was in prison in the Andaman Islands, while Gandhi had become the public face of the idea of a free India. More critically, Gandhi emerged as a spokesman for Indian Muslims who had rallied to the global cause of a restoration of the Caliphate after its fall. The initial encounter of the two men was in the context, detached from India, of London: the environment that occasioned Gandhi's feverish shipboard composition of his *Hind Swaraj*. Indeed, his encounter with anticolonial radicals, including Savarkar, inspired and clarified Gandhi's own political convictions. His response to the insurgent, but inchoate, politics that he encountered in London amongst young Indian men became the motivation for his brief but, in terms of its significance monumental, political manifesto. An emphasis on the subject as the foundation of the political was common to both men—and it was in this vein that Savarkar initially inspired the Ghadar's sacrificial politics. Moreover, as is further discussed below, they shared the invocation of celibacy as a condition of the political subject; it was deployed to divergent ends, however, which further marked out the lineaments of their enmity.

14. Christophe Jafferlot, *The Hindu Nationalist Movement in India* (New York: Columbia University Press, 1996).

By the time of their second and final encounter, Savarkar was a figure trans-formed. He had spent over a decade exiled to the notorious Andaman Islands, serving a long prison sentence. Then in 1923, at the whimpering end of the Khilafat movement, he had published *Essentials of Hindutva*, his own political manifesto. The second meeting was not a success.[15] Through the interwar pe-riod, Gandhi was chastised by Savarkar's followers who begrudged the fact that he had done little, if anything, to secure Savarkar's release from the Anda-mans. Gandhi defended himself by stating that although Savarkar's release from the penal colony was inevitable and despite their 'differences' on 'certain fundamentals', he could 'never contemplate' Savarkar's 'incarceration' with any 'equanimity'.[16] By 1939, Gandhi was dismissive of Savarkar, though perhaps also resigned, even reconciled, to their divergence. When asked again about their relationship by one of Savarkar's acolytes, he confessed, 'I have tried to woo him and his friends. I have walked over to Savarkar's house. I have gone out of my way to win him over. But I have failed.'[17]

Thus, as indicated above, Savarkar and Hindutva, though closely identified with Gandhian politics, essentially remained in parallel and a shadow to Gan-dhi. At the same time, if not for Savarkar himself, then certainly for his follow-ers and acolytes, Gandhi was not simply seen as hostile, but was also recog-nised as superior: a superiority evinced at the very least in the Mahatma's ability to effect change—whether in having a prison sentence revoked or something on a grander scale; and this only confirms the ambivalent nature of 'identification'. Significantly, too, both Gandhi and Savarkar named their political ideas in such a way as to designate them as both novel and specific. Gandhi's political vision was founded on and named for truth (*satya*), the insistence upon and visibility of which made *Satyagraha* (insistence on truth) both the precept and practice of his politics.[18] And 'Hindutva', like 'Satya-graha', was a neologism.

15. Dhananjay Keer, *Savarkar and His Times* (Bombay: A. V. Keer, 1950), 175–77. Under house arrest in Ratnagiri, Savarkar had launched the *shuddhi* (purification) movement that sought to convert Muslims and bring them into the Hindu fold. In a city associated with Sa-varkar and his new politics, Gandhi explicitly damned and castigated *shuddhi*, and also offered to meet him; Gandhi, 'Speech at Ratnagiri' and 'Discussion with Savarkar', 1 March 1927, *CWMG* 38, 176–79 and 179–80.

16. M. K. Gandhi to Shankarrao Deo, 20 July 1937, *Bombay Chronicle*, *CWMG* 72, 50–51.

17. M. K. Gandhi to Haribhau G. Phatak, 12 October 1939, *CWMG* 76, 403.

18. Shruti Kapila, 'Gandhi before Mahatma: The Foundations of Political Truth', *Public Cul-ture* 23:2 (2011), 431–48.

Quilting Hindutva

As a theory of violence, Hindutva institutionalised the form and logic of secret societies and was a genealogical successor to the internationally dispersed cellular activities of the Ghadar. This line taken in this chapter, then, is in contrast to the dominant description of Hindutva as a 'conspiratorial' or 'crypto-' nationalism. Rather, Hindutva embraced the logic of open secrets discussed in the last chapter. Hindutva, unlike the Ghadar, institutionalised secrecy, via the formation of the paramilitary volunteer organisation the RSS (Rashtriya Swayam Sangh), created soon after the publication of Savarkar's manifesto, in 1925.[19] If the Ghadar has been seen to be akin to anarchism, Hindutva, and specifically the RSS, has been compared with fascism, by both critics and followers.[20] What is significant here, however, is not the simple mutation of one ideological form into another, but rather the work of secrecy in the conjuring of a fraternity that endured. Savarkar did not merely embody a genealogical link or node between the Ghadar and Hindutva; here, he is presented as the arch-theorist of violence, who marshalled and institutionalised the power of secrecy in creating new conditions for the eruption and manifestation of a new brotherhood.

Secrecy and fraternity were fundamental to the conceptual repertoire of Hindutva, along with blood and the significance of history and the writing of history. The overarching idea of war and the political as a manifestation of warfare rendered Hindutva a specifically twentieth-century ideology, privileging combat and confrontation.[21] Hindutva is, above all, a confrontation with the history of India, for its political mastery.

First articulated in the interwar era, Hindutva can best be understood as a form of 'quilting'. Quilting, it has been argued in the domain of ideology, is a process of 'totalisation', through which disconnected elements can be 'fixed', thus producing a structured set of connections and meaning. 'Hindutva' as a neologism gained significance in such a context, in that by being named, it created an object, inasmuch as it became a 'rigid designator': that is, a totalising force-field, that disallowed the sliding away of any of these elements into

19. Walter K. Anderson and Shridhar D. Damle, *The Brotherhood in Saffron: The Rashtriya Swayamsevak Sangh and Hindu Revivalism* (Boulder, CO: Westview Press, 1987).

20. Jairius Banaji (ed.), *Fascism: Essays on Europe and India* (New Delhi: Three Essays Collective, 2013).

21. Badiou, *Century*.

another set of meanings.[22] Discrete elements of India's history and geography, whether the Maratha Empire, or the Indus river, or even Hinduism itself, became nodal points within the totality of Hindutva. Creating connections and equivalences, but also displacements, among its constitutive elements, the word 'Hindutva' emerged as a rigid designator, aiming as such to express meaning that brooked no interpretation, only demanding either affirmation or negation, as it sought to capture an entire field of meaning.

To approach Hindutva thus is especially insightful, in that through its evocation, Hindutva created new content, connections, meanings and effects where none previously existed. Originating from a point of lack, Hindutva had neither antecedents nor history.[23] It was a name created to bridge the gap or void between the political and Hinduism. The obsessive recourse to history writing by its ideologues, and especially Savarkar, aimed ultimately to fill this gap, or remedy the lack of history itself. Though loss featured prominently in the recounting of history, as this became the vehicle for conveying Hindutva's ideology, what became apparent was in fact the absence of Hindutva in the long story of India. War became the crucial category for Hindutva: war as a decision-making event marked out enemies, but, equally importantly, was seen as the central element that framed the history and geography of the subcontinent. As a confrontation with India's past, Hindutva sought to convert and absorb historical elements and episodes under its own insignia. As a method of, as a disposition towards and, above all, as a confrontation with the past, history became the register through which Hindutva's political ideas of mastery were articulated.

The War of History

Hindutva is not a word but a history.

—SAVARKAR[24]

Completed a couple of years before his suicide in 1966 and published in independent India, Savarkar's final work, *Six Glorious Epochs of Indian History,* was a striking antithesis to his first publication, *The Indian War of Independence.*

22. Žižek, *Sublime Object,* 87–100.

23. Thomas Blom Hansen, *The Saffron Wave: Democracy and Hindu Nationalism in Modern India* (Princeton, NJ: Princeton University Press, 1999), 60–88.

24. V. D. Savarkar, *Essentials of Hindutva* (Hindi Sahitya Sadan, Delhi, 2005 [1923]), 3.

Written nearly sixty years apart, and despite divergent ideological orientations, his historical works nevertheless betrayed an abiding attachment to the significance of war. In clarifying the logic of historical rhythm, Savarkar declared in his final book, 'by the "Glorious Epoch" I mean the one from the history of that warlike generation, . . . who ultimately drive away the enemy'. In a sweeping account ranging from the classical to the contemporary, the flow of time was marked by war. Opening with Alexander the Great and ending with the British in India, millennia and centuries were punctuated by six major wars or 'glorious epochs' in which new enemies emerged, each one, in this account, meeting its match in a new 'warlike generation'.[25]

The practice of history writing as a modern and professional occupation, as Dipesh Chakrabarty has argued, is a relatively recent and specifically twentieth-century phenomenon in India.[26] Chakrabarty has focused on the full-time academic historian and the figure of Sir Jadunath Sarkar, who, notwithstanding his fidelity to empiricism and to Ranke, could not entirely escape political proclivities—he memorably cast the Mughal Empire as a historical epoch that began in syncretism and ended with the violent exclusion of Hindus. Political ideologues and practitioners, conversely, were far from dismissive of historical methods, and were particularly preoccupied with the writing of Indian history, Savarkar being, in this respect, an early practitioner for whom the writing of history became essential for articulating and conveying political ideas.

The Indian War of Independence, Savarkar's account of the Indian Mutiny, had been politically radical in the opening decade of the twentieth century. Explicitly written to mark the fiftieth anniversary of the Indian rebellions of 1857, and armed with imperial documentary evidence from the India Office Records then housed at the British Museum, it was a rare type of historical work on the Mutiny: in English, but written by an Indian.[27] Previously, the Muslim political thinker and educationist Sir Syed Ahmed Khan, who had witnessed the Mutiny, had written a widely read account. His The Causes of the Indian Revolt (Baghawat-e Hind, 1858) was striking for at least two reasons.

25. V. D. Savarkar, Six Glorious Epochs of Indian History, in V. D Savarkar, Selected Works of Veer Savarkar, (Chandigarh: Abhishek Publications, 2007), 3, at 2–3.

26. Dipesh Chakrabarty, The Calling of History: Sir Jadunath Sarkar and His Empire of Truth (Chicago: Chicago University Press, 2015).

27. V. D. Savarkar, The Indian War of Independence: 1857 (Bombay: Phoenix Publications, 1947 [1909 (banned)]).

Firstly, it was an early articulation of the political triangulation of Hindus, Muslims and the British as separate and unequal entities. Primarily concerned to unhitch Islam from its centrality in accounts of the Mutiny's causation, Khan sought to demolish and revise what had become the standard British imperial stereotype, of the Muslim as the default subject of the rebellion. Instead, he aimed to give a historical explanation of hatred. Singling out the lack of intimacy between the British and their Indian subjects as the principal cause of the Rebellion, Khan extolled the virtues of intimacy and friendship as the basis for successful rulership in India.[28] It was commonplace, he wrote, to witness 'strifes [sic] and enmities' between 'peoples of the same race, religion and custom'; 'friendship, intercourse and sympathy', meanwhile, were not necessarily dependent upon religion or race, and friendship and its possibilities, heartfelt and with 'instinctive feeling', were open to those who shared no primordial substance such as 'blood'. Thus, the course of friendship had been open to Hindus and Muslims, as it was indeed open to the Muslims and the British, upon whose relationship he was primarily focused.

Secondly, and significantly, Khan interpreted the history of Muslim, including Mughal, rule in India as not one of creeping amalgamation or syncretism of distinctions, whether of 'blood', 'faith' or 'customs', but as the progress of an uneven, contingent and unequal friendship: Hindus and Muslims were indeed distinct, but not separate, which allowed for cordiality, kindness and friendship. Such dispositions were conspicuously absent in the British Empire in India, however; a state of affairs which in turn had fuelled anger, fear and hopelessness.[29] This is not to present Khan's political tract as one marked by notions of love and friendship in contrast to Savarkar's focus on hatred and antagonism. The point for emphasis is rather that for Khan, intimacy and kindness converted the estrangement even of the 'foreign' ruler into a form of friendship, through which empires endured. What the Mutiny thus represented, in his view, was the terminal failure of any such imperial bonding in British India.

A quarter of a century later, Savarkar recast 1857 as a 'revolutionary war'. In his robust and fast-paced narrative of military campaigns between the British and the Indians, the events of 1857 emerged as a concrete instantiation of a dramatic historical confrontation that unfolded across northern Indian cities

---

28. Syed Ahmed Khan, *The Causes of the Indian Revolt*, trans. G. Graham and A. Colvin (written originally in Urdu in 1858) (Karachi: Oxford University Press, 2000 [1873]), 6–38.

29. Ibid., 40–49.

and villages. He organised his account in the mode of the military histories that had long dominated imperial treatments of the Mutiny. At the same time, however, his was an early version of what was to become the prevalent framing narrative of modern Indian history, presenting it as a struggle between nation and empire. He deployed a predominantly violent historiographical register. Significantly, his account was introduced as a narrative of the conjoined historical purposes of *Swadharma* (one's own religion) and *Swaraj* (self-rule),[30] wherein the religious persuasions of Hindus and Muslims were neither transcended nor cast—as they were to be later, in his *Six Glorious Epochs*—as antagonistic. Savarkar did not at this stage portray Hindus and Muslims as primordially opposed; writing, for instance, on the role of one particular rebel, Ahmed Shah, he commented that 'the life of this Mahomedan [*sic*] shows that a rational faith in the doctrines of Islam is no way inconsistent or, or antagonistic to, a deep and all powerful love of the Indian soil; and that the true believer in Islam will feel it a pride to belong to, and a privilege to die for, his mother-country!'[31] Thus, inconsistently with Savarkar's overall elaboration of the ideology of Hindutva, simultaneous attachments to Islam and to India were not seen as mutually exclusive, nor even as an obstacle. It was perfectly possible to love and be attached to more than one powerful precept at a time.

While such a view may be atypical, and even somewhat counter-intuitive, in relation to Savarkar's writings on Islam, this is not entirely inexplicable, for at least three reasons. In the first place, *The Indian War of Independence* predated Savarkar's proclamation and elaboration of Hindutva sufficiently to escape—to state an obvious categorical distinction between his first and his later historical works—its 'quilting' effects. Secondly, while enmity remained central to Savarkar's political conceptions, the identity of the enemy was unstable: a moving target through history. Buddhism, as is further discussed below, featured almost equally in the litany of historical enmities, even if Islam and the Muslims remained the primary antagonist and the focus of most subsequent histories of Hindutva. Finally, even though Savarkar's account of the Mutiny was a chronicle of collaboration between Hindus and Muslims, 1857 represented neither a forgotten nor a repressed ideal of fraternity. Instead, history as war emerged and remained pre-eminent for Savarkar's political concepts. In this preoccupation with history as war, Savarkar was at odds with his nationalist peers.

30. Savarkar, *Indian War of Independence*, 1–12, 107–302.
31. Ibid., 456.

For the initial generation of political actors as historians, historical scholarship was a juridical exercise. The initial foundational historical works by political actors primarily addressed the economy. Dadabhai Naoroji, founder of the Indian National Congress and Liberal British parliamentarian, was followed closely by the civil servant and Congress leader-turned-historian R. C. Dutt. Both framed the economic case against the Empire as a set of historical arguments and evidence: statistics were the armature of the argument that imperial expansion of the economic frontier had left India impoverished and exploited. The overall and powerful effect of political economy as history was that the economic, whether it was trade, agriculture or manufacturing, was given a distinctly national form and territorial unity, with a reconstituted liberalism lending it political coherence.[32]

An older strand of historical thinking was rooted in a species of idealism. A form of what C. A. Bayly has termed 'counter-preaching', nineteenth-century historicist ideas invoked specifically Indian conditions and the Indian civilisational inheritance in a quest to absorb, whilst opposing, ideas deriving from a dominant scientism and universalism. The sense of the antiquity of Indian civilisation that characterised what was to become known as the 'orientalist' view was detached from its imperial and world-historical moorings, brought home and anchored within Indian philosophy in general, and Hinduism in particular. Deriving from evolutionary theory and coalescing around the doctrine of Vedanta, neo-Hinduism emerged as a powerful doctrine that privileged the imperceptible over the manifest. Historicism in this guise, whether embodied in the nineteenth-century celebrity figure of Swami Vivekananda or lesser-known but equally voluble public moralists, went beyond mere mimicry of the prevailing notion of the 'spiritual' superiority of India, actually to lay claim to it as heritage.[33] The *longue durée* of India's history thus became a testament to the power of the spirit to evolve and endure transformation. In this understanding of history, the 'soul' of India featured as an intangible but potent unity that unfolded through time.

Savarkar's writing of history, by contrast, cohered around a conception of war that eschewed both the dominant materialist and the idealist approaches.

32. Chandra, *Rise and Growth*; Bayly, *Recovering Liberties*, 132–87; on Naoroji, see Vikram Visana, 'Liberalism, Imperial Citizenship and Indian Self-Government in the Political Thought of Dadabhai Naoroji' (unpublished doctoral dissertation, University of Cambridge, 2016).

33. Bayly, *Recovering Liberties*, 161–87; Gyan Prakash, *Another Reason: Science and Reason in the Imagination of Modern India* (Princeton, NJ: Princeton University Press, 1999).

The notion of history as a grand struggle was not in itself particularly novel or unique to its twentieth-century conception, but Savarkar's works were notable nevertheless insofar as they presented India as a pre-eminent site of war. This was as true of his book on the Maratha empire, *Hindu-Pad-Padshahi*, as it was for the manifesto of Hindutva elaborated and apotheosised in his *Six Glorious Epochs*.

Six conflicts that had determined the history of India, from antiquity to the twentieth century, were selected in Savarkar's final and sweeping account, according to which her historical identity emerged through 'invasions' and 'confrontations'. As an amplification of his political manifesto, it is striking that the term 'Hindutva' is conspicuous by its absence in his final work. In *Six Glorious Epochs*, Savarkar aimed to give a history to Hindutva which in fact did not have a past. The book, in short, sought to satisfy the claims made in the name of what was an entirely novel phenomenon. 'The radical contingency of naming' in the field of ideology, as Slavoj Žižek argues, is the fact that naming 'retroactively constitutes its reference'.[34] By his turn to history—history as war—Savarkar set out not merely to fill in content, but, more importantly, to designate, and provide with meaning, through historical description, the name 'Hindutva' itself.

Naming the War

By Savarkar's own admission, Hindutva was a 'powerful' yet 'elusive' name. Written while its author was under house arrest in Ratnagiri after spending more than a decade in the penal colony of the Andaman Islands, *Essentials of Hindutva* in 1923 constituted the conjuring of a new political formation through naming. At the outset of the pamphlet-sized polemic, Savarkar states,

> But a name by its nature is determined not so much by what one likes to call oneself but generally what others like to do. In fact, a name is called into existence for this very purpose. Self is known to itself as immutable and without a name or even without a form. But when it comes into contact or conflict with non-self then alone it stands in need of a name.[35]

The initial and essential issue for Savarkar was that the term 'Hindu' was a received one and had accrued meaning given to it by others over millennia. In

34. Žižek, *Sublime Object*, 95.
35. Savarkar, *Hindutva*, 15.

short, the substance of what a Hindu was or could be was outside itself. The identity and even unity of the Hindu was estranged from itself. The tract proceeds, as has been well acknowledged, to invoke blood, soil, race, language and religion—the classic constitutive elements of both nationalism and fascism—in a bid to overcome the initial and fundamental estrangement of the term 'Hindu'. At first glance, the pamphlet appears to express a desire, even itself to attempt, to discover and formalise a Hindu variant of Nazism and fascism; and indeed, several interpretations of it have argued to this effect.

The ideological structures of Nazism or fascism present in Hindutva do not represent a quest for a mimetic realisation of fascism in India. Instead, in seeking to formalise the history of India in terms of blood, race, linguistic unity and even religion, the problem for Hindutva was that the history of India was one of miscegenation, mixture and multiplicity of beliefs.[36] Hindutva, as the following discussion elaborates, deployed the elements of soil, blood and race, but understood as obstacles to rather than as aspects of its realisation. These became vectors in declaring and waging a war on the past, as Savarkar recast the idea and image of India as a battlefield. This is not equivalent to Nazism or fascism; it is entirely novel. By taking blood in particular as its focus, Hindutva theorises violence and war as a permanent condition for the expression of a political fraternity.

In the opening lines of his manifesto *Hindutva*, Savarkar declares the Hindu to be a function and derivation of geography, and determined by 'foreigners'. This was because the term 'Hindu' was derived from 'Sindhu', referring to the Indus river that formed, according to him, the 'frontier' of the subcontinent. A large body of people had been given an identity and a name by virtue of a river. The term 'Hindutva', meanwhile, appears initially in Savarkar's polemics as a geographical designation, denoting a territory bounded by the Indus (or Sindhu). This meaning slips gradually in the course of the text into the related register of race. In the spectrum marked out between the two poles of a geographical frontier and a racial typology, the term 'Hindutva' remained for Savarkar unassociated with Hinduism, however. Categorically excluding from Hindutva as a political formation any theological significance, Savarkar declared that

36. See Luna Sabastian, 'Indian Political Thought and Germany's Fascism, ca. 1918–1950' (unpublished doctoral dissertation, University of Cambridge, 2020) for a brilliant and highly original revision of Hindutva's relationship with German fascism.

when we attempt to investigate into the essential, we do not primarily—and certainly not mainly—concern ourselves with any particular theocratic or religious dogma or creed. Had not linguistic usage stood in the way then 'Hinduness' would have certainly been a better word than Hinduism as a parallel to Hindutva. Hindutva embraces all the departments of thought and activity of the whole Being of our Hindu race.[37]

Linguistic usage was not, however, the only obstacle to the proper articulation of Hindutva. Hinduism itself was a crucial hurdle to be overcome. Hindutva was not the political articulation of a religion alone, but a total history that encompassed India. Time and history together with race, blood and soil were reoriented in novel directions wherein violence became pre-eminent. India, as will be seen, was a source of identity, but crucially also of a privation that Hindutva sought to overcome through war. As this chapter proceeds to demonstrate in its reconstruction and interpretion of Savarkar's manifesto *Hindutva* together with his final exercise in historiography, namely the *Six Glorious Epochs*, his re-ordering of India's history aimed to found a violent fraternity.

India as a Temporal Plot

Hindutva rendered India as a temporal plot to be rescued. This was the purpose of Savarkar's history of the *longue durée*. As an outcome of time, India receives her identity as one that is repeatedly attacked and rescued. Though under siege from the earliest times to the present, the key plot that typifies the place—its history—was not, he wrote, an 'unbroken chain of defeat after defeat of the Hindus', but an account of those who 'vanquished aggressors from time to time'.[38] Hindutva thus emerges as the ideal wherewith to counter the siege-history of Hinduism, and the force that could redeem the narrative of defeat that hovers over the subcontinental terrain. Through the delineation of enmity and war, Savarkar's *Six Glorious Epochs* was, in the final analysis, a search for a subjectivity for India that was expressed and clarified only through confrontation.

Whether in victory or defeat it is in the churning of war that, for Savarkar, India's historical character is to be identified; and war equally enabled the

---

37. Savarkar, *Hindutva*, 4.
38. Savarkar, *Six Glorious Epochs*, 5.

identification of historical aggressors or enemies. The first and third encounters in Savarkar's history of India, interpreted as wars of struggle for political control, involve Alexander and the Greeks, then the Sakas or Indo-Scythians.[39] The second epoch was associated with Buddhism and identified in terms of internal enmity. The fourth and fifth epochs, by contrast, were characterized as struggles between Muslim and Hindu rulers, religion emerging as a powerful form of enmity. The sixth and final 'epoch', that of domination by the British, is notably shorter than any of the others, and was narrated in relation to Savarkar's own role, the author thus writing himself into India's latest chapter of history.[40] Though Hindutva remained unnamed throughout, *Six Glorious Epochs* was, in effect, a history organised in support of its claims.

The most prominent mid-twentieth-century narrative, sweeping through the centuries as it invested the spatial expanse of India with a temporal identity, was Jawaharlal Nehru's best-selling *The Discovery of India*. Written twenty years before Savarkar's *Six Glorious Epochs*, Nehru's influential account of India's history was likewise a search for India's subjective identity, but in direct contrast to Savarkar's narrative of history as war. Positioning India's as an open civilisation, and with more than a third of the book devoted to the struggle against the British, Nehru's account was characterized by a play of binaries of progress and decline, matter and spirit, the national and the international, the old and the new, power and dominion, the past and the future, and above all, unity and diversity. He synthesized the prevalent idealist and materialist methods to mount India as exceptional and uniquely destined in world history to forge nationality out of diversity.

Strikingly, enmity was not, for Nehru, a matter of inimical insiders or aggressive outsiders. If there was enmity in history, then it was neither individual in nature nor given a collective identity in terms of religion or class. Instead, abstract, cumulative outcomes and processes of human action such as 'economic conditions' or general 'decline' took explanatory precedence over individuals, groups and even ideologies: foe-like general 'forces' became the organising causes of the rise and fall of the fortunes of India. A linear, historicist and evolutionist account allowed Nehru to identify India as a 'geographical and economic entity'; in short, as a nation; India was nevertheless greater than her material unity, since for Nehru she was famously an 'idea, a dream and a

39. Vinayak Chaturvedi, 'Rethinking Knowledge with Action: V. D. Savarkar, the *Bhagavad Gita* and Histories of Warfare', in Kapila and Devji (eds.), *Political Thought in Action*, 155–76.

40. Savarkar, *Six Glorious Epochs*, 467–75.

vision.[41] History, in this view, was a testament to India's distinctive national identity, as the historical outcome of a kinship of diversity. The telos or goal of this account was India's freedom and place in the world of nations—the inevitable conclusion to her recent centuries of strife.

For Savarkar, by contrast, war was not only the constant theme that unified the history of the subcontinent, but also a force that through confrontation interrupted stasis, and was thus definitive of dynamism over millennia. Drawing out details of campaigns and modes of warfare became Savarkar's signature-style of history writing. *Six Glorious Epochs* offered little exposition of the forces of history or the clash of ideologies. Rather, the expansive grandeur of long and deep historical time was to be apprehended in the minutiae of military manoeuvres and campaigns.[42] Unlike for Nehru, and notwithstanding Savarkar's own earlier account of the Mutiny, history neither testified to a past, nor comprehended a future, in which Hindus and Muslims could together constitute a single and distinctive nationality.

As an intervention in the temporal framing of India's identity, Savarkar's historical writings and Hindutva amounted to more than a historical theory or style of historiography. Hindutva was concerned with the conditions of possibility for the production of new histories.[43] It was not a 'regime of historicity', to borrow Francois Hartog's term, nor did Savarkar's deployment of the historical method reflect a straightforward disposition towards the past. In terms of the nature of time, his works delved into both its remoteness and its proximity, and of scale, both its vastness and compression, in identifying India over two millennia. Equally, a straight line running through India's past that was broken only by wars that inaugurated new epochs remained central to Savarkar's historiographical enterprise. Through such a deceptively simple view of historical time, and for all his focus on the past, Hindutva was oriented to the future.

Hindutva, especially as rendered in *Six Glorious Epochs*, was the anticipation of the future through historical writing. This prognostic form and disposition distinguished Savarkar's historical writing from that of the standard

41. Nehru, *Discovery of India*, 597–98.

42. Savarkar marshalled military history for a narrative account of the Maratha Empire: V. D. Savarkar, *Hindu-Pad-Padshahi, or, A Review of the Hindu Empire of Maharashtra* (New Delhi: Hindi Sahitya Sadan, 2003 [1925]).

43. François Hartog, *Regimes of Historicity: Presentism and the Experience of Time*, trans. Saskia Brown (New York: Columbia University Press, 2015).

historian. His historical works had the markings of a utopia, however positive or negative;[44] devoid, however, of any apocalyptic reckoning such as became the hallmark of the ghadri pamphlet and was a feature even of his mentor Tilak's commentary on the *Gita*: Savarkar's writings avoided or circumvented the deathscape and eschatology of the sacrificial political subject.[45] *Six Glorious Epochs* and *Hindutva* were likewise distinct from other *longue durée* approaches to India as a civilisation, whether idealist, liberal, orientalist, nationalist, overtly Hindu or a combination thereof, that sought to make the past proximate.[46] Instead, the permanence of a time that was structured by war operated as a mirror for identification and aggression. The stasis of time was interrupted only by the dynamism of war.

Anti-National Ashoka

At the outset of *Six Glorious Epochs*, Savarkar dismissed the question of the antique origins of India as a civilisation, or even the study of Hinduism, as irrelevant to the historian's enterprise. Though he considered Puranic history as symbolically significant, he swiftly demarcated it as beyond the bounds of historical 'authenticity' and 'evidence'.[47] His focus was thus upon 'historic periods' of 'national life'; questions of origins were significant, nevertheless, as the subcontinent had been a crucible for more than one religion. This nullified any potential Hindu claims to a monopoly on origins in India. The key themes of origins and departures, linearity and ruptures intersected with the historical record of Buddhism that posed significant problems for Hindutva.

Conflict with Buddhism was awarded special prominence in the elaboration of Hindutva, selected by Savarkar as marking the second of the 'glorious epochs' each of which was understood as a defining confrontation for India's destiny. He cast Buddhism, the mirror to Hindutva, and its patron the emperor Ashoka in particular, as an internal alterity characterised by heightened aggression: deriving, in part, from the excessive hostility that marks Savarkar's

44. This partly explains why academic history is at odds with and even in opposition to the histories organised around the claims of Hindutva.

45. On temporality and utopianism as both negative and positive, see Reinhart Koselleck, *The Practice of Conceptual History: Timing, History, Spacing Concepts*, trans. Todd Samuel Presner et al. (Stanford, CA: Stanford University Press, 2002), 84–99.

46. For instance, the works by R. C. Majumdar and K. M. Munshi; though concerned with the reconstruction of a Hindu past, these histories are not structured by war.

47. Savarkar, *Six Glorious Epochs*, 1.

narrative of Ashoka. His combative prose betrays envy, however, as he vies for
an India as the cradle of origins, the crucible—that Buddhism denies to Hinduism in exclusivity. Buddhism indeed became for Savarkar the principal obstacle
to the establishment of a total equivalence between India and Hinduism. The
lack of sole symbolic ownership of India was cast in terms of both enmity and
intimacy, and of a struggle between the virtues of violence and the vices of
nonviolence. Savarkar decried the prohibition of killing under Ashoka that rendered the imperial grandeur of the Mauryan Empire vulnerable,[48] and castigated Ashoka specifically for pursuing political power after his conversion to
Buddhism, positing a powerful counterfactual to the effect that, had the emperor Ashoka pursued the life of a renouncer, his Buddhism would have been
properly 'tested', and the 'Indian empire . . . spared a great calamity': the calamity being, indeed, the pursuit of nonviolence.[49]

Singled out by Savarkar as the original enemy, Buddhism had in his view
militated against the formation of nationality in India. The Emperor Ashoka's
conversion and the Buddhist commitment to total *ahimsa*, or nonviolence, had
disrupted the development of a 'political outlook' and 'political independence'
in India. As elaborated above, the absolute necessity of war and violence as a
condition of politics was Savarkar's framing principle, and the Buddhist nonviolence that came to prevail under Ashoka, depicted as being in confrontation
with Vedic Hinduism and its ritual adherence to sacrificial killing, made the
subcontinent vulnerable to aggression from beyond its frontiers.[50] It is to be
noted that under Nehru's leadership, Ashoka became the symbol of the republican and sovereign order of independent India, whilst Savarkar, in his historical
retelling, decoupled political violence from the classical languages and orders of
ritual and sacrifice that regulated and controlled violence.[51] For B. R. Ambedkar,
meanwhile—as is discussed in Chapter 5 below—the conflict between Buddhism and Hinduism was significant precisely insofar as it institutionalised
sovereignty and violence in the form of caste; whilst for Savarkar, violence was

48. For historical studies of Ashoka, Mauryan empire and Buddhism see especially the clas-
sic work by Romila Thapar, *Asoka and the Decline of the Mauryas* (Delhi: Oxford University
Press, 1997); more recently, Nayanjot Lahiri, *Ashoka in Ancient India* (Cambridge, MA: Harvard
University Press, 2015).

49. Savarkar, *Six Glorious Epochs*, 62.

50. Ibid., 62–64 and 66–87.

51. Veena Das and Ashis Nandy, 'Violence, Victimhood and the Language of Silence', *Contributions to Indian Sociology* 19:1 (1985), 177–95, discusses the problem of sacrifice and violence
in the nationalist imaginary.

empty of any significance beyond its status as pure confrontation. Such an emptying out and prising apart of meanings and connotations subsumed historical events and personages such as Ashoka—and the Mughals and Islam, too, with all their complexities, under the powerful single category of violent confrontation. This enabled the foreclosing of interpretations, inasmuch as it made the past not merely proximate, but alive: historical wars part of a conflict in the present.[52]

Perhaps most significantly of all, in Buddhism Savarkar was able to identify an enmity that was not foreign, but decidedly domestic. Claiming Buddhism as internal to India but nevertheless 'anti-national' rendered such enmity potent and ever-present. Singling out Buddhism as the clause prefatory to the exposition of the necessity of Hindutva, Savarkar explained the potential for intimacy to become a source of vulnerability:

> Moreover, everything that is common with our enemies, weakens our power of opposing them. The foe that has nothing in common with us is the foe likely to be most bitterly resisted by us just as a friend that has almost everything in him that we admire and prize in ourselves is likely to be the friend we love most.[53]

He acknowledged the power of identification, the more so since, for him, history ventriloquised the present. He positioned Buddhism as the nemesis of Indian nationality.[54] This was in direct contrast to the Indian jurist and Dalit leader Ambedkar's rendition of the Indian past in his *Annihilation of Caste* (1936), which had anchored Buddhism rather as the historical nemesis of caste in India. Gandhi, likewise, once more operated as a silent referent in Savarkar's declamations on *ahimsa*.[55] The intimacy of the enemy, while it made him more powerful in Savarkar's reckoning, became a critical form of identification.

---

52. See Hartog, *Regimes*, 23–38 for an excellent discussion on the heroic, the mythic and the event in forging historical regimes. Savarkar deploys various registers, such as the heroic and including the autobiographical, to highlight the primacy of confrontation, in V. D. Savarkar, *The Story of My Transportation for Life: A Biography of Black Days at Andamans* (Bombay: Sadbhakti Publications, 1950), which narrates his relations and experiences with Muslim warders as a contemporary repetition of a historical conflict; see especially 52–55.

53. Savarkar, *Hindutva*, 24, and *Six Glorious Epochs*, 63.

54. Savarkar, *Six Glorious Epochs*, 4, 62–81.

55. David Hardiman, *Gandhi in His Time and Ours: The Global Legacy of His Ideas* (New York: Columbia University Press, 2004), 175.

Enmity and friendship, whether distant or intimate, performed the work of a mirror, enabling self-recognition. The historical past imagined as warfare between antagonists also took the form of a mirror enabling recognition: a glimpse into and image of the present. The manoeuvres of ventriloquism and mirroring became ways of, on the one hand, not-naming, and not uttering, whilst on the other hand facilitating a recognition that conveyed the contemporary nature of enmity: they allowed Gandhi and Ambedkar to be construed as foes, without being named and identified. Thus, *Six Glorious Epochs* was consistent in naming neither the organising identity and object of its historical account—Hindutva—nor its antagonists, whether Gandhi or Ambedkar. Arguably, the identity of Savarkar's contemporary opponents was in any case so obvious that to name them would be redundant.

By designating enemies only retroactively, however, Savarkar constituted Hindutva as a political ideology that claimed and spoke for the future. Completed in 1963, *Six Glorious Epochs* was not merely a coded or veiled account of independent India but served as a chronicle of a future foretold. In both its spatial and its temporal dimensions, India, in Savarkar's account, is only nominally defined, but its history is filled out as a sequential account of violence. India was converted into a narrative of warfare and emerged as a permanent battlefield. Thus Hindutva, though never overtly named in *Six Glorious Epochs*, worked as its animating ideal: the history it narrated was not a triumphal account of Hindutva, but rather illustrated the ideal it represented, whose time was in the future. Deploying the past, *Six Glorious Epochs* spelt out the conditions of Hindutva's existence and the possibility of its fulfilment.

India as Privation

While temporality, though constitutive of Hindutva, is an aspect of it that has been largely neglected, territory, rendered by Savarkar as 'fatherland' (*pitribhumi*) and 'holy land' (*punyabhumi*) in the context of the ideology, has received considerable attention. In his manifesto, Savarkar was concerned to forge a mutually defining and fixed relationship between land and religion. Hindutva appears at first sight as a consideration of the congruence between religious identity and the claims of territorial nationalism.[56] India, as noted above, could not be monopolised as the original home of Hinduism alone: it

---

56. Janaki Bakhle, 'Country First? Vinayak Damodar Savarkar (1883–1966) and the Writing of *Essentials of Hindutva*', *Public Culture* 22:1, 149–86.

had lost its 'national centre of gravity', Savarkar wrote in *Hindutva*, because of its 'identification with Buddhism'.[57] In this, his most famous and influential text, after prefacing his manifesto with a brief account of wars that he was to amplify separately in *Six Glorioius Epochs*, he turned directly to the question of the difficulty both of disentangling and of establishing equivalence between Hinduism, Hindu and Hindustan. The overall aim of the manifesto was to present Hindutva as a category and a form of attachment that overcame the obstacles to an easy equivalence between nation, religion and territory.

Crucially, it was Hinduism that proved the main obstacle to the realisation of this claimed identification with the subcontinent's expansive territory: primarily on account of the religion's ambivalent and shifting nature, Hindutva needed to create a new political vocabulary of violence for the forging of nationality and fraternity, in which the theme of blood would seek to take the place of Hinduism itself.

At the end of his manifesto, Savarkar declared, 'A Hindu is most intensely so when he ceases to be Hindu.'[58] This somewhat extraordinary statement, which calls for identification through abdication of identity, was, although paradoxical, merely a repetition of and gloss upon a major theme of his politics: the decoupling of Hinduism from Hindutva, under the claim that the latter was no 'ism'.[59] Elaborating upon this severance, arguably as a homage to his own atheism, Savarkar aimed to clarify the categorical distinction between Hinduism and Hindutva in this remarkable passage:

> The objection that is levelled against the appellation, Hindu and Hindusthan on account of the mistaken notion which attributed their origin to foreign sources could, if left to itself, be easily laid low by advancing indisputable historical facts. But as it is, this objection is in some cases backed up by a secret fear that if the epithet be honoured, and owned, then all those who do so would be looked upon as believers in the dogmas and religious practices that go by the name 'Hinduism'. This fear, though it is not often admitted openly, that a Hindu is, necessarily and by the very fact that he is a Hindu, a believer in the so-called Hinduism, makes a man determined not to be convinced that the epithets are not an alien invention. Nor is this fear unjustified. . . . The superficial similarity between these two terms Hindutva

57. Savarkar, *Hindutva*, 28.
58. Ibid., 141.
59. Ibid., 81.

and Hinduism is responsible for this regrettable estrangement that, at times, alienates well-meaning gentlemen in our Hindu brotherhood.[60]

If Hinduism was not equivalent to Hindutva, Savarkar insisted instead that the latter was concerned only with a new set of principles, or what he termed 'essentials', as a means to identify 'who is a Hindu', and stipulated that 'the discussion of Hinduism falls necessarily outside of our scope'.[61] History as warfare was, therefore, constituted as an essential concept of Hindutva. The repositioning of relations between blood and territory, fortifying the identity of India as a battlefield, became equally essential in elaborating Hindutva.

The issue of racial descent, or blood, that was the 'essential' of Hindutva also proved to be a complex one. The notion of the 'commingling of races' was raised, but after a long if circular discussion of 'common blood', the inescapable diversity of India made unavoidable the conclusion that 'common blood cannot exhaust all the requisites of Hindutva'.[62] Moreover, the history of Islam in India testified to miscegenation. Variously characterised as a series of 'foreign invasions', as a conflict between 'life and death' and 'self-and non-self', and ultimately as a foreignness that 'weld[s] peoples into a nation' through a 'hatred [that] unites', in the final analysis Islam's intimacy with India, dubbed by Savarkar 'forcible conversion', militated against any complete identification between blood, race and Hindutva.[63]

Working on two axes, of the superficial or manifest, and the latent or libidinal, Savarkar's arguments and polemics were geared towards constituting Islam and the figure of the Muslim as foreign or 'the Other': several historians and commentators have attested to the plausability of such an interpretation.[64] Likewise, Nazi Aryanism, in its obsession with the purity of blood and race, expressed it as a phantasmic necessity to overcome and extinguish foreignness. This analysis of Hindutva as a variant of National Socialism breaks down, however, at the point where Savarkar identified the fate of Hindu with

60. Ibid., 80–81.

61. Ibid., 105; a view echoed by the firebrand journalist-editor and Hindutva ideologue Arun Shourie, who confessed an affinity with Buddhism to Martha Nussbaum: Nussbaum, *The Clash Within: Democracy, Religious Violence, and India's Future* (Cambridge, MA: Harvard University Press, 2007).

62. Savarkar, *Hindutva*, 28, 86, 9, and on 'common blood', 28–90.

63. Ibid., 42–43, 91.

64. Gyanendra Pandey (ed.), *Hindus and Others: The Question of Identity in India Today* (New Delhi: Viking, 1993).

that of the Jew.[65] This paradoxical identification with both the vanquisher and victim underscores the centrality of violence for Hindutva as he stripped out the historical context of the Holocaust. The notion of the Hindu as akin to the Jew was premised in their shared principle of religious affiliation by virtue of birth, and their expansion not being a function of the type of political and imperial power that had historically made Christianity and Islam alike, albeit antagonists.[66] Savarkar drew a key distinction between his own conception of territoriality, with its essential, indeed constitutive, relationship to Hindutva, and that of his mentor Tilak, often seen as the originator of a concept of Hindu nationality, whom he chided for a lack of conceptual clarity. Tilak, according to Savarkar, had mistaken Hindutva for a derivation of Hinduism, which had led him to a definition 'not . . . of Hindudharma, much less of Hindutva, but of Sanatan Dharma [eternal tradition]' alone.[67] In critiquing Tilak, Savarkar in effect claimed authorship of the term 'Hindutva' as a specifically political category. Hindutva, as Savarkar expounded it, was neither, on the one hand, the political expression of Hinduism nor, on the other, a war between pure races.

Beyond being possessed 'in common', albeit mixed, blood features in a more complex manner in the conceptual repertoire of Hindutva than has hitherto generally been acknowledged. Blood, for Hindutva, represented not simply a fantasy of racial purity.[68] To be sure, it was the merging fluid of nationality, fraternity and territory; yet it was neither descent, nor purity, nor even common origins, but rather the shedding of blood that was essential to Hindutva, along its latent axis of meaning.

The Hindu and the Muslim in India were united, in a perverse manner, through privation: for Hindutva, although India was the object of complete identification, she yet denied or frustrated any claims or aspirations to exclusive attachment. The geographically determined 'Sindhu' corresponded too to the frontiers of Islam in India—'al-Hind'; and discussion of the unamenability of India to putative and exclusive attachment that lies at the heart of Savarkar's

65. Satadru Sen, 'Fascism without Fascists? A Comparative Look at Hindutva and Zionism', *South Asia* 38:4 (2015), 690–711.

66. V. D. Savarkar, 'Glad to Note that Independent Jewish State Is Established, 19 December 1947', in S. S. Savarkar and G. M. Joshi (eds.), *Historic Statements of V. D. Savarkar* (Bombay: Popular Prakashan, 1967), 219–20.

67. Savarkar, *Hindutva*, 109.

68. On Hindutva and miscegenation, see Sabastian, 'Indian Political Thought'.

discussion of territoriality therefore employs the dual terminology of *pitrib-humi* (fatherland) and *punyabhumi* (holy land). Hindutva's idea of territoriality was informed by the perception that India represented discrete forms of privation for Muslims and for Hindus respectively: a loss of sacrality for the former, and the loss of a 'centre of gravity' for the latter. Whilst India was undoubtedly for Indian Muslims the land of their ancestors, or fatherland, they were detached from their holy land (*punyabhumi*). By contrast, the presence of Hinduism's holy places (*tirthas*) in India designated her as the Hindus' *punyabhumi*, but the lack of a political centrality had rendered claims to India as their *pitribumi* weak and contested. The Hindu as a category was marked neither by exclusive purity nor by political mastery, and this obstructed any congruence between India as holy land and as fatherland.[69] By Savarkar's curious, not to say perverse, logic, in being tied to India in this manner, Hindu and Muslim alike incurred loss and privation.

Total Attachment

If territory and soil were inadequate referents, if Hinduism did not equal Hindutva, and if blood lineage could not identify the Hindus as a race, then the inadequate and incomplete form of attachment to which India had consigned its inhabitants could only be rendered complete by the spilling of blood. War, that had captured Savarkar's imagination and framed his political ideas, had identified enmity and had converted India into a battlefield. Blood as kinship, but above all its shedding in wars, became paramount. Blood was, indeed, the 'mysterious surplus of attachment', to borrow Arjun Appadurai's famous reformulation of nationalism; and the shedding of blood, as Appadurai explains, contextualises a 'full attachment', which is sourced from neither some 'primordium', such as soil, nor a 'prior sense of shared community'. Rather it is violence, he argues, that is constitutive of 'the people'.[70]

For Hindutva, then, total attachment was to be forged through the shedding of blood, to circumvent or overcome the historical context of loss, the mixed nature of their own blood and a lack of monopoly over origins that had consigned India's inhabitants to incomplete forms of attachment. The search for equivalences between history and soil, religion and land, had its source and

69. Savarkar, *Hindutva*, 137.

70. Arjun Appadurai, 'Full Attachment', *Public Culture* 10:2 (1998), 443–49, at 445–46; Appadurai's focus is on the modern state in relation to nationalism.

solution in blood and war. Hindutva was thus both the name and the outcome of confrontation or the spilling of blood, forging a fraternity that had neither existed historically nor been suppressed by another force. Blood and its shedding were ultimately preconditions for the founding of a new brotherhood.

Such a conception of a new brotherhood premised on bloodshed explains Savarkar's admiration for the erstwhile Maratha and Sikh warrior-states as instantiations of an ideal fraternity.[71] As regards the latter, by going as far as to say that 'by ceasing to be Sikhs alone . . . they may, perhaps, cease to be Hindus', Savarkar at once absorbed them while recognising Sikhism as distinct. The Sikh as warrior and martyr, forging a new brotherhood as an outcome of confrontation, appealed to Savarkar as a model of fraternity for Hindutva.[72] In a similar vein, the Marathas represented an ideal whose history, Savarkar wrote in his *Hindu-Pad-Padshahi*, was a form of revelation.[73] As in his other works of history, military campaigns and war—both on the battlefield and as a trope—framed this narrative, the Marathas, creating 'internal externalities' through the figure of the Muslims and Islam. The most striking element of the book, written in 1925, was a mirroring and mimicking of Pan-Islamism: Savarkar deployed the term 'Pan-Hindu' to denote the master category through which details of the campaigns and political intrigues of the Marathas in confrontation with the Mughals were given a new meaning.

Important to note is that the Maratha Empire did not simply represent Savarkar's second 'key enmity', between Hindus and Muslims, for he articulated an aspiration for what he termed 'Hindu-dom' to be more like its imperial precedent of the Marathas. He claimed that the aim of writing a triumphal history of the Marathas was not to 'borrow hostilities and combats of the past only to fight them out into the present', which he dismissed as 'suicidal and ridiculous'. Their example, nevertheless, was instructive. He underscored in particular the 'imminent fact' of the consolidation of 'larger social units' that would be made on the 'anvil of war'.[74] An instance of a form of prognostics that he tended to deploy in his histories, this should not be taken to mean that

71. Savarkar, *Hindu-Pad-Padshahi*.

72. Savarkar, *Hindutva*, 120–28. Savarkar had also written a history of the Sikhs that was lost and in the Andamans had penned a long poem on the tenth Sikh guru, Guru Gobind Singh: Savarkar, *Story of My Transportation*, 8–9.

73. Savarkar, *Hindu-Pad-Padshahi*, Part 1 narrates the military campaigns, and Part 2 is a set of disquisitions on the 'ideal' and 'means' of a Hindu empire, 193–238 passim.

74. Savarkar, *Hindu-Pad-Padshahi*, 20–21.

Savarkar had divined the civil war of partition; it is rather an articulation of his constant theme of the transformative power of violence, and of war in particular, which, in this scheme, was not only a 'law of nature', but a necessity that alone could forge a unity between Hindus and Muslims. He expanded explicitly:

> Before you make out a case for unity, you must make out a case for survival as a national or social human unit. It was this fierce test that the Hindus were called upon to pass in their deadly struggle with the Muhammadan powers. There could not be an honourable unity between a slave and his master. Had the Hindus failed to rise ... even if the Muhammadans stretched out a hand of peace, it would have been an act of condescension and not of friendship, and the Hindus could not have honourably grasped it with fervour and sincerity and confidence which a sense of equality alone breeds.[75]

Hindutva sought through warfare not the extermination or annihilation of a race, but the aggressive incorporation of distinction. The logic of its violence thus pointed to the fomenting of civil war, but not of genocide. War and confrontation were preconditions to equality and friendship, laying the foundations, as argued earlier, for the eventual fulfilment of Hindutva. This furthermore explains the relative lack of hostility and even a degree of cooperation that Hindutva ideologues evinced towards the British, testifying once again that enmity remained a condition of intimacy. In a curious echo of Syed Khan's notion, decades earlier, of political rulership born out of friendship, Savarkar envisaged the forging of friendship—but as an outcome of war: warfare created the conditions for the conversion of foes into friends, premised on their defeat and incorporation. It should be noted, à propos, that Gandhi too characterised the Hindu–Muslim relationship as a friendship; for the Mahatma, however, only self-sacrifice enabled it.[76]

'Mother India' was Hindutva's supreme object from the outset, and the focus of Savarkar's oath for the Abhinav Bharat; while the warfare, blood and sacrifice that her service demanded were imperative for the creation of the Fatherland: the privation that informed the relationship between India and Hindutva could only be overcome, for Savarkar, through a shift in the object

75. Ibid.
76. Devji, *Impossible Indian.*

of attachment from Mother India to Fatherland, fuelled by martyrdom and the cult of the warrior-martyr.

Hindutva was not simply an expression of nationalism, Hindu or otherwise, either authentic or fabricated, as historians and public figures have often understood it to be. A wholly distinct theory of violence, as developed by Savarkar, it indeed represented rather a struggle *against* Hinduism. Hindutva demanded, through warfare, not passive homogeneity, but the vanquishing and annihilation of India's mixed past. In this context, the motif of 'blood' signified not an immortal racial purity, but its violent shedding, that could alone conjure into being a new fraternity.[77] Lacking a past, Hindutva expressed a view of the future, but in the historical register; and in a similarly paradoxical way, it sought its visibility and propagation through secrecy.

Secrecy and Fraternity

If discipline, organised centralization and organic collective consciousness mean Fascism, then the RSS is not ashamed to be called Fascist.

—ANTHONY ELENJIMITTAM OF THE RSS[78]

Admirers and critics alike often compare the Rashtriya Swyam Sangh (RSS)— the earliest affiliate of Hindutva and today the world's largest volunteer body—with fascism.[79] While fascism projected its power in an architectural monumentality that made it very distinctly visible, however, the RSS, it is argued here, derived its power from secrecy.

As early as 1909 and in his *Indian War of Independence*, Savarkar discussed the 'wheels of secret machinery' as a critical arsenal in 'revolutionary' warfare.[80] With an active role in his own Abhinav Bharat and in Krishnaverma's India House in London, secret societies contextualised Savarkar's political thought and action. Secrecy, as the last chapter argued, offered a second world of alterity with the potential to form fraternal bonds. Savarkar was not alone,

77. Jacob Copeman, 'The Art of Bleeding: Memory, Martyrdom and Portraits in Blood', *Journal of the Royal Anthropological Institute* 19:1 (2013), 149–71; P. Gassem-Fachandi, 'Ahimsa, Identification and Sacrifice', *Social Anthropology* 18:2 (2010), 155–75.

78. Anthony Elenjimittam, *Philosophy and Action of the RSS for the Hind Swaraj* (Bombay: Laxmi Publications, 1951), 197.

79. Marzia Casolari, 'Hindutva's Foreign Tie-up in the 1930s: Archival Evidence', *Economic and Political Weekly* 35:4 (2000), 218–28; Banaji (ed.), *Fascism*.

80. Savarkar, *Indian War of Independence*, 94, esp. 'Secret Organisation', 71–99.

as the founder of the RSS Dr Keshav Balram Hedgewar, or Doctorji as he was known, also had an early if short-lived association with secret, anti-imperial revolutionary cells, and knew the firebrand Ram Prasad Bismil.[81] Starting out as a member of the Hindustan Revolutionary Association (HRA), Hedgewar was inspired by its constitution. Deriving the RSS's organisational structure from the communist-leaning HRA, Hedgewar, who was closely associated with Savarkar, was instrumental in establishing Hindutva as a brand of secret politics, with publicity and propaganda playing a distinct role.[82] The aim here is not so much to retrace the division of labour of its institutional architecture, however, as to contextualise the import and work of secrecy for Hindutva and its transfiguration of sacrifice.[83]

Two years after the publication in a limited edition of Savarkar's *Hindutva* in 1925, Hedgewar founded the RSS, starting out with 'ten boys'. This moment has been likened by at least one admirer to the foundation of the Christian church. 'Self-sacrifice', 'renunciation' and an 'insistence on organization, discipline, efficiency, canalization and utilization of the youthful forces' formed the core principles of the RSS.[84] A fixed daily routine with designated time for political thinking (*baudhik*: literally, 'intellectual'), matched by convivial congregation, physical exercise and military drill practice together embodied the practices of the RSS.[85] Its constitution was written only in 1949: for the preceding two and a half decades, only members were privy to its oath and constitution. Both the oath and the secrecy that bound its members in effect created a boundary between the RSS and the outside world within which the new organisation operated as a secondary structure in relation to the political context.[86]

81. H. V. Seshadri (ed.), *Dr Hedgewar, The Epoch Maker: A Biography* (Bangalore: Sahitya Sindhu, 1981).

82. Anon., 'Constitution of the Hindustan Republican Association', in Shiv Varma (ed.), *Selected Writings of Shaheed Bhagat Singh* (Kanpur: Samajwadi Sahitya Sadan, 1996), 140–43; Walter Anderson, 'The Rashtriya Swayam Sangh', *Economic and Political Weekly* 7:11 (1972), 589–97.

83. Anderson and Damle, *Brotherhood in Saffron*; Tapan Basu et al., *Khaki Shorts, Saffron Flags: A Critique of the Hindu Right* (New Delhi: Orient Longman, 1993).

84. Elenjimittam, *Philosophy and Action*, 21–22.

85. M. S. Golwalkar, 'Disha-Darshan', in *Shri Guruji Samagrh: Prabodhan* (Collected works of M. S. Golwalkar, in Hindi) (Noida: Suruchi Prakashan, n.d.), 3, 3–111.

86. George Simmel, 'The Sociology of Secrecy and Secret Societies', *American Journal of Sociology* 11:4 (1906), 441–98.

Self-declared a 'new national army', the RSS was a counter-formation to dominant and mainstream political structures of representation such as the party, and generated its own symbols of submission and allegiance. With its own flag, an oath of service for life, commitment to secrecy and the principle of obedience to one leader (*ek chalak anuvartiva*), it formed a counterpart precisely to what it took as its own antithesis, namely the dominant Indian National Congress and Gandhi.[87] Operating in the manner of an archetypal secret society, although its foundation and institutional structure were public knowledge, the identities and relationships of individual members were concealed. As a result, it escaped the type of imperial surveillance that shadowed the cellular secret societies: internal secrecy within an otherwise known or public body affords and facilitates, according to the arch-theorist of secrecy Georg Simmel, 'a transition stadium between being and not being', for the preservation or instantiation of ideas and bodies of knowledge that are either dying or yet to become normative and dominant.[88] Whether or not Hindutva was radically insurrectionist, it was certainly, and by its own admission, a secondary force, especially in relation to Gandhi, in the context of interwar India.[89] The RSS became the 'transition stadium' and vehicle for Hindutva in relation to its future (public) life.

Secrecy was not an end in itself but became a distinctive form of bonding and socialisation. The detachment from the mainstream that was premised upon it moreover induced an inner coherence and strict structures of obedience that, as is typical of secret organisations, fostered homogeneity, autonomy and confidence. The RSS's deliberate detachment from what it took to be its antithesis, the Congress and Gandhi, was understood and theorised in terms of complementarity vis-à-vis the political, and compensation for the latter's inadequacy. As is well known, Hedgewar was explicit in seeking to keep the RSS separate and removed from what was regarded as the political sphere. Yet this detachment, with the internal secrecy of the organisation tracing its line of demarcation from the mainstream, worked not merely to produce an irregularity in relation to the norm, or even a new partisan entity. In critiquing

87. Elenjimittam, *Philosophy and Action*, 21; on the RSS as secret organisation, see Sardar Patel Papers cited in Casolari, 'Hindutva's Foreign Tie-up', 218.

88. Simmel, 'Sociology', 472.

89. See, for instance, 'Why I Cannot Enter the Congress: Swatantra-Vir Savarkar Explains His Position', *Hindu Outlook*, 30 March 1938; and Indra Prakash, *Where We Differ: The Congress and the Hindu Mahasabha* (Delhi: Federal Trade Press, 1942).

and dismissing the given (political) world as inadequate, the RSS elevated its own work as fundamental and eternal, its secrecy imbuing it with mystical power and purpose. Hedgewar warned aspiring volunteers,

> If it is the lure of office or rank which has brought you here, you will be sadly disappointed. For that you can find fertile field elsewhere outside the Sangha. Here it is selfless service and sacrifice unqualified, ungrudging and absolute ... [RSS] is the greatest Havana Kunda [Sacrificial Fire] ... Swayamsevak [Volunteers] plunge themselves, like so many sandal sticks, unmindful of which burns faster or first. They all burn without sound and smoke. Here burning is the essence.[90]

With echoes, at respective ends of the political spectrum, of both the Ghadar and Gandhi, self-sacrifice, both violent and nonviolent, was thus militarised, and became a constitutive element of an organised and anonymous structure.[91] For self-sacrifice was central to both the Ghadar's and Gandhi's brands of militancy, although categorically distinct from the form it took in the context of the RSS, given the highly individuated nature of both these political projects. The individual, or subject, was indeed both the means and the end both for the ghadri and in Gandhi's rendition of the political, which militated against their reproduction and embodiment in institutional forms.

Hindutva, through the RSS, converted this highly individuated principle of self-sacrifice, through which it maintained a genealogical connection to the Ghadar's secret societies and its own adversary Gandhi, into a collective, anonymous and cumulative force suffused by a heightened awareness of organisation and institutional perpetuation. Likewise, the cellular structure that formed the basic unit of a fraternity solemnised by oath, and the armed agility that had been the hallmark of the radical, mobile and small but secret anticolonial societies of which the Ghadar had been the global spectre. This form of cellular fraternities was replicated and stabilised in the RSS *shakhas* (branches) that emerged across neighbourhoods, creating a distinct political topography of twentieth-century India. While the cabals of the Ghadar dwindled, the RSS

90. Hedgewar, quoted in Elenjimittam, *Philosophy and Action*, 101. Other semi-official accounts include H. V. Seshadri, *RSS: A Vision in Action* (Bangalore: Sahitya Sindhu Prakshana, 2000) and a first-person account of a former volunteer, Partha Banerjee, *In the Belly of the Beast: The Hindu Supremacist RSS and BJP of India: An Insider's Story* (Delhi: Ajanta Books, 1998).

91. B. S. Moonje, 'Militarisation', speech in Nasik, 12 July 1945, B. S. Moonje Papers, NMML.

proliferated, with nearly five hundred branches and seventy thousand members on the eve of the Second World War.[92]

Belief in the potential, amounting to a cult, of the young as the proper subjects and agents of political work was a genealogical thread that ran from the opening years of the twentieth century and across the revolutionary spectrum, conservative and Communist alike. Immortalised in Lajpat Rai's *Young India*, the young male was a promissory note to the future;[93] both metaphorising and incarnating the new, the young were invested with a projected—and urgent—agency that had the capacity to alter the direction of historical destiny. In the interwar era, the young, and the potential of politics embodied in youth, were understood and valued, in their differing ways, by leaders from Savarkar to Har Dayal, and marked out as instructive and even iconic in the case of Bhagat Singh.[94] For the RSS, the young constituted an anonymous aggregate, characterised by submission, self-abnegation and service that reflected a highly centralised subordination, to a single leader, and subsumed the individual into an institutional unity.

In replicating, institutionalising and further promoting the Ghadar's emphasis on specifically male work as a founding principle, celibacy—*brahmacharya*—was deemed the 'esoteric' but everlasting and 'purifying' source of individual strength.[95] Indeed, the internal hierarchy of highly organised cells, moving up from the local to the regional and national levels, enshrined leadership also in relation to degrees of abstinence, with the supreme leader, whether the founder, Hedgewar, or his successor M. S. Golwalkar, remaining absolutely abstinent.[96] In a striking final departure from dominant moorings, the RSS displaced the conjugal ideal that had been the preferred, indeed fetishised, anchor of modern political life, along with domestic life as metonym for the nation's functioning: the loving couple or family were replaced by the abstinent man leading an army of young men. Emerging as what Simmel terms a 'life-totality', Hindutva, especially as rendered in the RSS, was the intensification of brotherhood and fraternity shrouded in an open secret.

92. Anderson, 'Rashtriya Swayam Sangh'.

93. Rai, *Young India: The Nationalist Movement* (New York: B. W. Huebesch, 1916).

94. Chris Moffat, *India's Revolutionary Inheritance: Politics and the Promise of Bhagat Singh* (Cambridge: Cambridge University Press, 2019).

95. Elenjimittam, *Philosophy and Action*, 90–108.

96. Partha Chatterjee, *The Nation and Its Fragments: Colonial and Post-Colonial Histories* (Princeton, NJ: Princeton University Press, 1993).

The highly visible and increasingly old and frail Gandhi represented the antithesis of such a life-totality.[97] Gandhi's assassination by a former member of the RSS forced the latent to become manifest, the clandestine into the open, and gave a name to the essential enmity that had constituted and contextualised Hindutva. A welter of paired antagonisms, of visibility and secrecy, Hinduism and Hindutva, violence and nonviolence, and even the Motherland and the Fatherland, were distilled into the prime confrontation between Hindutva and the Mahatma.

Confessing Hindutva

[T]he event of 30 January 1948 was wholly and exclusively political.

—NATHURAM GODSE[98]

With the assassination of Gandhi, Hindutva found its voice, which made its underlying hostility explicit. The long if silent and hostile dialogue of differences between Gandhi and Savarkar found its expression in the assassin's confession. Bowing to mark his respect for Gandhi before shooting him, Nathuram Godse, a former member of the RSS, made no attempt to flee the murder scene. Instead, he admitted that it was his 'ardent desire' to express and 'vent [his] thoughts in an open Court'. He then had a doctor summoned who could attest to his rationality, so that he could not be labelled or dismissed as a 'fanatic, maniac [or] lunatic'.[99] Perhaps, as has been suggested, Gandhi was explicitly courting a violent end to his life; for his assassin, certainly, the murder was committed to express secret and ardent desires.[100]

Godse's confession became public only decades after his hanging, thereby eventually realising one of his dying wishes written at the gallows, in which he had requested its publication. His other wish was for the scattering of his ashes on the river Indus. Bequeathing his confession to the future, Godse's instructions from the gallows bequeathed his confession 'to posterity', with the purpose of translating 'desire into reality'.[101] With the sealed courtroom becoming

97. Nandy, 'Final Encounter', 70–99.
98. Nathuram Godse, *Why I Assassinated Mahatma Gandhi* (Delhi: Surya Bharti Parkashan, 2003), 36; Manohar Malgaonkar, *The Men Who Killed the Mahatma* (Delhi: Macmillan, 1978).
99. Godse, *Why I Assassinated*, 101, 5.
100. Nandy, 'Final Encounter', recognises the assassination as also Gandhi's death-wish, 88.
101. Godse, *Why I Assassinated*, 186.

in effect a psychoanalytic clinic, the confession, fully admitting his guilt, was an exercise neither in apologetics nor simple justification. Rather, the act of assassination afforded Godse the opportunity that he craved: to be able to recount the recent history of the Indian subcontinent as a series of misnomers. The confession first and foremost rearranged the cause and effect of the tumultuous and defining events of decolonisation and independence in line with the essential elements of Hindutva.[102]

Godse explicitly paired Gandhi with Hindutva, as antagonists. He admitted that, although he had 'studied tolerably well the tenets of Socialism and Communism', he was most partial to Savarkar and Gandhi: 'I studied very closely whatever Veer Savarkar and Gandhiji had written' as, to his mind, 'these two ideologies had contributed more to mould the thought and action of modern India during the last fifty years or so, than any other single factor had done'. Rehearsing the ideas and illustrations delineated in *Essentials of Hindutva*, while he went to great lengths to distance Savarkar from the assassination and own it as his own individual act, he nevertheless declared that he had 'never made a secret about the fact that I supported the ideology or the school which was opposed to that of Gandhiji'.[103]

Premonitions and articulations of Hindutva's defining animosity towards Gandhi had preceded his assassination, which took place in public at a prayer gathering in Delhi a few months after India gained its independence on 30 January 1948. In particular, over the preceding decade, the English-language newspaper *Hindu Outlook* had expressed and shaped Hindutva's antagonism towards Gandhi, under its editor, Savarkar's associate Bhai Parmanand.[104] Bhaiji, as Parmanand was known, might be called Savarkar's double, sharing as he did the same trajectory as an itinerant, international anti-imperial insurgent, who on being convicted was confined to the Andaman Islands simultaneously with Savarkar, and who upon his release from the penal colony became the key publicist for Hindutva.[105] He also, like Savarkar, wrote history. While the latter's expansive historical tomes emphasised the role of war in forging combative fraternity, the former's pithy, popular volumes, primarily in the 'heroic' mould,

102. Ibid., 41–110.

103. Ibid., 26, 19.

104. For instance, A Hindu Nationalist, *Gandhi-Muslim Conspiracy* (Poona, R. D. Ganekar, 1941).

105. Bhai Parmanand, *Aapbiti: Kale Pani ki Karawas Kahani* (New Delhi: Prabhat Prakashan, 2007 [1934]).

privileged the theme of the warrior as martyr.[106] In a final series of resemblances to Savarkar, Parmanand had met Gandhi in the opening years of the twentieth century in South Africa: upon his facing official difficulties, Gandhi had facilitated his lecture tour there.[107] A few years prior to the assassination, Parmanand pointedly articulated the nature of the problem that Gandhi posed for Hindutva:

> Fortunately, or unfortunately, for better, for worse Gandhiji looks upon himself as the sole deputy of the peoples' living in India. . . . A majority among the Hindus look upon Gandhiji as their leader, though he himself denies the position. He wants to be the leader of the Muslims, but the Mussalmans refuse to accept him as their leader. This is the most puzzling dilemma. Hindus wish to see Gandhiji as their leader, but he declines their demands. He wants to be the leader of the Mussalmans but the latter are not prepared to recognize his leadership.[108]

This lays bare the visceral identification at play in Hindutva's animosity towards Gandhi, a figure admired and despised in equal measure. Intimately identified with Hinduism, while yet openly expressing Islam's intimacy with India, Gandhi embodied the obstacle par excellence to the pursuit of the putative congruence between India and Hindutva: he was, in this respect, akin to the history of India itself, whose diversity and lack of exclusivity to Hinduism had constituted the major barriers that Hindutva sought to overcome. As a political idea, Hindutva was entirely dependent on the Other; Buddhism initially, and latterly Islam, had been retroactively identified as the conditions and causes militating against its ascendancy. Now, notwithstanding invocation of the Muslim as the source of betrayal, it was the Hindu Gandhi who emerged as Hindutva's nemesis, and this confrontation turned India into a battlefield anew. Gandhi's politics had occasioned the promulgation and elaboration of Hindutva, and his assassination lifted the smokescreen over historical enmities and rendered Hindutva a recognisably contemporary idea.

Nathuram Godse's aim in carrying out the assassination was to consummate the inter-identification between India and Hindutva as he understood it. Invoking the theme of betrayal, his brother and convicted co-conspirator

---

106. Several figures associated with the Ghadar and radical anti-imperialism, notably Rash Behari Bose himself, recast their politics as Hindutva.

107. M. K. Gandhi to Ravishankar Bhatt, 21 July 1905, *CWMG* 4, 360.

108. Bhai Parmanand, 'Pt. Madan Mohan Malaviya', *Hindu Outlook*, 22 July 1941.

Gopal deemed the killing an 'unhappy' but necessary act to extinguish 'enmity': it was an act of violence, a confrontation, the annihilation of a life, that would turn the page of history and bring 'finality' to India's journey to independence.[109] For the assassin, the Mahatma, guilty of the partition, had to die, for he had 'failed' as the 'Father of the Nation'; and it was Godse's claim in his confession that he had only enacted a widespread covert fantasy, since others too 'knew in their hearts the reason why Gandhiji was assassinated'. An eyewitness account of his trial indeed contends that its audience would have returned a verdict of 'not guilty', had it been judge or jury.[110] The assassin, in short, had fulfilled a widely shared, if prohibited, desire.

If Nathuram Godse had become the vehicle of secret fantasies, then Savarkar, the assassin's inspiration, acquitted of any role in or guilt for the assassination, was reconfirmed as Gandhi's shadow. Gopal Godse attested to the psychological charge of the event, and Ashis Nandy has interpreted it as a function of the assassin's homosexual identification with Savarkar.[111] While a psychoanalytic perspective may well be of crucial relevance, however, the theme of sexuality between Savarkar and Godse is not to be read in any facile or puerile way. It is in relation to the psychic significance of parricide, rather than homosexuality, that the act of assassination must be assessed. Contra Nandy, then, it is interpreted here in terms of the Oedipal complex. Gandhi's murder compels us to consider some of the implications of overcoming and killing the Father.

Parricide and Political Monotheism

He [Gandhi] has failed in his paternal duty.

—GODSE[112]

Forty years after Dhingra, Godse too pulled the trigger wishing to avenge the Mother (India) who it seemed had been failed and betrayed by the Father.

109. Gopal Godse, *Gandhiji's Murder and After*, trans. S. T. Godbole (Delhi: Surya Prakashan, 1989), 3–7, at 6.

110. G. D. Khosla, *The Murder of the Mahatma and Other Cases from a Judge's Notebook* (London: Chatto and Windus, 1963), 234.

111. On masculinity and the psychic charge of homosexuality, see Nandy, 'Final Encounter', 85–86.

112. Godse, *Why I Assassinated*, 111.

Echoing Dhingra, Godse arrogated to himself the role of the dutiful son. For Dhingra, the fettered and bonded Mother had incited sacrifice. For Godse, on the other hand, betrayal and neglect by the Father had motivated parricide. His confession infamously concluded thus:

> He [Gandhi] has proved to be the Father of Pakistan. It was for this reason alone that as a dutiful son of Mother India I thought it my duty to put an end to the life of the so-called Father of the Nation, who had played a very prominent part in bringing about the vivisection of the country—our Motherland.[113]

The overtly familial language used here to explicate the political matrix impels us to take a psychoanalytic detour, via the psychic issues of paternity. As outlined above, the assassination of Gandhi, as Father, in pursuit of the restoration of India, the Mother, by Godse as a son, is precisely equivalent, in Freudian terms, to Oedipal parricide. Gandhi is perceived as the obstacle preventing Godse the son from establishing a proper or fulfilling relationship with the nation-mother; to kill him was 'necessary' in order for this to be achieved, and Godse's confession was the admission of his parricidal guilt.

The overcoming of the father, as Freud elaborated in his writings on the psychic structures of political life, presaged meanwhile the production of future generations and the establishment of horizontal bonds of fraternity. In his classic discussion of the origins of constellations, whether of fraternity or religion and paradigmatic morals and ideas, Freud singled out the prime significance of mythic parricide. The figure of the father, as the primary passage into life and language, invites both reverence and envy, love and fear, and his extinction or banishment, in myths of parricide, determines matrilineal descent and fraternal bonds. The father's very exclusion, however, by natural death, exile or killing, itself becomes incorporated into the symbolic system of the clan, religion or nation, providing meaning insofar as it conditions kinship bonds. Though murder is stained by prohibition, the murdered father nevertheless becomes emblematic of the new order.[114] Gandhi's assassination replays the mythic structure of parricide—but, crucially, as a historical event.

113. Ibid.

114. Sigmund Freud, *The Origins of Religion: 'Totem and Taboo', 'Moses and Monotheism' and Other Works*, trans. gen. ed., James Strachey, ed. Albert Dickson (Harmondsworth: Penguin Books, 1985). Freud discusses the ubiquity of this primary myth: not only with regard to the figures of Moses and the formation of Judaism or Christ, but across religions and cultures.

Gandhi is thus totemic for the Indian nation and in particular for its newly fraternal (and independent) dawning, while the transgression of his assassination, less than six months later, is marked by guilt.

For Godse, the assassination instantiated Hindutva's primary theme of bloodshed. The assassin brothers admitted that the murder was 'not occasioned by war', but was distinctive, exceptional and of a 'peculiar quality', a pure event that occurred 'once in an age or sometimes never . . . for ages together'. Killing Gandhi was explained as a 'dire duty', an 'ominous obligation'.[115] The shedding of blood represented for the Godse brothers the mechanism for the hastening, if not indeed the full articulation, of Hindutva. In one of his final letters, Godse affirmed his conviction of the rightness of his act, writing that 'My Motherland will, I am quite sure, accept the sacrifice of my life with great love'.[116]

In a crucial sense, it is his murder that has allowed the figure of Gandhi as 'Father of the Nation' to loom so large. It is death that, in effect, guarantees the perpetual return of the Father. As the insightful, if controversial, psychoanalyst Jacques Lacan avers, once dead, fathers become more potent: the dead father is perpetuated through his name, and it is this name that reproduces familial or symbolic orders. The patriarchal weight of such an ordering is felt particularly in the case of a nation that is often, as with India, imagined in terms of the Mother. It may be easy to dismiss this as psychobabble; it is telling nevertheless that, precisely because Gandhi is deemed to embody and represent the symbolic order of the nation, his name and its commemoration have become virtually synonymous with Indian nationhood, his status both as Father and—to invoke Freud once more—as superego of the nation guaranteed.[117]

The assassination and its afterlife reconstituted the symbolic order of the nation. There were two mutually reinforcing effects. The betrayal that Godse imputed to Gandhi returned to haunt Hindutva itself, and has been neither owned by the acolytes of Hindutva nor fully exorcised from its annals. Through Godse, it would forever be associated with this primal crime that curiously but

115. Godse, *Gandhiji's Murder*, 38–39.

116. Nathuram Godse to his parents, 12 November 1949, in ibid., 353–54.

117. Jacques Lacan, *On the Names-of-the-Father*, trans. Bruce Fink (Cambridge: Polity Press, 2013); Slavoj Žižek, 'The Big Other Doesn't Exist', *Journal of European Psychoanalysis* (Spring/Fall, 1997), www.lacan.com/zizekother.com; Alireza Taheri, 'Of Fathers and Sons: From the Name/No Name of the Father to the Paradoxes of Paternity', *Journal of the Centre for Freudian Analysis and Research* 27 (2016), 65–89.

assuredly re-established Gandhi as 'Father of the Nation'. The act of parricide leading to his reinstatement as father meanwhile marked the transmutation and absorption of brute force into symbolic structure, as the assassination became a founding event in the development of the mythic structure of independent India.

Gandhi and Savarkar were as deeply identified with each other as they were ideologically opposed. As antagonists, Gandhi projected Hinduism and Savarkar invented Hindutva. Celibacy for Gandhi was a means of Swaraj and individual overcoming; for the RSS, it became the principle of fraternal and institutional unity. Above all, Gandhi represented nonviolence, and Savarkar's Hindutva was a theory of violence. Cast in opposition, their mutual hostility was central to their individual identities.[118] Crucially, their ideas, though to a significant extent mutually constitutive, were not easily reversible, but marked by an irreducible gap, and remain resistant to any harmonious synthesis.

It would be too easy, and erroneous, to dismiss Hindutva as being merely a reflection of its antithesis, whether Gandhi, as it was for his assassin, or Hinduism itself, as it was for Savarkar. Articulated in a declaratory polemics, Hindutva forged a new political language, for the eruption of a new fraternity. As a future-oriented theory of violence and a political proposition, Hindutva sought to rearrange and overcome history, summoning the dominant twentieth-century motifs of blood, soil and war to establish a new brotherhood and found itself as a political monotheism.

118. The inability to exit from strong and imaginary identification structures contains the potential for murder and suicide, and it is thus striking that Gandhi was murdered, while Savarkar committed suicide. On psychic structures and their categories, see Darian Leader, 'The Real, the Symbolic and the Imaginary', CFAR Lecture Series, London, 2015–16 (unpublished), and Slavoj Žižek, *How to Read Lacan* (London: Granta Books, 2006).

4

Gandhi and the Truth of Violence

I am not God.

—M. K. GANDHI[1]

1933 SAW THE PUBLICATION of a distinctly critical biography of Mohandas Gandhi. Such a critique of Gandhi was notable at the time, for at least two reasons.[2] First, thanks to Romain Rolland in the West and to his acceptance in the Indian heartlands, Gandhi had by the 1930s come to be known generally as 'the Mahatma' (Great Soul). Second, and more striking, was that this work was written not by one of Gandhi's proclaimed or secret enemies, but by one of his ardent admirers, Indulal Yagnik. Yagnik, like Gandhi, was from Gujarat, and he had spent more than a decade in Gandhi's service, in ashrams and in public life. He had been instrumental in Gandhi's early experiments in organising mill workers in Ahmedabad, as a sequel to his satyagraha in South Africa. The later enmity Gandhi faced, engendered by Hindutva, related to divergences on the questions of Hindu–Muslim relations and territorial nationalism; and it should be recalled here too that in the early decades of the twentieth century Hindutva, though already potent, eschewed a public life: as the previous chapter recounted, it was in the wake of the shooting of Gandhi in 1948 that his assassin Godse named publicly the enemy that had hitherto remained, if not nameless, then certainly secret.[3] Yagnik was no enemy in this sense. His grudging assessment of Gandhi is rather symptomatic of an

1. M. K. Gandhi, 'One Year's Time-Limit', 11 December 1921, *CWMG* 25, 227–30, at 229.
2. Indulal K. Yajnik, *Gandhi as I Know Him*, rev. enlarged edn (Delhi: Danish Mahal, 1943).
3. Nandy, 'Final Encounter'.

incoherent and inarticulate frustration that Gandhi engenders amongst his admirers, particularly in Marxist accounts, which has to do with his usurpation of revolution: if Gandhi is considered a revolutionary, then his was a revolution that was like no other, to the extent that its mention had to be prefixed by reference to its distinguishing feature of nonviolence. 'Nonviolence' thus became the byword for the revolution itself, not merely its style.

This chapter argues, however, that the central category of politics for Gandhi was truth, rather than nonviolence or even freedom. In nationalist historiography, Gandhi emerges as a genealogical successor to the protagonists in the debate over violent extremism versus polite petitioning; whilst in the international context, Hannah Arendt famously argued for a perception of Gandhi's nonviolence as a mirror image of the violent power of the imperial state.[4] Violence and nonviolence, in short, have been seen as antithetical twins. But for Gandhi himself, truth, rather than nonviolence per se, was the arm by which to oppose the violence of the political. His politics amounted to a radical critique of violence, rather than simply its negation or refusal;[5] and the negative precept of nonviolence was entirely dependent upon, and gained its force from, grounding in the positive precept of truth.

In excavating the political Gandhi, there are three main issues for elaboration. The first is the matter of evil and the experience of it, a concern that is foregrounded in his thinking. The second concerns why and how a proper name, *Satya* (truth), comes to be assigned to the political, the more so since Gandhi sought to circumvent the available conventions in term of rights, representation and revolution. This is to address the why and how of the political salience of truth for Gandhi. The foundation of his idea of the political lay in a direct linking of the problem of truth to the formation of the modern subject, or selfhood. What makes Gandhi the super-subject, the superman or, simply, the Mahatma? I will consider this theme of truth as foundational to politics by examining Gandhi's seminal text *Hind Swaraj* in relation to the question of visibility that Satyagraha took as salient. The third point for consideration, finally, is that Gandhi's politics of fraternal intimacy arose not from

4. Arendt, *On Violence.*

5. I am mindful that nonviolence if interpreted as opposition to violence can only be circular in nature. If approached as negation, nonviolence can only be a product of a prior violence, without effectively breaking that circle. See Judith Butler, *The Psychic Life of Power: Theories in Subjection* (Stanford, CA: Stanford University Press, 1997), 63–82.

the transcendence of hostility or difference, but rather, through what has been termed 'extimacy'—referring to a specific coalition of the interior and the exterior—from the quest for a new kind of subject: one who inhabited their religion fully yet without any dependence on the antagonism that is all too often the concomitant of identity.[6] The chapter concludes by reprising Gandhi's iconic debate with Ambedkar on caste and self-transformation. In the final analysis, what Gandhi's politics of truth and the orientation of its subject involved was an eruption of the abstract into the immediate and experienced. Truth emerged as a visible interruption of the accepted and the consensual that consequentially recast political norms.

The concern here is neither to add to the vast library of Gandhi biography nor to decipher the instrumentality of nationalist negotiations with imperial officals. Instead, our focus is on Gandhi's influential intervention with regard to violence and its potential for political transformation. As was elaborated in Chapters 1–2, the question of the role of violence had animated foundational and formative thinking on political life and its horizons in the wake of failure of the Swadeshi movement of 1905–8 and in the context of the First World War, whether in the form of the ideological innovation of a thinker of revolution such as Tilak—the key figure prior to Gandhi, who created a new and normative vocabulary of politics that made violence possible—or of the Ghadar, which understood the act of violence in terms of a philosophy of self-making, and pitted the individual subject against the planet in its wartime collision with empire. Tilak, as discussed earlier, did not simply inspire the Ghadar, but addressed the 'event' of war and the ethics of killing in a philosophical vein that had made the law its initial theatre of confrontation.

Strikingly, Tilak's commentary on the *Gita* was written around the same time as Gandhi's *Hind Swaraj*, and while both texts were to become foundational of the twentieth-century political in India, they also mark essential ideological distinctions. For Tilak, the crux of the political lay in a notion of the enemy and the legitimacy of a suspension of ethical norms in the cause of initiating a new historical sequence. Violence in this instance was transformative of the political: not, significantly, violence against the 'outsider', but politically meaningful only when directed towards familiar kin or the intimate. Thus, enmity was understood as fraternal in nature. The powerful idea

6. Jacques Lacan, *The Seminar of Jacques Lacan, Book VII: The Ethics of Psychoanalysis*, trans. Jacques-Alain Miller (London: Routledge, 2008 [1992]), https://www.lacan.com/symptom/extimity.html.

of 'detached action' (*nishkaam-karma*) added to Tilak's conceptual repertoire the notion of the political subject whose existence was entirely dependent on the event of violence. Consequently, the political emerged as the exception to the everyday, the former marked by violence and the latter by ethical norms including nonviolence.[7] Contemporary with Tilak's *Gita*, at a period of growing significance of war and militarism, was also Savarkar's initial historical account, of the Indian Mutiny; over subsequent decades, Savarkar through his writings rendered India as narrative of aggression and resistance. Whether in Savarkar's political manifesto *Hindutva* or other writings, history became pre-eminent as it laid out the conditions for the violent birth of political fraternity.

Gandhi shared with Tilak the crucial concept that life and death were properties exclusively of the individual, and for him, unlike Savarkar, or even his own protégé Nehru, history held little in the way of precedent or prospect, precisely because he understood it essentially to be an account of violence.[8] This explains in part Gandhi's commonality with, but more importantly his alienation from, Savarkar. Whether in regard to history, or celibacy, or even Hinduism, the two were animated by some of the same precepts of politics and life, but were diametrically opposed regarding their value and purpose. For Gandhi, as this chapter will elaborate, truth was a visible aspect, condition and outcome of political remaking; while Savarkar took secrecy to be the essential condition for the making of a new and potent fraternity.

Gandhi's political philosophy, and especially his *Hind Swaraj*, was articulated in a context in which violence, fraternity and an anti-statist political subject had emerged in the form of powerful, operable and enacted precepts. This is not to downplay the potent novelty that Gandhi brought to the political landscape, but rather, if anything, to underscore the audaciousness of his originality, as he presented his own precepts within a given force-field of political vocabulary and concepts. Gandhi and Tilak were co-travellers to the extent that both charted questions of fellowship and sovereignty and the horizon of the political without taking the modern state as the ultimate destiny of politics. While Tilak remains hidden from our view, however, Gandhi is by contrast over-visible: indeed, ubiquitous.

Ther figure of Gandhi and his ideals are constantly commemorated in independent India. As the nonviolent 'Father of the Nation', he is habitually

7. Kapila, 'History of Violence'.
8. Devji, *Impossible Indian*.

invoked in particular after any bloody riot or pogrom. An anti-capitalist thinker, it is his face that adorns the Indian rupee. He serves as an ethical counterpoint, and necessary corrective, to the violence of the political. He has thus emerged as a supplement to the political, occupying a place 'above it all', as it were. This excess of attention is also to be witnessed in Gandhi's influence in animating contemporary Hindutva and causing a rift within its fold, as his assassin is celebrated even as the Mahatma is also piously adopted as a figure of inspiration for New India.[9] Significantly, too, Gandhi faces increasing denigration from Dalit ('untouchable') leaders and their acolytes for his position on and politics of caste, especially in contrast to his political nemesis, B. R. Ambedkar. Gandhi is thus a figure both excessively identified with and actively disavowed, his status as 'Father of the Nation' contested, with other figures zealously promoted to occupy that foundational position. Gandhi continues to incite and inspire; he remains 'alive' and pivotal, to an extent that still makes reconstruction of his political thought particularly difficult: scholarly writings, too, are not immune to the divisive potency of the Mahatma.

Indeed, it comes as no surprise to find Gandhi positioned at two poles in academe. One view sees him as a saint of almost Christian pedigree; the other as a wily negotiator, the Mephistopheles, if not the Machiavelli, of Indian freedom. The excoriation by the Marxist celebrity writer Perry Anderson cited in the Introduction above is a pithy portrayal of Gandhi as the arch-manipulator who sacrificed higher, better, greater emancipatory ideals upon the altar of his own personality cult: Anderson's 'Indian ideology' can be summed up as a petty form of Indian nationalism, an amalgam of bad faith and lashings of false consciousness fostered and embodied by its leaders, and especially Gandhi.[10] Gandhi, in short, for Anderson—and he is not alone—is the primary component or the fulcrum of the myth of a specifically Indian 'ideology' that hides, under a cloak of ethics and nonviolence, its essential commitments to brutal violence and an exclusionary vision. Clearly then, Gandhi is exceptional: even if for nothing else, then for a form of immortality that continues to incite, vex, divide and inspire.

9. Report on Pragya Thakur, recently elected Member of Parliament and a Godse apologist, https://www.bbc.co.uk/news/world-asia-india-50583728; and Gandhi as the symbol of 'Clean India' campaign launched by Prime Minister Modi, https://www.bbc.co.uk/news/world-asia -india-29441052.

10. Anderson, *Indian Ideology*.

More than a decade ago, Akeel Bilgrami made a compelling call for Gandhi to be understood first and foremost as a philosopher who laid the foundations for a 'politics of integrity'.[11] In answering that call, recent interpretations of Gandhi, with new insights, have re-signified Gandhi and his radicalism primarily in the domain of the ethical.[12] Faisal Devji's rendition of Gandhi as the 'impossible Indian', by contrast, squarely faces the question of violence and repositions him as a figure above and beyond the matter of national freedom.[13] His legacy, moreover, as Devji assesses it, is not merely superficially global: it transcends India in more than the simple sense of his influence being etched upon the civil rights movement in America, or anti-apartheid politics in South Africa, or the interwar Khilafat movement. Devji instead portrays Gandhi as ambitiously 'universal'—referring to a universality that by definition neither required nor was beholden to history. This claim rests mainly on the grounds that Gandhi returned to and resurrected, especially, the concept of life and death as possessions of the individual human being that amplified the power of sacrifice, and in doing so replaced the over-wrought languages of rights, representation and contract with that of duty and sacrifice. The labours of Bilgrami, Devji and others have had a curious effect, in that Gandhi is now one of the very few non-Western figures to have successfully stormed the zealously policed bastion of the canon of Western political thought. Ironically then, the contestation, even decline, of Gandhi's public stature is inversely related to his rise as a political philosopher.[14]

It is no easy task to reconstruct Gandhi as a political thinker, however. This is not only because of the multiplicity of received Gandhis. It is primarily because of Gandhi's own unsystematic, aphoristic and somewhat slippery style of writing and argumentation. It is precisely this style, however, that allowed him to circumvent the available political languages of the day, be it that of liberalism, of historicism, or of communism. To be sure, Gandhi's politics were fashioned in a transnational context—and not the one that has gained ascendancy in scholarship in recent years, whereby the metropolitan and the

11. Akeel Bilgrami, 'Gandhi the Philosopher', *Economic and Political Weekly* 27 (2003), 4159–65.

12. It is not, needless to say, the separation of the political from the ethical, but the specific relationship between them that is significant for the argument.

13. Devji, *Impossible Indian*.

14. Mishra, 'Gandhi for the Post-Truth Age' is a remarkable essay on Gandhi's reputation in our times.

colonial are conjoined, or one deriving simply from the fact that the British Empire itself was a transnational polity. Significantly, it was in the Transvaal and South Africa, rather than in London, that Gandhi forged and fashioned his novel concepts and practices;[15] India, it could be argued, was the beneficiary of a South African innovation. Not merely this, however; for it was certainly the main stage for the later performance of all things Gandhian.

What's in a Name?

Gandhi wrote *Hind Swaraj* in a dramatic context. In the opening decade of the twentieth century, violence had become central to the understanding of the political in the Indian and imperial contexts. Whether it was Tilak in India, the revolutionaries scattered across Europe or the Hindutva ideologue Vinayak Savarkar, who was assumed to be the 'Reader' addressed by Gandhi's 'Editor' in *Hind Swaraj*, the case for violence to effect transformation, be it liberation or revolution, seemed to have gained in persuasive power. A related context lay in the fact that by 1908, Gandhi had attached himself to a certain form and practice of politics.[16] The Transvaal Campaign in the opening years of the century had demanded a new form of commitment to action, though its ideological contours had defied any easy labelling or name.

Prior to his feverish completion of *Hind Swaraj*, on a shipboard journey from London back to South Africa, Gandhi had devoted considerable attention to the problem of truth. Apprehending it as a category of experience rather than in terms of its value as a virtue, truth for Gandhi was neither empirical nor transcendent. It was an insistent form of visibility. In searching for a name for his politics during the Transvaal Campaign, Gandhi's initial idea was to appropriate 'passive resistance', a term that had been adopted across a wide spectrum of thinkers, ranging from the arch–laissez-faire Herbert Spencer to other-worldly Romantics such as John Ruskin.[17] The point for emphasis here is the manner in which Gandhi seized upon dominant ideas, took

15. Isabel Hofmeyer, *Gandhi's Printing Press: Experiments in Slow Reading* (Cambridge, MA: Harvard University Press, 2013).

16. M. K. Gandhi, *Satyagraha in South Africa*, trans. Valji Govindji Desai (Madras: S. Ganesan, 1928).

17. Numerous studies have traced different 'influences' in Gandhi from both the Indic and Western traditions; see, for instance, Lloyd I. Rudolph and Susanne Hoeber Rudolph, *The Postmodern Gandhi and Other Essays: Gandhi in the World and at Home* (Chicago: University of Chicago Press, 2006).

possession of them and radically transformed them, thus inaugurating his own political philosophy.

The transition from 'passive resistance' to 'Satyagraha' was, then, not one of linguistic or conceptual translation, or even one that indigenised or vernacularised a western or universal concept. Rather, it radically introduced Truth as a condition and consequence of the political. It was a transition from a politics of negation to a positive philosophy for the founding of political truths.

In 1907, Gandhi set up a competition, through his journal *Indian Opinion*, in a search for an appropriate name for the Transvaal Campaign. While 'resistance means determined opposition to anything', he wrote, '*agraha* or firmness and insistence' specified an affirmative quality and action; by conjugating this 'insistence' with 'truth', or *satya*, he at last found (with a little help from a correspondent) a name for his politics.[18] Then, within a year, in 1908, he became the exclusive author of another concept or a set of ideas, that went under the name of *Hind Swaraj*.

The division of voices between a hostile 'Reader' and Gandhi's 'Editor' in *Hind Swaraj* was prefigured during the Transvaal Campaign, the actual 'Satyagraha in South Africa'. The campaign sought to question the compulsory registration of Indians through thumb and digit impressions. Registration raised issues of culture, class and race, and ended in a compromise between Gandhi and Jan Smuts whereby, though the law was not repealed, registration was made voluntary. It is this compromise that prompted Gandhi to write a dialogue whose form was to be repeated in *Hind Swaraj*. He fully reccognised the hostility to his own position, and his deliberate dividing of voices became the basis for his articulation of his own language of politics. He was also deeply concerned, moreover, in both of his dialogic pamphlets, that the nature of political consciousness be accurately identified. 'A Dialogue on the Compromise', seeking to explain the Gandhi–Smuts pact and published in *Indian Opinion*, opens somewhat strangely with the topic of the nature of the Reader and sleep. Gandhi writes,

> There are two kinds of readers: first, those who pretend to be asleep, that is to say those who read not indeed to be enlightened but with malicious intent and in order to pick holes; the other kind are those who really fail to see the point and are therefore truly asleep. This dialogue is addressed only

18. M. K. Gandhi, 'Johannesburg Letter', before 10 January 1908, *CWMG* 8, 80–88.

to the second kind. We can wake up those who are asleep. As for the others who feign sleep nothing can be done.[19]

A few months later, he opened the dialogue in *Hind Swaraj* once again with this issue of sleep and wakefulness. Referring to the violent agitations during the nationalist Swadeshi movement of 1905–8 he states,

> When a man rises from sleep, he twists his limbs and is restless. It takes some time before he is entirely awakened. Similarly, although the Partition has caused an awakening, the comatose state has not yet disappeared. We are still twisting our limbs and still restless, and just as the state between sleep and awakening must be considered to be necessary, so may the present unrest in India be considered a necessary, and, therefore, a proper state. The knowledge that there is unrest will, it is highly probable, enable us to outgrow it. Rising from sleep, we do not continue in a comatose state, but, according to our ability, sooner or later, we are completely restored to our senses.[20]

The problems for the assumed Reader in South Africa and in India, it can be seen, were not of the same order, despite the fact that they both were Indians. While the satyagrahi in South Africa had to be metaphorically shaken and woken up through the very act of reading the dialogue, the Reader in *Hind Swaraj*, by contrast, had a mistaken sense of his own wakefulness. The agitation of limbs—the Swadeshi movement—was misrecognised as the state of consciousness, or even a state of Swaraj. Gandhi not only pointed out that this was mistaken, but would go on to apprehend, amplify and apply what he took to be true Swaraj.

While 'Satyagraha' was Gandhi's own term, 'Swaraj' had a controversial prior authorship and meaning, and it was Gandhi's aim in his pamphlet to rescue it from its original liberal and radical associations.[21] For this reason, he begins by acknowledging the awakening, but not its naming—leading to its misconstrual—as Swaraj, by both the liberal Naoroji and the radical Krishnaverma. Gandhi's refusal to use the term that he wished to appropriate is instructive.

---

19. M. K. Gandhi, 'A Dialogue on the Compromise', 5 February 1908, *CWMG* 8, 136–47, at 136.
20. Gandhi, *HS*, 24.
21. Anon., 'Home Rule is "SVARAJYA"', *The Indian Sociologist* 3:3 (March 1907), 11.

Hind Swaraj opens with the acknowledgement that a seed, remaining below the ground and therefore unseen, had been sown. This seed, or what Gandhi called 'the awakening' in India, was for him either hidden or, more accurately, had a deceptive appearance, on account of the soil in which it had germinated. So the seed itself, as he put it, 'is never seen': it is destroyed for the sake of 'the tree which rises above the ground . . . such is the case with the Congress'.[22] This audaciously simple sentence encapsulates the problem of the hidden nature of evil (addressed in the next section), the issue of sacrifice and its appearance and, above all, the idea of truth as a form of visibility that Gandhi would chart first in *Hind Swaraj* and then in his various campaigns through the next thirty years.

As regards Swadeshi-era politics, the problem had thus been not only the issue of violence, but the mistaking of a state of agitation for one of freedom. This mistaken identity had resulted in the splitting of the Congress, not between moderates or the 'timid' party and extremists or the 'bold' party, so much as between, as Gandhi put it, the 'slow' and the 'impatient' party. A break with the historicist reckoning of time informs *Hind Swaraj*, inaugurating what Uday Mehta terms 'the politics of patience'.[23] At the height of such a momentous campaign as the Swadeshi, Gandhi 'hit the pause button', as it were, to survey the scene anew for the sake of an entirely different narrative. This pause is instructive in terms of why subsequent Gandhian campaigns too were punctuated and paused at the height of mobilisation: from Non-Cooperation, through Khilafat and Civil Disobedience, to Quit India and, eventually, 1947.

The Experience of Evil

In clearing the conceptual ground for his unique notion of Swaraj, Gandhi made explicit the nature, as he saw it, of evil. Evil, unlike the seed of awakening, and contrary to truth, had a definite appearance that was highly alluring. This manifestation of the blatantly evil was also misrecognised, however, and went by another name: that of 'civilisation'. He compared this evil to 'consumption' (tuberculosis): a force that sucked life out of the afflicted. Like consumption, this evil could hide itself, while at the same time being potentially

22. Gandhi, *HS*, 19.

23. Uday Singh Mehta, 'Gandhi on Democracy, Politics and the Ethics of Everyday Life', in Kapila and Devji (eds.), *Political Thought in Action*, 88–106; also Uday Singh Mehta, 'Patience, Inwardness, and Self-Knowledge in Gandhi's *Hind Swaraj*', *Public Culture* 23:2 (2011), 417–30.

contagious: 'Consumption', Gandhi wrote, 'even produces a seductive colour about a patient's face, so as to induce the belief that all is well. Civilization is such a disease.'[24] Through its vertiginous speed, the techno-dystopia, or what Gandhi called the 'wings of evil', had provided humanity with hitherto unknown capacities for destruction. Yet because its appearance was alluring, and because it offered a sense of momentum to human life, civilisation could be fundamentally misconstrued as an enhancement of the human condition.

His strident critique of technological life or modernity more generally has been interpreted to position Gandhi as a romantic, a traditionalist and even an anti-modern. What has been missed, however, is his anticipation of a number of classic themes that were to preoccupy philosophers as various as Adorno, Benjamin, Bataille and Foucault who have been central to our understanding of the twentieth century. To excavate and reconstruct Gandhi as a philosopher, we will at the very least need to do as he himself did in his writings,[25] insofar as, while he deployed available terms such as 'Swaraj' and 'civilisation', he transformed their meanings and points of application. Notwithstanding the range of 'influences'—Ruskin, for example, or Tolstoy—that might be traced in his thinking, Gandhi's own statement is illuminating: while not claiming to be 'original', and confessing to having 'read much', Gandhi at the outset of *Hind Swaraj* states that 'these views are mine . . . They are mine because I hope to act according to them.'[26] As readers, we will have to hold the binaries of East and West, nation and empire, tradition and modernity in suspension so as to reverse, or rather to relate anew, the philosopher as prime political actor.

Gandhi equivocated between the categories of evil and civilisation. While 'civilisation' and 'evil' were used interchangeably, evil did not correspond simply to the contemporary condition, nor was it purely the visualisation or aestheticisation of an abstraction. Equally, evil was not a historical context or epoch, as it was commonly understood in the Indian context: that is, as the apocalyptic or black age of the present (*kailyug*), or the age of non-morality, or even simply the modern age. Gandhi's immersion in Christian theology, in which evil prefigures moral codes and ethics, is far from irrelevant here.[27] Yet,

---

24. Gandhi, *HS*, 47.

25. Bilgrami, 'Gandhi the Philosopher'.

26. Gandhi, *HS*, 9–10.

27. Several commentators have noted the connection with Christian theology: see Parel's 'Introduction' to Gandhi, *HS*, xxi–xlvii, and also David Hardiman, *Gandhi: In His Times and*

evil was for him both more capacious and pointedly specific: capacious with
regard to the range of conditions that were productive of evil, and specific in
that evil was a set of embodied experiences that limited the possibilities of
being human. The notion of evil was thus for Gandhi central to the twentieth-
century theme of 'the destruction of experience' itself.[28]

The problem of evil lay in the fact that it was 'consumed', or was an aspect
of experience (*bhog*). The present times or the contemporary, as described in
Hind Swaraj, brought to salience certain 'conditions' and the nature of the
'experiences' that these conditions engendered.[29] In this respect, the condition of India was paradigmatic—and it is striking that the 'condition of India'
was understood here not in terms of poverty, famines, government jobs, education and missionaries—the standard litany of grievances of the nationalists—
but rather referred to the very things that nationalists and contemporary men
had accepted and celebrated as features of the new world that had vastly enhanced human power over nature. Railways, for example, as we know, were
central to Gandhi's own life: not only was the railway the site, for him, of the
revelation of race and its concomitant exclusions in South Africa, but in *Hind
Swaraj*, the railways were singled out in particular for their acceleration of the
contagion of evil.

Nor was evil in the Indian context restricted to the British presence or to
Britain itself. Money and commerce, according to Gandhi, had been accepted
into India and had consequently made the rule of the Company Bahadur and
the British Raj possible and perpetual: 'We like their commerce', he explained, and 'it was not [through] the sword' that British suzerainty had been
established. The British might be 'kept' by Indians, as he often said, but the
fundamental issue was that their presence had had the effect of an enchant-
ment, in the form of the satisfaction of appetites. In citing bodily appetites and
their satisfaction, Gandhi conveyed the fate of the human subject in the capi-
talist empire. If the enjoyment of *bhang* (marijuana) had become addictive,
however, then merely 'getting rid of the retailer', Gandhi argued, would not

---

Ours: The Global Legacy of His Ideas (London: Hurst & Co., 2003); on evil and politics, see Paul
Kahn, *Out of Eden: Adam and Eve and the Problem of Evil* (Princeton, NJ: Princeton University
Press, 2007).

28. Martin Jay, *Songs of Experience: Modern American and European Versions of a Universal
Theme* (Berkeley: University of California Press, 2005).

29. *Hind Swaraj* thematised conditions that were allotted separate chapters, such as 'Railways', 'Doctors', 'Lawyers', 'The Condition of England', and so on, with 'The Condition of India'
occupying a central position.

alter the situation, since another retailer would simply step into the role. Likewise, though 'excess of food . . . causes indigestion', simply blaming the British for the 'indigestion' would achieve little by way of remedy; indigestion could not be relieved by 'drinking water'; and so on.[30] Colonialism, for Gandhi, was not a matter of political, economic or governmental power relations alone; rather, it was an embodied experience of particular appetites and their gratification, a cycle of addictive desires.

Money and commerce, then—the market and exchange—were taken to be the key conditions that produced new experiences of excess, and this experience of 'consumption' and fulfilment of desires in turn, of course caused illness. The sensual satisfactions of these experiences disguised their true nature as afflictive, however. Empire, market and exchange, for Gandhi, produced a vicious cycle of desires that could not be satisfied but, crucially, led to the mistaking of illness for enjoyment.

The fundamental problem, in Gandhi's view, was thus that the unity of the subject was destroyed by the nature of its own experience: the tearing apart of the self was experienced as pleasure and enrichment. Evil, then, was the dense and hidden set of mediations that oriented the conditions and nature of experience. At the same time, the overt form that these mediations, or the connection between the self and the world, took alienated the self not only from itself, but, significantly, from relations of intimacy and familiarity.

Gandhi's critique of lawyers is apposite here, as it is illustrative of his wider critique of nationality as a legal and liberal category.[31] The practice of lawyers—described by him as 'lazy' and 'leeches'—epitomised for Gandhi this double estrangement. The essence of the matter was that the language of the law and practice of courts had redefined the Hindus and Muslims as confrontational juridical categories. Gandhi did not of course naively assume that the fraternal relationship between Hindus and Muslims had always been peaceful prior to their legal classification as communities. This legal classification had, however, forcefully established them as estranged from, if not indeed overtly hostile to, each other. He wrote,

30. Gandhi, *HS*, 39–41.

31. Gandhi himself practised law, with relatively greater success in South Africa than in England, and he recalled that over twenty years in practice he had resolved hundreds of cases through private compromises.

The Hindus and the Mahomedans have quarrelled. An ordinary man will ask them to forget all about it, he will tell them that both must be more or less at fault, and will advise them no longer to quarrel. They go to lawyers. . . . It was certainly a sign of savagery when they settled their disputes by fighting. Is it any less so if I ask a third party to decide between you and me? Surely the decision of a third party is not always right. The parties alone know who is right. We in our simplicity and ignorance, imagine that a stranger, by taking our money, gives us justice.[32]

Intimacy was destroyed, and replaced by a set of obligations of exchange that alienated the familiar. Lawyers and doctors embodied to perfection this role of mediation as a contract conditioned by the exchange of money. In a similar vein, Gandhi argued that while the railways had speeded journeys to sites of pilgrimage, they had made those places unholy. Thus, although the railways had connected India as a mass of territory, they had in effect divided the people.

The audaciousness of Hind Swaraj lay in its simple dialogue that related the subjective, or the experiential, to the abstract. It was not a conventional political manifesto, instructing the reader and arousing him or her into a new state of consciousness. Hind Swaraj was more like Nietzsche's writings, seeking through the plainly aphoristic to re-evaluate all values. What had been experienced, as opposed to the argument and abstraction that had formed the basis of nationalist polemics, became the prime modality of truth as an aspect of the political. This fundamental break from the abstract would allow Gandhi to deploy truth as action and as a form of politics that could not be contained within the national.[33]

Hind Swaraj was, however, a 'Trojan' text. It was neither declaratory, in the vein of a political theology, nor confessional in nature.[34] Rather, like the Trojan horse, it was meant to be a 'vehicle' for the Reader, a vehicle to 'effect a transformation in self-conception'. Evil and truth were conjoined, not as opposites of darkness and light, as they were often rendered in religious and moral doctrines, but rather in that they shared the quality of hiddenness. The visibility of truth for Gandhi required an insistent pursuit that would become the key mode and symbol of his politics. This politics would be dependent

32. Gandhi, HS, 59, 61.

33. Kapila, 'Self, Spencer'.

34. This distinction between 'Trojan' and declaratory texts is from Jonardon Ganeri, The Concealed Art of the Soul: Theories of Self and Practices of Truth in Indian Ethics and Epistemology (Oxford: Oxford University Press, 2007), 97–102.

entirely on the quotidian; and Gandhi would commit to a specific set of techniques in the pursuit of truth as a means to access self-transformation. Increasingly, then, for Gandhi, truth would not be about veracity, but about breaking away from the consensual, resulting in entirely radical perspectives on any given condition.

The Truth of Swaraj

All sins are committed in secrecy.

—M. K. GANDHI[35]

In almost all interpretations of Gandhi's thought, insistence on truth, or Satyagraha, and self-rule, or Swaraj, are seen as separate projects, a separation that ultimately derives from their relative efficacy. Swaraj, and Gandhi's notion of its nature, has proven to be unamenable to available political languages: *Hind Swaraj*, while recognised as original, is regarded as 'out of its time', and unrealistic, and tends to be largely dismissed as a weak and romantic set of ideas—a rant at worst and a dream at best. By contrast, Gandhi's political technologies, in particular his ability to mobilise, are seen, precisely on account of their novelty, as effective. This commonly asserted distinction marks Gandhi as less of a philosopher and more of a practitioner.[36] To identify in this a gap between ideas and practice is, however, fundamentally to misconstrue him, and perception of such a gap has furthermore led to his neglect and obfuscation as a political thinker. Certainly, however, it is plausible, even to a degree convincing, to claim that Gandhi's main interest as a philosopher was in the subordination of the political to the ethical. Here, in what follows, Swaraj will be placed *in the context of* Satyagraha, as a means to illuminate the political in Gandhi.

Satyagraha is seen to be particularly potent as a form of mobilisation, and especially as a weapon of the weak. This indeed to an extent reflects Gandhian techniques of mobilisation. His most successful campaign, the salt-satyagraha of 1930, demonstrates the power of the plain and simple: the mere act of walking became a form of political mobilisation that was directly available to one and all. Starting out from his ashram in Sabarmati with less than fifty people, Gandhi walked over two hundred kilometres to Dandi, by which point several

35. M. K. Gandhi, *Hindu Dharma* (Ahmedabad: Navajivan Publishing House, 1950), 122.
36. Perhaps asserted by none more than Nehru himself, who carved out this distinction to great effect throughout his writings: for instance, Nehru, *Discovery of India*, 379–86.

hundred thousand people were walking with him. This was a radically simple and universally accessible form of political action. The end of the walk too was simple, culminating as it did with the making of salt, the production of which from the open seas required—unlike cotton manufacture—no complex technology or machinery. The making of salt, a commodity at once essential and prohibitively taxed, exposed a true paradox of power. Such disruption of the abstract by means of the immediate epitomises Gandhi as a political thinker. Insistence on truth—Satyagraha—was the interruption of the accepted or the consensual aspect of the real; and we are far too accustomed to viewing this form of politics as primarily or purely a form of mobilisation. Undoubtedly, it *was* effective mobilisation; but citing its effectiveness alone is not sufficient to demonstrate its full nature or political import.

Indeed, by the simple act of making salt, under the banner of Satyagraha, Gandhi made visible the oppression of abstraction. It was precisely those who lived on the impoverished shorelines of the sea who were the least able to access this essential commodity. Yet the available languages of alienation of labour from the product, which had been the hallmark of the critique of capital, were not the answer for Gandhi. In such critiques, among which Marxism provided the most cogent set of arguments, the solution involved a mere inversion of the relationship between the producer and the consumer. These views took the commodity to be central, with the emancipatory ideal being that of restoring ownership of the commodity to the producer. As will be further exemplified in the case of cloth, Gandhi was as opposed to liberal capitalism as he was to Marxist socialism. His critique of both concerned the nature of the subject, in that both regarded possession, whether of labour or commodity, as the central problematic.

The claim here is that Gandhi understood truth not as a function of speech or aspect of conduct and cultivation, but rather—in its most ordinary manifestation—as revelation. Truth was a visible form of the political, whereby all that was hidden came to the surface to display the ordering that made the practical world; yet could only be displayed as such within a sequence of actions and events, such as the Transvaal, Champaran or salt satygrahas. All these mobilisations took place in order to uncover, to make visible, the 'real' nature of relations between Indians and Whites, cultivators and planters, the poor and the Empire. This was a mirror image of the mode of operation of the radical terrorists who, in their defined targets of assassination and bombings, identified or made visible through the narcissism of violence the perpetrators by whose power the many were being oppressed.

Truth was the opposite of evil and violence. Truth and evil, as argued above, were both hidden. Yet while evil was a matter of false or misrecognised appearances, truth in the Gandhian political was constituted through the event. Just as the individual, subjective act of an assassination focused attention upon the objective structures of domination, Gandhi intervened radically within these sets of relations between the subject, truth and the politics of visibility. In the case of public satyagrahas, the simple and nonviolent acts of making salt or walking miles laid power equations bare, while at the same time inverting the subjective and the objective. In the case of assassinations, however, while the event of violence indeed made the power equation visible, it maintained and reinforced the inequity. In Gandhian satyagrahas, it was likewise intended that the truth of inequity be made visible; but here the resemblance ended. The aim was not simply inversion or negation, but the transformation of the equation itself.

What were considered the commonsense, the accepted or the consensual terms of reference, thus stood transformed. In the South African satyagraha, to take one example, while the law of registration was implemented, registration in itself was recognised, not just by the satyagrahis but by the imperial authorities themselves, as an unequal form of relations between Indians and the white South African government. As a result of the long-drawn out satyagraha, the registration of indentured and non-indentured Indians alike could not be made compulsory; and by voluntary submission to registration, Indians made the white South African authority responsible for the relationship. Accepting the law as a compulsion meant, Gandhi insisted, acceptance of the oppressive as truth, with no assignment of responsibility. By getting compulsion revoked, on the other hand, and insisting that his Indian compatriots register voluntarily, Gandhi ensured that every single act of submission to this unequal arrangement was an enactment too of the true nature of the inequity. Making the oppressors responsible for their actions furthermore potentially allowed for a transformation or change of heart on their part. At the same time, Gandhi sought to define and name, rather than abstract, the true nature of the relations that sustained the Empire.

The Subject of Swaraj

There were two axes of transformation for Gandhi. One related to the critique of exchange, reconstituted as a question of sacrifice. The argument here is that, for Gandhi, the one human capacity or experience that was unamenable to the calculus of exchange was death. In other words, while death could be an act of sacrifice for others, even for a cause, one's own death was beyond exchange, and death was thus the sole possession of the individual. This made the body, for Gandhi, not an ensemble of the sensual, but the ultimate habitation of truth, and the only gift to give. Devji has alerted us to the Gandhian idea of sacrifice as duty, and its relationship to nonviolence.[37] To extend that discussion: for Gandhi, sacrifice, or more specifically self-sacrifice, thus did not assume life and its enhancement to be central. Sacrifice is a notoriously elusive and ambiguous political category that raises questions of exchange, economy, meaning and purpose. As the basis of religion, nation and even family, sacrifice can be reduced to neither ritual, exchange nor pure combat, but is best understood as a way of participating in the sacred and a means of consecrating both death and desire.[38]

Gandhi's second technique of relevance here was that of fasting. Fasting encompassed the usual disciplines of extreme self-control. The aim at one level was through this control actually to expunge the body; or at the very least to detoxify it, to eliminate excess. This was the mortification of the body as a direct counterpoint to the consumptive 'civilisation' that had the satisfaction of the body as its primary aim. Fasting was a 'limit-experience' that tested life and death, but also a state between ingesting and expunging that took the form of self-control. Fasting stood as the mirror image of famine, in which a lack of control over resources and exchange had made millions vulnerable, deprived of the ability even to take responsibity for their own mortality.

Once more, what is consistent in Gandhi is the interruption of the abstract. Whereas economic nationalists had made an almost juridical case for the uneven relationship between economy and empire, through a battery of statistics and argument, Gandhi broke away fundamentally from this mode of argument.[39] He did so by making the abstract part of the embodied and experienced. Fasting increasingly became such an act, lying between the gift of death and ordinary life, that revealed the underlying but true nature of oppression.

37. Faisal Devji, *The Terrorist in Search of Humanity: Militant Islam and Global Politics* (London: Hurst & Co., 2008), 97–135.

38. Paul W. Khan, *Sacred Violence: Torture, Terror and Sovereignty* (Ann Arbor: University of Michigan Press, 2008); and, especially, René Girard, *Violence and the Sacred*, trans. Patrick Gregory (London: Bloomsbury Press, 2013 [1977]).

39. See, for instance, M. K. Gandhi, 'Indian Economics', *Young India*, 8 December 1921, *CWMG* 25, 213–16.

In a related way, he also subordinated the key colonial commodity of cloth to the act of spinning itself. The violence at Chauri Chaura in the early 1920s, in conjunction with the failure of the Khilafat movement and ongoing famine in the Madras area, made Gandhi into an icon. This was the point at which he famously reduced his clothing to the simple loincloth: a declaration of the bareness of life, the power of sacrifice and the belief in everyday activities such as spinning. It was also the making of Gandhi as a superlative image of the twentieth century; we know, meanwhile, that he blamed the outbreak of violence and the collapse of solidarity in part on the simple fact that people had stopped spinning *khadi*.[40]

Our discussion so far has focused on Gandhi's ideas of truth that encompassed its public enactment, revealing the hidden and abstract nature both of oppression and of evil more generally. This was to designate truth as a gesture towards power and responsibility. Truth was undeniably related to power; and insistence on truth revealed collective facts or conditions. Yet for Gandhi, this was only one, and perhaps not the most important, aspect of truth.

In the face of violence, Gandhi called off the Non-Cooperation and Khilafat campaigns at their very height. This has been construed primarily as evidence of his insistence on and fidelity to nonviolence. Declaring that 'I am not God', he went on to remind his followers of his conception of Swaraj:

> Those who believe, and those who have spread the belief, that Gandhi will somehow get them Swaraj . . . are, whether or not they know it, their own and the country's worst enemies; they have not understood the meaning of swaraj at all. Swaraj means self-reliance. To hope that I shall get swaraj for them is the opposite of self-reliance. . . . I am a *vaidya* [doctor]; I prescribe the medicine, explain the manner of taking it, mention other things to be taken with it and specify the quantity to be taken every time. It is ultimately for the patient to act and do the best he can.[41]

Swaraj, or self-reliance, was a repertoire of therapeutics. While mediation and exchange were hidden forces that could only be revealed through the visibility of truth, the truth of Swaraj was the domain of non-mediated practices of the self that were to be cultivated in a state of retreat. The end of a public movement signified—quite literally—a retreat. Gandhi's acolytes were often left frustrated, and most such public gestures led to accusations of betrayal and

---

40. M. K. Gandhi, 'Speech at Madras', *The Hindu*, 15 September 1921, CWMG 24, 238–46.
41. Gandhi, 'One Year's Time-Limit', 228.

compromise. It is pertinent here to point out that for Gandhi, the end of action meant a return to the ashram; for, as Ajay Skaria points out, the ashram was not for him a refuge, or escape, or alternative, but rather a component of the ethical-political.[42] Ashrams, whether in Sabarmati or at the Phoenix and Tolstoy Farms in South Africa, were in fact precursors to public mobilisations, and the institutional context for Gandhian ideas of selfhood.

Swaraj was understood, then, as 'self-reliance', as opposed to its nationalist rendering as 'freedom': as Gandhi noted, 'self-transformation', and not 'the expulsion of the British', was its 'essence'.[43] It was 'to be experienced by each one for himself'. This self-reliance was not only to be experienced 'internally', however, but was also a non-sociological programme for action. Truth, which for Gandhi inhabited the body, was a will-to-selfhood. It is relevant that in Sanskrit and Sanskrit-derived languages, 'truth' (*satya*) shares its root with 'being' (*sat*); yet the fundamental problem remained that there was no access to truth simply because one was a subject. Swaraj, or self-reliance, involved recognising, indeed, that transformation derived from a compulsion to be something other than what the subject was.

Gandhi sought a particular construction and image of the self in his politics of modernity. This was not the superman of iron and steel who vanquished evil on behalf of the weak through supernatural powers. It was rather the *Ubermensch* of an overcoming, whereby violence, in the form of self-mortification, was turned to the interior, the very limits and frailty of the body becoming symbolic of the power of restraint. An ascetic body—in contrast to the militarised body of a Hitler or a Stalin—marked Gandhi out as a global icon of the potency of self-sacrifice.

It also marks out his divergence from Tilak, who shared the principles of sacrifice and a subject-oriented horizon of the political, whereby the individual's duty to the 'event' was paramount. For Gandhi, however, by contrast, the techniques described above, from spinning and fasting to walking and celibacy, took the everyday as the only temporal framework. *Hind Swaraj* subordinated history to the creation of a new self; and this subordination, or de-historicising, took the everyday, as opposed to the eventful, as the context for the therapeutic subject. As Yagnik notes in his biography, Gandhi's ashrams were spartan and were notable for an absence of books. A new and unique moral and

---

42. Ajay Skaria, 'Gandhi's Politics: Liberalism and the Question of the Ashram', *South Atlantic Quarterly* 101:4 (Fall 2002), 955–86.

43. Gandhi, *HS*, 72–76.

political language of the self was signified for Gandhi through radical technologies of the self, from spinning to celibacy. Gandhi shared in the nationalist idea that spirituality, or what he often called 'soul force', was a this-worldly force that was transformative of the self and the world. However, unlike for nationalists such as Tilak, this 'soul force' was not embedded in the collective and repressed past, but was to be constituted and realised anew through the rigours of self-construction. Further, political instrumentality and the realisation of the nation-state were subordinated to this new, overcoming subject. Gandhi's repeated subordination of the political movement to the matter of the transformation of the self is what has earned him his apparently contradictory characterisation as Mahatma/Mephistopheles.

Sacrifice and fasting were, however, not oriented towards the Empire alone. Their most fateful reckoning was to be in the domain of fraternity, in relation to Hindus and Muslims, and Hindus and caste.

Killing/Dying: The Extimacy of Hindus and Muslims

I want both Hindus and Mussalmans to cultivate the cool courage to die without killing.

—GANDHI[44]

Gandhi sought to transform a political domain that he saw to be rife with conflict, power and antagonism by positing a challenging, overcoming subject. Identified by a commitment to the plain and the everyday, Gandhi wrested the most arcane concepts of truth and being from their metaphysical perches and recruited them to a visible vocabulary that helped prosecute a new politics of selfhood. Crucially, this was not expressed in the seductive terms of self-love and self-esteem that characterised the cult of individualism, or the ego-psychology, of the twentieth century. Attuned and oriented to the most pervasive and dominant structures of empire, Gandhi's presentation of the overcoming subject was instead geared towards reanimating the grand potential of religion itself.

In most accounts, and to take Anderson again as indexical, Gandhi's embrace of religion is seen to be noxiously hypocritical to a degree only surpassed by the diffusion of his pious sanctimony. If for his assassin Gandhi had

---

44. M. K. Gandhi, *To the Hindus and Muslims*, ed. Anand T. Hingorani (Allahabad: Allahabad Law Journal Press, 1942), 70 ('The Meaning of the Moplah Rising').

betrayed Hindus, then for his scholarly critics such as Anderson, it was precisely his commitment to Hinduism that had not only distorted the potential for emancipation, but has given credence to the powerful myth and iconic representation of India as nonviolent. New perspectives by Devji and Skaria, among others, have succeeded in presenting Gandhi's religion as a form both of challenge and of power that allowed the subject, as Skaria puts it, to 'surrender without subordination', which ushered in a radical form of equality. Though Devji is focused on the question of violence rather than equality, he nevertheless convincingly re-evokes Gandhi's as a philosophy committed to the principle of a subject who could die but not kill. Both these renderings highlight and underscore the principles of death and sacrifice, as opposed to life and its enhancement through contractual rights, that made Gandhi a potent but ultimately a paradoxical figure, the paradox of his legacy lying in a form of 'radical conservatism', in that he accepted the conditions of religion and society even as he sought to transform them.[45]

While the issue of Hindus and Muslims was of primary importance across the entire spectrum and in the density of detail of the hectic years of action, mobilisations and the partition, the discussion here is limited to explication of three key elements that are definitive of Gandhi's idea of Hindu–Muslim relations, premised once again on the new truth of the subject.

Firstly, Gandhi's apprehension of religion was as a totality that could neither be bifurcated between private and public articulations nor policed, and this has been widely acknowledged in scholarship. The point for emphasis here, however, is that in Gandhi's rendition of the concept, the subject could neither deny nor ever entirely overcome the symbolic world into which she or he had been born. Without becoming mired in the technicalities of the rich if controversial related psychoanalytic discussion, suffice to note here—in agreement with Freud and Lacan—that the human subject is uniquely marked by the fact of being born into a given, and dense, symbolic structure.[46] For Gandhi, the individual's inheritance of religion was primary in the construction of

45. Ajay Skaria, *Unconditional Equality: Gandhi's Religion of Resistance* (Minneapolis: University of Minnesota Press, 2016), 10–15, and 'Gandhi's Radical Conservatism', https://www.india-seminar.com/2014/662/662_ajay_skaria.htm; Faisal Devji, 'Gandhi, Hinduism and Humanity', in Gavin Flood (ed.), *Hindu Practice: The Oxford History of Hinduism* (Oxford: Oxford University Press, 2020), 375–97.

46. Jacques Lacan, *The Four Fundamentals of Psychoanalysis*, trans. Alan Sheridan (London: Penguin Books, 1984).

a true and even of a political subject. Whether in his own confessions in his *Autobiography* or in his near-daily sermons, he sought to radicalise this inheritance, not only for the individual but more consequentially for a new relationship between Hindus and Muslims. This helps to explain why he took the most powerful symbols as central to his politics of religion: if cow-protection went to the core of Hindu symbolics and totems, then the Caliphate and its demise became the inspiration for the launch of the Khilafat movement. These had, in effect, the same value for Gandhi, and not at all because they were so close as to be amenable to amalgamation through a multicultural 'fix'; on the contrary, in Devji's understanding it was precisely because they were so different that the cow and the caliph could enter into a moral rather than merely materialistic relationship of self-interest.[47] Such a view then amplified Gandhi's suspicions and disavowals of the mediating powers of contract, the negotiations of a third party or even of the state. Significantly, this view was overtly related to, and made explicit, the subject-oriented horizon of the political; but this time, in relation to distinction and even hostility.

Secondly, although they were intimates and even 'brothers' of 'the same Bharat Mata' (Mother India), relations between Hindus and Muslims could only be ethical for Gandhi, it is argued here, if they were marked by what has been termed 'extimacy'—a neologism invented by Lacan to convey the notion of a coalition of the interior and the exterior.[48] Extimacy, crucially, is not the antonym of intimacy. Both the estrangement of separation and the intricacies of intimacy carried the potential for violent hostility. Extimacy here refers to the establishment of distance in a claustrophobic intimacy, while throwing a bridge over a chasm of violence.

'I have known', Gandhi wrote, 'deadly enemies dine, and chat together heartily and yet remain enemies.'[49] The intimacy of sharing bread and relations was no barricade against violent hostility; indeed such intimacy could in itself cause wars, as he expounded by taking the example of the Kauravas and Pandavas: even though their intimacy extended from inter-dining to intermarriage, it failed to 'disbar a disunion', and their epic fratricide was in fact provoked by it.[50] A distant aloofness, even exclusiveness, alone created the possibility of fraternal

---

47. Devji, 'Gandhi, Hinduism', 385–89.

48. Lacan, *Seminar of Jacques Lacan, Book VII*, https://www.lacan.com/symptom/extimity .html.

49. Gandhi, *Hindus and Muslims*, 63 ('Inter-Dining Again').

50. Ibid., 60 ('Hindu–Mahomedan Unity').

companionship. In this regard, while the cow was Hinduism's totem, Gandhi was explicit in resurrecting intermarriage as its taboo, respect for which could underlie a union.[51] In contrast to Savarkar, for whom, as incisive new work by Luna Sabastian shows, miscegenation was the primary mode for the realisation of the new political formation of Hindutva,[52] Gandhi sought to re-state the given precepts and limits of Hinduism. Despite declaring his undying friendship for and understanding of the Khilafat leader-duo of the Ali brothers, Maulana and Shaukat, Gandhi explained that he would never 'give his daughter' to them, nor would his Muslim friends give theirs to his family in marriage; and it was precisely the respecting of this taboo, that recognised and even enshrined distinction and exclusion, that in Gandhi's view made the 'union' of friendship possible.[53]

Gandhi's repeated calls for 'love' and 'union' between Hindus and Muslims, especially in the interwar period, referred to such a project of extimacy. Take for instance his appeals for 'unity': these can easily appear pedantic and sanctimonious against a background of repeated conflagrations between followers of the two religions. Yet underlying them was the difficult demand to ignore and resist the force of the Other, as only internal strength—in both the individual and the collective sense—could realise, not peace, so much as the potential for both Hindus and Muslims fully to live as Hindus and as Muslims.

In the wake of violence and even forced conversions in what came to be known as the Mopalah riots in southern India in 1921, Gandhi berated those Muslims who had sought to convert Hindus by force and the fear of violence. At the same time, he hectored those Hindus who claimed victimhood over this episode for their failure to defend their own faith. Both the Muslim as 'bully' and the Hindu as 'coward', as Gandhi termed them, were exemplars of a fear that expressed itself in violent if unwinnable struggle. 'As a coward,' he wrote, 'which I was for years, I harboured violence.' It was cowardice and the 'unwillingness to die and suffer injury', rather than their belief in nonviolence, that had rendered Hindus weak and themselves easily given to violence. In the face of conversions, Gandhi declared, 'If the Hindus wish to convert the Mussalman bully into a respecting friend, they have to learn to die in the face of the heaviest odds.'[54] It was in this context above all that death as sacrifice acquired for Gandhi its most

51. Ibid., 57 ('Hindu Muslim Unity—A Camouflage?').
52. Sabastian, 'Indian Political Thought'.
53. Gandhi, *Hindus and Muslims*, 57 ('Hindu Muslim Unity').
54. Ibid., 108, 111 ('Hindu–Muslim Tension: Its Cause and Cure').

profound value. In insightful writings on Gandhi, and recently on the nature of his religion in particular, Devji has expounded the notion that it was only in the event of violence that the precept of sacrifice gained salience, not only disallowing the calculus of interest and exchange, but also instituting the primacy of moral duty. Such a centrality of sacrifice alone elevated religion.[55]

Thirdly and finally with regard to his view of Hindu–Muslim relations, Gandhi proposed an empowering if difficult path out of the mutual play of identification and envy that led to brutal violence and depleted any capacities for transformation. The exit lay in seeking a brave relationship with one's own and given religion as the effective way to forestall and neuter the provocations of the Other. Whether in the form of inter-dining or intermarriage, by peaceful incorporation or conversions that obliged it, over-zealous intimacy, for Gandhi, portended violence. This was because it was not merely a matter of maintaining food and marriage taboos; distinction of religion especially was the quintessential inheritance of the subject, and incorporation and amalgamation or mixture negated this distinction. Incorporation, most significantly, whether peaceful or forced, especially of the Other, only empowered and ensured an endless competitive play in search of 'superiority'.[56] Invoking both cow-protection and conversion, Gandhi stated starkly, 'Virtue lies in being absorbed in one's prayers in the presence of din and noise. We [Hindus and Muslims] shall both be voted irreligious savages by posterity, if we continue to compel one another to respect our religious wishes.'[57]

The subject was, in short, duty-bound to be fearless in the pursuit of his own faith or religion rather than in seeking to convince, let alone convert, the Other. Such a commitment demanded a practice of restraint and sacrifice that could only be cultivated within the framework of daily living, but only put to the test in the extremities of violent events. In strengthening the self, the Other's capacity to provoke envy and emulation was automatically diminished. Gandhi recognised, however, that the demands of restraint and reflection that alone could render Hindus and Muslims companions, friends and brothers were exacting. He was all too aware of the hostility to his particular and demanding creed of nonviolence.

Far from being a mask for hypocritical impulses and manipulations, then, Gandhi's embrace of religion was open, total and radical. Such a radical

55. Devji, 'Gandhi, Hinduism'.
56. Gandhi, *Hindus and Muslims*, 64 ('Inter-Dining Again').
57. Ibid., 108 ('Hindu–Muslim Tension').

embrace of not only his own religion but also that of the Other led to his assassination by one of his own co-religionists. This at the very least instated him
as an authentic practitioner of his own truth. It was caste, however, and the
question of Hindu fraternity and its own intimate hostilities, that was to mark
out a new and defining departure for the Indian Age. It was Gandhi and the
caste question that ended the near-total fixation on the anti-statist subject of
this era; it was his defining debate with Ambedkar that steered anti-statism
towards a republicanism that was based on a political reappraisal of caste.

Gandhi's Death-Wish

I am used to misrepresentation all my life.

—GANDHI[58]

Fasting, for Gandhi, was the technique and act that interrupted the continuum
of life and death that was related to sovereign power. Death, especially in the
form of sacrifice, as argued above, became the basis of life with others, whether
it was family or fraternity, or friend or foe. In highlighting death as the ultimate
individual capacity, Gandhi aimed to rescue sovereign power from its mediating and all-encompassing cages of law and institutions: or, bluntly, the modern
state. Fasting emerged as the primary practice that not only disrupted the
norms of sovereign power, but also, crucially, became the pivotal technique of
the self-transformation that remained for Gandhi the ultimate end of human
endeavour, whether political or ethical. It is thus not entirely surprising that it
was one of his fasts that occasioned the emergence of a new and highly consequential debate on caste and was to become a landmark event.

At the high-level imperial negotiations of the Round Table Conference in
1931, Gandhi staked his life to stall and scupper the official identification of
untouchables—Dalits—as a 'minority' in the way that Indian Muslims had
been designated. In a speech to the Minorities Committee in London in November, he declared,

Those who speak of the political rights of untouchables do not know their
India, do not know how Indian society is today constructed, and therefore

58. M. K. Gandhi, *All Men Are Brothers: Life and Thoughts of Mahatma Gandhi*, ed. Krishna
Kripalani (Ahmedabad: Navajivan Publishing House, 1960), 50.

I want to say with all the emphasis that I can command that, if I was the only person to resist this thing, I would resist it with my life.[59]

'This thing' that Gandhi would go on to 'resist with his life' was B. R. Ambedkar's proposal to provide separate electorates for the untouchables of India.[60] The precedent for separate electorates had been set and was in operation for the Muslims. Though the consequences in terms of political representation were comparatively meagre, the principle defined the ideological divide between Gandhi and Ambedkar,[61] and Gandhi went so far as to wager his own life in a foundational debate that encompassed divergent perspectives not only as to what India was, but how it might be transformed. This transformation was not to be limited to jettisoning the imperial for a national yoke. It equally, if not indeed to a greater degree, signified the making of a new relationship between Indians themselves. At stake was the question of how freedom and liberty could inaugurate a new fraternity.

The issue of separation was at the core of the differences between Gandhi and Ambedkar. Ten months after his speech in London, made in the context of the Round Table Conference set up to frame the representational institutions for India, Gandhi dramatically announced his fast unto death. The British imperial authorities had ignored his initial intervention. On 17 August 1932, the British prime minister had declared the 'Communal Award' and proposed separate electorates for minorities, encompassing not only Muslims but also for the first time recognising Dalits as separate and a minority. The following day, in a letter to the prime minister reminding him of his previous announcement, Gandhi declared his intention to act on his threat.[62] In a public statement, he sought to explain the audacious move whereby his life would stand between the proposal for separate electorates for Dalits and its realisation. The

59. M. K. Gandhi, 'Speech at the Minorities Committee Meeting', London, 13 November 1931, *CWMG* 48, 293–98, at 298.

60. Memorandum by B. R. Ambedkar and R. Srinivasan to the Round Table Conference, 4 November 1931, ('Political Safeguards for Depressed Classes'), B. R. Ambedkar, *What Congress and Gandhi Have Done to the Untouchables* [1945], in B. M. Ambedkar, *Dr Babasaheb Ambedkar, Writings and Speeches*, ed. Vasant Moon (Bombay: Government of Maharashtra, 1991; hereafter *BAWS*) 9 (= 9.1), at 304–6.

61. D. R. Nagaraj, *The Flaming Feet and Other Essays: The Dalit Movement in India* (Ranikhet: Permanent Black, 2010) was one of the earliest philosophical engagements with this political difference.

62. M. K. Gandhi to Ramsay Macdonald, 18 August 1932, *CWMG* 56, 347–48.

phrase 'over my dead body' certainly acquires in this context an uncustomary political seriousness.

Announcing his resolve to the press, Gandhi clarified, 'Since there appears to be a misunderstanding as to the application of my fast, I may repeat that it is aimed at a statutory separate electorate, in any shape or form, for the "depressed" classes. Immediately that threat is removed once for all, my fast will end.'[63] Though he did not name Ambedkar, it was the latter's cause of caste that Gandhi had singled out as the focus of his death-wish, presenting an explanation of Hinduism that denied the Dalits' own desire for separation in a bid to nullify the social import of caste:

> [M]y intimate acquaintance with every shade of untouchability convinces me that their lives, such as they are, are so intimately mixed with those of the caste Hindus in whose midst and for whom they live, that it is impossible to separate them. They are part of an indivisible family. Their revolt against the Hindus with whom they live and their apostasy from Hinduism I should understand. But this so far as I can see they will not do. There is a subtle something—quite indefinable—in Hinduism which keeps them in it even in spite of themselves. And this fact makes it imperative for a man like me, with a living experience of it, to resist the contemplated separation even though the effort should cost life itself.[64]

Gandhi's deadly threat overtly deployed a description of the relationship between caste Hindus and untouchables as a 'subtle' or 'indefinable' familial bond; he also taunted untouchables for their lack of apostasy, enabling him to claim the presence of the untouchable as integral to Hinduism. Untouchables, for Gandhi, as part of one religious family, were caste brothers of Hinduism, marked by their inferiority but nevertheless children of its god. It was in this vein that he had termed them 'Harijan' (children of God) assigning a theological-spiritual meaning to people who by contrast were identified in political terms variously as 'depressed classes', Dalits or, most starkly, untouchables, by Ambedkar.

On the first day of what was dubbed 'the epic fast'—though it lasted no longer than five days—Gandhi explained his act as an appeal for 'repentance and repararation' on the part of the 'suppressors', so that some 'understanding'

---

63. M. K. Gandhi, 'Statement to the Press', 16 September 1932, *CWMG* 57, 39–42, at 41.
64. Ibid., 40.

could be forged between the suppressors and the suppressed.[65] He declared that he was aiming for a 'brotherly embrace', and went on to claim that the proposed separate electorates for untouchables were 'a huge obstacle' in the way of religious 'reform'.[66] Untouchability, thus, was a domestic issue for Hinduism, to be resolved through forgiveness and internal transformation. Ambedkar's initial response was one of bemused anger. Gandhi's death-wish was a deliberate exaggeration and, as Ambedkar fully understood, was aimed at undermining the import of the caste question. The demand for separate electorates, Ambedkar retorted, was 'only an appendix to the book of India's constitution and not the main chapter. It would have been justifiable, if Mr. Gandhi had resorted to this extreme step for obtaining independence for the country. . . . His determination to fast himself unto death is worthy of a far better cause.'

Branding Gandhi's intervention a form of 'terrorism', Ambedkar defiantly added that 'coercion of this sort will not win the Depressed Classes to the Hindu fold if they are determined to go out'.[67] Gandhi would later admit to his fast being 'coercive' in pushing 'some people into action which they would not have endorsed without my fast', but explained it away as ultimately a 'force . . . used against myself'.[68] To be sure, Gandhi had positioned his own life as the boundary and force between Hinduism as a unity, as he understood it, and the caste that internally divided it.

Not quite apostate yet, Ambedkar had nevertheless clearly proclaimed the separation of the untouchable. Amidst global publicity and imperial anxiety, Gandhi's fast ended within six days with the signing of the infamous Poona Pact between himself and Ambedkar. The Pact achieved Gandhi's immediate aim, in that Ambedkar abandoned his demand for the separation of untouchables, at least in terms of electorates.[69] But his 'victory', as Ambedkar had warned, would 'not [be] worth having':[70] the Poona Pact has gone down in

65. M. K. Gandhi to P. N. Rajobhai, 20 September 1932, *CWMG* 57, 89–90, at 90.

66. M. K. Gandhi, 'Interview to the Press', 20 September 1932, *CWMG* 57, 94–98, at 96, and 'Statement to the Press', 23 September 1932, ibid., 109–10 at 110.

67. Statement on Gandhi's fast by Ambedkar, in Ambedkar, *What Congress and Gandhi*, 311, 316.

68. Gandhi, *Hindu Dharma*, 100, 102.

69. On the international and national attention that the fast received, see Pyarelal, *The Epic Fast* (Akhil New Delhi: Bharat Anusuchit Jati Parishad, 1984 [1932]), 223–74.

70. Ambedkar, *What Gandhi and Congress*, 316. The main emphasis of the brief nine-point Poona Pact, signed between Gandhi and Ambedkar on 24 September 1932, was upon joint electorates: Pyarelal, *The Epic Fast*, 153–56.

Indian history as Gandhi's betrayal, even if it was not over the caste question—notwithstanding his willingness to die for it—that he was to lose his life at the hands of his Hindutva adversaries.[71] The Pact impelled Ambedkar to reprise the event and rewrite the political in such a manner as to become impervious to the Mahatma's logic. It forced Gandhi, meanwhile, to articulate what had hitherto been an assumed relationship between caste and Hinduism.

Gandhi remained steadfast in his views, three elements of which in particular mark out their contrast with the principles informing Ambedkar's project. First, the relationship between the Hindu social and the untouchables, as noted above, was for Gandhi an internal matter, and a given. His attitude towards this relationship was characterised by an equivalent approach whatever the institutional domain to which it was applied, whether the question regarded the disputes raging over temple entry, or the matter of education for the untouchables or, above all, the question of a separate dispensation in the form of electorates: all appeared to Gandhi to demand a similar response, in terms of internal reform.[72] This is to say, and secondly, untouchability for Gandhi could only be overcome through a transformation of disposition. In keeping with his subject-centred vision of the political, and underscoring the power of self-transformation at the height of the fast, Gandhi would repeatedly recite the mantra that he was 'touchable by birth but untouchable by choice'. A change in disposition could alter the choicelessness inherent in caste as it was ordained by birth. Conduct, as the practice of an altered disposition could, for Gandhi, convert the unconvertable.

Caste Hindus, Gandhi would repeatedly urge, could not be 'forced' to dine or marry untouchables, since what was required was a sense of willingness and a change of heart. Forgiveness on the part of the untouchables, and penance and reform on the part of the caste Hindus, became the motif and mantra of Gandhi's politics of caste. The 'spiritual', as the force that would enable becoming something other than what is given, was invoked once more as expressing the quality and character of his opposition to Ambedkar's challenge. Gandhi's defense of Hinduism amounted above all else to recognising and keeping untouchables within the religion.

71. The major Dalit leader of independent India Kanshi Ram marked the Pact's fiftieth anniversary by republishing the Pact, citing it as the cardinal event of modern Dalit political history, inaugurating a new Dalit politics; see his *The Chamcha Age: An Era of Stooges* (New Delhi: Vedic Mudranalaya, 1982).

72. For instance, Gandhi, *Hindu Dharma*, 103 ('A Purificatory Chain of Fasts').

In a perverse manner, what untouchability and Ambedkar's challenge offered for Gandhi was an opportunity for Hinduism not only to reform but also
to redeem itself. This was essentially because for Gandhi the victim was
marked by a lack of choice. Yet, an ethical disposition and morality in Gandhi's
vision had the potential to circumvent and convert even the most abject and
passive condition into an active and moral force.[73] In such an outlook, disposition was key, and consequently untouchability could be transformed by respective acts of will by caste Hindus and by untouchables. Transformation was
thus for Gandhi a matter of choice, and as he argued, it was for caste Hindus
to 'permit' untouchables to 'enjoy' the same things as caste Hindus ordinarily
and routinely did.

Whilst the above was in keeping with Gandhi's political philosophy, what
remained intractable was the matter of religion, as a category, but above all as
a horizon of human ideas and action. As a category, Gandhi had willingly recognised its import for Muslims, as at the Round Table Conference he had
accepted separate Muslim electorates: his non-recognition of the untouchables as separate, by contrast, only served to emphasise the distinction that he
drew between them and the Muslims. This was certainly no mere matter of
numbers and demographics, the legitimacy or adequacy of which as a language whereby to understand the relationship between Hindus and Muslims
Gandhi rejected.[74] It was rather that for him, Muslims represented a truly
radical alterity. Hindus and Muslims might be bound in a fraternal intimacy,
but the two were not the same, even though, historically, they had been, and
therefore contained the potential again to be, one and united.

It would be precisely such a scheme of distinction and incorporation in the
name of religion that Ambedkar would dismantle and redistribute along a
different trajectory. Gandhi's ethical emphasis would be replaced with a focus
upon power as violence in relation to the historically dispossessed. Through
an analysis of antagonism and violence, and in a spirit of neither forgiveness
nor penance, but rather of anger and a sense of betrayal, with caste as its cen-
trepiece, Ambedkar promulgated, as the next chapter recounts, a nonviolent
but agonistic and radical account of fraternity and nationality that endures to
the present day.

Finally, it is instructive here to consider the distinction between symbolic and
systemic violence. For Gandhi, untouchability resided in the symbolic structure
of Hinduism that was shared between high and low castes and could be

73. Devji, *Impossible Indian*.

74. Faisal Devji, *Muslim Zion: Pakistan as a Political Idea* (London: Hurst & Co., 2013).

transformed through subjective practices. To cite his preferred examples in relation to caste, entry into temples by low castes, or the cleaning of toilets by upper castes, could alter the all-powerful symbolic order of caste. The inherent violence of the separation that the practice of caste entailed, being symbolic in nature, could potentially be neutralised or nullified by transgression of the established prohibitions. The potency of the prohibitive symbolic order of caste could, through conduct, gesture and transgression defuse its capacity to exclude. For Ambedkar, however, these symbolic prohibitions only made visible the 'invisible background of systemic violence'.[75]

Ambedkar emphasised that Hindus and Muslims, on the other hand, were united under a common symbolic order. He did not, of course, posit this in relation to religion; the crucial point he understood, however, was that caste Hindus and Muslims shared a history of power and rulership, and that tied them symbolically. Despite religious differences, their shared historical experience of power had rendered them not antagonists belonging to separate symbolic orders, but merely estranged. As a new dispensation of power became imminent, Ambedkar explained, their estrangement had engendered anxiety leading to violence and competition for political control over their collective destiny.

The chasm between untouchables and caste Hindus, by contrast, was in Ambedkar's view categorical and complete, and foreboded 'political disaster'. Untouchability was the quintessence and source of a separation that was not characterised by 'difference on non-essentials', but foundational. Explaining the systemic, hidden yet obvious nature of the violent hostility that framed the relationship between Hindus and untouchables, Ambedkar wrote, in a book published a month before Gandhi's assassination,

> It is a case of fundamental antagonism and antipathy. No evidence of this antipathy and antagonism is necessary. The system of Untouchability is enough evidence of the inherent antagonism between the Hindus and the Untouchables. Given this antagonism it is simply impossible to ask the Untouchables to depend upon and trust the Hindus to do them justice when the Hindu [sic] get their freedom and independence from the British.[76]

Political freedom and liberty were indeed the potent context for debates around untouchability, the failure of the initiative for separate electorates

75. Slavoj Žižek, *Violence: Six Sideways Reflections* (London: Profile Books, 2008), 8.

76. B. R. Ambedkar, 'Mr. Gandhi and the Emancipation of the Untouchables: Caste and the Constitution' [1948], *BAWS* 9, 425.

notwithstanding. Critically, in addressing the issue, Ambedkar rebalanced the relationship between the social and the political, respecifying the nature and amplifying the extent of the latter. In different forums, from legal-constitutional committees to public meetings, and in historical-philosophical writings, he developed a comprehensive critique of caste such as to render it a political category. As the next chapter discusses, he transcended the subject-oriented horizon of the political that achieved its apotheosis in Gandhi. By focusing on violence not as an individual capacity for death or sacrifice but rather revealing it as the basis of the separation of castes, Ambedkar's project laid the republican foundations of India and, indeed, of Pakistan.

But to return to Gandhi: his politics, as this chapter has shown, amounted to the performance of truth. This took the visible as the essential aspect and consequence of truth, which was dependent not on elections and representation, but upon technologies of the self, ranging from restraint to sacrifice. It was a politics that required attachment to truth as action, as opposed to the detachment as a disposition for action (*nishkaam-karma*) that had been dominant in nationalist and other contemporary Indian political thinking.

The aim of this politics was to transform not the nation, economy, community or class, but the self, or the subject itself. This radical politics of truth remains problematic, however. In the first place, such a political philosophy produced an 'excess of the subject': the term 'Mahatma' could indeed be viewed not so much as a translation of 'saint', but as pointing to the literality of the excessive subject. Most strikingly, while only the subject or the self was capable of truth, truth in itself was not sufficient or even redemptive for the subject. What remained was the excess that was witnessed in the power of the image of Gandhi himself: indeed, it is not entirely possible to separate Gandhi from his image. Nevertheless, beyond the image, the excessive emerged increasingly as a supplement to the violence of the political. Precisely because Gandhian politics was premised on the revelatory and the ordinary, reliant on the eventful as much as on the visible, it proved to be unsustainable and impossible to institutionalise or reproduce—or rather, the only way it could be institutionalised was, as in contemporary India, through a series of ritual commemorations. Thus, as the 'Father of the Nation', Gandhi became the object of neglect and betrayal. The act of his assassination, above all, installed him as the Father, and each instance of complaint or disavowal only confirms that status anew.

5

The Triumph of Fraternity

SOVEREIGN VIOLENCE AND
PAKISTAN AS PEACE

They hate me . . . I know that the Hindus are sick of me.

—B. R. AMBEDKAR[1]

THE RECOGNITION OF HOSTILITY and violence was a central problem in the life and works of B. R. Ambedkar. The Hindus might be, as he himself remarked, 'sick of him'; he was also the sole founding figure to write a monumental account of the idea of Pakistan in the divisive and violent decade of the 1940s, but this, again in his own words, was 'unowned' by the Muslims—and so it remains.[2] Today Ambedkar is widely 'owned': appropriated and lauded primarily as a messiah of the lower castes and the marginal, and identified too as the Mahatma's political nemesis. Yet caste and the cause of the untouchables were but a point of departure that led Ambedkar effectively to rewrite the political foundations of violence and power, sovereignty and fraternity, nationality and republicanism. His political ideas proved to be not only radical but also crucially consequential for the formation both of the Indian republic and of the first avowedly Muslim nation in world history, namely Pakistan.

The differences between Ambedkar and Gandhi proved definitive for the political foundations of India. The Poona Pact and the failure to designate

---

1. B. R. Ambedkar, 'Annihilation of Caste' [1936], *BAWS* 1, 23–96, at 37.

2. B. R. Ambedkar, *Pakistan or the Partition of India: The Indian Political What's What!* [1946 edn] = *BAWS* 8, at 2.

the 'depressed classes' or untouchables as a minority caused Ambedkar to undertake a fundamental reconsideration of what constituted the political. As this chapter elaborates, he focused on the notion of violence as systemic and foundational, and by uncovering the historical source of sovereign violence, he developed a new and radical language of fraternity and sovereignty that endures to date. Most significantly, he made a decisive move away from the anti-statist fixation of contemporary political practice that had privileged the individual political subject that was attached to the themes of violence and nonviolence. Disrupting and dismantling this vision of politics, associated above all with Gandhi, Ambedkar repositioned violence and power as not only systemic, but also historical, and in doing so, inaugurated a new future of sovereign fraternity.

In focusing primarily on Ambedkar, this chapter reconstructs and interprets the work on violent hostility and antagonism that was central to his political thought and writings. As a thinker, Ambedkar remained singular in taking account of the full and potential measure of violence, predominantly in caste relations but also beyond, in the comparative contexts of revolutions and the formation of nation-states in the modern world. As I have elaborated elsewhere, Ambedkar's idea of the political involved a radical appraisal of social antagonism, whereby inherent hostility and the potential for violence became institutionalised competition, and antagonists thus became adversaries: in short, antagonism was converted into agonism.[3] (To reprise: 'the political' here refers to the consideration and the domain of power, conflict and antagonism, rather than to either the institutional management or representation of 'interests' commonly understood as 'politics', or to the domain of deliberation and freedom associated with a wide range of traditions from classical liberalism to Hannah Arendt.[4])

Ambedkar was a pre-eminent thinker of nonviolence precisely because he understood the full measure and consequences of violence. Crucially, and unlike his global and historical interlocutors, be they constitutional experts or Karl Marx, he identified the nation as the 'container' of the political, in the form of a radical republican democracy. For democracy 'the people', or popular sovereignty, remains the basic unit of politics, as opposed to 'humanity',

3. Kapila, 'Global Intellectual History'.

4. Mouffe, *On the Political*. But see Steven Lukes, *Power: A Radical View*, 2nd edn (London, Palgrave, 2005), who integrates power with deliberation, or aims to stitch together the registers of the political and politics.

which for cosmopolitanism is the basis of political ethics and a form of universality. Ambedkar's agonism was constitutively elaborated and attached to the concept of nationality as it related to democracy or popular sovereignty rather than to any universalistic framework or notion of human rights, and is most clearly elaborated in his book on Pakistan and equally, if not more so, in his disquisitions on caste. Moreover, Ambedkar's political vision, unlike that of his rival Mahtama Gandhi, was staked on the reproductive capacity of political ideas through an institutional design in which the subject—national and Dalit—was embedded in popular sovereignty. Agonism, or the recognition of hostile distinctions as opposed to their violent eradication or wilful neglect, in effect became the nonviolent condition for the life of the Indian nation and democracy.[5]

While cognisant of extensive discussions of agonism in relation to democracy and liberalism, this chapter departs from those perspectives in its focus on modern India. For the modern West, the question of agonism has re-emerged, after its initial treatment by Nietzsche, to dislodge the coercive emphasis of consensus in the so-called post-political era of globalisation and late capitalism, enabling the recognition of distinctions and promising to renew liberal democracy.[6] The political foundations of India, by contrast, were framed by considerations of distinction, whether of caste or religion—especially as regards their potential for antagonism and hostility and the forms these might take. For Ambedkar as for Gandhi, the issue of violence in the context of these distinctions remained pre-eminent and constitutive rather than one that emerged as an after-effect of a history of consensus. Moreover, and significantly, the enmity or even active antagonism were identified in the intimate and familiar, rather than by reference to the category of the foreigner—however much fabricated

5. Chantal Mouffe, *Agonistics: Thinking the World Politically* (London: Verso, 2013); for related discussions of agonism, see William E. Connolly, *Pluralism* (Durham, NC: Duke University Press, 2005), and Hannah Arendt, *Crises of the Republic* (New York: Harvest Books, 1969). My argument stands also in opposition to multiculturalism and equally its Nehruvian rendition of a 'unity in diversity' that recognises but surrenders to the cultural domain. For the contemporary consequences of this debate and Indian democracy, see Shruti Kapila, 'The Majority of Democracy', *Social Text* (Periscope digital issue on 'Politics under Modi'), 27 February 2015, https://socialtextjournal.org/periscope_article/the-majority-of-democracy/.

6. Bonnie Honig, *Democracy and the Foreigner* (Princeton, NJ: Princeton University Press, 2003); James Tully, *Strange Multiplicity: Constitutionalism in the Age of Diversity* (Cambridge: Cambridge University Press, 1995); James Tully, *Public Philosophy in a New Key* (Cambridge: Cambridge University Press, 2008), esp. vol. 2.

or invented—as the potential enemy or oppositional figure that has animated modern political thought elsewhere, and particularly in the modern West.[7]

In this regard, however, the resurrected, controversial works and ideas of Carl Schmitt on the dimensions of the political in the contemporary appraisal of both democracy and communism on a global stage cannot be avoided. To clarify: for Schmitt, antagonism animated the political horizon that was identified by the distinction between friend and enemy with the possible and real destruction of the enemy as its condition. The salience of antagonism for the political domain is integrated into this chapter, but herein primarily lies the point of departure from Schmitt, regarding the central role of homogeneity in forging unity. In fact, Schmitt interprets unity and homogeneity not only as interchangeable, but also as the ultimate ends and goal of order and sovereignty. He concluded his famous book *The Concept of the Political* by quoting Virgil's verse 'ab integro nascitur ordo' (from unity/integrity/homogeneity order is born).[8] The Indian political by its very conditions of heterogeneity and division militated against the instituting of sovereignty towards a homogeneous end while retaining a focus on unity. Ambedkar's agonism became a salient precept for Indian sovereignty and his critique of Savarkar's *Hindutva* in this regard, discussed below, remains instructive. Precisely because Ambedkar's political thought was animated by an interest in antagonism in relation to sovereignty or even unity, consideration of Pakistan proved to be inescapable.

Highlighting the issue of separation and antagonism, Ambedkar provided a candid assessement of caste in comparison with religion:

[T]he chasm between the Hindus and Muslims, between Hindus and Sikhs, between Hindus and Christians is nothing compared with the chasm between the Hindus and the Untouchables. It is the widest and the deepest. The chasm between the Hindus and the Muslims is religious and not social. That between the Hindus and the Untouchables is both religious *and* social. The antagonism rising out of the chasm existing between Hindus and Muslims cannot spell political disaster to the Muslims because the relationship between Hindus and the Muslims is not of master and slave. It is one of mere estrangement. On the other hand, the chasm between Hindus and the Untouchables must spell political disaster for the

7. Kapila, 'History of Violence'.
8. Schmitt, *Concept of the Political*, 96.

Untouchables because the relationship between the two is that of master and slave.[9]

The above extract tellingly encapsulates the range and ambitions of Ambedkar's political project. With clarity and candour, he argued that caste was a political formation marked by inequity of power and the experience of subjugation. Although he departed fundamentally from Gandhi, in one crucial respect Ambedkar accorded with his adversary: he recognised the relationship between Hindus and Muslims as intimate, inasmuch as only a close bond could transform into one of 'estrangement'. The 'chasm' between the Hindus and Muslims thus was categorically different—more in the nature of a drifting apart—from that between untouchables and caste Hindus, characterised as this was by a complete lack of intimacy, an absence of relations, that had ensued from the casting out of the untouchable.

This separation between the Brahmin and the untouchable was steeped in violence. Identifying caste as a historic political order that had installed the Brahmin as an immortal sovereign, Ambedkar sought to both reveal and undo what I term here 'the dispersed monarchy of the Brahmin', in a bid to inaugurate a new fraternity. As this chapter aims to demonstrate, fraternity was not merely a matter of kinship or society, but was rooted in sovereignty and violence. To elaborate, however, it is necessary here first to contextualise Ambedkar's exposition of the Hindu social that he took to be the central obstacle to the establishment of both a new fraternity and the republic.

Moreover, as also elaborated below, Ambedkar was concerned with violence equally as it related to the maintenance of sovereign order—that is, as it had emerged in relation to caste—and as a force for disorder, especially in terms of Hindu–Muslim relations in the twentieth century, albeit that, in light of his understanding of natural rights, he appreciated too the generative power of violence. If too few had the means to inflict violence, however, as in the case of upper-caste Brahmins, this would militate against the formation of and/or destroy the social order. If, conversely, the practice of violence was widespread, that too would destroy the social order: a state of affairs he described at length as pertaining to Hindus and Muslims in interwar India.

The point for emphasis here is that Ambedkar, unlike natural rights theorists such as Hugo Grotius and even the foremost foundational thinker on sovereignty, Thomas Hobbes, was not seeking an Archimedean point of

9. Ambedkar, *What Congress and Gandhi*, 249 (original emphasis).

equilibrium with regard to violence.[10] Rather, he was making explicit the altogether radical potential for discovering and instituting sovereignty anew, and was forthright in his treatment of the issues both of separation and of violence. In such a perspective, Ambedkar is less amenable than has often been assumed to being cast as a 'communitarian liberal' or a proponent of 'group rights.'[11] He can be more fruitfully approached and accurately understood as a thinker of modern sovereignty.

Fratricidal Fraternity, or The Hindu Social

Far from working in a spirit of fraternity the mutual relations of castes are fratricidal.

—AMBEDKAR[12]

The critique of caste that Ambedkar developed in the interwar period aimed not so much to obscure the nationalist preoccupation with political liberty as to foreground fraternity. In so doing, however, he shifted the focus to the more fundamental yet more intractable issue of political formation: that is, the relationship between violence and power. Savarkar had devoted his intellectual capacities to elaboration of the 'essentials' of the new political fraternity of Hindutva; for Ambedkar the delineation and destruction of what he termed 'the Hindu social order' was 'essential' to create the possibility of a new fraternity.

With one eye on the French and American revolutionary era that had produced the powerful vocabulary of modern politics and the other on the rise of Nazism and fascism in contemporary Europe, Ambedkar placed caste within the bounds of this historical and contemporary horizon. In referring to the revolutionary era, his aim was to situate the problem of the social squarely within the context of the political. Nazism and fascism, on the other hand, became a foil in his writings, to situate the violence that had led to the powerful

10. Richard Tuck, *The Sleeping Sovereign: The Invention of Modern Democracy* (Cambridge: Cambridge University Press, 2016); Leo Strauss, *The Political Philosophy of Hobbes: Its Basis and Genesis* (Chicago: University of Chicago Press, 1952); Quentin Skinner, 'Hobbes on Sovereignty: An Unknown Discussion', *Political Studies* 13:2 (1965), 213–18.

11. Bayly, *Recovering Liberties*; Rochana Bajpai, *Debating Difference: Group Rights and Liberal Democracy in India* (Oxford: Oxford University Press, 2011).

12. B. R. Ambedkar, 'India and the Prerequisites of Communism' [n.d., published posthumously] = *BAWS* 3.2, at 104.

persistence and preservation of the caste order in the monarchical form. The revolutionary potential of a fraternity of equals, in the Indian context, thus had to confront caste. The Hindu order as it emerged in his disquisitions was both the source of the social and an obstacle to the possibility of 'associated life'.[13]

In her influential writings on the 'social question', Hannah Arendt too returns to the eighteenth century to interpret the revolutionary era as the foundational moment of the creation of the modern politics of the people.[14] For her, the social question, as the revolutionary era made manifest, was bound up with necessity primarily understood as poverty or, in Marx's rendition, exploitation. The social, as Arendt elaborates, was embedded in necessity and 'man made violence'. Marx, she argues, aimed posthumously to rehabilitate the oppressed 'to whose injured lives history had added the insult of oblivion'.[15] Further, though the French revolution failed to answer the 'social question' satisfactorily, the era nevertheless produced the sentiment—however politically inconsequential—of 'compassion' for the 'suffering' of others, as a means to overcome the 'distance' between unequals.[16] Finally, and relevant to the discussion here, immanent in the failure of the social in the French revolution was the emergence as a political category of 'the people': a successful outcome of the revolution, according to Arendt, but a failure of the republic, the category of 'the people' was equated with the 'general' and 'indivisible' will that was ultimately dependent on the idea of a 'common national enemy'.[17]

In delineating the social, Arendt makes a crucial connection between the revolutionary discovery of the people and its simultaneous splitting along social and political lines. In other words, the abrogation of the monarchy resulted in its replacement by 'the people' embodying a popular or general will. Marked by unanimity of the general will, such a revolutionary discovery of the people, Arendt argues, 'meant the enduring unity of the future political body was guaranteed not in the worldly institutions which the people had in common but

13. Ambedkar, 'India and the Prerequisites', 95–129.

14. Hannah Arendt, *On Revolution* (New York: Penguin Books, 2006 [1963]), 49–105.

15. Ibid., 59.

16. Ibid., 67–72. But see Uday Singh Mehta, 'The Social Question and the Absolutism of Politics', *Seminar* 615 (November 2010), https://www.india-seminar.com/2010/615/615_uday_s_mehta.htm. On Ambedkar, see Jesús Cháirez-Garza, 'Nationalizing Untouchability: The Political Thought of B. R Ambedkar, ca. 1917–56' (unpublished doctoral dissertation, University of Cambridge, 2014).

17. Arendt, *On Revolution*, 66–67.

in the will of the people themselves'.[18] It was only under these conditions, or in a 'republic', that the equality of people was possible. Significantly, the corralling together of, in Arendt's words, 'the multitude into the place of a single person' was the work of the 'general will' that 'was nothing more or less than [the conversion of the] many into one'.[19] It was in this precise context that the 'unifying power of the common national enemy' became salient. In short, 'only in the presence of an enemy' and conditions of potential hostility can an indivisible and general will become manifest. Thus, national and foreign affairs were constitutive of 'the political', while 'human relations as such became the realm of "the social"'.[20]

The above Arendtian detour was necessary in order to explicate the matter of the social and its rendition as the political in Ambedkar's project, and not only because Ambedkar wrote in full awareness of the revolutionary fallout of this for the modern language of politics. Ambedkar, unlike Arendt, did not interpret the social as distinct from the political. Rather, the social, in the Indian context, was itself the source of distinction and separation. In Ambedkar's understanding, the social primarily militated against the formation of the 'people', or fraternity. Significantly, and as elaborated below, the conversion of the one by the many or the monarch by the general will was the central obstacle: an obstacle identified with the Brahmin. The social, marked by its very absence of bonds, yet ubiquity, had nevertheless, according to Ambedkar, produced the Brahmin not as a sovereign in the singular, or monarch. Indeed, as will be recounted below, the Brahmin and Brahminism as a caste had itself been constituted by a regicide. Dispersed, rather than concentrated in an individual monarch, and yet separate from the society it dominated, Brahmin caste power had been rendered permanent as it was premised on a total control of violence. In elaborating this important intervention regarding caste as sovereign order, the discussion synthesises and interprets Ambedkar's several historical and philosophical writings on caste in relation to the political.[21]

18. Ibid., 66.

19. Ibid., 67.

20. Arendt, *On Violence*, 67–68.

21. Here Ambedkar's 'Annihilation', 'India and the Prerequisites', 'Philosophy of Hinduism' = *BAWS* 3.1 and *Who Were the Shudras?*, *BAWS* 7, 11–227 are salient. His earliest writings included 'Castes in India' [1916], *BAWS* 1, 3–22, which is often cited as a pioneering essay in Indian sociology.

Caste thus posed a specific problem. It was the fabric of the social, with a pervasive and inescapable power; yet it was sustained by, and fostered, principles that were the antithesis of the social: namely, separation and isolation. It was, in Ambedkar's words, 'the most extensive and wild manifestation of the spirit of isolation and separation'.[22] In delineating the Hindu social, Ambedkar defined its essential principle as 'graded inequality'. Its vertical arrangement with the Brahmin at the top, the untouchable at the bottom and the Kshatriya and the Vaishya in the middle was, he argued, not 'merely conventional', but utterly pervasive: 'no sphere of life . . . is not regulated by this principle of graded inequality'.[23] Encoded in 'spiritual, moral and legal' precepts, fixity of both occupation and people made each caste separate and exclusive; and the ban or taboo on intermarriage and inter-dining between castes moreover fossilized immobility. The Hindu social order did not merely enshrine inequality, but actually defied relationality between unequals.

Such a spirit of isolation and exclusiveness was distinctive of and specific to caste, as opposed to social class, which Ambedkar understood as universal to human and social life.[24] Caste, as he put it, is 'not so much the existence of classes as the spirit of isolation and exclusiveness which is inimical with a free social order'.[25] Moreover, the power of separation and the taboo on relationality between castes allowed Ambedkar to dismiss any notion of caste as race, in the sense of an affinity derived from descent and blood that had become the staple of early twentieth-century colonial ethnography and public debate.[26] 'Indeed the ideal Hindu', he wrote, 'must be like a rat living in his own hole refusing to have any contact with others.'[27] Lacking in a spirit of the 'common'— the 'Hindu's public [being] his caste' and the suffering of others evoking 'no response'—the Hindu social was ultimately, in effect, 'anti-social'.[28]

Separation as the basis of the social was, moreover, an outcome of systemic and historic violence. This militated against the formation of fraternity, and the relationship between castes was neither reciprocal nor peaceful, but antagonistic and hostile.[29] Castes were 'self-enclosed', with the key antagonism

22. Ambedkar, 'India and the Prerequisites', 102.

23. Ibid., 107.

24. Ibid.

25. Ibid., 113.

26. Ambedkar, 'Annihilation', 49; also, Ambedkar, 'Castes in India', 9–14, 21–22.

27. Ambedkar, 'Annihilation', 50.

28. Ambedkar, 'Annihilation', 51, 56.

29. Ambedkar, 'India and the Prerequisites', 99–148.

being that between the Brahmin and the untouchable at the two ends of the vertical social scale. A related feature of separation inherent in the caste principle was, moreover, according to Ambedkar, the 'distance'—a term he borrowed from the early twentieth-century sociologist Gabriel Tarde—between the two extremes. This distance, he explained, was intended to ensure that any 'infection of imitation' of superiors was impossible.[30] The Brahmin emerged as the category that held imperative sovereignty over others regardless of religious distinction. Ambedkar thus wrote,

> [W]hile making themselves into a caste, the Brahmins, by virtue of this, created non-Brahmin caste; or to express it my own way, while closing themselves in they closed others out. . . . Take India as a whole with its various communities designated by the various creeds to which they owe allegiance, to wit, the Hindus, Mohammedans, Jews, Christians and Parsis. Now barring the Hindus, the rest within themselves are non-caste communities. But with respect to each other they are castes . . . Symbolically, if Group A wants to be endogamous, Group B has to be so by sheer force of circumstance.[31]

In describing and understanding the nature of India and the Hindu social through the 'fissiparous' character of caste, Ambedkar addressed the possible nature of the future fraternity of independent India, and a form of fraternity that was to be embedded in nationality. It is important here to focus on the element of antagonism between the Brahmin and untouchable.

The force, or categorical sovereignty, of the Brahmin rendered hostility internal to the social itself. For Ambedkar, and unlike Arendt, it was not the presence of the external or the outsider that had the potential for an enmity and hostility that further enabled the emergence of the general will of 'the people'. By contrast, hostility was instead inherent in the nature of the Hindu social, in the form of the antagonism between the two ends of the caste, the Brahmin and the untouchable; and confronting, indeed 'annihilating', this hostile relationship became for Ambedkar the precondition for the creation of a fraternity.

The untouchable, or *shudra*, was not only marked by the greatest degree of distance from caste Hindus, and isolation, but was essentially without any rights. Moreover, precisely because untouchables did not constitute a 'class',

30. Ambedkar, 'Castes in India', 18.
31. Ibid., 20–21.

albeit untouchability was a function of labour, their predicament was not simply a matter of poverty. To be sure, the untouchable's condition was akin to that of the poor and the exploited, but was not the same, as Ambedkar pointed out in his critique of Marx. In fact, as a figure of necessity and want—but, crucially, due to hostility and isolation—the untouchable had become the abject subject of the Hindu social.[32] This abject condition of extreme separation was, according to Ambedkar, the outcome of historical civil wars engendering a systemic violence premised on the disarming of the untouchables, who were thus themselves denied any means of violence.[33] This had ensured the perpetual power of caste and the Brahmin, regardless of changing imperial dispensations.[34] In turning to the historic past of civil wars, Ambedkar's aim, as elaborated below, was to forge a future in which distance and separation were replaced by a relationship of competition between castes. To put it differently, only once the full measure of the violence of the social had been apprehended could the conditions for a democratic fraternity come into existence; otherwise there was no possibility of, in Arendtian terms, the conversion of the single monarch to a general will, given the fratricidal and antagonistic nature of the Hindu social. Only the emergence of agonism—the conversion of internal hostility mired in isolation into an adversarial and competitive relationship, as envisioned by Ambedkar—could summon the force of the social to become the basis of the political.

Ambedkar achieved the transfiguration of the social as the political by directly addressing the issue of violence and power. Arguably, he was unconvinced that violence was capable of creating power.[35] Rather than taking an ethical view with regard to violence, he turned, like several of his political peers, to history. In excavating the historical source of sovereignty, he identified its origins in what he termed India's 'counter-revolution', which had installed a perpetual power of the Brahmin that over the ages had become not only invisible, but indeed immortal. Turning to the historical conflict between Buddhism and Brahminism, or the revolution and counter-revolution, as he termed it, in Ancient India, entailed furthermore the critique and rejection of both Marxism and Nazism, which in Ambedkar's own century had become the dominant languages of revolution and violent power.

32. Ambedkar, 'Annihilation', 44–48.
33. Ambedkar, 'India and the Prerequisites', 126.
34. Ibid., 273–79.
35. Arendt, *On Violence*, 56.

The Sovereign Order of Caste

The Nazis had indeed a great deal to learn from the Hindus. If they had adopted the technique of suppressing the masses devised by the Hindus, they would have been able to crush the Jews without open cruelty and would have also exhibited themselves as humane masters.

—AMBEDKAR[36]

In the mid-twentieth-century world-historical context of Nazism and the Holocaust, Ambedkar elaborated the nature of the violence that premised and had made perpetual the power of the Brahmin. He described the Hindu social as 'nothing but Nietzsche's Gospel put in action'.[37] In tackling the issue of violence and power, he presented the Brahmin as sovereign, but—importantly—not in the form of a king or monarch: in Ambedkar's rendition of caste, the Brahmin emerged as the Superman, a figure who could kill but not die; and violence was portrayed as historically systemic, by pointing to its means, instruments and ends.

In showing the intersection between Nietzsche's idea of the Superman and the Brahmin, and the catastrophic violence that this idea entailed, Ambedkar starkly articulated the position of the untouchable. 'As against the Superman' or Brahmin, the untouchable 'has no right to life, liberty or property or the pursuit of happiness. He must be ready to sacrifice everything for the sustenance of the life and dignity of the Superman.' Sacrifice here was understood in terms of life itself, and the belief was inculcated in the untouchable that he should 'respond to such call for sacrifice in the interest of the superman as his supreme duty'.[38] The ability to take life, in other words, was integral to the Brahmin as sovereign. The untouchables, by contrast, were 'the weariest, most loathed the most miserable people that history can witness . . . a spent and sacrificed people'.[39] Whereas Nietzsche was interested in creating a brave new 'race', the Hindu order of things was centrally concerned rather with 'maintaining the privilege' of the Brahmin, who had already 'come to arrogate to [him]self the claim of being Superman'.[40] (While it goes beyond the bounds of this discussion, it is important to reiterate that Ambedkar had repeatedly dismissed the

36. Ambedkar, 'India and the Prerequisites', 127.
37. Ibid., 116.
38. Ibid., 123.
39. Ambedkar, 'Frustration', *BAWS* 12.6 ('Miscellaneous Notes'), 733–35, at 733.
40. Ambedkar, 'India and the Prerequisites', 116.

notion of caste being a form of race, disputing the claims of colonial ethnographers and critiquing emerging anthropological debates in this regard.[41]) Equally, for Ambedkar, as discussed above, caste was a phenomenon unique to India, that 'marks off Hindus from other peoples'.[42]

The Brahmin's arrogation of supremacy was the outcome of a regicide. Its origins lay in the mists of India's antiquity, in the killing of a Buddhist king.[43] This turn to history by Ambedkar was not antiquarian or recuperative in intent: as for other ideologues of the period, be it Tilak, or Nehru, or indeed Savarkar, history was the template through which a political future was imagined. This history, Ambedkar explained, is 'even more than a past of the present . . . a 'living past [and therefore] as really present as any present can be'.[44]

Given that the Hindutva ideologue Savarkar, as discussed in Chapter 3 above, had identified Buddhism as the original cause that had militated against the formation of nationality in India, it is striking that in Ambedkar's interpretation of India's past it is the destruction of Buddhism in particular that is seen as constitutive of the violent power of the Brahmin as sovereign. The necessity to reprise this historical event for Ambedkar, however, by contrast with Savarkar, was in order to forge a fraternity of equals in India. With a rhetorical flourish and considerable conviction, and contra Hindutva, Ambedkar wrote,

> [T]he effects of Muslim invasions on Hindu India have been really superficial and ephemeral. The Muslim invaders destroyed only the outward symbols of Hindu religion such as temples and Maths [i.e., seminaries] etc. They did not extirpate Hinduism, nor did they cause any subversion of the principles or doctrines which governed the spiritual life of the people. . . . To alter the metaphor the Muslims only stirred the waters in the bath and that too only for a while. Thereafter they got tired of stirring and left the water with sediments to settle. . . . [In contrast] . . . Brahmanism in its conflict with Buddhism made a clean sweep. It emptied the bath with the Buddhist Baby in it and filled the bath with its own waters and in it its own baby.[45]

41. See for instance 'Brahmins versus Kshatriyas', *BAWS* 3, 419, whereby Ambedkar argues that Aryans were not a race. He also argued that there were no racial differences between Brahmins and untouchables. Ambedkar, *The Untouchables: Who Were They and Why They Became Untouchables? BAWS* 7, 233–382, at 242, 303–7.

42. Ambedkar, 'India and the Prerequisites', 141.

43. Ambedkar, 'Revolution and Counter-Revolution', *BAWS* 3.3, at 269–70.

44. Ambedkar, 'Manu and the Shudras', *BAWS* 12.6 ('Miscellaneous Notes'), 719–25, at 719.

45. Ambedkar, 'Revolution', 274.

Thus, for Ambedkar, as previously discussed, Hindu–Muslim relations were not necessarily antagonistic, primarily due to their common historic experience as rulers, which had at the very least tied them symbolically. More significant was that caste, and especially the power of the Brahmin, had remained intact regardless of any change in imperial dispensations. In short, in turning to history, Ambedkar's aim, unlike Savarkar's, was not to foment antagonisms anew, but rather to explain the source, preservation and perpetuation of power. It is in this perspective that he identified Buddhism as the Hinduism's crucial antagonist.

'The history of India', Ambedkar wrote, 'is nothing but a history of mortal conflict between . . . Buddhism and Brahmanism'.[46] The regicide of the Buddhist king Pushyamita and the destruction of the Buddhist state in the classical past were understood by Ambedkar as the originary moment of the installation of the Brahmin as sovereign. A key consequence was the promulgation of caste laws and taboos, as enshrined by Manu, that had rendered untouchability permanent.[47] Ambedkar delineates and details several features of this phenomenon, whereby Brahminism was deemed the 'counter-revolution' to the Buddhist 'revolution' in India. He likewise raised the matter of the historic conflict between Brahmins and Kshatriyas (the warrior caste), especially with regard to kingship and power. Three related issues emerging from Ambedkar's disquisitions are pertinent here.

Firstly, as a consequence of the regicide, taboos and codes between castes were redistributed, especially in relation to the rights to bear arms. According to Ambedkar, the taboos against Brahmins bearing arms and exercising kingly power were lifted.[48] Moreover, the Brahmin was made immune from capital punishment, whatever the nature of the crime,[49] and the rights to bear arms and to rule were further amplified by the right to regicide and rebellion, although this right was circumscribed by the significant condition that the (Kshatriya) king or ruler must have failed to uphold the social order.[50] The king or ruler nevertheless became, as Ambedkar put it, 'liable for prosecution and punishment like a common felon'.[51] Thus, with the destruction of

46. Ibid., 267.
47. Ibid., 269–71.
48. Ibid., 276–77.
49. Ambedkar, 'Manu and the Shudras', 722.
50. Ambedkar, 'Revolution', 277.
51. Ambedkar, 'India and the Prerequisites', 124–25.

Buddhism, codes and taboos enshrining and embedding the sovereignty of the Brahmin, while not exactly rendering direct rulership or kingship irrelevant, subordinated the king to the Brahmin.

Secondly, a separation was enforced between Brahmins and non-Brahmins. Applying the principle of 'graded inequality', the motive force and key outcome of this separation was the disarming of the shudra, who was not only deprived of the means of violence by restriction of the rights to bear arms, but was specifically barred from exercising it.[52]

These combined developments meant that the isolation and fixity that represented both the nature and principles of the Hindu social, as elaborated above, were sustained by division: a division not only of labour or occupation, but in terms of capacity for and legitimacy of violence, and as a definitive aspect of sovereignty. Ambedkar described, with nuance and complexity, how erstwhile hostility between Kshatriyas and Brahmins was converted into an entente that ultimately closed ranks on the lower orders, and the shudras in particular, who were once warriors but through internecine warfare and as an outcome of the banishment of Buddhism were reduced to the lowest and the most abject subjects of Hinduism.[53] The two enduring effects of the regicide and consequent redistribution of ritual and sacrament were, in summary, the dilution of the sovereignty of the king, making him dependent on the Brahmin,[54] and the monopolisation and control of the instruments and means of violence; with the end result that one whole group (*varna*) was made into the untouchable caste.

Ironically, the Buddhist commitment to nonviolence had itself furnished new norms for the Brahmin, especially in relation to meat-eating; and this too could be projected against the untouchable.[55] Thus, the Brahmin incorporated principles of nonviolence from the very regime—Buddhism—that it displaced, with strict taboos in favour of vegetarianism. This allowed for the distinction of the Brahmin to emerge as one of sovereignty, but without killing, or indeed, dying.

The third and final relevant point emerging from Ambedkar's historical account is that, unlike other versions of kingship (Western and Islamic) that

52. Ibid., 126; Ambedkar, 'Revolution', 308–20.

53. Ambedkar, 'Revolution', 392–415.

54. Ambedkar describes the difficulty of Shivaji's coronation and the conflict of Kshatriyas and Brahmins: see Ambedkar, *Who Were the Shudras*, 175–85.

55. Ambedkar, *The Untouchables*, 318–55.

derived some of their status from the divine, the laws of Manu, as interpreted by Ambedkar, had made caste, not kingship, divine. Caste, Ambedkar wrote, 'is sacred, not open to abrogation, amendment and not even to criticism'.[56]

The net result of these three factors, whereby the Brahmin had the capacity punish and even kill the king, no means of violence or rebellion were available to the lower orders and caste was the dispensation of the divine, was that the Brahmin emerged as sovereign, though not in the form of an individual monarch. This made the power of the Brahmin perpetual, with the responsibility of the social deposited on the king as ruler. Significantly, the 'social' was not only isolated and separate in nature but incorporated the diffused monarchy of the Brahmin. Such an interpretation of history, while it was geared specifically towards the problem of untouchability in India, nevertheless helps to elucidate the wider context of the formation of the modern Indian republic. As will be discussed in greater depth in the final chapter below, establishing the republic would not only be a question of displacing the various kings and princes, or monarchy. It would require the accomplishment of another, at least equally ambitious, task: namely, the creation of 'the people', or a fraternity; and for such a fraternity to be constituted, it was necessary first of all to recognise the antagonism and violence between the Brahmin and the untouchable as the true crucible of sovereignty in India. As already noted, Brahminism, for Ambedkar, had been the counter-revolution to the revolution of Buddhism that had enshrined equality and nonviolence, establishing in its place the perpetual and systemic power of caste, rooted in violence, wherein there was no necessary identification between the sovereign and the monarch. With a polemical flourish, Ambedkar wrote that this system was perfected to the extent that the Nietzschean doctrine of 'Realise the ideal and idealise the real' had been actualised in India.[57] As a 'permanent difficulty', caste cut through the time's arrow of the present and the past.[58] Historically understood, (Brahmin) caste as sovereign power and its perpetuation was thus a doctrine neither of 'social utility' nor of 'individual justice'.[59] In short, it could be understood as political only in the stark sense that it essentially concerned and was rendered coherent by violence and power. This is why Ambedkar felt able to compare caste, however heuristically, with Nazism, the critical point of divergence

56. Ibid., and Ambedkar, 'India and the Prerequisites', 127.
57. Ambedkar, 'Philosophy of Hinduism', 67.
58. Ambedkar, *Who Were the Shudras*, 16.
59. Ambedkar, 'Philosophy of Hinduism', 71.

between the two being only, as pointed out in the epigraph to this section, that the violence of caste was as hidden as it was obvious. Deploying the modern triad of liberal politics in relation to caste and Hinduism, however, Ambedkar denounced it as 'inimical to equality, antagonistic to liberty and opposed to fraternity'.[60]

Systemic and with its legitimacy enshrined in ritual and sacrament, the denial of freedom of opportunity or knowledge and above all the denial of the right to bear arms was not only a 'cruel wrong' but was also the 'most shameless method of preserving the established order' and power.[61] While the lower and subjugated orders experienced this powerful order of things as 'fate', there was in fact nothing random about caste. Detaching the arbitrariness of fortune that is assumed in understandings of violence and power, Ambedkar denaturalised the familiar, accepted and consensual understanding of caste.[62] Through a study of the classical past, or what he termed the 'exhumation of debris' of Ancient Indian history, he came to understand that violence was not necessarily equal to power. Instead, in uncovering the systemic conditions of violence including its means and ends, Ambedkar repositioned caste as political doctrine that legitimised violence rather than a social institution of rank and labour.

Though preoccupied by history, it was only later in his life and during the twinned moments of the Second World War and the coming of Indian independence that history became a sustained focus of Ambedkar's writings. The history of Buddhism became his template for a departure from the past, and a prospectus for the future. For Nehru, the past was the testament to and the unique credential for India's claims to a distinct nationality. For Savarkar, by contrast, as was discussed in Chapter 3, history converted the identity of India into a battlefield for a new fraternity of Hindutva to emerge. For Ambedkar, the past most overtly carried revolutionary potential. Having qualified the French revolutionary tradition and critiqued Marx on the question of the social and the political, he identified the source of revolution in the history of the vanquished original religion of the subcontinent.

History, above all, allowed Ambedkar to identify the source of sovereignty in India, which, as explicated above, lay with the Brahmin. Precisely because caste militated against fraternity and also because the Brahmin was dispersed

---

60. Ibid., 66.
61. Ambedkar, 'India and the Prerequisites', 126.
62. On fortune and the arbitrary nature of violence, see Arendt, *On Violence*, 4–5.

but above the monarch, the discovery of 'the people' as a byword of fraternity became essential to Ambedkar's political project: unlike the case of the French revolution, there could be no automatic replacement of the individual monarch or sovereign by the general will. It was in the course of discussions of nationality that the notion of a revolutionary discovery of 'the people', or a commitment to the idea of the republic premised on popular will, could be most forcefully and fully expressed: nationality entailed not only identifying the source of sovereignty but also demanding the recognition of a new nationality and its 'people': namely, that of Pakistan.

Pakistan and Peace

> If Pakistan has the demerit of cutting away parts of India, it has also the merit of introducing harmony in place of conflict.
>
> —AMBEDKAR[63]

Ambedkar's discussion of caste uncovered the violent source of sovereignty in India; Pakistan, on the other hand, opened up for him the possibility of peace between Hindus and Muslims. It was Ambedkar, rather than one of the major ideologues and protagonists—Nehru, or even the architect of Pakistan, Mohammad Ali Jinnah—who was to write a powerful treatise on Pakistan. A second, expanded edition of his *Pakistan or the Partition of India* appeared in 1945. Structured as a set of arguments, the book lacked the anger and polemical vibrancy which spilled from the pages of his writings on caste, but shared nevertheless the candid style of prose that characterises his disquisitions. In the context of the eventful and complex politics in the 1940s, the clarity of his position is noteworthy, even exemplary.

Notwithstanding the overwhelming complexity of detail, an abstract quality especially marks the nature of the political in the defining decade of the 1940s.[64] This had much to do with the imminent future becoming real, even as its details remained unknown. In Ambedkar's case, the abstract nature of the political was applied towards giving a clear conceptual language to the empirically crowded nature of politics of that time. Though as foundational as his *Annihilation of Caste*, his text on Pakistan is not widely cited; its interpretation here will concentrate upon the reconstruction of his idea of 'the people'

63. Ambedkar, *Pakistan*, 220.
64. Devji, *Muslim Zion*, 103.

or popular will as a national category, and it should be noted in this connection that he saw the question of caste, or recognition of the Dalit, as the founding act of India's independence, and the foundation of Pakistan as being linked by more than mere chronology: it was for him an established yet under-explained historical fact that both developments related to the same issue of fraternity, and had done so since at least the Poona Pact. Aware of the singular nature of his enterprise, Ambedkar warned the reader that his book was 'disowned by the Hindus and unowned by the Muslims', a reaction that he took to be evidence of the 'independence of [his] thought'.

The lengthy and full-blown account that Ambedkar undertook operated on two levels. On the one hand, it documented the nature of the demands and details of specific contentions relating to the various institutional provisions that have gone down in history and historiography as the 'bargaining counters', tending to highlight and overstate the mechanistic role of interest between dominant protagonists and parties. Even as he assiduously recorded the contentious views and issues of all parties, however, he rightly asserted that the book was not limited to the intricate details of a new political settlement or what he termed 'the X,Y,Z of Pakistan'.[65] On its second level, the book sought to provide a conceptual framework for analysis of the issue of Muslim nationality in relation to the political—as its sub-title, *The Indian Political What's What!*, overtly declared. As he put it, as an 'analytical presentation', the book intended 'to explain the A, B, C of Pakistan'.[66] The following discussion will engage primarily with this second aspect of the work, elaborating upon the horizons of hostility, the potential for war and the promise of Pakistan as peace. With the exception of Devji's *Muslim Zion*, the conceptual history of Pakistan remains under-historicised and under-theorised. The scholarship on partition and the birth of Pakistan remains transfixed by issues of guilt and blame, and overhung by the sense of a historical mistake. Few if any, apart from Ambedkar, have taken into account the full measure of ideological momentum, will and imagination that went into the making of the first avowedly Muslim nation in world history, especially in the critical years leading up to its foundation.

In the course of providing an account of the 'Hindu' and 'Muslim' cases against and for Pakistan respectively, Ambedkar reprised the recent history of relations between the two communities. Armed with a battery of statistics on

65. Ambedkar, *Pakistan*, 2.
66. Ibid.

killings, he noted that the interwar period had seen Hindus and Muslims 'engaged in a sanguinary warfare':[67] the high nationalist era—the decades between 1920 and 1940—had been, despite Gandhi's efforts to 'bring unity', an era of 'civil war between the Hindus and Muslims of India ... interrupted by brief intervals of armed peace'.[68] By the critical moment of the end of the Second World War, the 'depth of antagonism', he wrote, had ensured that the 'mirage' of Hindu–Muslim unity had vanished 'out of sight and also out of mind'.[69] With this context before him, Ambedkar appraised the question of unity, analysing the inter-communal relationship in terms once more of the social and the political, in the manner in which he had treated the issue of caste.

When couched in terms of the possibility of an Indian union and separation in the form of Pakistan, however, the relationship of the social to the political emerged in Ambedkar's book as being the contrary of the situation pertaining to caste. As elaborated above, caste for Ambedkar amounted to a political union rooted in graded sovereignty within the divine dispensation of social separation. Hindus and Muslims, by contrast, had had throughout their long mutual history a complex social union. Yet, in the contemporary era of the nation-state, their social relationship defied translation into a political union.[70]

In a significant departure from all other nationalist leaders, Ambedkar fully recognised the power of sentiment and will. This was done in specific awareness of the contentious debates that had equated the question of Pakistan with institutional provisions ranging from separate electorates to various schemes that were under discussion to determine the shape and power structure of the imminent independent state. The opening premise of his treatise was indeed that discussion of Pakistan could not be restricted only to matters of mechanisms and instruments, but must recognise the nature of the 'dynamic expression' of nationalism, it being declared at the outset that the 'Muslims have developed a "will to live as a nation"'.[71]

Official discussions focused on the colonial census that had corralled and constituted 'groups' as opposed to a 'people', and this had an overwhelming power in setting the terms of a debate that repeatedly treated nationality as a

67. Ibid., 184.
68. Ibid.,
69. Ibid., 186–87.
70. Ibid., 26–35.
71. Ibid., 39.

function of demographics.[72] Its most powerful effect was that the national question was considered through the prism of 'majority' and 'minority'. Ambedkar notably argued that once the principle of separate electorates had been accepted, recognition of a 'minority' had created a 'statutory majority'.[73] To be sure, Ambedkar rejected the claims of the 'majority' to constitute an actual political unit, aware that such aspirations were associated with Hindutva. He dismissed such claims partly because he saw Hindutva's then political body, Hindu Mahasabha, as a mirror image of the Muslim League, and believed, rather presciently, that both would disappear with the recognition of Pakistan. More importantly, as argued here, caste militated against any imagined unity within the Hindu social. The emphasis fell instead, therefore, on the question of the 'minority', and Ambedkar understood the 'minority' not only in the terms ordained by colonial rule, but as related centrally to hostility and violence between Hindus and Muslims. In the first place, however, he recognised the salience of the national question in Muslims' own political aspirations.

The extent of 'national feeling' prevalent among Muslims, Ambedkar wrote, though recent, was nevertheless such that Muslims were no longer 'content to call themselves a community'.[74] The 'fundamental difference' between these two conceptions, he pointed out, lay in the category of a 'people', popular or general will, or sovereignty itself. Hitherto, he argued 'political philosophers' had been satisfied, if not complacent, in recognising 'communities' as differentiated, but nevertheless components of 'the governed'; under conditions of distress, these 'communities' had given rights to 'insurrection', but these were limited to the seeking of changes in modalities of government. Only the 'nation', by contrast, had the 'right to disruption [and] secession' which went beyond the right of insurrection. The distinction between community and nation was 'fundamental', but where it lay could only be determined on the basis of 'ultimate destiny', or goals.[75] In this vein, Ambedkar concluded that both 'prudence and ethics demands that bonds shall be dissolved', so that potentialities are

72. Arjun Appadurai, 'Number in the Colonial Imagination', in Carol Breckenridge and Peter van der Veer (eds.), *Orientalism and the Postcolonial Predicament* (Philadelphia: University of Pennsylvania Press, 1993), 314–39; more recently, Devji, *Muslim Zion*, 49–88.

73. Ambedkar, *Pakistan*, 107.

74. Ibid., 37.

75. Ibid., 326–27.

'freed' in such a manner as to 'pursue [their own] destinies'.[76] The nation, as opposed to community, Ambedkar realised, was the crucible of the idea of 'the people'; or, more precisely, it was the nation that converted 'the people' into a political category. This transformation, in his view, and as recognised by historians of nationalism, was above all a work of the imagination. 'The delay in discovering the philosophical justification for Pakistan', Ambedkar argued, was precisely 'due to the fact that the Muslim leaders had become habituated to speaking of Muslims as a community and as a minority'. This terminology had taken Muslim aspirations in a 'false direction and had brought them to a dead end'. The recent philosophical discovery of Pakistan represented 'a complete transformation' amongst Muslims, and it was 'brought [about] not by any criminal inducement but by the discovery of what is their true and ultimate destiny'.[77]

Based on a futurity, rather than being the belated expression of a repressed ideal in the subcontinental script, Pakistan as an idea was not possessed by the past: the future by definition cannot be 'observed' or 'checked', let alone 'experienced', and futurity is thus a feat of the imagination that 'breaks free [from] spatial controls'.[78] While—unsurprisingly, given the density of imperial negotiations and related settlements—territorial issues have dominated standard historical accounts of the creation of Pakistan, Ambedkar was distinctive in recognising that Pakistan represented, even more than a spatial idea or territorial telos, an entirely future-oriented temporality: a futurity that was a break in historical time as much as it was a departure from imperium, both Mughal and British, and that ultimately revealed the inadequacy, if not indeed encompassing the destruction, of prevailing categories, whether of 'community' or 'minority', that had stifled Muslim aspirations.

In its most recent appraisal, by Faisal Devji, Pakistan as a political idea is likewise seen as best understood in terms of the apprehension of the future. Radical in its capture of an untold future, the formation of Pakistan was only made possible, Devji argues, by the rejection of dominant political languages, such that putative attachments to soil, blood and even history are forsaken for the negation of both Indian nationalism and imperial endgames. For Devji, though, the emphasis lies upon the postwar reconstitution of the world order:

76. Ibid., 328.
77. Ibid., 336–37.
78. See Koselleck, *Practice of Conceptual History*, 87, and Hartog, *Regimes*, for two very different treatments of temporality and political utopias.

a 'Muslim Zion', Pakistan operates as a fitting if contrasting complement to Israel as the 'minority' form acquired the historical destiny of the national.[79]

It was Ambedkar's view, then, that neither official designations in terms of majority and minority nor recognition of the status of Indian Muslims as a 'community' could contain the will towards a distinct and political entity that, though belated, had nevertheless become salient. As Ambedkar recognised, the philosophical discovery of Muslim republicanism was associated above all with the pre-eminent Muslim thinker Muhammal Iqbal, who influentially rejected global Islam, the Caliphate and the idea of the 'minority' in favour of Muslim republicanism; and the next chapter rehearses Iqbal's ideas of new fraternal and sovereign political horizons for the Muslims. Virtually unnoticed, however, but strikingly worthy of note, is that Ambedkar marked out Jinnah, often seen as the arch-manipulative leader of the time, as entirely 'incorruptible'.[80] It can clearly be seen, then, that the notion of Muslim nationality as politically separate was not, for Ambedkar, an outcome of machinations or bad faith.

At least since the days of, and perhaps as a result of, the Poona Pact, Ambedkar was not troubled by the issue of separation—so pivotal to his understanding of caste—in relation to Hindus and Muslims. In the context of the Round Table Conference and the Poona Pact, indeed, and as discussed above, he had argued that Hindus and Muslims, unlike caste Hindus and Dalits, although estranged were not categorically separate, and he did not revise this position or ever argue, in the imperial mode, that Hindus and Muslims were primordially distinct, such that the newly demanded nation-state would simply enable the fulfilment of separate historical destinies. Ambedkar recognised that Hindus and Muslims had a long history of what he termed 'social union'. Whether in terms of language, 'race' or custom, there was, he argued, considerable commonality between Hindus and Muslims, and in several social and cultural respects their relations were 'honeycombed'.[81]

---

79. Devji, *Muslim Zion*. See also Faridah Zaman, 'Futurity and the Political Thought of North Indian Muslims' (unpublished doctoral dissertation, University of Cambridge, 2014); Adeel Hussain, 'Legal Antagonism and the Making of Muslim Political Thought in India' (unpublished doctoral dissertation, University of Cambridge, 2017).

80. Ambedkar, *Pakistan*, 328; he further dismissed Gandhi's claim that Jinnah did not represent all Muslims of India, going so far as to describe him as having become 'a man of the masses': ibid., 407.

81. Ibid., 32.

Yet history, and particularly the 'inability to forget', militated against any political union between the two. Building once more on insights from the French experience, and in particular the nineteenth-century philosopher Ernest Renan's works on nationality and nationalism, Ambedkar posited and privileged the necessity of forgetting the past in order to constitute a national union.[82] Unlike for other nationalists—whether Nehru or Savarkar—who turned to history as testimony of India's credentials for modern nationality, for Ambedkar, the grip of history had become the obstacle to Hindu–Muslim union. 'The crux of the problem', he wrote, was that 'common historical antecedents' were difficult to 'share together'. Whether it was shrouded in memories of violence or of rulership, history had become the insuperable barrier. 'The pity of it is', he continued, 'that the two communities can never forget or obliterate their past.'[83] He cited Renan to the effect that 'deeds of violence have taken place at the commencement of all political formations', even those whose 'consequences have been most beneficial', reiterating the latter's contention that 'forgetfulness and I shall even say historical error, form an essential factor in the creation of a nation.'[84] The Hindus and Muslims, Ambedkar surmised, had 'no such longing' whereby the past and its antagonisms should be forgotten in the interests of forging a union.[85] The implication was that when it came to caste, history had obfuscated and repressed the true nature of sovereignty that Ambedkar assiduously retraced and revealed. For Hindus and Muslims, by contrast, the past was ever-present and constantly articulated, leaving little or no potential for the repression or forgetting that would have enabled the suturing of remembered wounds for the sake of a new relationship of unity. This was now not to be.

The power of history coupled with the 'tyranny' of numbers had rendered the Hindu–Muslim relations hostile and antagonistic. The 'communal problem' was not a matter of disposition, whether this was expressed in the much-rehearsed polemics of 'insolent' demands on the part of Muslims or 'meanness' on the part of Hindus. Instead, Ambedkar directly addressed the question of majority and minority, the potential for violence between Hindis and Muslims, and through it, peace.

82. Ibid., 33–36.
83. Ibid., 35, 37.
84. Cited in ibid., 36.
85. Ibid., 37; and, citing the issue of 'invasions' and the fear of becoming mere subjects as critical to Hindu and Muslim anxieties rooted in history, 49.

[The communal problem] exists and will exist wherever a hostile majority is brought face to face against a hostile minority. Controversies relating to separate vs. joint electorates, controversies relating to population ratio vs. weightage are all inherent in a situation where a minority is pitted against a majority. The best solution of the communal problem is not to have two communities facing each other, one a majority and the other a minority, welded in the steel frame of a single government.[86]

As this extract clarifies, coercion or 'the steel frame of a single government' could not on its own assuage the depth of antagonism nor satisfy the powerful will to nationhood which was present on both sides. In fact, the political mechanisms described by Ambedkar as 'controversies' would only create conditions in which hostility would be perpetuated.

In Ambedkar's reckoning, as elaborated above, relations between Brahmins and untouchables and between Hindus and Muslims were diametrically opposed in nature. A separation founded on and preserved in violence had constituted the order of things for caste. The work of the republic, then, would be to ensure that even though castes could not be 'dissolved', a relationship, however competitive and adversarial, could be established between castes that had hitherto been marked only by separation. By contrast, while a density of social relations indeed existed between Hindus and Muslims, their antagonism when it arose could not be sublimated, but only expressed in violence. From his work on Pakistan, it is clear that 'for Ambedkar, only political separation offered the possibility of peace. 'Integral India', he concluded, was 'incompatible with an independent [India] or even with India as a dominion.'[87]

The antagonism between Hindus and Muslims, as Ambedkar interpreted it, was not of the same kind or even degree as that between Brahmins and untouchables. It was visible on the surface, pervading the ambience and prone to easy mobilisation: Hindus and Muslims were thus effectively in a state of civil war. This called for some form of separation between Hindus and Muslims whose historical brotherhood had been subsumed into a murderous logic. The violent antagonism in which the separation of castes was steeped, on the other hand, was so complete that it had become simultaneously both obvious and invisible. Caste antagonism could thus only be managed, perhaps even overcome, through a facing off of different caste groups within the bounds of

86. Ibid., 111.
87. Ibid., 339.

the same political horizon and the acknowledgement of a historical sovereign order that had to be displaced. Whether it regarded Muslin nationality or caste, however, Ambedkar's influential political project would be overwhelmingly agonistic and zealously nonviolent.

Read together, Ambedkar's interventions on caste and Pakistan, though in one sense diametrical opposites, had in common the recognition of separation. For caste, the principle of separation remained a deliberate blind spot, which he undertook to illuminate, summoning up history, social practice and the issue of deeply embedded violence. By contrast, although Hindus and Muslims were often described and recognised as a union or a fraternity, this, in his view, was merely 'display'.[88] Mutual antagonism was the *essential* form of this relationship and would constantly come to the surface in a 'common theatre'. 'It is the common theatre'—that is, united India—he argued, 'which calls this antagonism into action.' 'Pakistan' thus had the 'advantage' of 'defanging' the antagonism, by excluding the possibility of a common platform that was both the site and the cause of deadly confrontation. Pakistan offered the possibility of removing this 'disturbance of the peace' and ensuring an enduring 'tranquillity' through the separation of the antagonists.

Critiquing the Hindutva ideologues' hostility to the creation of Pakistan, Ambedkar directly reintroduced the question of caste.[89] Dismissing Har Dayal, whom he categorised not as an anarchist or a revolutionary but as belonging to the ideological world of Hindutva, he chastised him for his views on Muslim conversion, or what was termed *shuddhi* (reconversion/purification),[90] dismissing on the basis not of religion but of caste the Hindutva desire to incorporate the Muslim as a species of Hindu. The Hindutva idea of 'assimilation', he reminded Har Dayal and others, was an affront to Hinduism itself, since 'caste is incompatible with conversion'. More provocatively, he ironically identified Savarkar's claims as compatible with the idea of Pakistan itself: if, in accordance with Savarkar's assertion, 'Hindus are a nation by themselves,' Ambedkar argued, 'this of course means that the Muslims are a separate nation

88. Ibid., 339–41.

89. Ibid., 336–43, 129–33.

90. On Hindu nationalism, see Thomas Blom Hansen, *Wages of Violence: Naming and Identity in Postcolonial Bombay* (Princeton, NJ: Princeton University Press, 2001); Charu Gupta, *Sexuality, Obscenity, Community: Women, Muslims and the Hindu Public in Colonial India* (London: Palgrave, 2001).

THE TRIUMPH OF FRATERNITY 189

by themselves'.[91] In fact, he pointed out, precisely because of their belief in the existence of the Hindu and Muslim 'nations' in India, Jinnah and Savarkar were alike and in agreement. The key difference, once again, regarded separation and violence. Jinnah, he averred, wanted separation. Of Hindutva's proponents, on the other hand, he wrote,

> [Mr. Savarkar] wants Hindus and the Muslims to live as two separate nations, in one country, each maintaining its own religion, language and culture. One can understand and even appreciate the wisdom . . . because the ultimate aim is to bring into being one nation. . . . One can justify this attitude only if the two nations were to live as partners in friendly intercourse with mutual respect and accord. But that is not to be, because Mr. Savarkar will not allow the Muslim nation to be co-equal. . . . He wants the Hindu nation to be the dominant nation and the Muslim nation to be the servient [sic] nation. Why Mr. Savarkar, after sowing the seed of enmity between the Hindu nation and Muslim nation, should want that they should live under one constitution and occupy one country, is difficult to explain.[92]

These were not random or hapless remarks. Through a discussion of territory and nationality, Ambedkar had taken full account of raging polemics, party positions and constitutional considerations. The separation of caste, though immanent in Hinduism, had rendered the Hindu social an asocial body politic. Confronting that fact and ensuring the proper relation between castes had the potential to convert a separation that was singular to India into a political union. 'Unity', or 'the people', or popular sovereignty, Ambedkar astutely realised, was immanent in the national form.[93]

The central issue was the problem of hostility and antagonism, and its proper acknowledgement in order to achieve the nonviolent, even peaceful, emergence of a new politics. Ambedkar's recognition of Pakistan was constitutive of an agonistic politics that took two mutually constitutive directions: whether the antagonism was that of caste or of religion, he sought to convert that relationship, without the erasure of fundamental differences, into an

91. Ambedkar, *Pakistan*, 130, 141.

92. Ibid., 144; Ambedkar further warned that the international examples such as Turkey, Czechoslovakia and Austria that were approvingly cited by Savarkar only illustrated the problem of separation.

93. Chantal Mouffe, *Democratic Paradox* (London: Verso, 2005), 38–43, examines critically Carl Schmitt's work on antagonism and parliamentary democracy.

adversarial one, which would become peaceful. One dimension required the recognition of separation: namely Muslim nationality; and the other, the end of separation: namely a compact between castes. The overall concern that emerges from the totality of Ambedkar's writing is with the making of 'the people' as the subject of politics. Essentially, he sought the correct 'container' for the expression of popular sovereignty; his was thus a radical republican project.

In a major departure from the subject-oriented political thought and practice of Gandhi, or even Tilak, which had located sovereignty in the individual subject, for Ambedkar its rightful place was the general will. Ironically, the work of separation, in its full measure, enabled the philosophical discovery of the general will, or a true popular sovereignty.[94] Both the nature of caste and the recent deadly antagonism between Hindus and Muslims called for the recognition of violence and hostility; but in Ambedkar's case, this was not for an ethical resolution or personal transformation, but for the institution of a nonviolent politics. For him, in distinction from Gandhi, the existence of enemies and antagonists offered the opportunity not for self-transformation, but for the conversion of those relations into agonistic politics.

The destruction of the dispersed monarchy of the Brahmin and the recognition of Muslim nationality were two sides of the same political consideration. The conversion of violence and hostility into the nonviolent separation of historical brothers and the creation of a new fraternity—though not entirely recognised today as fruits of Ambedkar's political thought and work— effectively constituted the foundations for the establishment of not just one but two agonistic republics.

The single coin that bore these two sides was, of course, independence; and a declaration of independence was simultaneously a declaration of sovereignty—a moment of enclosure that marked out or defined a people. The only consensus that existed between all positions, Ambedkar wrote, regarded freedom: specifically, independence from British imperialism; but the 'obligation to maintain freedom' too was paramount, and understood also in relation to 'any other foreign power'.[95] In other words, to return to the theme of unity or 'the people', while it required constant vigilance against the 'foreigner', unity was equally defined against the outsider.

94. Devji, *Impossible Indian*; Kapila, 'History of Violence'.
95. Ambedkar, *Pakistan*, 272.

Pakistan as an expression of Muslim nationality was not 'foreign' in the sense that had been used since at least the French revolutionary period, noted earlier in this chapter. The new antagonism that was witnessed between Muslims and Hindus in the early decades of the last century was not an immanent feature of India, but had by then become openly expressed and volatile. Its containment involved not so much the making of a 'foreign' Muslim nation as an evacuation of the common site that provoked the mutual antagonism. A single government, Ambedkar wrote, would not only render India weak, but would also be founded on an enforced union. Their 'differences', he stated, 'have the sure effect of keeping [Hindus and Muslims] asunder but also of keeping them at war'. What therefore must be eliminated was the presence of opportunity and root cause of civil strife.

Acceptance of Pakistan was presented in Ambedkar's work as a matter of historical urgency, necessary to transform two antagonisms, of religion and of caste, into an agonistic formation that addressed the problem of hostility and violence. Delay or denial of acknowledgement of Pakistan as the national 'destiny' for Muslims would indeed result in a civil war. With Pakistan finding philosophical utterance—separation, in this instance—the moment of new sovereignty had the political capacity to convert antagonists into adversaries, staving off confrontation and civil war. The need for this was all the more imperative 'since every possible attempt to bring about union [had] failed'.[96] The 'dualism', once expressed, was, in Ambedkar's view, 'sure to call for a life and death struggle for the dissolution of this forced union'.[97]

Ambedkar fully recognised that Pakistan was not the expression or natural outcome of any historical tradition of separatism, and thus did not represent the identification or construction of a hostile foreigner for the purpose of defining who was 'inside' a people under the insignia of a nation. Quite the opposite. The 'starting point' in India 'at all times' has been 'unity'; 'partition', therefore, he admitted, could only be 'shocking', given India's historical experience and relations between Hindus and Muslims.[98] He furthermore recognised that while Pakistan would be characterised by the 'homogeneity' of its people, the very nature of India, given its range of diversity and remaining Muslim 'minority', was to be 'composite'.[99] Most strikingly, surveying the recent history of the

96. Ibid., 304–5.
97. Ibid., 339.
98. Ibid., 348.
99. Ibid., 117.

nation-state across the world, Ambedkar concluded that Pakistan would have
to be constituted through an exchange of population, so as to convert the minority into a majority within a territorial boundary.[100] Neither 'safeguards' nor
'ruthless war', he surmised, could adequately address the national aspirations
of minorities across the globe; conversion of the minority into a recognised
nationality through migration into a territorial unit, however, possibly presaged
the creation of a politics of peace.

For Ambedkar, then, an anti-social spirit at best, at worst an animosity, was
definitive of the social in the Indian context. Pakistan, or Muslim nationality,
was recognised as the 'constitutive outside', rather than as representing the
hostile outsider or foreigner that catalysed the general will into a collective
and indivisible force, or made a 'people'. Hostility, as discussed above, was
immanent in the Hindu social, inverting the self/other distinction that was
common to Hindu nationalists. Whether in regard to untouchability or Muslim nationality, the aim of Ambedkar's agonism was to recognise, through
excavation and elaboration, the imperatively political nature of difference.
The antagonism was hidden in the case of caste, while Hindus and Muslims,
historically agonistic, had become openly hostile in the age of the nation-
state. Both oppositions had to be acknowleged as political, and it was in part
through such acknowledgement that antagonisms could be rendered merely
adversarial. Most significantly, such recognition and transformation alone
could enable the discovery of the popular will and identify the desired object
of politics, namely the people, living in a republic. This project had as much
to do with the dispersed monarchy of the Brahmin as with the imagination
and recognition of Pakistan.

If Savarkar had defined the essentials of Hindutva, then Ambedkar, the
arch-critic of Hinduism, delineated essential and unique features that made
the Hindu social unamenable to fraternity and republican sovereignty. A
Robespierre vis-à-vis the monarchy of Brahmanism, he took to the pen rather
than to arms to understand and then destroy its systemic power steeped in
violence. Gandhi and Ambedkar, meanwhile, despite their mutual hostility,
were bound by a common recognition of radical difference, though for Gandhi, this lay in the domain of religion, whereas for Ambedkar it was identified
in caste, conditioned and contextualised by his recognition of Muslim nationality. In significant ways, Gandhi's denial of the political nature of untouchability prompted Ambedkar to take a full account of of caste as separation in

100. Ibid., 115.

a starkly violent form. The work of the republic of which Ambedkar was the key architect would be to replace violent separation with a competitive relationship between adversaries, thus recruiting the social to the political. The spectre that Ambedkar above all hoped to avoid by his promotion of Pakistan was that of civil war. It was to be civil war, however, and the cause of separation, that visibly inaugurated the new era of the people.

6

The Philosophical Discovery of Muslim Sovereignty

A Prophet is only a practical poet.

—MUHAMMAD IQBAL[1]

IN HIS FORTHRIGHT TREATISE ON PAKISTAN, Ambedkar expressed a degree of exasperation with the belatedness of the philosophical discovery of Muslim political aspirations. Filing these aspirations under the category 'Pakistan', he simultaneously both exaggerated what was then but a 'scheme' conjured up by a Cambridge student, Rahmat Ali, and attributed the idea of a separate Muslim state to arguably the greatest and certainly the most celebrated poet and philosopher of twentieth-century India, Muhammad Iqbal. Ambedkar was astute in recognising that the political aspirations of Muslims could no longer be articulated, let alone represented, in terms of the established form and language of 'community'. As argued earlier, he understood the categorical transformation of the community into a 'nation', which licensed secession and separation. He was, nevertheless, hasty in holding Iqbal solely responsible for this conversion of community to nation. Although Ambedkar invoked the significance of the philosophical, his terse account of the genesis of the idea of Pakistan obscured the philosophical aspect, reducing it, in all its force and innovation, to the level of a powerful caricature.[2]

1. Muhammad Iqbal, *Stray Reflections: The Private Notebook of Muhammad Iqbal*, ed. Javid Iqbal, 3rd edn (Lahore: Iqbal Academy, 2006 [1910]), 113 ('A Prophet').
2. See Devji, *Muslim Zion*, for an especially incisive history of ideas of Pakistan.

The closing or shutting out of philosophy, as we have been reminded recently by Alain Badiou, is the greatest obstacle faced by any, but especially a new, political formation. Philosophical enterprise entails the work of producing abstract propositions that are, however, mediated and obscured by the interventions of history. The philosophical kernel at the heart of new political imagination is thus obscured and can only be recovered through a form of 'clearing'. Without the philosophical, and bereft of the potency of imagination, political ideas can all too easily be reduced to a historical caricature. The power and form of this clearing, in Badiou's words, 'inscribes into History the destiny of a thought'; as he warns, the caricature, however flattering or obscene, obscures or even replaces the philosophical kernel that is nonetheless essential to the politics.[3] The reduction of philosophy is particularly disastrous, he warns, for any political emancipation. It would not be unfair to assert that the idea of Pakistan has suffered precisely such a fate, for all that Iqbal remains a celebrated figure.

Iqbal's political thought, it is argued here, was precisely oriented towards the opening of the enclosure of 'community', expanding from its substance as religion, culture or language to discover its political moorings through an ambitious form of clearing that ingested but departed from the range of Western political thought to embrace the precepts of Islam and the place of India in the twentieth century, and as a futurity. By the time he was invited to become the president of the Muslim League in 1930, Iqbal was a noted public man of letters. As much a philosopher as he was a poet (and a lawyer too), little was beyond his intellectual prowess, be it Muslim theology, Hindu epics or British and German idealism.[4] Whether in the form of the philosophical tome, the essay, the poem or the pamphlet, his writings were not imprisoned by any one genre, or even language, as he wrote in Persian, Urdu and English, without ever incurring dismissal as a dilettante, and is still today regarded as one of the most influential political thinkers and literary figures of the twentieth century.[5]

3. Alain Badiou, *Conditions*, trans. Steven Cochran (London: Continuum, 2008), 147–76.

4. Iqbal Singh, *The Ardent Pilgrim: An Introduction to the Life and Work of Muhammad Iqbal* (Delhi: Oxford University Press, 1997 [1951]) remains a sympathetic and illuminating biography.

5. Recent works include Javed Majeed, *Muhammad Iqbal: Islam, Aesthetics and Postcolonialism* (Delhi: Routledge India, 2009), which is insightful on the question of subjectivity in relation to Iqbal's global imaginary, and Iqbal Singh Sevea, *The Political Philosophy of Muhammad Iqbal: Islam and Nationalism in Late Colonial India* (Cambridge: Cambridge University Press, 2012), which firmly positions Iqbal as a 'third world intellectual' who critiqued state-oriented

As a political thinker, Iqbal remains singular in comparison to other figures whose thought has been elaborated in this book, in that his primary pursuits were philosophy and poetry, with an involvement in institutional politics, especially of the Muslim League, that was only hesitant and fitful. Interpretations of and commentaries on Iqbal have emphasised the global dimensions and application of his philosophy, connecting him with a diverse range of thinkers, from Bergson to McTaggart to Nietzsche, in a bid to annex him to the cosmopolitan expanse of modern philosophy. His critique of territorial nationalism has moreover been interpreted as a genealogical predecessor and anticipation of a global Islam in which the retrieval of Islamic precepts gains significance as a form of purity aiming to purge history.[6]

India, and not only Islam, remained the pre-eminent preoccupation and subject of Iqbal's imagination, as typified by his *Taran-e-Hind* (*Song of India*) that remains the most famous of all paeans extolling the country's singularity and beauty. The global potential of Islam, as he wrote, lay in its expansion beyond its desert origins: its potential for greatness and magnificence, spiritual or otherwise, 'was due to the genius of people other than the Arabs'.[7] India thus represented, among other virtues, the grandeur of Islam. This chapter rejects the dominant interpretations that characterise Muhammad Iqbal as both national and equally, if not more, a thinker of the global, especially in its sense of circumventing the bounded. Whilst acknowledging the extensive range of his writings, its attention is confined to his political thought in particular, as it reconstructs and interprets the centrality to this of republicanism for the fostering of a fraternity conditioned by sovereignty. In doing so, it approaches the global in Iqbal's imagination as a lens upon the world or a vision, rather than in terms of the physical scale of history. The chapter further contends that in his prose and in his poetry, Iqbal innovated and amplified key concepts of modern politics by clarifying and separating out deep structural antagonisms, whether those of the immediate versus the immortal, the self versus selflessness, or the hearth versus the earth. In resisting the temptation

---

nationalism. Although this chapter departs from their interpretations, these works are crucial to an understanding of Iqbal.

6. S.V.R. Nasr, *Mawdudi and the Making of Islamic Revivalism* (Oxford: Oxford University Press, 2001).

7. Muhammad Iqbal, 'The Muslim Community: A Sociological Study' [1910], in Muhammad Iqbal, *Speeches, Writings and Statements of Iqbal*, ed. Latif Ahmed Sherwani, revised 2nd edn (New Delhi: Adam Publishers, 2006 [1977; 1st edn 1944]), 118–37, at 122.

to resolve or synthesise oppositional dualities, be they Indian or global, the chapter aims to capture a crucial gap between oppositional poles of thinking: in clearly delineating the separation or gap between the national and the universal, Iqbal forced an opening that remade the Muslim subject as political, rather than communitarian. The trope of separation animated his philosophical and poetical works. In one of his poems, he writes,

> Two planets meeting face to face
> One to the other cried 'how sweet
> If endlessly we might embrace,
> And here for ever stay! How sweet
> If Heaven a little might relent,
> And leave our light in one light blent!'
> But through that longing to dissolve
> In one, the parting summons sounded.
> Immutably the stars revolve
> By changeless orbits each is bounded;
> Eternal union is a dream
> And severance the world's law supreme.[8]

A key separation existed between subjectivity, selfhood (*khudi*) and a global vision of Islam. Such a global vision, as Javed Majeed alerts us, undermined and circumvented, even entirely rejected, the power of the national. To be sure, Iqbal's corpus provides a triangulated understanding of subjectivity, the global or the universal precepts of Islam and the problem of sovereignty. As argued here, however, the question of sovereignty did concern, for Iqbal, an ethical precept of the subject alone, with its attendant powers to transcend the immediate or the territorial. In this respect, Iqbal is comparable with Gandhi in his critique of and dissatisfaction with the national as the conclusion or the ultimate goal of an ethical existence. But for the life of fellowship or fraternity, or even just to attain the conditions for ethical self-realisation, political freedom was for both these innovators of modern politics essential. Such freedom, or to be more accurate sovereign conditions, was not conceived by Iqbal in the purely negative terms of anti-imperialism, whereby the rejection and demise of empire was a sufficient condition for sovereignty. Iqbal's ideas and interventions, as this chapter expounds, discovered philosophically the potential of the

---

8. Muhammad Iqbal, 'Two Planets', from *Bang-i-Dara: The Call of the Marching Bell* [1924], in V. G. Kiernan (trans.), *Poems from Iqbal* (London: John Murray, 1955), 14.

proximate and the intimate that articulated concrete contours for life with others, or fraternity, as he demarcated the idea of the Indian Muslim as a political subject.

Iqbal's significance, at least for the arguments of this book, lies first and foremost in his departure from contemporary Muslim politics and ideas that were the mainstay of the *ulama* (religious scholars) and even of leaders like the Indian nationalist Maulana Azad, who often sourced their political ideas from scripture.[9] Equally, however, Iqbal's political ideas neither emanated from nor ended with the imperial-liberal language of negotiation and institutional representation that has come to be seen, somewhat mistakenly, as the hallmark of M. A. Jinnah, the founder of Pakistan. Yet the verses, words and actions of Iqbal as a poet, philosopher, polemicist and politician made their mark in the arenas of both scripture and the imperial negotiating table, articulating a new and powerful political vocabulary for Islam and India. The discussion here is restricted to an exegesis of Iqbal's ideas and elaborations of sovereignty and fraternity that rendered the category of the Muslim not merely religious or cultural, but—and primarily—political, in its relation to co-religionists and others.

For Ambedkar, caste was above all a political relationship embedded in power and violence that had militated against the formation of fraternity, while the national horizon, as argued in the last chapter, allowed for the disintegration of a sovereign order based in caste and its replacement by an agonistic fraternity. For Iqbal, the question of fraternity and sovereignty was historically and theologically equivalent to and synonymous with Islamic precepts. As he put it, Islam had bequeathed the idea of civil society to the world.[10] One of the hosts of Iqbal's now famous lectures in Madras in 1929 likewise opined that 'whatever be the teachings of Islam, it is an acknowledged fact that it has taught the concept of fraternity and brotherhood to the world. . . . It is, therefore, necessary that the Hindus have to learn the principles of fraternity, brotherhood and equality from Islam.'[11]

---

9. Venkat Dhulipala, *The New Medina: State Power, Islam and the Quest for Pakistan in Late Colonial North India* (Cambridge: Cambridge University Press, 2015) re-emphasises the power of the *ulama* in the ideological formation of Pakistan.

10. Muhammad Iqbal, *The Reconstruction of Religious Thought in Islam* (Lahore: Hafeez Press, 1977 [1931]), 155.

11. P. Subbaroyan's introduction to Iqbal's address 'The Philosophy of Islam', 7 January 1929, in Muhammad Iqbal, *Letters and Writings of Iqbal*, ed. B. A. Dar (Karachi: Iqbal Academy, 1967), 50–51.

In the twentieth century, neither a nostalgia for the glories of the past nor the comforts of decline—renunciation, withdrawal or passivity—offered Iqbal, again, unlike his peers, any intellectual or political solace. Ironically, it was precisely because fraternity and sovereignty were synonymous with the precepts and history of Islam that, in the new century, Muslims had become estranged from a new vocabulary of brotherhood. In the case of caste, as Ambedkar elaborated, violence was structural to the point that obvious power had become invisible; Islamic precepts of fellowship and dominion, by contrast, had arguably become too absorbed or digested for Iqbal's co-religionists to derive from them any visible application. Iqbal's ideas would address and reconfigure key concepts of modern politics, with regard to which Islam had been pre-eminent historically, in both its imperial and regional reflections, but was proving unamenable in the context of the new and encompassing national dimension. The question of the Caliphate and its revival for a global Muslim fraternity became unavoidable, and Iqbal targeted this idea to forge a new and visible political imaginary.

Killing the Caliph

The Indian Muslim is likely to play a very important role in the future of Islam.

—IQBAL[12]

In the opening years of the twentieth century, prior to any disintegration of the Caliphate, Iqbal had declared that the 'Caliph of Islam is not an infallible being', but was 'subject to the same law' as every other Muslim.[13] He undermined any notion of the Caliph's permanence as the figurehead who signified the universal brotherhood of Muslims: taking an entirely representational view of the Caliph's role, he asserted that he could be deposed for misdeeds, and cited examples to that effect that testified to Islam's intimacy and collaboration with 'democracy'. In fact, for Iqbal, the ossification of the institution of the Caliphate had undermined that democracy that Islam 'regarded as a political ideal': indeed, the British Empire's 'spirit' of democracy, he claimed rhetorically, had enabled it to become the 'greatest Muhammadan empire in

12. Interview with the *Bombay Chronicle*, 1931, in Iqbal, *Letters and Writings*, 60.
13. Muhammad Iqbal, 'Islam as a Moral and Political Ideal' [1909], in Iqbal, *Speeches, Writings*, 97–117, at 114.

the world'.[14] Equally, the notion of consent (*ijma*) was, as several commentators have appreciated, central to Iqbal's understanding of the tenure of the Caliph: as an 'elective monarch', with no divine dispensation and dependent entirely on the approval of his co-religionists, the Caliph's dominion was as contingent on consent as he himself was fallible. If this represented the dominant Sunni view of the Caliph, Iqbal was quick to point out that even Shiite rulers, for whom the authority of the Imam (Caliph) derived not from election and consent but had 'divine origin', elevated the twelfth Imam as an 'absent Imam', whose appearance might be awaited but who had an 'absolute authority' that relegated earthly representatives (mullahs) to the status of mere 'guardians'. This nevertheless instituted the authority of religious leaders or mullahs over secular rulers, and Iqbal highlighted as evidence the contemporary constitutional reforms that were afoot in Persia: Persia only represented a variation in the division of power in relation to institutions, rather than any fundamental difference in the ordering of a brotherhood.[15]

For Iqbal, then, the Caliph was all too human, prone to error, and subordinate to the will of his electors—a creature of his context. The burden of his early writings on the subject was to the effect that any limitation or 'reform' or even the abolition of the Caliph was enshrined within the tenets of Islam and not exogenous or a 'borrowed ideal of political freedom'.[16] While this testified to some democratic principles within Islam, however, the overall emphasis of Iqbal's political philosophy was upon the role of the Prophet as the unique and ultimate source of sovereignty; this is discussed further below. Meanwhile, if the Caliphate was but a product of Muslim political history, the call for its restoration in the twentieth century signalled ignorance to a new world-historical age in which, he noted, nationalism had become dominant, albeit dangerous.

Turkey thus represented an instructive example for the future of Islam in the national age. A little over a decade after Iqbal first wrote of the limited powers of the incumbent of the Caliphate, that institution had been undone in the aftermath of the First World War. The fall of the Caliphate and the new place of Turkey in the Muslim imagination redrew the political landscape of Indian nationalism. In January 1920, Jinnah, in concert with the widest

14. Ibid.

15. Muhammad Iqbal, 'Political Thought in Islam', in Iqbal, *Speeches, Writings*, 138–54, at 143–54.

16. Ibid., 154.

possible range of political actors of the day, including Hindu nationalists such as M. M. Malviya, the soon-to-be assassinated Swami Shraddhanand and Congress and League grandees like Motilal Nehru and Gandhi, along with the Ali brothers and a smattering of princely rulers and Muslim religious leaders, petitioned the viceroy of India to forestall any drastic imperial redesigning of the Muslim sacred landscape. Iqbal, however, was conspicuously absent from the long list of signatories, though other public men of letters who were not necessarily political figures had added their weight to this initial broad coalition.

Alluding to a degree of Arab support for the imperial initiative, the petition clarified that 'Indian Musalmans' sought instead to eliminate 'every cause of friction that may tend to separate Arab from Ajam and Turk from Tajik'. It appeared that India's Muslims, 'supported by practically the whole of enlightened Hindu opinion', aimed to bridge emergent separations wrought by empire and war in the world of Islam.[17] But this, as is well known, instead provoked the exit of Jinnah from Indian nationalism. In September that year (his ally Tilak having died in August), addressing a heavily attended Muslim League meeting as its president, Jinnah—though rarely given to hyperbole—declared the Khilafat (Caliphate) a 'life and death' question.[18] One day later, Gandhi launched the twin Khilafat and Non-Cooperation movements that demanded Swaraj. Jinnah, in his last speech to the Congress in December 1920, amidst jeers and disruptions, defiantly excoriated Gandhi's method and movement: 'Mr. Gandhi thinks . . .', and before Jinnah could even complete his sentence he was shouted down by attendees and instructed to address Gandhi as the Mahatma. Unfazed, Jinnah continued,

> Yes, Mahatma Gandhi thinks that by peaceful methods, having declared complete Independence for India, he will achieve it. With very great respect for Mahatma Gandhi and those who think with him I make bold to say in this Assembly that you will never get your independence without bloodshed (cries of no, no). If you think that you are going to get your Independence without bloodshed I say that you are making the greatest blunder (cries of no, no—a voice nonsense). Therefore I say at this moment you are

17. Khilafat deputation to the Viceroy, in Mohammad Ali Jinnah, *The Collected Works of Quaid-e-Azam Mohammad Ali Jinnah*, vol. 1: *1906–1921*, ed. S. S. Pirzada (Karachi: East and West Publishing Co., 1984), 374–82.

18. Speech by Jinnah, AIML session, 7 September 1920, Calcutta, in Jinnah, *Collected Works* 1, 390.

making a declaration which you have not the means to carry out. On the other hand, you are exposing your hand to your enemies.[19]

Jinnah was acutely aware that violence suffused questions of sovereignty or political freedom. This was no mere divergence over moderation of methods at a time of heat and noise—of 'outraged feelings'. The conjoining of the issue of Indian freedom with a project for the global unification of Islam that did not entail the question of sovereignty for Indians in any immediate way only made visible the power of religion that he feared had the potential to jeopardise and render suspect the authenticity of both religious and political ideals. For Jinnah, while the cause of the Khilafat belonged to the global life of Muslims and necessitated support from all Indians as subjects of Empire, the question of Indian independence or sovereignty was a distinct matter, urgent, proximate and with the potential for violence. The confounding of the immediate with a profound but long-distance bond, as exhorted and practised by Gandhi, only exposed, as Jinnah stated, the vulnerability of colonised Indians, a form of weakness that was pregnant with violence. In other words, Jinnah's divergence from Gandhi had little to do with any so-called loyalism to the Empire, or hankering after office, but had everything to do with his concern to avoid a mistaking of the global for the immediate. Making religion a bridge between these two— identifying the Khilafat with Indian independence—could in Jinnah's eyes only constitute a context of conflict. Turning his back on what he called Gandhi's 'pseudo-religious approach to politics' and expressing a refusal to 'work up mob hysteria', Jinnah left the Congress and withdrew to London for a few years in self-imposed political exile.[20]

The impression of a lack of authenticity and 'true' representation has not only haunted Gandhi's afterlife, but, as articulated by Jinnah at that time, points once more to the problem of the 'excessive' nature of Gandhi's politics. The excess of Gandhi's politics—whether in terms of whipping up collective hysteria or of not being true to a cause so much as merely dedicated to a form of action and mobilisation, by ethical appeals or otherwise—nevertheless forced new political truths to emerge. It was a form of politics that might be construed as insincere or purely instrumental, but that incited a sincere remaking of political ideals and concepts. This was especially true of Gandhi's bitter opponents: Ambedkar's anger at the Mahatma forced him to elucidate the

19. Jinnah's opposition to Gandhi's resolution, Nagpur Congress, December 1920, in ibid., 403.
20. Ibid., 402.

truth of caste as violence; and Jinnah, with his much-vaunted coolness of head, would articulate a new truth of Muslim sovereignty and its fraternal horizons. Gandhi came, if briefly, to represent the cause of the Khilafat in concert with the Ali brothers in what Devji calls his 'boldest experiment' in politics: one that elevated the choice and common suffering of friendship over the violent temptations of fraternity.[21] The fall of the Caliphate and the Khilafat mobilisation had strained the friendship between Hindus and Muslims; but these events equally incited an imagining of Muslim fraternity in its global and national dimensions.

Away from the hullaballoo of party intrigues, alliances and conferences, Iqbal returned not to the question of the Caliph, but to Turkey, in its new incarnation as a nation rather than as a repository of a global brotherhood. In his most famous and oft-cited work, *The Reconstruction of Religious Thought in Islam*, published in 1931, which ranged widely over philosophical history and Muslim thought, he expended considerable effort in situating the 'Turkish nation' in both world history and the history of Islam. Significantly, the recent Khilafat movement was neither endorsed nor criticised overtly: the book ignored it entirely, as perhaps not worthy of mention in a grand disquisition on Muslim thought. Through this philosophical history and in public lectures and debates, Iqbal initiated and amplified a new political vocabulary that clarified the stakes that faced Muslims in a post-Caliphate order. In so doing, and in evaluating enduring foundations and emergent possibilities, Iqbal's ideas and words were instrumental in opening a future for and directing the political fate of Muslims in India, primarily in relation to their co-religionists, and to others only by extension.

Instruction by Turkey

If the renaissance of Islam is a fact, and I believe it is a fact, we too one day, like the Turks, will have to reevaluate our intellectual inheritance.

—IQBAL[22]

For Iqbal, the new republican order in Turkey, marked by an absence of any lament for the fall of the Caliphate, had demonstrated her singularity in

---

21. See Devji, *Impossible Indian*, 92, and Zaman, 'Futurity', for an insightful discussion of the politics of the Khilafat and global Islam and interwar India.

22. Iqbal, *Reconstruction*, 153.

shaking off a 'dogmatic slumber' and was 'alone' in claiming a 'right of intellectual freedom'. As a riposte to the well-worn European idea of the inherent stasis of Turkey, he highlighted the 'power' of *ijtihad*, literally 'exert oneself', the independent reasoning deployed in the interpretation of Islamic law, that was 'manifested' in the contemporary 'thought and activity' of Turkey. Through 'fresh interpretation', Turkey, for Iqbal, had not only enabled the evolution of Islamic law, but also, importantly, recognised the centrality of polity and power in Islam. Rehearsing once more the contingent nature of the Caliphate, he argued that the new republican order represented neither a contradiction of nor a deviation from any given norms. Endorsing the republican form of government as 'perfectly sound' and 'thoroughly consistent with the spirit of Islam', he noted nevertheless that the 'religious doctors' of Egypt and India had been silent on the subject. Interestingly in this context, he invoked the iconic thinker of republican sovereignty: none other than Thomas Hobbes—not simply to justify Turkey in the mirror of Western liberalism, but to assert that to 'have a succession of identical thoughts and feelings' amounted to 'having no thoughts or feelings at all'. In refusing to repeat 'old values', the Turk, he wrote with a degree of cautious enthusiasm, 'is on the way to creating new values'.[23] Turkey's identity, in short, lay in claiming sovereignty but not replicating older or other, foreign forms of it.

Through the virtues of exertion and interpretation (that is, *ijtihad*), Turkey had fundamentally re-evaluated the work of the state, or sovereignty itself. In providing an account of Turkish nationalism, Iqbal noted that the Caliph had not so much prevented as generated Turkish, Iranian or Arabian 'national egoism', making 'localisation' visible while obscuring the 'universality of Islam', much to the vexation of Turkey's religious leaders. The Turkish nationalists, on the other hand, shorn of the 'symbolic overlordship' of the Caliph, and in the absence of an empire, sought an opportunity to organise and make 'modern Islam workable . . . by way of a reunion of modern Muslim States'. With an eye on to vigilance and prudence, Iqbal saw in this a glimpse of the 'birth of an international idea which though forming the very essence of Islam has been overshadowed or rather displaced by the Arabian Imperialism of the earlier centuries of Islam'.[24] Turkey had thus displaced Arabia in outlining a possible political order of the twentieth century.

23. Ibid., 157, 162.
24. Ibid, 158.

In displacing Arab imperialism, the future as foretold through Turkey had made independence imperative. For Turkish nationalists, Iqbal noted, any effective political unity of Islam was dependent on Muslim countries achieving an independence that deferred their 'totality' and consequently impelled the Caliph to 'reduce his own house to order and lay the foundations of a workable modern state'.[25] Iqbal avoided synthesising, or resolving any apparent contradiction between, the national and the universal in this instance, concluding instead:

> It seems to me that God is slowly bringing home to us the truth that Islam is neither Nationalism nor Imperialism but a League of Nations which recognizes artificial boundaries and racial distinctions for facility of reference only, and not for restricting the social horizon of its members.[26]

As will be discussed shortly, for Iqbal neither blood nor race qualified as meaningful in forging fraternity or nationality: grudging recognition was here deployed only as a nominal indicator of distinction. Iqbal's concern was to boost the greater principle of spiritual realisation as a political idea, and he identified this as the domain of the unique and all-encompassing figure of the Prophet. Turkey's achievement fell short of this ideal, but her significance lay above all in creating conditions for such political realisation by exhorting interpretation of Islamic law, in particular, over and above any repetition of the past. This was not merely yet another plea to 'move on', or even simply to adjust or calibrate Islamic precepts in line with the current of history—though that too required intellectual labour, which he acknowledged had been the work of contemporary liberal Muslims. Turkey for Iqbal was instructive in highlighting Islam's intimacy with power, the concrete and the material.

Iqbal was equally forthright in his dismissal of Pan-Islamism as superfluous to the idea of Islam, inasmuch as it failed to capture the nature of political Islam. In public statements in 1931–33, he clarified that Pan-Islamism was a term adopted by those either ignorant or dismissive of Islam, coined to lend credibility to 'European aggression', akin to the term 'yellow peril' that had animated and legitimised imperial propaganda, and its use only served to diminish political aspirations to the status of Muslim 'intrigue'. He acknowledged that Pan-Islamism had somehow become associated with the writings of the nineteenth-century political ideologue and activist Jamaluddin Afghani,

---

25. Ibid., 159, citing and interpreting the Turkish nationalist poet Zia.
26. Ibid.

but specified Afghani's use of the term, and its historical meaning, as referring to a plea for unity between Afghanistan, Persia and Turkey against the tide of European expansion.

Divesting Pan-Islamism of any import as a 'political project', Iqbal interpreted it rather as a 'social experiment' that was central to the message of the Quran. Islam did not 'recognise caste, or race or colour', and to the extent that the idea behind Pan-Islamism was universal, Islam being equivalent to 'humanity' itself; any prefix to that effect was redundant, and Iqbal urged that it 'be dropped'.[27] In a bid to distance himself from contemporary Pan-Islamism and any mobilisation associated with it, Iqbal restated that even Afghani 'never dreamed of a unification of Muslims into a political state'. Returning from the Round Table parleys in London and urging that attention be turned to the immediate and the interior, Iqbal advised that for

> Indian Muslims to stand on their legs as an Indian nation is perfectly sound [advice] and I have no doubt that Muslims fully understand and appreciate it. Indian Muslims, who happen to be a more numerous people than the Muslims of all other Asiatic countries put together, ought to consider themselves the greatest asset of Islam and should sink in their own deeper self like other Muslim nations of Asia in order to gather up their scattered sources of life.[28]

For Iqbal, Turkey's new order would inspire a re-evaluation of republicanism as a new political language for the Muslims of India. It would be a categorical error to conclude, however, that he asserted the primacy of the bounded or the territorial in Islam. The transcendence of territory, or race or caste, in Islam was not to be equated with the aims of its political instantiation. It is arguable whether for him the transcendent 'social' was the greater or lesser principle in relation to the 'political'; but what should be noted is that he did not equate the two. This was in direct contrast with Ambedkar and his conversion of the social *as* the political relationship, truth, and instantiation of caste.

Islam's immortal precepts of the social brooked no boundaries, but in the twentieth century, Iqbal warned, it was Bolshevism that had produced a new

27. Interview to the *Bombay Chronicle*, September 1931, in Iqbal, *Letters and Writings*, 55–56.

28. Muhammad Iqbal, 'Statement . . . regarding Pan-Islamism', 19 September 1933, in Iqbal, *Speeches, Writings*, 283–84, at 284.

and political articulation of social and territorial transcendence, one that brought it dangerously close to Islam:

> Since Bolshevism plus God is almost identical with Islam, I should not be surprised if, in the course of time, either Islam would devour Russia or Russia Islam. The result will depend, I think to a considerable extent, on the position which is given to the Muslims under the new constitution.[29]

Evidently, for Iqbal, the future of Islam, especially in its political articulation, rested entirely with Indian Muslims and their fate. The point for emphasis here, however, is his assiduous refusal to conflate the social with the political for a remaking of Muslim political fraternity. Dismissed by some of his critics as a 'reactionary' for a perceived inability to apprehend the social foundations of the political, and cast by others as a sympathiser of socialism, he can only be interpreted in either of these ways by eliding what were for him two separate issues: the centrality of republican sovereignty, and its role as the mooring for a new form of brotherhood.[30]

Before developing this discussion, it is important to note in conclusion that Iqbal remained steadfast with regard to Turkey's republican order. In a long retort to Jawaharlal Nehru in 1936, on the nature of Islam and the political aspirations of Muslims, he reasserted the lack of any contradiction in Turkey's new order even as under Ataturk it displaced Arabic in favour of Turkish and segregated the religious from affairs of the state. In fact Ataturk, for Iqbal, in banishing 'mullahs' had dignified the principles of Islam and 'would have delighted [religious radicals like] Shah Wali Ullah'.[31] Jinnah, too, returned from his exile and again at the helm of the Muslim League, called for a day of mourning by Indian Muslims at Ataturk's death in November 1938; and Ambedkar noted both the vanishing influence of any Caliphate and the recognition of Turkey as a sovereign entity in orienting Jinnah's politics. Jinnah's refusal to join the Khilafat Conference has been understood primarily in terms of his unease at or disdain for the 'orthodox' and his lack of 'religious fire', but

---

29. Iqbal to Sir Francis Younghusband, published in the *Civil and Military Gazette*, 30 July 1931, in Iqbal, *Speeches, Writings*, 253.

30. See W. C. Smith, *Modern Islam in India* (Lahore: Ashraf Press, 1963 [1943]), 143–54 for a discussion of Iqbal's philosophy as 'reactionary' and 'unoriginal'; and as utopian socialist, Sevea, *Political Philosophy*, 115–20.

31. Muhammad Iqbal, 'Islam and Ahmadism' [1936], in Iqbal, *Speeches, Writings*, 214–40, at 234.

Ambedkar was correct in surmising that Jinnah in fact broke loose from both the Congress and the heady politics of the Khilafat movement that had engulfed India and beyond for a number of years because 'he was opposed to the Indian Mussalmans engaging themselves in extra-territorial affairs relating to Muslims outside India'.[32] Turkey contra the Caliphate would clarify, through example but not emulation, the lineaments of Muslim sovereignty in India.

Iqbal, for his part, remained resolutely anti-imperial, and his supportive disquisitions on the Turkish republic were not mere introversion or nativism, but rather testified to the instructive potential of this novelty in the history of Islam for the political ordering of the century. At the same time, he avoided being a representative of Muslims as a culture or religion alone. In the highly charged context of the Khilafat movement, Gandhi offered Iqbal the vice-chancellorship of the new university of Jamiah Milliah Islamiyah in Aligarh, but this invitation he politely declined, ostensibly on account of lacking the 'necessary qualifications' and disposition, as 'infant institutions' were prone to 'struggles and rivalries', and his preference was to be a 'peace-time worker'. Though he thought the work of education to be important, Iqbal made it clear to Gandhi that 'political independence must be preceded by economic independence and in this respect the Muslims of India are far behind other communities in India'.[33] In the heat of the Khilafat enthusiasm, and keeping their own counsel, Iqbal and, increasingly, Jinnah were forging the language of a sovereign fraternity that detached Muslim aspirations from their long-held communitarian articulations as social, cultural, economic or even global forms and launched them decisively into the political domain.

The Prophet's Republic

History knows but one monarch whose rule over man may justly be called a rule by divine right and that one man was the Prophet of Islam.

—IQBAL[34]

If *ijtihad* (interpretation) had fostered new ideas amid the demise of old institutions, then the centrality of *tauhid* (unity), premised on the finality—that

32. Ambedkar, *Pakistan*, 318.
33. Iqbal to M. K. Gandhi, 29 November 1920, in Iqbal, *Speeches, Writings*, 245–46, at 245.
34. Muhammad Iqbal, 'Divine Right to Rule' [1928], in Iqbal, *Speeches, Writings*, 163–67, at 167.

is, his status as the final prophet—of Muhammad, encouraged a rethinking of freedom or, more to the point, of sovereignty. As 'humanity's true actor', the Prophet was not for Iqbal, as Devji notes, a figure of miraculous powers: his assertive polemics consistently evoked his preoccupation with the finality of the Prophet as representing the 'vanishing moment of particularity out of which universality emerges'[35]—a principle that allowed, incidentally, for the demise of the Caliph. As will be argued, however, this 'ruling concept' of Iqbal's, which would embroil him in a serious dispute with the Ahmadis that also drew in Nehru, had more to do with Iqbal's conception of a political fraternity than with fidelity to theocratic dogma.

If, for Iqbal, 'prophecy [in Islam] reaches its perfection in discovering the need of its own abolition', then this was only because the Prophet represented humanity.[36] The principle of Muhammad's finality as Prophet that had set free the Muslims in particular, and by extension all humanity, forestalled any possible reproduction. Describing prophecy as a 'unitary experience' that overflowed and transcended boundaries, Iqbal argued that it was, nevertheless, marked by excess. Such an overflow or excess had the capacity to redirect 'collective life' and was 'calculated to completely transform the human world'. He recognised that the form of prophecy belonged to the 'ancient' world, but the Prophet Muhammad's status as final could only point to the ordering of the modern world. The Prophet, according to Iqbal, stood at the mid-point in this perspective of time, annihilating the ancient and inaugurating an endless futurity. Iqbal castigated the Sufis and Persian 'magicism' and Spengler's widely read *Decline of the West* alike for confusing this 'ancient' form of prophecy with the supernatural.[37]

For Iqbal, the finality of the Prophet, in the form of its own abolition, had universalised sovereignty and was everywhere, by virtue of which Muslims had been tied into an *ummah*, or brotherhood, and Islamic law, as a form of contract that was open to interpretation, had constituted Muslims as a civil society. Yet this civil society could not be equated with, nor was it even a sufficient basis for, a political union. The Prophet, on the other hand, as the sole sovereign, had inspired a distinctly republican form of politics. It was not merely that the reproduction of his image was forbidden; this prohibition occasioned a form of freedom, as human beings could only be truly free in a republic. The prohibition

35. Devji, *Muslim Zion*, 158.
36. Iqbal, *Reconstruction*, 126.
37. Ibid., 124–45.

on the replication of the Prophet's image extended to and depleted the powers of representation more generally; thus, and as Iqbal repeatedly argued, the abolition of the institutions of priesthood and kingship was faithful to this core idea of prophethood, as these institutions were based on the principle of representation. As a political idea, then, the Prophet's finality contained a nihilism, and testified to Islam's radical potential.

Freedom from 'idolatry', as boundless and limitless potential, had nevertheless through the Prophet created a 'collective will in a heterogeneous mass'.[38] This spoke of the global nature of Muslim brotherhood, and it is thus unsurprising that subsequent interpretations of Iqbal have underscored this transcendent and international dimension. Yet he himself was equally concerned with the finite, the concrete and the material that he took to be central to the instantiation and manifestation of Islam's principles. Rendering *tauhid* (unity) that was constituted by the finality of the Prophet as a republican triad of 'equality, solidarity and freedom', but one that 'demands loyalty to God, not to thrones', Iqbal rendered the power of unity 'as a polity' and as a set of pragmatic principles.[39]

It should not be assumed, however, that, in investing the principles of unity, finality and solidarity with the form of a pragmatic polity, Iqbal was, as has occasionally been surmised, only conveying a call for a theocratic state. His writings on the potential and power of the Prophet privilege the republican order over a theocratic centralisation of sovereignty, and Turkey and its republican sentiment was for him the manifestation of the principal precept of Islam that enshrined the indivisibility and the finality of the Prophet. Though Iqbal cited the English Civil War and the French Revolution as marking the republican drift in world history, 'the people', or the popular as the indivisible unit of republicanism, were absent from his disquisitions. Instead, the Prophet as monarch and sovereign emerged as the singular principle and source of rule. In this vein, he advanced the argument that, albeit the state was a necessity that need not itself be 'mere domination', all states were nevertheless in effect 'theocratic', and especially those conceived in terms of the 'self-realisation of spirit'.[40]

The Prophet was thus emblematic of the radical abolition of despotism, whether of priests or of kings. If the power of blood and lineage created

38. Ibid., 167.
39. Ibid., 154, 147.
40. Ibid., 155.

spurious forms of solidarity, then kingship as a hereditary form of rule was neither justified nor enabled by Islam. For Iqbal, hereditary rulership in the form of monarchy or aristocracy only signified brutality, not divinity.[41] Dependent on violence and wealth, kingship separated the ruler from the ruled by means of performative rituals whereby the monarch was kept 'out of the gaze of people' and cultivated distance by making rare appearances in 'small openings in the palace [or from a] balcony', in order to inspire 'awe and veneration'. Such ploys, he wrote scornfully, far from being evidence of any divinity, were 'artificial human methods' that were 'open to all', available to any 'knave who may get the opportunity and the means to do the same and perhaps much better.'[42] The Prophet, however—the only true monarch—was everywhere, not attached to any throne or idol, such as to make 'the whole earth into a mosque' through the dispersal of his sovereign power.[43]

For Iqbal, contemptuous and dismissive of kingship understood as a form of divine representation, the efficacy and extension of Muslim rulership, though it had made many a Muslim empire possible, was not equivalent to the political power of the Prophet's republic:

> The history of Islam tells us that the expansion of Islam as a religion is no way related to the political power of its followers. The greatest spiritual conquests of Islam were made during the days of its political decrepitude. . . . Islam gained greatest and most lasting missionary triumph in times and places in which its political power has been weakest, as in South India and Eastern Bengal.[44]

History for Iqbal offered neither precedent nor pattern for the pursuit of new political ideas. His thinking on the theocratic basis of all states, however, was but a reworking of Hegel, insofar as the state was seen as embodying the highest ideals, rather than functioning simply to contain violence—of which he says little, although it is clear that he was more than familiar with Hobbes. One way of approaching and clarifying this apparent contradiction in Iqbal's political thought is to reprise his dismissal of religious states in Europe: because Christianity was in origin 'monastic', with little or no initial involvement in 'civic affairs', its subsequent identification with the state led to division, confrontation

41. Iqbal, 'Divine Right', 163–64.
42. Ibid., 164.
43. Iqbal, *Reconstruction*, 155.
44. Muhammad Iqbal, 'Islam as a Moral and Political Ideal', 111–12.

and the eventual separation between the state and the church. For Iqbal, such a separation of the political from the religious was the sum total of, and equal to the history of, modern European political ideas.[45]

Islam, for Iqbal, who in this regard compared the Quran to Plato's *Republic*, had bequeathed in its very origins a civil society and the republic of the Prophet. Islam's origins and its precepts were in effect altogether political, circumventing any need for a separation between religion and state.[46] His dismissal of divine kingship, on the other hand, cautions us against any easy conclusion that for Iqbal the state was a representation of religion: that is to say, if the republic was everywhere, and the state was not a mirror of the Prophet's sovereign order, the political was in effect not an expression of religion. As discussed above, Islam provided the template for the social, which for Iqbal was not synonymous with the political, and religion was too great a category to be equated with and exhausted by the political.

Even if the history and power of Islam was not equivalent to its empires, Iqbal was nevertheless forthright in disassociating virtue from vulnerability. Contra Hobbes, he took human nature to be 'naturally good and peaceful', in accordance with the precepts of Islam; at the same time, however, he clarified that 'virtue is power, force, strength', while 'evil is weakness'. Weakness and vulnerability emanated from a fear that was engendered by the natural world itself, and Islam in his view was categorically distinct from other world religions, and especially Buddhism and Christianity, in that it did not elevate poverty, otherworldliness or renunciation as virtues to be cultivated. 'God', he noted in his *Stray Reflections*, 'reveals Himself in history more as power than love [. . . and] on the basis of our historical experience, God is better described as power.'[47] Most significantly—and here Majeed's work on Iqbal's pre-eminence of subjectivity is particularly relevant—the subject was not merely the container of will and experience, but was the ultimate figure of realisation and freedom. Thus, in Islam, in direct contrast to Christianity, 'there was no mediator between God and man': the subject or self was the 'maker of his own destiny' with 'salvation as his own business'. Discussion of violence as such is otherwise conspicuously absent from or muted in Iqbal's extensive corpus; his disquisitions on fear, vulnerability and power, however, were directed against the despotisms of religion and state that through fear engendered 'dependence', and

---

45. Iqbal, *Reconstruction*, 155.
46. Ibid., 166.
47. Iqbal, *Stray Reflections*, 24 ('The God of Islam').

cultivated a vulnerability that was compensated for by a blind form of obedi-ence.[48] A recurrent feature of Iqbal's writings is the articulation of antagonistic categories that clarify the place and range of a conceptual category. His famous epic poem in Persian *Asrar-i Khudi* (*The Secrets of the Self*) was followed up by *Rumuz-i Bekhudi* (*The Mysteries of Selflessness*), the latter being a disquisition on Islam focused especially on the Prophet and the ordering of the collec-tive.[49] He thus gave the oppositional categories of self and selflessness expres-sion in the form of an extreme distinction that was reflected in two different book-length poems. It would be erroneous to read the self or individuation as being in opposition to the collective. Instead, in clarifying the work of the self in one poem and the powers of the Prophet in the other, Iqbal aimed to force open a gap between these two categorical philosophical concepts that defied easy reconciliation or synthesis.

While the strength of the subject was the ultimate end of freedom, the political matrix of power and the republic of the Prophet was not simply a dispersed form of sovereignty. Without mediation, and as the 'eternal princi-ple' that regulated 'collective life', the power of finality aimed to provide a 'foothold in the world of eternal change'.[50] Much has been written on Iqbal's philosophy of time, elaborated in dialogue with the French philosopher Henri Bergson, among others; what is of relevance here is the notion that the figure of the Prophet was beyond the transitions and vagaries of history and his simultaneous abolition and finality for Iqbal enabled escape from the con-straints and conventions of serial time. Such a turn to the 'origins' of Islam conveyed not retrieval, but a radical futurity.[51] This contrasts with the ap-proach of the Hindutva ideologue Savarkar, whose zealous engagement with the ancient was directed towards making all that was remote proximate, for the unfolding of a new history. History, as Iqbal mused in his provocative and pithy *Stray Reflections*, was rather a 'sort of huge gramophone' blaring out a cacophonous record of human motives and powers that could only be 'ac-cepted with great caution'.[52]

48. Iqbal, 'Islam as a Moral and Political Ideal', 104–5.

49. Iqbal, *The Mysteries of Selflessness: A Philosophical Poem*, trans. A. J. Arberry (London: John Murray, 1953), esp. 21–39 on the Prophet and 14–19 for a denunciation of despair.

50. Iqbal, *Reconstruction*, 147.

51. Devji, *Muslim Zion*, 111–12.

52. Iqbal, *Stray Reflections*, 97 ('The Gramophone of History'), 77 ('The Interpretation of History').

The figure of the Prophet alone enabled the radical rejection of history, as it provided a form of futurity that was detached from the serial and cyclical time of defeats and revolutions, of wounds and triumphs alike. And precisely because the Prophet's own future was prohibited from replication, as a form of finality this sovereign and its republican order was immune to the creeping 'barbarism' of the flow of time that was the lot of all other regimes.[53] Final and immutable, the Prophet summoned a totality of sovereign conditions that was imbued with power that potentially encompassed the entire planet; and since this sovereign power was everywhere, it could also be anywhere. To put it differently, the Prophet's regime informed and centred the subject, and simultaneously dispensed with any fixed territorial sacrality that demanded restoration or return as symbolised in the form of an empire. Neither incarcerated in a church nor enshrined in a sacred kingdom or holy land, such a form of sovereign order potentially encompassed the entire planet.

Tauhid, or the unity enabled by the finality of prophethood, has been interpreted primarily either as Iqbal's endorsement for the international (that is, non-national) life of the Muslim or as a call for a theocratic Islamic state. Closely argued, and involving a philosophical case for (and fulsome approval of) modern Turkey and a repudiation of the newly announced prophethood of the Ahmadis, the principle of finality and the work of the prophet was, however, to underscore the republican virtue that could summon sovereignty. Yet this principle of the finality of the Prophet Muhammad was marked by categorical, even violent, limits. As will be argued below, fraternity and fellowship as afforded by the finality of the Prophet was for Iqbal a form of sovereign foreclosure that specified not so much the source of sovereignty, as its boundaries.

By detaching any fixed or centralised form of sovereignty from either an imperial past or divine kingship, Iqbal redistributed political precepts along distinctly novel trajectories. It is perhaps a more than merely biographical fact, and one with significance in terms of redirecting the immediate fate of Muslim political subjectivity, that Iqbal's own life, notwithstanding extensive travels to Europe and elsewhere, was firmly rooted in Punjab. Born to a tailor in Sialkot, in his repudiation of inherited forms of rule, whether landed or otherwise,

53. Iqbal, *Reconstruction*, 156; see Christopher Clark, 'Time of the Nazis', in Alexander C. T. Geppert and Till Kossler (eds.), *Obsession der Gegenwart* (Bristol, CT: Vandenhoeck & Ruprecht, 2015), 156–87 for an incisive discussion of political regimes and temporal orders in the mid-twentieth century.

Iqbal resorted not to social critique, but to the tenets of Islam that had provided a powerful template of rule that resisted the hereditary principle. More immediately, his political thought signified the circumvention if not the denunciation of the north-Indian Muslim aristocracy that had hitherto dominated intellectual and political leadership in the reworking of political ideals. Iqbal's writings, unlike those of his predecessors such as the famous Sir Syed Ahmed Khan, are remarkable for an absence of lament for the passing of Muslim empires in India:[54] in Punjab, the Sikh empire had preceded British suzerainty and in contrast to the United Provinces, or even Bengal, Punjab offered neither the restoration of a continuum nor a simple possession of the past. If, as argued here, Muslim sovereignty was for Iqbal ahistorical and radically grounded, this arguably made Punjab a particularly appropriate site for Muslim political aspirations.

In the highly charged atmosphere of elections and constitutional debates on enumeration and its territorial representation in the 1930s, Iqbal steered Jinnah towards Punjab and the formation of Pakistan.[55] Jinnah's friendship with Iqbal in the poet's final decade would forge the political project of Muslim nationality in a context of hostility and strife. Yet it is striking that Iqbal, not unlike Tilak, would turn to the intimate and the internal to define the hostile lineaments of fraternity anew.

Fraternity as Sovereign Foreclosure

Let not the sorry plight of the garden
Upset the gardener.

—IQBAL[56]

The last decade of Iqbal's life, up to his death in 1938, was an eventful one, engulfed in public and political controversy, during which questions of Indian representation and freedom gathered constitutional momentum. In a context

54. C. W. Troll, *Sayyid Ahmad Khan: A Reinterpretation of Muslim Theology* (Delhi: Oxford University Press, 1978); Singh, *Ardent Pilgrim*.

55. Iqbal to Jinnah, 28 May 1937 and 21 June 1937, in Muhammad Iqbal, *Letters of Iqbal to Jinnah with a Foreword by M. A. Jinnah* [1942] (Lahore: Ashraf Press, 1974), 16–25.

56. Muhammad Iqbal, *Shikwa and Jawab-i-Shikwa (Complaint and Answer): Iqbal's Dialogue with Allah*, trans. Khushwant Singh (Delhi: Oxford University Press, 1981), 86. The epigraph is taken from the *Answer to the Complaint*.

that was marked by widespread violence, considerations of fraternity, particularly in terms of religion and caste distinctions, became urgent. Echoing Ambedkar, Iqbal deemed India to be 'actually living in a state of civil war'.[57] The interwar period witnessed several controversies, both legal and violent, between Hindus and Muslims and Muslims and Sikhs in which offence and desecration created the contours and contexts of an ambient antagonism.[58]

Iqbal's ire, however, was directed specifically towards the immediate and intimate question of the Ahmadis. As is well known, late nineteenth-century Punjab witnessed a zealous new proselytising Muslim movement that took the charismatic figure of Mirza Ghulam Ahmed Khan as its prophet. The aim here is not to rehearse the violent controversy that led to the eventual de-recognition of the Ahmadis as Muslims in Pakistan—as had famously been demanded by Iqbal himself in the mid-1930s. The main emphasis of interpretations of the dispute has been upon the issue of the 'legality' and 'ownership' of Islam. For Devji, Iqbal in his excoriation of the Ahmadis adopted 'an orthodox mien in a specifically rabbinical way' that served to reveal an affinity between Zionism and Iqbal's political philosophy and project.[59]

To be sure, though Iqbal admired Spinoza, in his long disquisitions on Ahmadism he nevertheless endorsed the philosopher's excommunication from Judaism on grounds of heresy. Iqbal had urged the British imperial authorities to identify and segregate the Ahmadis as a distinct community. The Ahmadis were quick to point out that Iqbal's position was analogous to that of the Romans who had crucified Jesus. In an escalating polemic, Iqbal retorted that it was a 'matter of surprise' to him that 'a community [the Ahmadis] which has, for its birth and growth, depended entirely upon the liberalism of a modern State should resent my demand for the protection of Islam against religious adventurers'.[60] The accusation was not only untrue, but disingenuous, in that Iqbal himself had little faith in liberal legal structures, which in his view displaced 'moral' languages such as to 'make the illegal and the wrong identical in meaning'.[61] The equivocation between morality and legality was arguably

57. Iqbal to Jinnah, 28 May 1937, in Iqbal, *Letters of Iqbal to Jinnah*, 21.

58. Adeel Hussain, 'Legal Antagonism'.

59. Devji, *Muslim Zion*, 152–61.

60. Muhammad Iqbal, 'Jewish Integrity under Roman Rule' [1935], in Iqbal, *Speeches, Writings*, 211–14, at 213; see too Iqbal, *Stray Reflections*, 44 ('Christ and Spinoza'); Kenneth Jones, *Socio-Religious Reform Movements in British India* (Cambridge: Cambridge University Press, 1989), on the rise of the Ahmadiyya movement in Punjab.

61. Iqbal, *Stray Reflections*, 108 ('Democracy').

a lesser problem, however, as Iqbal, much like several Hindu ideologues including Tilak, advocated the 'non-interference' in religion 'by the rulers of
India'. Exclusion and excommunication, Iqbal argued, would not only make
the Ahmadis 'consistent' with themselves but, significantly, would allow Indian Muslims to 'tolerate' them in much the same way as they did those of
other persuasions.[62]

His part in the debate over theological validity and its legal recognition did
not, however, represent a retreat into orthodoxy by Iqbal, who recognised the
issue as entirely 'political', insofar as the new claimants disrupted the boundaries of fraternity. Rather than viewing the emergence of the Ahmadis as an
extension of the frontier of Indian Islam, Iqbal clearly considered it in a spirit
of hostility and animosity that was entirely internal and intimate. In a context
of raging hostilities between Hindus and Muslims and Muslims and Sikhs, his
turn to the inner and 'familial' intra-Muslim world aimed to clarify the external
ends and antagonistic bounds of fraternity. While for Tilak—for whom, too,
as argued in Chapter 1, the political domain was identified primarily by delineating the boundaries of the intimate—the discovery of fraternity rested on
the conversion of kinsmen into enemies, for Iqbal fraternity, though centred
again on the intimate, was a form of foreclosure clarified above all through the
exclusion of the proximate. The proximity of the Ahmadis as Muslims was
precluded as they had sought to pluralise the primary source of sovereignty,
namely the Prophet.

Arguing from 'perfectly defined boundaries' and the finality of prophethood as the categorical 'line of demarcation' that 'enables' the contours of Muslim fraternity, Iqbal likened the Ahmadis to the Brahmos of Bengal, who also
regarded Muhammad as a prophet, but without belief in his finality, and were
therefore outside fraternal bounds.[63] Clarifying that this was no ethical dis-
putation over the 'good or bad', or even about 'toleration', Iqbal steered the
debate into a political register. Invoking the distinctive precepts of sovereignty
as either 'life-giving' or 'life destroying', he posited the 'essential' and 'biologi-
cal criterion' as the only basis for the evaluation of fraternal solidarity, thus
configuring the Ahmadis as representing a choice for Islam between life and

62. Muhammad Iqbal, 'Qadianism and Orthodox Muslims' [1935], in Iqbal, Speeches, Writings, 197–203, at 203.

63. Muhammad Iqbal, 'A Letter to The Statesman', [10 June 1935], in Iqbal, Speeches, Writings,
208–11, at 209.

death.[64] By boycotting congregations and even marital bonds with their co-religionists and in abstracting themselves from the social while still claiming membership of Islam, the Ahmadis had rendered the dispute entirely 'political' and amenable only to a partisan resolution: Iqbal thus called for the exclusion of the Ahmadis from the fold of Islam for the procurement of internal peace precisely because they pulled at shared totemic strings of attachment.[65] The regime of the Prophet's sovereignty might indeed, as argued above, countenance no boundaries; but infidelity to the principle of finality as the singular source of this sovereign order inevitably incited the barring, the ruling out, the prevention of a union of the near and intimate. For all his pouring of invective upon Ahmadism as a form of 'medieval revivalism', moreover, Iqbal's insistence on foreclosure highlighted the contemporary political concerns of fraternity and violence.

Categorically, and in contrast to Hindutva, this form of fraternity was not constituted through blood lineage, nor did the shedding of blood create attachment. For Iqbal, Islam was 'much more than a religion', especially in the manner in which it alone elevated the potential and prospects of internal and external peace. In its 'external' dimension, the principle of 'deracialisation of man', and through its 'internal' organisation that ordained 'equality', Islam offered and ensured unrivalled forms of peace and security.[66] The coherence of Islam as a 'nationality', Iqbal repeatedly reminded his readers, did not derive from the 'territory, marriage, birth, domicile or naturalization' that had been the cause of much bloodshed in human history. Aligned rather with peace, 'membership of this nation', he had written earlier, 'was determined by a public declaration of "like-mindedness" and would terminate when the individual has ceased to be like-minded with others'. This affirmative communion was, moreover, structured 'not by physical force but by the spiritual force of a common ideal'.[67] Exacting, expansive but exclusive, this 'ethereal' fraternity preferred separation and forsaking as a peaceful if declaratory form of hostility to the violent aggression of confrontation. Enmity and hostility ultimately remained immanent, rather than vested in any power of the external or the outsider.

64. Muhammad Iqbal, 'Islam and Ahmadism' [1936], in Iqbal, *Speeches, Writings*, 214–40, at 218.

65. Iqbal, 'Letter to *The Statesman*'.

66. Plan [1933] for a book to be entitled Muslim Polity and Muslim Jurisprudence (unwritten due to failing health), in Iqbal, *Letters and Writings*, 89.

67. Iqbal, 'Political Thought', 141.

One of Iqbal's earliest poems, *Shikwa* (*Complaint*), and its companion *Jawab-i-Shikwa* (*Answer*), written soon after the attack on Ottoman Turkey by Bulgaria in 1912, is particularly insightful as regards the nature of enmity and brotherhood. Written in the author's own voice as an address to Allah, the *Complaint* lyrically portrays the political and material degradation of Muslims while their tormentors experience and enjoy the full splendours of earthly magnificence and dominion in what has been called an 'audacious criticism of God'. The *Answer*, written in the voice of Allah, foregrounds—as Majeed argues, and like his later epic poem the *Javid-Nama* that also concludes with the voice of God—the excesses and transgressions, but primary significance, of the subject.[68] It would be erroneous to interpret the *Complaint* and the *Answer* as representing a conflict between the material and the spiritual over the sovereign claims of the self. Rather, the *Answer* assigns an immutability and immortality to the subject even in the face of loss at the hands of antagonists. Crucially, the external, the Other or even the hostile enemy (*aada*) is disempowered and voided of any import in defining the subject, including in its political dimensions. The 'Bulgar aggression' incited 'action' and 'sacrifice', but as the following couplet from the *Answer* clarifies, the truth of the subject was beyond the reach of even its most virulent aggressors:

Why tremble at the snorting of the charges of your foes?
The flame of truth is not snuffed out by the breath the enemy blows.[69]

Although not too much should be made of the similarity, the *Complaint* and the *Answer* nevertheless bear a resemblance to the *Bhagavad Gita*, in that they are structured as a dialogue between a trembling, defeatist and despairing subject (like Arjuna) and a God who exhorts to action as duty and essential to the identity of the subject. Arjuna's despair had reduced him to inaction on the battlefield on the eve of the commencement of a fratricide, only for Krishna to remind him that the war would take place regardless, and his despairing inaction would only deprive him of his selfhood. Iqbal deployed rather the metaphor of the earth as a garden in which 'countless plants wither' or 'remain forever green', where 'countless more hid' and were 'yet to be seen'. The significant point was not, however, the inevitability of change, but, as highlighted in

68. Majeed, *Muhammad Iqbal*, 24; Javed Majeed, *Autobiography, Travel and Postnational Identity: Gandhi, Nehru and Iqbal* (London; Palgrave, 2007), 269–83.
69. Iqbal, *Shikwa and Jawab-i-Shikwa*, 90.

the epigraph to this section, God's exhortation to the 'gardener' not to be 'upset' at the 'sorry plight of the garden'.[70]

However, while both the *Gita* and the *Jawab-i-Shikwa* (*Answer*) made the subject primary, regardless of context, here the similarity ends. Their divergence arose when it came to the nature of fraternal enmity. In the *Answer*, fraternity is presented as the principal category and condition of the subject. While the *Gita* construed the brother as the potential antagonist, for Iqbal, the subject without the brother was not merely incomplete, but suicidal. The essence and logic (*sheva*) of self-destruction (*khudkushi*) were inextricably linked to the absence and alienation of fraternal sentiment and duty. It was precisely absence of brotherhood (*akhuwat*), and the inability to make any sacrifice for the sake of brotherhood, that the Bulgarian attack had made visible. The significance of the attack for Iqbal, ventriloquising Allah, thus lay not so much in a call to combat, but in an opportunity to discover and renew the fraternal bond through sacrificial action.[71] For the *Gita*, it was only in the event of war that the brother was converted into an enemy, because in peace or unexceptional conditions, by contrast, fraternity was normative, the bond being expressed through a system of ethical duties, sentiments and attachments.[72] For Iqbal, however, war was on the contrary a *consequence* of weakened bonds of brotherhood, and in this sense, however damaging it might be, it was unexceptional, as it emanated from and signified a political loss already sustained.

Thus fraternity, both as foreclosure and bond, framed the essentially political nature of Islam, with incorporation as its related principle, whereby the external or the outsider was of little consequence. Soon after the infamous Poona Pact between Gandhi and Ambedkar, the question of a coalition between Dalits and Muslims acquired significance. With Ambedkar's call in 1935 to Dalits to sever their connection with Hinduism at the Depressed Classes Conference in Nasik, several Muslim religious leaders sought their conversion to Islam. Without fully endorsing such a move, Iqbal nevertheless wrote to the rector of Al-Azhar, the leading seminary in Egypt, which had sent its representatives to India for this purpose, pointing out both the obstacles to and

---

70. Ibid., 86–87. On the garden as a master metaphor in Islamic imagination, see, for instance, Ronald Inden, 'Paradise on Earth: The Deccan Sultanates', in Daud Ali and Emma J. Flatt (eds.), *Gardens and Landscape Practices in Precolonial India: Histories from the Deccan* (London: Routledge, 2011), ch. 4.

71. Iqbal, *Shikwa and Jawab-i-Shikwa*, 82.

72. See Chapter 1.

opportunities for such conversion.[73] Incorporation, then, functioned as an open invitation, while the force of foreclosure determined fraternity not simply as a social or ethical form of fellowship, but as distinctly political inasmuch as it referred to violence and sovereignty.

The Luther of Islam

Nations are mothers of *ideals*, but ideals, in course of time, become pregnant and give birth to new nations.

—IQBAL[74]

In his *The Discovery of India*, Jawaharlal Nehru recounts meeting Iqbal a few months before the poet's death in Lahore in 1938. This meeting was at Iqbal's request and was all the more astonishing given that, just a few years earlier, Nehru and Iqbal had locked horns in a public and bitter debate on the question of the Ahmadis.[75] Moreover, by this point, relations between the Muslim League and the Congress had become irreconcilable over the question of Muslim political representation. Nehru felt 'pleased' to be 'liked' by Iqbal, whom he admired greatly as a poet, and represented Iqbal's political thought in a double-edged manner that has, to varying degrees, held sway to date. On the one hand, Nehru acknowledged Iqbal as an 'influential' poet, but not a 'mass leader', who had nevertheless inspired a 'separatist direction' amongst the Muslims of India that was born of a 'psychology of fear' and competition between Hindus and Muslims. Yet in the same breath he was keen to assert that Iqbal had confessed to him that though he had 'advocated Pakistan' as leader of the League, 'he [Iqbal] felt sure that it would be injurious to India as a whole and to Moslems specially'. Nehru concluded this vignette by recalling that the poet had judged Jinnah to be a mere 'politician', in contrast to his own anointment by him as the 'patriot'.[76] The seductive implication of this summary of the formation of Pakistan as a series of low-level political machinations is that if the country's now widely acknowledged spiritual and ideological founder— namely Muhammad Iqbal—did not on his deathbed go quite so far as to regret

73. Recommendations of Iqbal to the mission of Al-Azhar, 25 July 1935, in Iqbal, *Letters and Writings*, 83–85.

74. Iqbal, *Stray Reflections*, 39 ('The Modern Hindu'; original emphasis).

75. Jawaharlal Nehru, 'The Solidarity of Islam', *Modern Review* 58:5 (1935), 504–7.

76. Nehru, *Discovery of India*, 371–73.

his endorsement of Pakistan, he certainly sought to belittle it as something to which he was constrained by the political office that he held.

It is widely appreciated that Iqbal did not take attachment to blood or soil as primordial to nationality, nor consider it to be grounded in a coalescence of 'economic interest'.[77] And, as is equally well known, Iqbal's presidential address to the Muslim League, delivered soon after the ill-fated Simon Commission in 1930, was categorical in its assertion of territoriality, and can easily be cited and interpreted as the first articulation of Pakistan as it exists today, in that it called for the 'North-west' of India to be a 'consolidated' formation—indeed a 'consolidated State'—that was the 'final destiny of the Muslims, at least of North west India'.

Iqbal began this lengthy presidential address to the Muslim League—seen as a foundational moment for Muslim nationalism—by declaring that 'Muslim thought and activity' was at its most 'crucial turning point', and he went on to assert that the 'spirit of Islam' was a 'world fact'. However, the main content and emphasis of the speech was directed towards the place of India in the Muslim world, and the fate of the Muslims of India. The address strikingly positioned India in the Muslim world—indeed hailing it as 'the greatest Muslim country in the world'.[78] This was not mere national pride: India represented the global not only in its scale but in its history of diversity and the multiplicity of empires it had seen rise and fall, such that it alone was positioned to produce a new political language, perhaps not capable of universality, but of a form of futurity hitherto unknown but transcending its present.[79] In this sense, India and Indian Muslims carried a potential that could not be contained by the national alone.

Iqbal's address was thus not simply about territorial claims, even as the only principle for the realisation of modern political ideals, whether for Muslims or non-Muslims. As early as 1909, soon after his return from Europe, he had recognised the powerful advent of nationalism. 'Nationality with us [Muslims] is a pure idea', he wrote then, and 'has no geographical basis.'[80] But

77. Iqbal, 'Muslim Community', 121.

78. Muhammad Iqbal, Presidential address to the All-India Muslim League, Allahabad, 29 December 1930, in S. S. Pirzada (ed.), *Foundations of Pakistan: All-India Muslim League Documents*, vol. 2: *1906–1947* (New Delhi: Metropolitan Book Co., 1982), 153–71, at 154, 159.

79. Muhammad Iqbal, *Javid-Nama* [1932], trans. Arthur J. Arberry (London: George Allen & Unwin, 1966); for India and the global imaginary, see esp. Majeed, *Autobiography*, 76–121.

80. Iqbal, 'Islam as a Moral and Political Ideal', 116. Iqbal repeated and expanded some of the themes of this article in his presidential address.

the singular transformation in modern politics had been, in his view, the discovery of 'national outlook' that was 'finding expression through varying systems of polity . . . on lines which recognize territory as the only principle of political solidarity.' In reprising some of his earlier writings for the members of the Muslim League, Iqbal identified Luther and Rousseau as the innovators who had transformed Christianity and Europe by bequeathing it a 'national outlook' that was made possible through the 'break-up of the one into a mutually ill-adjusted many.'[81] As he put it somewhat rhetorically, 'The universal ethics of Jesus is displaced by national systems of ethics and politics.' This had led to the sequestering of religion as a 'private affair' that was separated from 'temporal life', a separation that mirrored the 'duality of spirit and matter' that 'Europe [had] uncritically accepted', resulting in what he argued were 'mutually ill-adjusted States' driven by 'interests' that were 'national' rather than 'human' in scale.

But Islam was not Christianity. 'A Luther in the world of Islam', he stated, 'is an impossible phenomenon; for here there is no Church organisation . . . inviting a destroyer.' Even though 'Islam is not a church', as Iqbal argued, the concept of the 'State' was, however, embedded in its ideas and precepts, as it operated as a 'contractual organism, long before Rousseau ever thought of such a thing.'[82] Bounded by an ethical ideal, Islam for Iqbal could not countenance a Manichaean separation of the temporal from the spiritual or the religious from the political, under national conditions. 'The truth is', he wrote, 'that Islam looks upon the universe as a reality, and consequently recognises as reality all that is in it.'[83] Embodying neither a contradiction nor a separation, Islam enshrined the powerful precepts of equality and democracy that the contract with God and his law, or the Prophet and the Quran, had enabled. Turkey, however, notwithstanding his endorsement of the republic, betrayed an intimacy with Europe that had led it, albeit superficially, to incorporate a degree of separation between church and state where none originally existed in Islam.[84]

For Iqbal, Europe, and by implication Christianity, had discovered sovereignty through the formation of national states. While Islam was suffused with sovereignty and conducted its lifeworld through a set of contractual

81. Iqbal, Presidential address, 155.
82. Iqbal, Presidential address, 153–71; and *Reconstruction*, 155.
83. Iqbal, 'Islam as Moral and Political Ideal', 101.
84. Iqbal, Presidential address; and *Reconstruction*, 155.

obligations for Muslims, the twentieth century and its political imperatives demanded an understanding and resolution of sovereignty in relation to its national dimension. To be sure, and as several authors have pointed out, Iqbal was critical of European nationalism. It does not follow, however, that he abandoned the pressing problem of the relationship between Islam and nationalism. Quite the opposite. In 1930, he was clear that the national principle had become a powerful idea whose 'final fate' he was unsure of 'in the world of Islam'.[85]

Nationalism was powerful, and dangerous. Iqbal saw it in its European incarnation as a successor to the Catholic Church that had not merely led to a mechanical separation of religion from the state, but had produced states that were actually irreligious. Nationalism was powerful precisely because it possessed novel and unprecedented powers of captivation such that it could disenchant without leaving a spiritual void. Muslim nationalism as a conjugated unity thus had the potential to calibrate the desacralised nature of nationalism. To put it differently, European nationalism evoked attachments to land and territory, whilst the potential of nationalism in its Muslim incarnation lay in its ability to enchant land and territory through the precepts of Islam. While European history had moved to a disenchanted but passionate nationalism of the soil whereby the church was replaced by the state, the Muslims of India had the opportunity to rewrite the script of nationalism.

Iqbal feared nationalism because it aroused sentiment for and attachment to the figuration of the nation and as 'deity'.[86] His dispute with Nehru, whom he correctly identified as a patriot, was less to do with the latter's call for 'toleration' towards the Ahmadis than with what Iqbal deemed Nehru's idolatrous notion of nationalism, which summoned distinctions only to sublimate them under the all-enveloping domination of the national.[87] Significantly, and unlike Ambedkar, for whom democracy offered the political recognition and nonviolent interplay of adversarial distinctions, Iqbal saw modern democracy as a matter of disputes and 'rows': a force and form of government that unleashed repressed 'aspirations and grievances' resolved not by 'authority', but by 'argument and controversy'.[88] Consent (ijma) remained for Iqbal the organising precept of political life, whereby change occurred through

85. Iqbal, Presidential address, 155.
86. Iqbal, 'Islam and Ahmadism', 215.
87. Iqbal, 'Muslim Community', 122.
88. Iqbal to Sir Francis Younghusband, 30 July 1931, 251.

interpretation (*ijtihad*), but not to the interpretation of any particular assembly, be that even of religious leaders, as this would entail the separation of religion from the political.[89]

Just as Islam was not Christianity, India was not Europe. In this regard, Iqbal's presidential address gains significance not for its invocation of territory alone, but mainly insofar as it sought to steer the charged currency of 'communalism' as a relationship with distinct others. Wrested away from its associations with the pathological expression of religious affiliation, communalism, in its 'higher meaning', was for Iqbal 'indispensable': understood as a 'culture' and 'cultural autonomy', it represented not merely diversity, or the Muslims alone, but the essence of nationality in India. As opposed to Europe, where language and blood had become the violent principle of nationality, India, though continental, was characterised by an absence of 'race-consciousness' defined by blood. This, Iqbal noted astutely, was as true of the Hindus as it was of Muslims. As a language evocative of distinctions, rather than animosity, communalism offered the contours for a contract with non-Muslims. Any transcendence or non-recognition of religion, whether Hinduism or Islam, would lead, he warned, to the 'blood-shed' that he identified as a consequence of Nehru's nationalism and social democracy.[90]

In his famous dispute with Maulana Husain Ahmad, shortly before his own death, Iqbal explained that groups without an anchor in either religion or law were merely that: groups. Be it a clutch of bandits or of businessmen, they were equivalent to the denizens of any city or locality that could be designated by the term *qaum*: a 'community', perhaps, but one shorn of any ideological force, with no internal powers of persuasion or attachment. For it was through ideology, law or, more specifically in this instance, religion that a union or group became elevated to the status of *millat*: a religious or ideological community, in its full partisan dimension in relation to others. The problem, as Iqbal interpreted it, was not the 'quibbling' over the freight and meaning of *millat*, but that the *millat* offered by Indian nationalism was a new political union that sought powerfully to obfuscate and absorb other such and contending forms of association.[91]

89. Iqbal, *Reconstruction*, 175.

90. Iqbal to Jinnah, 28 May 1937, in Iqbal, *Letters of Iqbal to Jinnah*, 19.

91. Iqbal, 'Statement on Islam and Nationalism in Reply to a Statement of Maulana Husain Ahmad', 9 March 1938, in Iqbal, *Speeches, Writings*, 300–313.

Of course, for Gandhi too the all-permeating aspects of religion could not be sequestered or rendered private; but although their politics of prejudice might be superficially similar, there was a critical distinction between Gandhi and Iqbal with regard to sovereignty: for the former, let us recall, it was the sacrificial politics of death that dignified the intimate other; whereas for the latter, sovereignty operated as a form of foreclosure, with its watchful hostility turned entirely inwards. Iqbal's political philosophy, moreover, was not by any means the mirror image of Savarkar's Hindutva: as argued above, Hindutva was a theory of violence in which the enemy, though a moving target, was salient for the creation of a new fraternity; while for Iqbal communalism, devoid of animosity, was an interface between distinct others. Iqbal noted the entirely novel nature of the ideological reconstruction that had seized the Hindu community and was transforming it into a 'new people' no longer 'dominated by ethical ideals' but a 'political' body impregnated with the ideal of a new nation.[92] The issue of political freedom and fraternity, Iqbal contended, was hitherto altogether unfamiliar to the Hindu; like many in the Muslim League, he took the Hindu Mahasabha as the true representative of Hindus that was bound to produce a new nation. Iqbal's endorsement of the Mahasabha undermined Nehru's inclusive conceptions of sovereignty as freedom and nationality based on diversity. For Iqbal, without the political, Islam faced a future that was ethical and individualised but would lack the power to manage its own fraternal bonds.

The aim here is not to square the circle of Iqbal's political philosophy, widely interpreted as embodying a contradiction between the global or universal and the national or territorial that amounts to an aporia: such is the outcome of interpretations that treat scale as historical argument in itself. Equally, Iqbal has been represented as a sequential political thinker, who transits from an earlier 'global' vision to a later 'national' outlook. Given the remarkable primacy of the political understood in terms of sovereign claims of fraternity and foreclosure, Iqbal's philosophy is characterised by a surprising coherence, however, and even consistency. If anything, and unlike the global Ghadar that subsequently became absorbed and folded into the national, Iqbal detached the global frontier of Islam and the cause of Khilafat in particular for the development of a new political vocabulary that philosophically discovered Muslim sovereignty.

92. Iqbal, *Stray Reflections*, 39 ('The Modern Hindu').

As this chapter has highlighted, Iqbal's political thought in the main deployed antagonisms between any two contending principles—whether between the Caliph and the Prophet, the abstract and the concrete, or even poetry and prose—to force open a space between the two opposing poles that gave concepts a unity. It has been argued, that is to say, that, rather than attempting to synthesise two opposing ideas, Iqbal pushed antagonistic ideas to a limit that forced not reconciliation, but rather a gap or separation that had the potential for the emergence of new concepts. This form of severance distributed the meaning and application of dominant oppositions in new directions; equally, in separating and disaggregating the social from the political, the religious and cultural from the political, Iqbal forced open the space of the political for new contents and meanings to emerge. Islam and its history had bequeathed political principles of sovereignty and fraternity deriving from its very origins, but these in the twentieth-century order seemed invisible. This invisibility had made Muslims primarily religious, cultural and even social in their collective outlook, and they were thus regarded as a 'community', but curiously estranged from the new political vocabulary of brotherhood and nationality that had become the currency of twentieth-century nationalisms.

Iqbal thus sought, through a philosophical history, to clarify and make visible the political by disentangling it from the social, cultural and religious realms—bringing him, ironically, closer to Luther, whom he despised, than to Spinoza, whom he admired. This process of conceptual clearing and separation opened a domain for Muslim politics and subjectivity that was understood distinctly in terms of modern sovereignty. For Iqbal, sovereignty did not emulate the order and control of violence, however, but operated through the force of foreclosure, involving possibilities of hostility, enmity and exclusion that referred primarily to the internal and intimate world of Islam.

To an extent, Iqbal's role as an ideological innovator can be seen as similar to that of Tilak, in that in seeking separation and departure from the given political currencies, they both opened new conceptual and political spaces that were not fully articulated or named but could retrospectively be occupied and named through rigid designation. This is not to compare or evaluate their relative statures or contributions as thinkers, but rather to point to the similarity of the positions their thought has occupied. Territory, for Iqbal, was neither exhausted by nor equivalent to Islam, yet in powerful interventions in the Muslim League and beyond he argued for the potential of sovereignty as separation and as an opening for the possibility of peace. It would be reasonable to claim, then, that Iqbal's ideas occupied the gap between the philosophical discovery of fraternity and sovereignty, or the political, and the name that came to designate it as a category. Pakistan, as separation and as a prospect of peace, and above all as a name, transformed fraternity for the inauguration of a sovereignty that was to be discovered and made concrete in civil war.

7

A People's War

1947, CIVIL WAR AND THE RISE OF REPUBLICAN SOVEREIGNTY

It is a question of civil war or partition.[1]

—SARDAR PATEL

Free India can be nothing but a republic.[2]

—JAWAHARLAL NEHRU

IN JANUARY 1947, the American news magazine *Time* put Sardar Patel on its cover, featuring inside a long report on the historic dilemmas and choices that faced India on the threshold of freedom. The choice was not odd, but it was striking in that it reflected the correct perception that, at that crucial moment, more than Gandhi—who had long been the 'face' of Indian freedom—or Nehru, who went on to institutionalise and direct the realisation of the idea of free India, or even Jinnah, the founder of Pakistan, it was Patel, anointed 'The Boss' by the magazine, who was central to the form free India would ultimately take.

Entitled 'Pieces of Hate', the January 1947 *Time* cover feature on Patel, in surveying the conundrum of India's decolonisation, suggested that 'something

---

1. Vallabhbhai Patel to Gandhi, cited in Rajmohan Gandhi, *Patel: A Life* (Ahmedabad: Navajivan Publishing House, 1991), 401; this remains an authoritative biography of Patel.

2. Jawaharlal Nehru, Resolution in the Constituent Assembly of India, 13 December 1946, https://www.constitutionofindia.net/constitution_assembly_debates/volume/1/1946-12-13.

more than' Jinnah's 'fanaticism', Gandhi's 'combination of mysticism and manipulation' and Nehru's 'eloquent idealism' was needed. 'India', it declared,
'needed an organizer'. And the historical moment had found that in Patel. The
profile cast Patel, a man for whom no detail was small or sordid, as an austere
figure who had never seen a movie, whose only recreation was bouncing a ball
across the room and who, although he handled the Congress party's funds,
had 'no love for money'. The profile noted the curious fact that 'the Boss' was
neither much of a writer nor indeed much of a reader: his less than substantial
collection of books, it reported, consisted entirely of works written by Indians,
and was exclusively concerned with India. Though uninterested in the world
beyond India, Patel, unlike most others, did not see India as being in a state of
'chaos', but rather as a 'puzzle to be fitted together'.[3] The 'chaos' undoubtedly
referred to the nature of the arrival of free India, born in partition, in a context
of overwhelming and unprecedented violence and strife. Understanding this
as 'civil war', this chapter reconstructs and interprets its profound political
significance as ushering in the republican age of the people.

In revising the notion of 'partition violence' in terms of civil war, the chapter argues that concern with fraternity, fellowship and life with others was
transfigured into the domination of the language and pursuit of sovereignty.
This transfiguration was grounded in the violence of civil war. The language
of—albeit fraught—'brotherhood' and fellowship was replaced by that of 'the
people', discovered and demarcated by repeated utterance in powerful pronouncements. As the new but dominant political category, 'the people' inaugurated and became the basis of the Indian constitution and the foundational
principle of the new sovereign power of India.

This chapter contends that violence was not incidental, but *integral*—
foundational—to this arrival of 'the people' as the proper subject of the political
in India. Over a million people were killed, and at least another ten million
moved between the new territories of India and Pakistan in less than a year—a
remarkably short period of time[4]—and the correlation between violence and
the arrival of the new nations on the subcontinent was not merely strong, but
mutually causative. While in the relatively cool chambers of the Constituent

---

3. Anon., 'Pieces of Hate' *Time*, 27 January 1947, 14–17.

4. Urvashi Butalia, *The Other Side of Silence: Voices from the Partition of India* (London: Hurst
& Co., 2000); Gyanendra Pandey, *Remembering Partition: Violence, Nationalism and History in
India* (Cambridge: Cambridge University Press, 2001); Mark Mazower, 'Violence and the State
in the Twentieth Century', *The American Historical Review* 107:4 (2002), 1158–78.

Assembly the term 'republic' was finding its first utterance as a reality, beyond them, in the streets, towns and villages, from at least August 1946, violence acquired a catastrophic power: the new territories were being enacted and demarcated in blood. The overall outcome was the migration and reassembling of peoples on a massive scale within the designated nations of India and Pakistan. The violence was not simply a corollary if thus processed, but actually constitutive of sovereignty. This civil war, as it is understood here, became the revelatory moment of the discovery of 'the people' as the primary source of sovereignty.

Prior even to the violent strife that marked the coming of freedom to India, Ambedkar had described relations between Hindus and Muslims in interwar India as a state of civil war; but his had been a lone voice, and it is striking that to date, this killing of over a million has been somewhat quaintly designated 'partition violence', alluding only to its cause and context, and thus obscuring, perhaps deliberately, its profoundly fratricidal nature. The period surrounding the transition of power between the regimes of British empire and the nations of India and Pakistan saw violence unprecedented in scale and intensity: mass murder started with the 'Great Calcutta Killing' in August 1946, with possibly a million killed in 1947, and lethal hostility only coming to an end with—significantly—the assassination of Gandhi in January 1948. Yet in both the historical record and its subsequent reception in historiography, partition violence features in two distinctly diverging registers, neither of which addresses its true political significance.

On the one hand, dense accounts of the details of negotiations between hostile parties and representatives of the outgoing empire, Indian nationalists and spokesmen for Pakistan are steeped in the concerns of the politics of interest, ranging from territorial boundaries and apportioning of natural resources to the division of government assets, be they office typewriters or army regiments. A second type of account, on the other hand, relays the details of violence recounted as memory and trauma: the subjective experience of violent division. If the former register is infused with the cold logic of realpolitik, the latter compensates for this with the pathos of the personal and emotional costs that history extracted. While in the former register the violence attendant upon the high politics of partition and the making of nation-states is addressed in terms of a revolving 'blame game', with historians apportioning guilt between key figures (primarily Jinnah, Congress leaders and the outgoing British masters), in the latter, by contrast—in the memory portraits of partition violence experienced as popular suffering of the consequences of high politics—no one is guilty: everyone is a victim of a violent history. It is the aim of this chapter to revise the thoroughly depoliticised understanding of the violence of 1947 that results, and in so doing to recover its full and profound political significance.

Eschewing the registers both of realpolitik and of pathos, this chapter will instead approach partition violence as an instance of civil war, and as the arch-paradigm of the political domain. Civil war as a category is premised on the politicisation of the familial and the fraternal;[5] emanating from the intimate, civil wars make, suspend and test the boundaries of any given order. Civil war has thus been characterised as the opposite of 'the law'. Sovereign legal regimes, as has been recently argued, have been forced historically only to play catch-up with the consequences of civil wars:[6] the law effectively displaces civil war onto a plane primarily of concern with its delimitation through regulation and codification of norms, after the violent event has in fact happened. More profoundly, as in the case of the Indian civil war of 1947, the suspension of law and the disruptive violence can occasion the discovery of sovereign power. The 1947 war, in short, for all its catastrophic violence, was revelatory, as it made visible 'the people' as the true subjects and basis of sovereignty. Retroactively, but tellingly, it was in the wake of the violence of 1946–47 that 'the people' were enshrined in the constitution that declared India a republic in 1950.

Focused primarily on Patel, this chapter charts the historical transformation of India's political horizon as sovereign with the aggressive incorporation of the people as the unitary basis of sovereignty. This chapter will reconstruct political ideas of and debates between key individuals to argue that the emphasis in the mid-twentieth century was on what can be termed the 'discovery of people'.[7] A distinction will be drawn here between formal sovereignty and deep sovereignty. Formal sovereignty denotes the territorial understanding of political power that is associated with the national form. Undoubtedly since the late nineteenth century a territorial imagining of India encompassing both the material and the spiritual had become standard currency, articulated through a range of knowledges, practices, aesthetic genres and political

5. Giorgio Agamben, *Stasis: Civil War as a Political Paradigm*, trans. Nicholas Heron (Edinburgh: Edinburgh University Press, 2015).

6. David Armitage, *Civil Wars: A History in Ideas* (New Haven, CT: Yale University Press, 2017) and Paul Cartledge et al., 'Special Issue: David Armitage's *Civil Wars: A History in Ideas*', *Global Intellectual History* 3 (2018).

7. On the elusive nature, but necessary political category, of 'the people', see Alain Badiou et al., *What Is a People?* (New York: Columbia University Press, 2016), esp. the 'Introduction' by Bruno Bosteels and essays by Badiou, Judith Butler and Jacques Rancierre.

ideologies.[8] At the moment of independence, moreover, the matter of territorial boundaries was pre-eminent, and this has been detailed and discussed extensively in relation to the partitioned provinces of British India;[9] indeed, both scholarship and popular perception have been primarily focused on the territorial aspects of the forging of the national project. This is understandable; without undermining the significance of territoriality, however, this chapter will focus on the more elusive, less 'visible' but constitutively necessary aspect of deep sovereignty, founded on 'the people'. 'The people', or general will, is both the subject and object of popular sovereignty. Yet, as Nehru's 'pledge' in 1946, cited in the epigraph to this chapter, testifies, while at that stage 'the people' had become the accepted primary category of politics in India, they had not yet been formally recognised as such in the constitution of a republic.

In December 1946, in the last winter of the British Empire in India, the Constituent Assembly of India was convened. It would meet for another three years, drafting the lengthiest constitution in the world to recast the institutional and political apparatus of India as that of a free country. On the third day of the Assembly, Jawaharlal Nehru tabled the first significant resolution. 'The resolution that I am placing before you', he declared,

> is in the nature of a pledge. . . . A great country is sure to have a lot of controversial issues; but we have tried to avoid controversy as much as possible. The Resolution deals with fundamentals which are commonly held and have been accepted by the people. . . . Unfortunately, our country is full of differences, but no one, except perhaps a few, would dispute the fundamentals which this Resolution lays down. The Resolution states that it is our firm and solemn resolve to have a sovereign Indian republic. We have not mentioned the word 'republic' till this time; but you will understand that a free India can be nothing but a republic.[10]

8. Matthew Edney, *Mapping an Empire: The Geographical Construction of India* (Chicago: University of Chicago Press, 1997); Chandra, *Rise and Growth*; Partha Chatterjee, *Nationalist Thought and the Colonial World: A Derivative Discourse* (London: Zed Books, 1993); Sudipta Kaviraj, *Imaginary Institution of India: Politics and Ideas* (New York: Columbia University Press, 2010); C. A. Bayly, *Origins of Nationality: Patriotism and Ethical Government in the Making of Modern India* (Oxford: Oxford University Press, 2001).

9. Ayesha Jalal, *The Sole Spokesman: Jinnah, the Muslim League and the Demand for Pakistan* (Cambridge: Cambridge University Press, 1985); Joya Chatterji, *Bengal Divided: Hindu Communalism and Partition 1932–1947* (Cambridge: Cambridge University Press, 1994); Tai Yong Tan and Gyanesh Kudaisya, *The Aftermath of Partition in South Asia* (London: Routledge, 2000).

10. Nehru, Resolution.

Nehru's declaration consciously conjugated sovereignty and freedom with the people and a republic. His statement to the effect that independent India would be, ineluctably, a republic was at once understood, even accepted, but represented a sudden departure from the political lexicon that had shaped the moment of arrival of free India. As Nehru confessed, it was perhaps the first time that the term 'republic', with all its transformative potential and future orientation, had been uttered in any powerful forum: it simply had not been part of the received vocabulary. Beyond the rooms and corridors of power within the confines of which Indian negotiations with the Empire took place, the notion of the republic had barely featured in the speeches, writings and political rhetoric of the interwar high nationalist era. 'Freedom' and 'independence' had been the watchwords in relation to sovereignty, while issues of fraternity, as discussed in previous chapters, had become the focus of the political.

The arrival in India of sovereignty in its classic sense of national determination, in August 1947, was the expression of three constitutive and related elements.[11] In the first place, and crucially, it represented the culmination of a historical struggle with a foreign power. Freedom and independence from a foreign ruler were central to the idea of sovereignty understood primarily in terms of territoriality and power and the making of the national project. Secondly, sovereignty entailed the more fractious and contentious issue of the making of what has been termed the 'constitutive outside'.[12] Detachment and freedom from a foreign power was imperative; equally requisite, however, in order to complete the claim to national sovereignty, was the delineation of its limits in relation to the external: 'the Other', or outsiders. For India, the simultaneity of independence and partition created at one stroke, dramatically and in the bloodiest fashion, both formal sovereignty and its immediate and constitutive 'outside', namely Pakistan. The combined event of independence and partition converted the fraternal relationship between Hindus and Muslims into one also of neighbours. Thirdly, and finally, the foundational republican

11. On forms of sovereignty, especially in its non-national form of bio-political power, see Antonio Negri, 'Sovereignty between Government, Exception and Governance', in Hent Kalmo and Quentin Skinner (eds.), *Sovereignty in Fragments: The Past, Present and Future of a Contested Concept* (Cambridge: Cambridge University Press, 2013), 205–21. Negri critiques, as he extends, the ramifications of Michel Foucault's understanding of sovereignty as disciplinary; for an overview of perspectives, see Thomas Blom Hansen and Finn Stepputat, 'Sovereignty Revisited', *Annual Review of Anthropology* 35 (2006), 295–315.

12. Mouffe, *On the Political* and *Democratic Paradox*; Arendt, *On Revolution*.

principle of the popular will—embodied in 'the people'—became the points both of emanation and of completion of sovereignty.

Critically, and unlike in revolutionary France or the earlier civil war era in England, the 'discovery' of the people or general will in India was not an out-come of a dualistic confrontation between a monarchy and its subjects. The overthrow of the imperial order entailed a triangular confrontation: firstly, civil war or the breaking out of open hostility between Hindus and Muslims and Muslims and Sikhs; which was directly related to, secondly, the making of the constitutive outside, or demarcation of the people, whereby the national was founded in relation to a new neighbour; and thirdly, the issue of inheri-tance and heritability (if not royalty) represented by the Indian princely order—deemed, crucially, to be a derivative of British suzerainty. Indian princes, whether the holders of large principalities or of minuscule territories, obstructed their incorporation into the union to varying degrees. The point for emphasis here, however, is that although the presence of Indian princes did indeed pose a limited problem for the coalescence and unification of internal sovereignty, primarily in terms of territoriality, in India, monarchy as the basis of sovereign power had little to no ideological force or momentum behind it: arguments in favour of monarchical power alone did not emerge as a central obstacle to the forging of the republic. Unlike his European counterparts, the king or the sovereign in colonial India was neither singularised nor specified as the site of ultimate power. Ambedkar, as discussed earlier, had in fact identified India's historic sovereignty as a curious case whereby caste and the Brahmin were identifiable as a dispersed monarchy. And although the mere existence of the nearly six hundred satraps, princes and nawabs who had come to represent the 'princely order' under the suzerainty of the British crown and empire—even if their claim to represent any body of people was distinctly questionable—was in practical terms problematic, the casting off of the foreign and imperial yoke that had held ultimate power licensed too the destruction of the Indian princely order that lay below it. Whether it was Nehru, Ambedkar or Sardar Patel who was the primary architect of the republican project, there was a consensus that since Indian 'princes' derived their power, or 'paramountcy' as it was called, from the British crown, they had lost, with the severance of that connection, their dispensation to rule.[13] Any residual claims to monarchical

13. V. P. Menon, *Integration of the Indian States* (London: Longmans, 1956) and *The Trans-fer of Power in India* (London: Longmans, 1957); Ian Copland, *The Princes of India in the Endgame of Empire, 1917–1947* (Cambridge: Cambridge University Press, 1997); Harshan

power were overwhelmed by the civil war and indeed by the considerations of caste that were gaining attention in India's republican moment. Neither gods nor even quite kings, Indian 'princes' were exhorted and eventually obliged by Patel to honour their responsibility to recognise freedom as the 'triumph of popular will'.[14]

Patel certainly merits his enduring reputation as a man of organised action. At the centre of the making of a sovereign order for India, and much like his adversary Jinnah, he did not articulate his political creed in essays or books: his ideas and vision only come into clear view in the speeches he delivered in those eventful years of freedom and partition. While Ambedkar had written a tome on partition and the idea of Pakistan that dealt with a wide variety of pertinent themes from natural rights and the distinction between community and nationality to the testing details of territorial division and population statistics, Patel's ideas, especially on sovereign order, can only be reconstructed from the rhetoric that he deployed in mass public meetings. His forthright speeches may have lacked a contemplative tenor, and were devoid of a conceptual vocabulary, but clarified, nevertheless, in plain and powerful terms, the lineaments of hostility, the work of violence and the stakes involved in historical choices.

Sardar Patel is not alone in his appearance on the cover of *Time*: the totemic figure of a cow, the sacred animal of the Hindus, edges forward from the background to join him.[15] This conjoined image has had a profound effect and powerful afterlife in terms of how the political thrust of the man who was to be India's first home minister is understood. A leading congressman, who left his legal practice in the interwar period to join Gandhi in his country's struggle for independence, Patel is unanimously considered the original strongman of India. Today, however, the image of the cow—the subject of visceral current political polemics in India—seems to have obscured that of the man. Overwhelmingly, the point of debate is whether Patel is indeed representative of Hindu nationalism; and this is the theme which will conclude this chapter.

In 2018, the world's largest statue, depicting Patel, was erected in his home state of Gujarat at the specific behest of Narendra Modi, the Indian

---

Kumarasingham, *A Political Legacy of the British Empire: Power and Parliamentary System in Postcolonial India and Sri Lanka* (London: I. B. Tauris, 2013).

14. Vallabhbhai Patel, *For a United India: Speeches of Sardar Patel, 1947–1950*, 3rd edn (Delhi: Publications Division, Government of India, 1967, [1st edn 1949]), 25.

15. *Time*, 27 January 1947, cover.

prime minister and leader of the Hindu nationalist Bharatiya Janata Party (BJP) who, like Gandhi, is from the same province. This memorial, which joins the global ranks of national statuary as a counterpart to the American celebration of its ideal in the Statue of Liberty, is named 'the Statue of Unity'; and this is a theme with which Patel is specifically identified. The symbolic identification is tellingly apt. As this chapter elaborates, India's freedom became transmuted into the pursuit of a powerful vision of sovereignty, and in historiographical and popular accounts alike, Patel is credited with uniting the country, with making India integral. From the incorporation of nearly six hundred Indian 'princes' and regional satraps to the defining of new borders, Patel remains the central figure in the forging of sovereignty with regard both to its internal depth and its external dimensions. Unity, indeed, becomes synonymous with sovereignty.[16]

The events of 1947 did not simply convert fraternity into the arrival of new and antagonistic neighbours: rather, the kinship of fraternity was aggressively incorporated and even dissolved into a unitary and popular sovereignty. To put it another way, ideas of freedom that had suffused politics for several decades was transformed into a concern with the exercise and experience of sovereignty. The earlier focus on fraternity was overwhelmed by and in favour of 'the people', as India became a republican democracy.

The Civil War of 1947

Pakistan is not in the hands of the British Government.
If Pakistan is to be achieved, Hindus and Muslims will have to fight.
There will be civil war.

—PATEL, JANUARY 1946[17]

Civil war executed the logic of partition as it forcefully blurred the line between the categories of brother and enemy. Through real and potential violence, the civil war displaced and pushed outwards elements and relations of

16. Carl Schmitt, *Political Theology: Four Chapters on the Concept of Sovereignty*, trans. George Schwab (Chicago: University of Chicago Press, 2005).

17. Sardar Patel, speech in Ahmedabad, 15 January 1946, reported in the *Hindustan Times*, in Sumit Sarkar (ed.), *Towards Freedom: Documents on the Movement for Independence in India, 1946*, Part 1 (New Delhi: Indian Council for Historical Research and Oxford University Press, 2007), 274.

proximity to forge a new externality. Civil war or partition violence expresses the paradox that the object of reconciliation and peace is the same as the object of hostility and violence. Hindu–Muslim relations alone guaranteed peace, but the conversion of the insider and the known into the estranged, the outsider and even the enemy violently factionalised the neighbourhood, the family, the circle of the intimate. Partition or division was not the abstract drawing of the line of a border: its most potent realisation took the form of violence. Civil war, as Giorgio Agamben argues, thus operates as the threshold of politics for the conversion and transformation of relations, and between the former solidarity of kinship and the abstract association of citizenship.[18] The personal and the known was shot through with division and violence, as variously recounted in memory portraits, and Gandhi rightly characterised this violence as a 'blood-feud' that was a 'fight between brother and brother'.[19]

As neighbours set upon neighbours, as journeys by train or on foot became perilous in the context of the announcement of boundaries, and as cities and fields smouldered with ambient antagonism, the intimate and the abstract became indistinct. Through a murderous logic, the division of nations and the intimacy of brothers and neighbours, the domestic and the civic, were dissolved. The nature of the division that violently prosecuted a new and national language of exclusion and inclusion was intimate; what historically had been intimate was at the threshold of becoming external.

Paradoxically, though intimate in nature, the perpetration of this violence was shrouded in the anonymity of the collective. The anonymity of the crowd militates against individual culpability and responsibility as it functions as an active agent in concretising new bonds of the collective.[20] The intimate nature of violence is significant when next-door neighbours rather than the army or state machinery become the bearers and perpetrators of aggression in the form of face-to-face combat, while civic institutions, and the police in particular, become entirely partisan. Nor was this dissolving into one of the crowd and the machinery of public order merely the temporary suspension of the norms

18. Agamben, *Stasis*, 7–16.

19. M. K. Gandhi, 'Letter to Jawaharlal Nehru', 7 June 1947, *CWMG* 88, 94–95, at 95; 'Talk with Visitors', 9 June 1947, ibid., 116–17, at 116.

20. Thomas Blom Hansen, 'The Political Theology of Violence in India', *South Asia Multidisciplinary Academic Journal*, special issue 2, http://samaj.revues.org/1872.html; Stanley Tambiah, *Leveling Crowds: Ethnonationalist Conflicts and Collective Violence in South Asia* (Berkeley: University of California Press, 1996); Gustave Le Bon, *The Crowd: A Study of the Popular Mind* (California: CreateSpace Independent Publishing Platform, 2018 [1895]).

of peace, or an exception to order: as Blom Hansen strikingly argues, the crowd in such a case, as it arrogates to itself the right to kill with impunity, becomes 'semi-sovereign'. The intimate and the individual was absorbed into the crowd, the collective, the 'mass' that was visible but, crucially, without culpability, as it became the effective and deadly 'anonymous agency' of the civil war. The crowd was, indeed, 'the dark matter', or the nucleus, of sovereign power in all its brutality.

Civil war, furthermore, and critically, generated a distinction between 'leaders', isolated in their helplessness, and, by contrast, 'the masses', deemed mad in their violent frenzy. 1947 operated as a threshold in which freedom arrived as sovereignty, and it was widely acknowledged that even 'leaders who started this trouble [were] now thoroughly frightened'.[21] The people, who had been the basis of the mass struggle against empire, were no longer the peaceful and pliant subjects of national projects but had become manifest in their most dangerous form.

Direct Action Day, to all intents the opening of the civil war, was declared from Calcutta for 16 August 1946, and the city witnessed large-scale violence that swiftly effected a dramatic reversal in the religious composition of its densely populated neighbourhoods.[22] The mobility of people was then only matched by the mobility of the violence as it spread into the eastern hinterlands of Bihar. Even though at that point the principle of partition had not been agreed upon, to say nothing of territorial specificities of imminent division, Direct Action Day violence proclaimed the depth of hostility and lethal force that would attend the drawing of boundaries in 1947. In the interwar era, violence between Hindus and Muslims and Muslims and Sikhs had already broken out at regular intervals, leading Ambedkar, as we have seen, not only to seek separation in order, as he saw it, to ensure peace, but to declare interreligious relations to be in a state of civil war. Even by the end of 1946, however, when what may have been for Ambedkar a potent metaphor had become devastatingly real, few if any political leaders, such as those who in November toured the wreckage left by the eruption of mass violence in the eastern state of Bihar, described the ongoing and catastrophic violence as civil war; and

21. Sir Evan Jenkins, governor of Punjab, to Governor-General Wavell, 6 March 1947, in Lionel Carter (ed.), *Punjab Politics, 3 March–31 May 1947: At the Abyss: Governors' Fortnightly Reports and Other Key Documents* (New Delhi: Manohar, 2007; hereafter Carter (ed.), *Abyss*), 59.

22. Janam Mukherjee, *Hungry Bengal: War, Famine, Riots and the End of Empire* (London: Hurst & Co., 2015).

they were far from being alone in this. Though a prevalent feature of history, civil war is rarely owned: discussing the profound reluctance to name it as such notwithstanding its historical ubiquity, David Armitage, in his recent historical genealogy of global civil wars, refers to it as a 'Cinderella' concept of politics. Seen primarily as pathological, even immoral, its potency is all the more intense, insofar as the disruption to order it entails is entirely internal. Due to its internal nature of strife and as disorder, civil wars have often been at best dismissed by rulers and philosophers as momentary aberrations and at worst denied altogether. Yet whether it concerns the conflicts within the Roman Republic or the modern world-historical event of the American Civil War, internal strife or civil war, Armitage contends, has been to a greater extent than war between states a determining factor in the making and unmaking of political orders.[23]

Histories of civil war, largely deemed to be war without winners, have obscured its political nature by rendering the issue of violence as one of management and manipulation. The existing historiography of the partition amply demonstrates the compulsion to explain the mass violence that accompanied the moment of transition from servitude to sovereignty either in terms of a concern with the administration of the partition arrangements or as a matter of individual or family experience, thus managing to evacuate what was in fact a civil war of any political potency. Though the prime text on the morality of fratricide—namely the *Mahabharata*, and in particular the *Gita*—had animated the political thought of various foundational figures, few if any invoked these texts at the historical moment of the fratricide of 1946–47. Rather, this violence rooted in intimacy has been treated as a family secret of Hindus and Muslims, and even of India and Pakistan, and never named as civil war. In the testimonies and memorial accounts that continue to proliferate, the violence is represented as something that just 'happened', almost as if the product of an external if exigent force of history, to erstwhile neighbouring groups that until that point had lived in comfortable proximity, even if not in harmony; or else the events are seen as a 'moment of madness' in which history as horror inexplicably overwhelmed humanity.[24] The profoundly intimate nature of this violence, in short, is displaced into the realm of an abstract externality, whether of 'history' or a collective irrationality. Ironically, the work and effect of this violence was precisely to produce an externality out of intimacy.

23. Armitage, *Civil Wars*.
24. Nehru to Patel, 5 November 1946, Patel Papers, NMML.

The official record testifies to the utter reluctance on the part of political leaders to call the violence by its true name, even as their notes at the same time detailed 'attempts to exterminate' religious rivals. Visiting and reporting on areas of Bihar where hundreds had been killed by erstwhile neighbours and tens of thousands had suddenly been totally uprooted by killings or the fear of them, Nehru was typically squeamish: describing the state of affairs as 'quite as bad and something even worse than anything' that any supposedly 'exaggerated' account may have reported, and the violence itself as 'incredibly brutal and inhuman', he was able at most to refer to it as a 'big uprising' that had generated a kind of 'ill-will' with 'terrible effects', making it a 'horror that [would] last a long time.'[25]

The structure and form of violence radicalised the force of the 'outsider', fulfilling the purposive logic of fratricide, which was to both expunge existing solidarity and form the lineaments of the new internal. To cite an illustration: a representative report from a large village of five thousand residents in Bihar, surveyed by leaders of both the League and Congress, points to core features of the fratricide that were typical of multiple sites from late 1946 to the early months of 1948. In this instance, Hindus comprised two-thirds of the original population of the village. Firstly, an exchange of rabid slogans and news from elsewhere—in this case from distant Patna city—of violent conflagrations precipitated firing and armed looting, as open conflict broke out between Hindus and Muslims with the active support of co-religionists from outside the village. Secondly, the piecemeal interventions of police and soldiers became entirely partisan, providing security only to co-religionists. Thirdly, 'private grudges' that existed between families in the village were integrated and settled by violence. Fourthly, the outnumbered party—here Muslims who had 'been living in a beleaguered state' and in 'fear of their neighbours'—gave in to apprehension and moved out, their 'evacuation' being completed within a few days as 'mobs' were still repeatedly threatening an attack even after the conflict had abated. Finally, and most significantly for our purposes here, as the report haplessly concluded, since the violence was enacted by 'crowds' who also 'usually took away the dead', it was impossible for authorities or leaders to count or know the exact number of casualties, let alone assign responsibility for the violence and killings.[26] Both the imperial archive and private testimonies confirm the widespread repetition of this sequence of violence, whereby former

25. Ibid.
26. 'Third Note on Bihar Disturbances', 8 November 1946, Patel Papers, NMML.

neighbours and those proximate and known to each other became lethally hostile. From such villages in Bihar to cities in Punjab, and across the eastern and western frontiers, the process of ruthless separation was prosecuted to create Hindu and Muslim majority territories in the very areas where Hindus and Muslims had been most inextricably intertwined.

The violence in Punjab, described as a 'slaughter-house', had made its people 'lunatic'. The perilous movement of people in fact was seen as a contagion of 'terror' and a violent mobility through which the new boundaries of the two new nations came into existence.[27] The widespread contagion of violence and hostility was such that, as Patel noted, 'Hindu, Muslim and Sikh cannot stay together amicably', rendering the 'terrorised' atmosphere one in which no appeal for peace, even by Gandhi, could have any effect.[28] This civil warfare was neither entirely unsystematic nor merely expressive of repressed hatreds, however: the means of violence that were mobilised ranged from the people's own household knives to batons, guns and other weaponry gathered by the armed volunteers of various political parties.[29]

The civil war had in fact unleashed the 'underworld' of political parties, whether in the form of the Muslim League Guards, the RSS or the organised *jathas* of various Sikh groups, in violent partisanship, leaving their leaders to deliberate or appeal sanctimoniously for peace in speeches. The absence of 'justice', or more precisely the evisceration of any authority capable of meting out punishment, completed the conditions for the perpetuation of violence as civil strife. At the height of killings, in June 1947, officials admitted that not one person had been hanged for any of the violence. The absence of sovereign authority was absolute: incapable of protecting life, it also lacked even the capacity to take life for the sake of civil peace.[30]

Patel recognised that civil war was but the absence of sovereign authority. The imminence of independence prior to the establishment of a new sovereign authority had produced a lethal hiatus. Patel was quick to stress, however, that

27. Patel to Gandhi, 24 August 1947, in Vallabhbhai Patel, *The Collected Works of Sardar Vallabhbhai Patel*, ed. P. N. Chopra and Prabha Chopra (New Delhi: Konark Publishers, 1998; hereafter *CWSVP*), 12, 170.

28. Patel to Gandhi, 27 August 1947, *CWSVP* 12, 172–73.

29. William Gould, 'Hindu Militarism and Partition in 1940s Uttar Pradesh: Rethinking the Politics of Violence and Scale', *South Asia* 42:1 (2019), 134–51.

30. Jenkins to Mountbatten, 25 June 1947, in Lionel Carter (ed.), *Punjab Politics, 1 June 1947–14 August 1947: Tragedy: Governors' Fortnightly Reports and Other Key Documents* (New Delhi: Manohar, 2007; hereafter Carter (ed.), *Tragedy*), 101, 105.

the assumption of power by free India would bring peace. Gandhi had rejected the presence and continued mediation of the British as a third party that was only capable of enforcing an armed intervention as opposed to real peace; Patel went further to argue that the British imperial position as a supposedly 'neutral' presence that nevertheless remained 'in power' was in fact a 'way of propagating civil war'. This was a classic statement and understanding of the necessary conditions of sovereignty, to the effect that the holding of power without the arrogation to itself of violence ('neutrality', in Patel's terms) was the short road to civil strife. Underscoring this ideal, Patel bombastically de-clared that there would be 'peace within a week' with the assumption of 'the necessary power to put down disorder'.[31] Recognising perhaps the sheer force of the civil war, the Empire's 'men on the spot' such as Evan Jenkins, the last governor of undivided Punjab, dismissed the accusation that it was British presence that was 'fostering chaos'. Speaking for others in his position, Jenkins confessed to Mountbatten that British officials were inclined to leave precisely because they were now in the midst of 'people who are out to destroy them-selves [in a] civil war'.[32] For Patel, however, such a position had been 'con-tributory' to the escalation of strife and not 'conducive to the restoration of peace and confidence'. As conflagrations raged and multiplied, this self-exculpatory perspective of the decamping rulers, 'distant' even in their depar-ture, he argued to be 'illegal'. Imperial 'prestige' he regarded as a function of a fake neutrality; it was no 'consolation' to those killed, nor even legitimate, but had instead only incited further 'hostility' amongst the people.[33]

By March 1947, the violent situation in Punjab had the potential to split even what remained of British imperial sovereignty in India. With the eruption of violence and Hindus and Sikhs in effect forming one side of the antagonism, the machinery of the outgoing imperial state, the British argued, would have to be 'involved on the Muslim side' in the 'civil war for possession'. In the face of this choice, British imperial self-extrication seemed preferable, and viable, with a powerful view asserting that 'constitutional niceties no longer matter' in what was after all a 'final struggle for power'. In its final throes of empire, the primary aim of British rule was thus to leave without itself being divided along the new national frontiers.[34] While Nehru and Patel were demanding martial

31. Bombay Chronicle, 10 May 1947, CWSVP 12, 85.
32. Jenkins to Mountbatten, 16 April 1947, in Carter (ed.), Abyss, 138.
33. Patel to Evan Jenkins, 27 June 1947, in Carter (ed.), Tragedy, 125.
34. Jenkins to Wavell, 6 March 1947, in Carter (ed.), Abyss, 58.

law, and Jinnah went further, ordering even his co-religionist Muslims to be shot to end brutality,[35] the Empire, in its final act, rather created conditions for the dispersal and multiplication of violence. As early as January 1947, a short-lived ban on the armed volunteers of both the Muslim Guards and the RSS was lifted in Punjab by the imperial authorities, and this was done in the name of freedom and the instituting of 'civil liberties'.[36] The people had indeed been set free: to fight and kill.

Precisely because the making of intimates into enemies actively engaged in hostile combat constituted a civil war, the British authorities were content to regard the state of affairs as one that did not concern them. The effect of their presence might well be, as Patel argued, to function as a third party that was actually stoking the civil war, yet in the face of catastrophic violence the Empire simply withdrew its sovereign presence from the scene. With its abandoning of any role for itself in enforcing peace, the primal scene of the birth of a newly distributed 'people' as 'national' was enacted in the most visibly brutal form possible. Identifying them as the third party involved, however, did not stop Patel, like Jinnah, from entreating the British to declare a state of emergency. Jinnah's right-hand man Liaqat Ali also urged that the British 'could not evade responsibility' and indeed 'could not possibly walk out' of the 'civil war'.[37] On the eve of the declaration of partition, however, the plea was rejected, and the violence classified as an entirely domestic matter. The 'difficulty' as understood by the retiring sovereigns of the Empire lay in the nature of 'facts', the most significant of these being, it was supposed, that 'hostility' was 'universal', such that even if emergency measures were to be introduced, the outgoing masters and rulers would not have the capacity to enforce them. Even martial law was judged to be impotent and 'unlikely to affect the situation materially'.[38] With the exception of Gandhi, all the main Indian leaders asked for martial law; but the British, dismissing the appeals from all such quarters and heeding instead Gandhi's historic call, had resolutely decided to 'quit India'. As a matter of policy, British troops had in fact been withdrawn from service and were being repatriated even prior to the official declaration of

35. Gandhi, *Patel*, 419.

36. Jenkins to Mountbatten, 16 April 1947, in Carter (ed.), *Abyss*, 136; for a description of the cycle of violence in the initial months of the year, ibid., 134–38.

37. Note by Jenkins, 25 May 1947, in Carter (ed.), *Abyss*, 214.

38. Jenkins to John Colville (acting viceroy for a fortnight), 25 May 1947, in ibid., 212.

independence.[39] Even under intense pressure from Nehru, Patel and Jinnah to account for the mass killings in Punjab on the British watch, the Empire freely owned up to being an absent sovereign forgoing the command of rule. In the face of intense criticism, the outgoing imperial authority dismissed calls to assume the responsibilities of power in the face of violence as fundamentally misplaced: a case of 'false premises' and misrecognition of the situation. It needed to be recognised, imperial officials contended, that the state of civil war could not be attributed to British rule: 'rule' implied a 'degree of permanence', and the 'troubles' of civil war were for the British a sign that the last 'remains' of that rule were 'now ending'.[40] The official record and political rhetoric of this year were replete with metaphors of beginnings and endings. The defining tropes of civil war and a revolution-like situation were repeatedly cited as forces oppositional and dangerous to sovereign order. Such invocations betrayed the British as being indeed essentially a third party, unable to contain hostilities, let alone enforce peace. The vanishing sovereign, as it continued to relay messages of its own demise, soon became merely a witness of catastrophic violence.[41]

These imperial authorities crucially understood the civil war as a choice in relation to control and 'conquest'. Evan Jenkins, the last imperial governor of Punjab, in briefing Viceroy Wavell a couple of months before the declaration of partition, initially dismissed the widespread talk of 'civil war', on the assumption that 'no one community can rule the Punjab with its present boundaries except by conquest'. He further thought that such premonitions of strife had existed for some length of time: 'There has been much talk about "civil war" with forebodings of suffering on a scale unknown . . . for more than a century.' It is striking that Jenkins thus compared the scale of the violence to the most violent event in nineteenth-century India. Though he did not name it, the dating of these forebodings makes it clear that the reference is to the Indian Mutiny and Rebellions. The Mutiny was instructive: that episode of violence had ended in full conquest and the formal recognition of imperial sovereignty. In his own time of 1947 and in the face of the civil war, however, Jenkins noted that in this new strife, 'conquest' would prove 'inconclusive', and

39. Gandhi, *Patel*, 344–45, 419.

40. Memorandum by Jenkins, 3 August 1947, in Carter (ed.), *Tragedy*, 206.

41. Agamben in *Stasis* separates revolution from civil war. For a firsthand account of the British quitting India, see Penderel Moon, *Divide and Quit* (London: Chatto & Windus, 1961).

that 'the result of a "civil war" would in fact be partition'. The comparison between 1857 and 1947 was relevant to the extent that these two violent moments
marked British conquest on the one hand, and departure on the other; at the
height of the violence in the summer months of 1947, the civil war had obscured the identity of any new power that could control the widespread violence. There was, however, a complete disjunction between the violence of the
Mutiny and that of 1947. Crucially, unlike the rebellion ninety years previously,
the violence now was between intimates: the British alone were spared its fury.
Such a hostile intimacy confirmed both the fratricidal nature of this violence
and the complete irrelevance of the Empire.[42]

The Empire's vanishing suzerainty had produced the conditions for popular sovereignty to emerge precisely through a blurring of law and violence.
Civil war contained within it both the evisceration and the emergence of
sovereignty, old and new, imperial and popular—a fact that was not missed
by the imperial authorities when they repeatedly asserted that 'Punjab is not
now in a constitutional but in a revolutionary situation'.[43] A revolutionary
situation had indeed come to pass, as officials anxiously noted that neither
law nor its representatives, civil or armed, were 'recognised' by the people.[44]
In June 1947, soon after the official declaration of the partition plan, Nehru
had raised publicly the issue of the nature of British power and control, noting that 'no authority [was] left in the country to enforce order', as the new
(national) sovereigns had not yet assumed power. Admonishing the Empire,
he wondered aloud where exactly imperial authority had vanished so quickly,
given that only recently it had controlled and quelled the national 'civil
disobedience'.[45] The outgoing Empire's fleeing officials for their part reminded
Nehru that earlier events through the 1940s were 'concentrated' acts against
the 'government'. 1947, they argued, was different, not only in degree but in
kind, as the Punjab, they categorically concluded, was in a state of 'revolution'.[46]
Depiction of the scenario as one of 'revolution' served to emphasise sovereign
dimensions in their disordered form. The breakdown enhanced the capacity
of violence to change the established order. The conflation of civil war with
revolution derived from the shared feature of violence, with 'revolution'

42. Jenkins to Wavell, 7 March 1947, in Carter (ed.), *Abyss*, 63.
43. Jenkins to Mountbatten, 16 April 1947, in ibid., 138.
44. Jenkins to Mountbatten, 30 April 1947, in ibid., 144.
45. Extract, *The Tribune*, 16 June 1947, in Carter (ed.), *Tragedy*, 81.
46. Jenkins to Mountbatten, 16 June 1947, in ibid., 80.

moreover strongly implying not simply disorder or the overthrow of the existing order, but, significantly, novelty.[47]

Patel too understood the full revolutionary potency of the moment and likened it to the 'light that is seen before the sun rises'.[48] Further metaphors adorned Patel's rhetoric to impress upon his hearers' minds his vision of the new political order of 'the people', whom he deemed 'anxious', because it was their sun that was rising. He compared this to the convulsion of the body that on rising after being 'suddenly cured' from a long illness is dangerously prone to ravenousness.

It is striking that metaphors of sovereignty took the form of the body itself, conflating it with the collective but also equivocating between the collective, the people, as the new sovereign power, even as protagonists, leaders or representatives sought to direct and discipline it. While the Hobbesian behemoth, or revolutionary potential of people, and even the leviathan, or machine of the state, remained distant, neither a monarch nor an emperor, the ambiguous yet pervasive presence of the people had conjured a new sovereign order: one that had arrived, but not quite arisen yet in its ordered form. For Patel, the 'ravenous' and dark convulsion signalled civil war or revolution in its violent dimensions with a distinct sequence of a beginning and end; he sought to absorb and convert this violence into an enduring body politic.

In June 1947, although partition had been announced, the boundaries remained indeterminate, and North India was violently mobilised and on fire. Nehru wrote that cities such as Amritsar or Lahore were 'ruins' and feared their turning into a 'heap of ashes'.[49] The skies were thick with smoke and the land disrupted by the movement of imperilled people, both heartlands and border territories strewn with camps.[50] In surveying the effects of the civil war, Nehru initially thought the 'human aspect' too 'appalling to contemplate'. Yet he did contemplate it, and understood it as the 'human capacity to endure

47. Arendt, *On Revolution*, 10–45.

48. Speech in Delhi, 14 May 1947, *CWSVP* 12, 94.

49. Nehru to Mountbatten, 22 June 1947, in Nicholas Mansergh and Penderel Moon (eds.), *The Transfer of Power 1942–7: Constitutional Relations between Britain and India*, vol. 11: *The Mountbatten Viceroyalty: Announcement and Reception of the 3 June Plan, 31 May–7 July 1947* (London: HMSO, 1982), 561.

50. Sunil Purushotham, *From Raj to Republic: Sovereignty, Violence, and Democracy in India* (Stanford: Stanford University Press, 2021) expands upon the centrality of partition violence and the settling of the refugees in forging India's new sovereign order.

misfortune'. Nehru rendered the horror as both acute and—significantly—immune from the assignment of individual responsibility:

> I do not know if it can be said that what is happening in Lahore is beyond human control. It is certainly beyond the control of those who ought to control it. I do not know who is to blame and I do not want to blame anybody for it. But the fact remains that horror succeeds horror and we cannot put a stop to it. Meanwhile vast numbers of human beings ... live in the midst of this horror. .... It is curious that when tragedy affects an individual, we feel the full force of it, but when the individual is multiplied a thousand-fold, our senses are dulled, and we become insensitive.[51]

Nehru was far from insensitive. Rather, in his ability to empathise with individual misery, he sought to numb its sheer horror by absorbing the force of violence into the capacities of the collective. Senses could only be understood as 'dulled' to the extent that they were overwhelmed by the force and the scale of violence. Such a force as was able to overwhelm the individual could only belong to the collective or masses, or, simply put, the people. In their manifest form, the people were imbued with both danger and possibility.

Dissolved into the collective mass, unindividuated violence defied a precise locus of perpetration and responsibility, and civil war was further understood as a function of time and a temporary breakdown. Ahistorical and a form of 'madness', its brutality perversely offered the potential of hope. Such hope, with which the civil war was pregnant, brought into sharp focus the coming of a new deity: namely, the people. If for the Indian national triumvirate on the one hand, and Jinnah on the other, partition was the price of sovereignty in its categorical national form, then it was civil war, spectre and enactment that produced its most crucial and constitutive element: namely, demarcation and delimitation of the people in their bounded and national sense.

Defying an easy sequence of cause and effect or the decision for partition and its consequent violence, 'civil war' instead was the dark matter and arguably even the nucleus that made coherent and propelled the moment of recognition of independence as sovereignty. Partition, in other words, was not a delayed reaction for protagonists, but would increasingly be associated with 'the people' who carried the cross as pliant keepers of a sovereign peace that constituted and completed the political subject of the nation; and much of the

51. Nehru to Mountbatten, 22 June 1947, in Mansergh and Moon (eds.), *Transfer of Power*, 561–62.

rhetorical labour of national leaders was directed to that end. The people, how-ever, was also the elusive yet potent force that through violent mobility, as neither quite agents nor perpetrators, but as an anonymous collective of civil war, carried the ambient potentiality of completing the project of national sovereignty. The rule of the people had to contend, however, with Gandhi's radical—and prevailing—understanding of sovereignty as self-mastery.

From Swaraj to Sovereignty

We have to shed cowardice, that is the meaning of fighting sword with sword. Except India the world fights sword with sword.[52]

—PATEL, JANUARY 1947

In the event of civil war, questions of life and death that had founded and ani-mated Gandhi's political project became pre-eminent. Though Gandhi himself would become increasingly powerless, Patel prevailed, and this was partly because he pirated a powerful Gandhian vocabulary, effectively appropriating and deploying Gandhian concepts as an arsenal in his own project to convert freedom into sovereignty. In instituting a new normative vocabulary and ex-perience of unitary sovereignty, Patel was instrumental in displacing the tenets of Swaraj as expounded by Gandhi. Gandhi's concept of Swaraj, as discussed earlier, had comprehended sovereignty, understood especially in terms of the ability to kill and to protect life, as a capacity of the individual. Detached from any abstract authority, the Mahatma's principles of self-mastery and sacrifice had made the anti-statist subject the pivot of an ethical and experiential poli-tics, and his political project radicalised nonviolence not as a passive principle, but through truth and civil disobedience, arming the individuated political subject against the temptations of violence. Patel's political rhetoric in 1947–48 redirected these powerful political precepts and integrated them into a new normative vocabulary of an all-encompassing sovereignty that opened and defined an ideological schism between him and Nehru, with echoes that have lasted to date.

Addressing the issue of violence as action and as a responsibility of the people in January 1947, in a speech purportedly explaining the 'edifices for swaraj erected by Gandhi', Patel wrested these entirely from the meaning in-vested in them by their author and revised the stated relationship between

52. Speech at Gujarat Vidyapeeth, 5 January 1947, CWSVP 12, 4.

violence and politics. 'Nonviolence also means that we shoulder the responsibility to protect the people and where there is danger, we need not hide, but
die while fighting the attackers.' Thus, 'to escape' when under threat, Patel went
on to assert, was to be worse even than an 'animal', and only betrayed cowardice. Concluding this exhortation to shun cowardice and take up the sword,
however, Patel added a caveat, admitting that to do so would be to propagate
a 'vicious cycle', and one that Gandhi had urged Indians to break out of.[53] This
would be typical of Patel's rhetorical style, as he invoked but simultaneously
displaced the meaning and content of Gandhi's precepts to create an opposite
series of effects and meaning. Fearlessness in the face of violence was undoubtedly central to Gandhi's philosophy, but to urge the bravery to act violently in
self-defence was to subvert Gandhism entirely. The conversion of courage as
moral action into the courage of violent defence at once deployed and remade
the Gandhian understanding of political action.

This speech by Patel led Nehru in January 1947 to declare haplessly to Gandhi his wish to relinquish office; Patel immediately dismissed Nehru's wish to
resign as an 'empty threat'. On being questioned by an irate Gandhi, who was
then at the epicentre of violence in Noakhali, Patel's initial plea was that his
speech had been reported selectively or out of context; but he admitted, as he
often did, that it was his 'habit to speak out unsavoury truths to people in the
plainest manner.'[54] What was this truth—in itself a primary Gandhian category of politics—that Patel took to be unsavoury yet worthy of plain expression? Deploying a species of doublespeak, Patel dismantled whilst invoking
Gandhi's understanding of violence, truth and, simply put, the political. It
would be inappropriate to understand his rhetoric as the mere destruction of
Gandhi's tenets, however. Rather, Patel opened a breach, splitting the
Gandhian foundations of the political that in fact had also been the Sardar's
own for over two decades; and by breaching the established Gandhian norm,
he was instituting the possibility of a new norm. His 'doublespeak' betrayed
the perplexity involved in his seeking now to depart from the freedom movement that Gandhi had spearheaded and to assume the task of founding the
nation as a new beginning. Such beginning or founding entailed either violence or the commandeering of violence, however; and in signalling thus a
breach from Gandhi's nonviolence, Patel was in effect announcing a transition
from freedom to its converted form as sovereignty.

53. Ibid.
54. Patel to Gandhi, 7 January 1947, *CWSVP* 12, 4–5.

Throughout 1947 and 1948, Patel steadfastly maintained that the potential, means and ends of violence rested with the people. A few months after the speech cited above, in April 1947, he once again pointed out the virtues of self-defence. This time, he urged even those villagers who were far removed from the epicentres of the civil war to 'no longer look to the Police for protection', but rather to organise their own 'patrol parties' that alone could ensure their safety amidst the 'problem'. The people were thus to be their own policemen and effectively themselves become the defensive cordon against a violence that was also generically of the people.[55] In a sense, of course, Patel's appeal was redundant, as it was common knowledge that members of all communities were already armed,[56] and the police was deemed incapable of any 'decisive action', being either part of the partisan conflict or simply devoid of any capacity to enforce order, let alone peace.[57]

Such as it was, policing reflected the new division of the partition: without any supervisory authority and fully partisan, the police were next to indistinguishable from the crowd. For Patel, it was the 'aggressive attitudes adopted by Muslims' in particular that remained the 'serious challenge to law and order'.[58] He took this to be the logic of separation and partition, and the blurring of the line between police and the mob exemplified for him the way in which Muslim officials were in effect all representatives of the Muslim League, and that even in the police force 'Pakistan was in action'. The formal declaration of Pakistan, he asserted, would entail the assumption of 'responsibility' for the violence that had broken out.[59]

In the event, Patel called on the one hand for 'clean fighting', and on the other, for a moment of hiatus in the violence to enable the opening of a relatively peaceful corridor for people to move across new borders and thereby exchange their minority status for membership of a 'majority'. In a speech in Amritsar in 1947, he went as far as to invoke the 'laws of war' that allowed for such a momentary pause. Both at the height of violence and in peaceful pauses, he continued to pursue the logic of division or partition as the necessary

55. Tribute to the people of Ras, *Bombay Chronicle*, 6 April 1947, ibid., 29.
56. Enclosure in a letter by Baldev Singh to Patel, 14 July 1947, ibid., 130.
57. Jenkins to Mountbatten, 25 June 1947, in Carter (ed.), *Tragedy*, 100.
58. Patel to prime ministers of various provinces, 15 May 1947, *CWSVP* 12, 95. Even civil appointments reflected the new division, and in overt terms of religious identity: see Patel to Mountbatten, 6 June 1947, cancelling appointments of Muslims onto the Tariff Board, ibid., 101.
59. Patel to Congress party delegates, 16 June 1947, ibid., 107.

condition for the attainment of national sovereign power. A few months later, soon after independence, he both invoked and qualified the effectiveness of the law as a weapon against violence: 'Ruthlessness or rigour of repressive machinery of Government can and has enabled us to gain a sudden improvement'; but, he warned, 'it is neither creditable to you nor to us to have recourse to such a distasteful course.'[60]

Recognising, even thereby legitimating, the civil nature of the strife, Patel demanded—in a mutilated echo of Gandhi—fearlessness of death. The language of peace was replaced by that of a protection that emanated from the civil order itself. Discounting any possibility of protection from the political order, whether the army or the police, Patel returned the potentiality of violence and nonviolence, protection and policing, to the body of the people. In the face of escalating violence, in May 1947 at a public meeting in Delhi, he declared,

> In such hard times we should keep our minds strong and learn to protect oneself and those around us. It is our duty to protect our family. Do not run after the police but do the work of policeman yourself. That means you must be fearless. Even police die. It is an undisputed fact that death is a surety for every living being. We must love to learn death. . . . If a third person does any harm to us, we should suffer ungrudgingly with a proper understanding. That is the Gandhian way. Either you go on Gandhian way [sic] or the way of the world. That is my advice to you in these hard times.[61]

If a few months earlier Patel's plain speaking had redirected the principles of Swaraj, now suffering and Satyagraha, the Gandhian precepts that underpinned nonviolence, whereby death was embraced as sacrifice, also underwent displacement and redirection. Most significantly, Patel wrested sovereignty away from Gandhi's understanding of it as experiential and a category of selfhood, and indeed death as sacrificial. Posing a stark choice between Gandhi and 'the way of the world', he sought instead to redistribute the available Gandhian language of sovereignty. Yet he did not seek to identify it with the state, or even government. Rather, the people as police, as both protectors and killers, became the custodians of life and death—that is, of sovereignty itself. As discussed in Chapter 4, and elsewhere, Gandhi had taken death, as opposed to life, as central to a sovereignty of the political subject that had elevated dying

---

60. Appeal to citizens of Delhi in the *Bombay Chronicle*, 13 September 1947, ibid., 200.
61. Speech at a public meeting in Delhi, 14 May 1947, ibid., 94.

over killing, as the Mahatma rendered death as indissoluble individual capacity and responsibility. Gandhi's Swaraj, though potent indeed, was nevertheless unamenable to an institutional and collective representation.

For Gandhi, fearlessness of the subject, individual and collective, ensured a recursive but necessary relationship between the ethical and the political domains that allowed for the discovery of their true meaning and limits. Ethics and politics were thus not merely co-constitutive, but mutually recognisable. Given Gandhi's emphasis on the individual as the preferred subject of a mutual discovery of politics and ethics, sovereignty was indivisible, as it emanated from and was deposited within the self. For Patel, by contrast—the archthinker of sovereignty, but in its more normative and national sense—the shores of the political were to be discovered in and through the people and the civil order more generally. The scenario wherein violence and law became dangerously blurred nevertheless attached this violence to the people as civil war conjured the new horizon of the political. For Patel recognised that both the potency of violence and the capacity for protection against it lay with the people, or collective civil order: extracted from its ethical encasement, political violence was deemed instrumental to popular sovereign power, and Patel asserted that the potential for both violence and peace resided not within the individual, but within the people. Such a displacement and revision of Gandhi's understanding of violence allowed Patel to transpose the representation of the disordered civic body into the institutional order of the new state, a purely political entity, and one that would now oscillate between the poles of the people and government. Such an ideological remaking did not merely displace, but rejected, the Gandhian opposition between the individual and the state. Patel articulated this remaking of sovereignty as a choice between ethics and politics, and, starkly, as one between Gandhi and the new order. Repeatedly he explained that the choice now was between the uniquely and distinctively Gandhian position and one that was more in keeping with the norms and ways of the world. Gandhi's distinctive idea of sovereignty was effectively rendered marginal. In articulating action as a form of choice between Gandhi's method and the way of the world, Patel sought a breach with, a transgression of, even a departure from, the principle of nonviolent action, a breach wherein India's new sovereign status, authorised by the people in its brute and violent form, would be more like that of the world of the nation-states than the unconventional individualised project of political subjectivity that Gandhi had proposed.

The logic of the political as national and sovereign, as Patel understood it, demanded the dismantling of Gandhi's Swaraj, as the new project was focused on the making of a unity out of the multiple, whereas the Mahatma's project had made the self the singular subject of the political, and this was a singularity that defied any 'gathering' into the unitary. The potential for the conversion of the multiple into a concrete unit lay within the civil war itself. The choice between a Gandhian idea of sacrifice and self-defence by violence indicated also a transition from a Swaraj based on the individual self and the new singularity of the people, or the general will, as the subject of sovereignty. Through a rhetoric that pirated Gandhi's understanding of violence as inherent in the individual subject and thrust it into the domain of the collective, Patel managed to render Swaraj synonymous with the sovereignty of the people. (This was a redirection of Gandhi's precepts that did not go unnoticed, however, and was precisely what opened an acrimonious rift between Nehru and Patel, deriving from differing understandings of the meaning of violence, and in particular the role of the RSS in the context of the civil war; this is discussed in the concluding section of this chapter.) Thus, in the context of widespread violence, Patel oriented the conditions of civil war towards the articulation a new sovereign order, of and by the people: he annexed the cause and context of this civil war—namely, the partition—as the founding moment of a new unity of the people, devoid of radical individuality, enabling the replacing of Swaraj by the aggressive pursuit of unitary sovereignty.

The Unity of Division: Patel and Sovereign Power

I was convinced that in order to keep India united it must be divided now.

—PATEL, AUGUST 1947[62]

Addressing mass public rallies in the defining year of 1947, the famously plain-speaking Patel emerged as the locus of authority and sovereign power in India. It was he who, in his deceptively simple but potently clear speeches, sought to normalise partition, identifying it with unity, and folding the people into the new dispensation of sovereignty.

In dealing directly with the paradox of the fact that partition and violence had been integral to the moment of freedom and decolonisation, Patel aimed to deplete the force of the unfolding contradictions not only between violence

62. Speech to citizens of Delhi during liberty celebrations, 11 August 1947, *CWSVP* 12, 152–54, at 153.

and freedom, but between unity and division. He did so neither by negating nor neglecting these. Instead, he repeatedly and directly presented the paradox as representing a choice that was suffused with the force of history. In his speeches, he sought to present partition as a momentous but considered decision: neither inevitable, nor the unintended consequence of the historical struggle between the Empire and India, but imbued with a sense of the historic decision-making that is generally associated with sovereign power. Patel folded in the historic with the personal, and this new unity born of division, by means of a plain and powerful rhetoric, became crucial to the development of a new language and norm of sovereignty.

In August 1947, a few days prior to the official date of independence, on the occasion of its celebration in New Delhi, Patel opened his address by co-opting the force of history as a political choice, stating,

> My colleagues and I have agreed to partition of the country not because of fear or out of a sense of defeat. Under the prevailing conditions in the country partition on the present pattern was the best thing possible and I have no qualms about it.[63]

He thus presented partition as the product of a conscious resolution, asserting ownership of it and approaching it in a realistic spirit that contrasted with the reaction of his political peers such as Nehru or Gandhi, who appeared overwhelmed by the pathos of the situation—by remorse, helplessness and a sense of tragedy. Curiously, the historical record of the same speech exists in two entirely different versions, both in officially authorised collections of Patel's papers, and it is unclear why this should be the case. In the works edited by Chopra and Chopra published in 1998, the overall thrust of the speech is towards Patel's exhortations for the 'consolidation' of a 'well-knit united power' for India; partition, in this version, is explained as the result of the Muslim League's 'obstructionism' and the solution to a vicious 'deadlock' in the face of violent strife. Ostensibly the same speech, however, as originally published in 1949 in a collection by the Government of India, and cited here, is shot through with a sense of personal responsibility for decisions taken with regard to the question of division and unity. Both versions of the same speech, nevertheless, give profound insights into the elements in play for the remaking

---

63. Speech in New Delhi, 11 August 1947 ('First Things First'), in Patel, *For a United India*, 125 (the same speech as that in *CWSVP* 12 cited in the epigraph to this section, but the two texts differ widely).

of sovereignty and its power that Patel assiduously assembled in order to re-alise the project of India as a united entity.

Partisan politics and current polemics in India have generated the accusation that Patel's foundational role has been deliberately and maliciously written out of history so as to present Nehru exclusively as the representative figure of free India. This perceived erasure of Patel is today being enthusiastically compensated for by his reinsertion into public life, with invigorated commemoration in statues and in public commentary, with some going so far as to declare him 'the man who saved India'.[64] It would be a mistake to interpret the dual official record of the same speech purely as a function of competitive commemoration of founding figures; though it does remain unclear why two very different versions of the same historic speech exist, something more fundamental is at stake. Minimally, the second version, published decades later, in which the element of personal decision-making that Patel originally articulated is expunged, might be taken as symptomatic of the realisation, indeed the normalisation, of sovereign India. More generally, however, a reticence regarding, even a distaste for, the personal is integral to the conceptual history of modern sovereignty itself.

In his pithy and highly influential exegesis of Hobbes, Schmitt suggests that in the modern articulation of sovereignty, impersonal rules and institutional perspectives have edged out the personal element that he terms 'decisonistic'. In uncovering the sway of the decisionism that underlies sovereign power, Schmitt argues that this denial of the personal, absorbed now into normative rules and institutional practices, derives historically from negation of the absolute power of the monarch. With the modern desacralisation of power, and the overthrowing of monarchy in particular, the people, or the general will, became sovereign, whereby the 'decisionistic and personalistic element in the concept of sovereignty was lost'.[65] While 'the people' represented a quantitative dimension and a national consciousness expressive of 'organic unity', the central category of sovereignty was thus rendered impersonal. Schmitt goes on to argue that, while the 'unity that a people represents does not possess this decisionistic character', decision and authority are nevertheless still immanent in and central to sovereignty. Moreover, in the modern rendition of sovereignty, the sacred was displaced from the monarch and deposited onto the

64. Hindol Sengupta, *The Man Who Saved India: Sardar Patel and His Idea of India* (New Delhi: Penguin Random House India, 2018).

65. Schmitt, *Political Theology*, 48.

people, most famously in the case of the American republic's equation of the voice of the people with the voice of God. Finally, Schmitt highlights infallibility as the essence of the decisionism that is grounded in authority: 'infallibility and sovereignty', he asserts, 'were synonymous'.[66]

Patel embodied and emerged as the locus of sovereign authority precisely in the sense that Schmitt has outlined. With his famed sense of realism, both at the negotiating table, as is now well established, and, most strikingly, in public declarations, Patel presented the policy of partition and division as infallible. The division was explained as the new but categorical condition for India's sovereignty. On the eve of independence, on 11 August 1947, he declared, 'Today the partition of India is a settled fact and yet it is an *unreal* fact!'[67] In the same speech, he described partition as a resolution to a 'duality' that he claimed had the capacity to violently fracture and fragment. The territorial division was to be regarded as a form of closure: 'Now that Pakistan has been established', Patel argued, there could be 'no quarrel between Hindus and Muslims.'[68] He thus sought to declare the end of partition at the moment of its inception, positing the inauguration of a new dispensation, at once real and incredible. Without precedent, both the closure of duality or partition and the arrival of two nations as a new but incredible fact referred to the sovereign subject of the people.

1947 was overwhelmingly represented as the original political moment of the classic form of sovereignty: namely, the national determination in India. In repeatedly accepting responsibility for partition by marking it as almost a personal decision, Patel arrogated to himself a sense of normative sovereign power that he sought to underscore as a new rule. Utterly vague, yet ubiquitous, the new form of sovereignty that had come in the form of two nations on the subcontinent needed and demanded its content. For Patel, acceptance of partition and its acceptance as a decision were categorical, and he sought this through repeated exhortations as he undertook a vigorous campaign of public speaking that year. His repeated pleas to accept partition, claimed as a policy decision, were geared towards rendering the new sovereign but unitary dispensation the 'new normal' political horizon.[69]

---

66. Ibid., 55.

67. Speech, 11 August 1947, *CWSVP* 12, 153 (original emphasis).

68. Patel, *For a United India*, 128.

69. On decision, exception and the norm of sovereignty, see Schmitt, *Political Theology*; also, Jüri Lipping, 'Sovereignty beyond the State', in Kalmo and Skinner (eds.), *Sovereignty in*

The June 3 Plan, as the partition came to be termed in official discussions, was in fact tabled to the Congress by Patel and Nehru precisely in these terms. The division or partition was stated by them to be a choice against 'complete Balkanisation and anarchy'.[70] Civil war had operated as a powerful spectre in the two short years leading up to the decision for partition and independence, and indeed not only that: it was also increasingly represented as a choice, a pure Hobbesian one, since the questions both of the division of the subcontinent and of civil war referred to arrangements and disarrangements with regard to sovereignty. In the summer of 1947, prior to the official date of independence and at the height of imperial negotiations, Patel said so in as many words in conversation with Gandhi, who had prevaricated on partition, and, as is well known, was unhappy about the imminent division. In a bid to convince him, Patel presented the Hobbesian choice:

> It is a question of civil war or partition. As for civil war, no one can say where it will start and where it will end. True, the Hindus might win in the end but only after paying an unpredictable and huge price.[71]

Partition or division as the price for peace became the dominant understanding even as most of the protagonists prevaricated over the precise details of that division. The prospect of ultimate peace brought even the Mahatma to prefer civil war to an 'armed peace' enforced by the Empire.[72] This is not to apportion blame so much as to underscore that deliberations regarding the logic of partition and its timing, and the negotiation of its detail, were conducted in the context of civil war. An 'agreed partition' was broadly understood as a 'peaceful solution' that was represented as, above all, 'rejection of civil war'.[73]

In arrogating to himself sovereign power over the decision for partition, Patel overtly linked this to an imagined future of endless civil strife without it. In a speech in December 1947, against the background of widespread ongoing violence, he once more announced that 'We are determined to put an end to all quarrels. That is why the partition of the country was agreed to.'[74] His

---

Fragments: The Past, Present and Future of a Contested Concept (Cambridge: Cambridge University Press, 2013), 186–204.

70. *Bombay Chronicle*, 16 June 1947, *CWSVP* 12, 103.

71. Patel to Gandhi, in (Rajmohan) Gandhi, *Patel*, 401.

72. Devji, *Impossible Indian*.

73. Jenkins to Wavell, 7 March 1947, in Carter (ed.), *Abyss*, 63.

74. Speech in Cuttack, 14 December 1947 ('Sink Differences and Work Hard'), in Patel, *For a United India*, 17.

decisionism regarded not only the territorial division represented by partition; more fundamentally, it involved a claim to ownership of violence in terms of both authority and responsibility as he demanded the cessation of hostilities. A new demarcation of the external via partition had brought the internal horizon into sharp relief. The internal sphere, however, was not inhabited exclusively by 'the people' that the civil war had brought into view. The singularisation of the people as a unity was obstructed by an inheritance from the old order in the form of the Indian princes, and the question of their incorporation into the new singularity raised anew the prospect of violence. In this context, Patel deployed 'the people' instrumentally as the bulwark against potential princely insurrections.

Absorbing the demise of the princely order into the emergence of 'the people', Patel annexed the division or partition as an inevitable new unity and claimed it as a triumph of popular will that was marked by an internal depth.[75] These were powerful metaphors, as the princely order was represented as a superficial overlordship that needed to be removed so that the depth of 'the people' as the new bearers of sovereignty could become visible, incorporating the diminishing princely power and associating the division of partition with the category of 'the people', the pressures of violence and the paramount need for 'unity'. This enabled Patel to articulate and stress republican sovereignty as the fundamental experience of freedom. Freedom was thus translated into popular sovereignty.

In his influential writings on republican liberty, Quentin Skinner explains that the 'absolute form of sovereignty' with the people as its basis was forged with the ultimate aim of peace and security. At even the most individual level, and via the reinterpretation of Hobbes, one of the central covenants for the establishment of popular sovereignty is, Skinner notes, submission to a sovereign power that is categorically distinguished from enslavement.[76] Thus, from Hobbes to Hannah Arendt, freedom or liberty is understood to be real, authentic and true only in a republic. Freedom, in this view, can only be experienced in 'self-governing regimes' or a democracy in which 'each individual becomes a subject but the people as a body becomes the bearer of sovereignty'. It is only under the conditions of a republic that sovereignty in its absolute and indivisible measure can enforce peace. As the historical and philosophical

75. Patel, *For a United India*, 25.

76. Quentin Skinner, *Hobbes and Republican Liberty* (Cambridge: Cambridge University Press, 2008), 43–55.

debates on the nature of modern political life unfolded, divided or multiple sources of sovereign power were predominantly understood to be the short route to strife and violence.[77]

Patel may not have read, and certainly did not cite, Thomas Hobbes or Jean Bodin. Nevertheless, it was the idea of a unitary sovereignty enacted through and in the name of 'the people' that animated his forceful political actions. On the one hand, division had potentially realised the unity of the new sovereign body of the people; on the other, multiple sources of sovereignty and violence within the new body retained a threatening potential. Patel was categorical: whatever the nature of sovereign authority that the princely order wielded or represented, it was derived entirely from the British crown. In the face of possible competition with or dissension from the emergent dispensation of republican authority, he warned that '[i]f any member of the Princely Order desires to establish paramountcy he is mistaken. They cannot establish that paramountcy which the British are relinquishing.' In the new order, he made clear, 'paramountcy' was 'vested in the people':[78] the princes or 'old rulers' were only 'inherited', and this vestigial 'heritage' was to be neither owned nor continued but instead entirely 'cleanse[d]'.[79] The crown and its representative Englishman, he asserted, were 'abdicating'. Patel did not view the abdication and departure of the British crown as leaving an empty centre or body politic without its head, but rather as creating a gap between two regimes of sovereignty. Though violent, this gap or interregnum had only made visible the transformed nature of the body politic, revealing most saliently the new horizon of 'the people'. Patel reminded Indians, and warned Indian princes whom he suspected of 'collecting arms and consolidating power', that '[t]oday India is not what it was when the Englishmen arrived'.[80] The abdicating Englishmen, though the true if illegitimate representatives of an old regime of sovereignty, were not simply replaceable by more such, because the body as a whole had changed, and thus its head too was transfigured. 1947 stood, in short, not for a mere transfer of power, but the transformation of sovereignty itself.

Patel worked assiduously to abolish any residual representative status that the princely order may have desired to maintain through the continuation of titles. He barred the term 'heritable' from its mooted inclusion in the Constitution,

77. Ibid., 72–76.
78. *Bombay Chronicle*, 4 April 1947, CWSVP 12, 25.
79. Speech at Karamsad, 6 April 1947, ibid., 30.
80. Speech at Vadodara, 15 April 1947, ibid., 43.

noting as chair of the Fundamental Rights Committee that he and others were 'legislating for the future not the past'.[81] The new sovereign head was not to be entirely visible, fully 'crowned', and sovereignty was not to be enshrined in the form of republican democracy, until 1950; the possibility of convulsion and division and the persistence of a plurality of forms remained salient features of the three crucial years prior to this.

Patel displayed a heightened awareness of the dispersal of violence and its multiple sources. The interregnum manifested the idealised goal of sovereign power as unitary as Patel zealously set about incorporating disparate sources of sovereignty. It was also clear to him, however, that princes, satraps and nawabs had the potential to incite and initiate violence. Whether in Kathiawar on the western frontier or in Hyderabad in central India, the existence of a multiplicity of sources of latent sovereign power, with the potential to become actively visible primarily through violence, remained starkly evident.[82] Invoking popular sovereignty, Patel insisted that 'peace and unification' of the political body was with 'the people' and warned that any resistance on the part of princely petty sovereigns to the authority of the people would only reduce them to becoming mere spectators to the 'march of events'. The princes and even big landlords or *taluqdars* (landed gentry) with princely pretensions, Patel declared, 'would have to enter the ocean' of the people.[83] The scale of India became both the argument and metaphor for the submission and 'merging' of principalities into the 'bigger and sizeable entity' of the nation.[84] Patel deployed the idea of popular will as he urged the princely order to recognise the 'writings on the wall'. Speaking in the name of the people, he warned the princes that any imagined or conspired separation from or contest with the new sovereign authority would only see the old princely order 'oppressed under the burden of the weak'.[85]

Civil war had established the category of 'the people of India' especially in relation to its new and immediate external dimension in the form of Pakistan, and Patel's rhetoric had exhorted and explained division as the prerequisite

81. Patel's resolution for abolition of titles, *Bombay Chronicle*, 1 May 1947, *CWSVP* 12, 73.

82. B. L. Mitter to Patel, on import of arms by Junagadh to conquer Kathiawar, 26 March 1947, ibid., 18; also, Sengupta, *The Man*, 322–24.

83. Speech at Vadodara, 15 April 1947, *CWSVP* 12, 43.

84. Speech in Alwar, 25 February 1948, in Patel, *For a United India*, 35.

85. Patel to Sardar Shrino Patro, 16 April 1947, on the continuing vacillation over accession to the Indian Union of certain states that wanted to come in under a separate union, in this instance the Kathiawar States, *CWSVP* 12, 49.

for an internal unity; the enfolding of the princely order then served as an opportunity to declare the people as the proper subject of the new sovereign national order. While negotiations with princes could be confrontational, the greatest effect of their incorporation was the amplification and aggregation of the people as a singularity. This singularity was premised on the idea of sovereignty as a form of reciprocity between the people and the new order.[86]

Eighteen months after Indian independence, with the incorporation of all princely states into the Union by early 1949, Sardar Patel repeated with conviction the view that he had held over the past couple of years, namely that the division of India had in fact brought about its unity. Seeking closure, Patel stated that 'partition is behind us. It has come to stay.' He went on to reaffirm the infallibility of the decision in its favour:

> It is good that we have agreed to partition in spite of all its evils; I have never repented my agreeing to partition. . . . I know we would have erred grievously and repented had we not agreed. It would have resulted in a partition not into two countries but into several bits. Therefore, whatever some people may say, I am convinced and remain convinced that our having agreed to partition has been for the good of the country.[87]

Patel's mantra of 'unity as the watchword for India' was executed through a triangulation involving the gamble of partition, the decapitation of princedom and the summoning of 'the people'—this last elusive of clear definition but central to republican sovereignty. The dangerous power of 'the people' had been manifested in all its brutality in civil war. In asserting ownership of partition, Patel sought not only to sublimate and convert that violence into a new order, of and by the people, but also to convert that violence into the language of power and authority. His rhetorical labour was thus directed towards executing the conversion of historical violence into power and order based on the singularisation of the people.[88] In placing himself at the centre of this epochal change as the figure overseeing the transition from violence to the rule of law, and in summoning and assembling the people as the new sovereign subject, Patel himself loomed large as the locus of sovereign authority.

86. Purushotham, *From Raj to Republic*.

87. Speech at Island Grounds, Madras, 23 February 1949 ('Build a Strong India'), in Patel, *For a United India*, 146.

88. Balibar, *Violence and Civility*.

Aggressive Incorporation

Those who are disloyal will have to go to Pakistan. Those who are still riding on two horses will have to quit Hindustan.[89]

—PATEL, JANUARY 1948

Patel extolled the virtues of a supposedly peaceful exchange of populations and of 'clean fighting' at its epicentre in Amritsar; at Lucknow he warned Muslims of the necessity of expulsion, attachment and loyalty. Opening a speech in early January 1948 that was to bring relations between the Indian triumvirate to a breaking point, he declared himself to be 'a true friend of the Muslims although I have been described as their greatest enemy.' He went on, 'I want to tell them frankly that mere declarations of loyalty to the Indian Union will not help at this critical juncture. They must give practical proof of their declarations.' Pointing out that Lucknow was the city where the 'foundation of the two-nation theory was laid', he once more overtly accepted the logic of partition.[90] The background to his strictures was the ongoing contest between India and Pakistan over Kashmir, and Patel sought the explicit denunciation of Pakistan from Indian Muslims.

This speech was the early and influential articulation of a new and powerful rhetoric that connected the formation of Pakistan with the demand for proofs of loyalty from Indian Muslims and that soon became the standard political vocabulary of what has been identified as 'communalism' in India.[91] Its significance lies in its illustration of the way in which Muslims as subjects in independent India were to be held hostage to the national frontier, and in particular Kashmir. Modern nation-states ensure the peaceful working of popular sovereignty by institutionalising violence at their armed borders and frontiers. Yet within the Indian body politic, it was the figure of the Muslim who was held as the frontier of violence.[92] The import of Patel's speech was

89. Speech at Lucknow, 6 January 1948 ('You Cannot Ride Two Horses'), in Patel, *For a United India*, 69. This sentence, together with Patel's invitation to the RSS to join the Congress, declaring them to be 'patriots', is surprisingly missing from the text of this speech in *CWSVP* 13, 18–20.

90. Ibid., 64–66.

91. Gyanendra Pandey, *The Construction of Communalism in Colonial North India* (Delhi and New York: Oxford University Press, 1990).

92. Kahn, *Putting Liberalism*.

that in accepting Pakistan, India itself was transformed, for which the Muslim bore the responsibility.

The key but unspoken transformation was in the nature of the minority, and specifically of the Indian Muslim minority. From the opening years of the twentieth century, the category 'minority' was articulated in terms of number and size. Anchored in a 'demographic' ideology, the minority as a quantifiable category licensed Muslim separatism and the equation, by Jinnah in particular, of India with the Hindu. While Iqbal had argued for Muslim nationality as a 'reduced universality', Jinnah pursued the logic of the enumerated minority as an 'enlarged particularity'. Jinnah's argument was 'segregative' in its force, militating against any possibility of a simple aggregation into popular sovereignty or 'the people'.[93] The principal actual effect of separation, however, was to split the Muslims themselves between the two contradictory registers of neighbour and brother, across both the external and internal divides: a form of splitting that effectively fragmented the Indian Muslim.

Having accepted the segregation wrought by partition, Patel turned to the aggressive incorporation of the Indian Muslims. This was focused primarily upon securing their detachment from Pakistan, extracted in the form of its denunciation. Patel's attitude in this matter would be enshrined in the Indian constitution: in short, with the advent of Pakistan, any further demands for separate political representation or reservations for Muslims in India were denounced and rejected. Even Chaudhury Khaliquzzaman, who had argued for the retention of separate electorates, recognised that Patel had become the 'final arbiter of the fates of minorities'.

Patel and his followers, notably G. B. Pant, argued that the repealing of separate electorates in independent India was both a recognition of Pakistan and the end of 'isolation' of the minority. Pant went as far as to present Muslims as the bulwark against a 'Hindu State' and warned that it would be 'suicidal for Muslims to uphold separate electorates', implying that it would only strengthen the religious majority. Patel, on the other hand, reasserted the principle of partition as the moment that defined the making of the political body in its sovereign measure of exclusion, inclusion and, above all, incorporation.

Incorporation, or what Patel repeatedly termed 'unity', involved neither the agonism of adversaries that Ambedkar had envisioned in terms of caste, nor

93. See Pierre Rosanvallon, *Democracy Past and Future*, trans. Samuel Moyn (New York: Columbia University Press, 2006), 52–54, on aggregation and segregation of general will; on Jinnah, see Jalal, *Sole Spokesman*.

the constitutional arrangements that Nehru sought to privilege to safeguard against the extremities of hostility and weaknesses that existed in the Indian social and religious fabric. In his summation to the Constituent Assembly that repealed separate electorates and any political rights specifically for the minority, Patel reasserted that Pakistan represented the fulfilment of the logic of separate electorates and that India now 'shall be One Nation'. In dismissing any claims to political rights specifically for the Indian Muslims, he declared that such claims were now exhausted 'as safeguards had been enjoyed for a long time', and concluded—without naming the Dalits openly—with the observation that 'there are other communities who are not well organised' and 'deserve protection and safeguards and, therefore we want to be generous to them'.[94] In his speeches, whether in Lucknow or Kathiawar, for Patel partition had fulfilled the 'two nation theory' that disallowed any remainder or residual effect.

The arrival of a Muslim nation as India's neighbour dramatically transformed the question of fraternity between Hindus and Muslims. With partition, for the first time, the brother acquired a distinctive sense of the 'foreigner' in the midst. Patel made a habit of addressing rallies and making speeches where there was a significant Muslim presence, or in principalities that were nominally ruled by outgoing Muslim monarchs. When the nawab of the western Indian state of Junagadh initially opted for Pakistan, Patel publicly asked Muslims to 'introspect': much as in his speech in Lucknow, he reminded Indian Muslims that the presence and formation of Pakistan was to 'put an end to this dual loyalty' between faith and nation. For those who 'preferred in that [to choose Muslim] faith' there was indeed now a 'place to pursue it', but, he declared categorically, 'in India there is no place for such persons'. The question of fidelity was articulated as a threatening choice between seamless incorporation and expulsion. Patel insisted that Muslims were free to 'go to the country which claims their allegiance'. If they remained in India, though, total allegiance was required: Muslims with dual loyalty would 'have to be treated as foreigners with all attendant disabilities'.[95]

A practitioner of sovereignty in its most normative, national and unitary sense, Patel was thus noticeably aggressive on the question of incorporation. The figure of the Muslim did not for him represent only a religion, such as to render him 'communal' in any simplistic sense. His idea of 'unity' was certainly

94. Patel's reports on minorities and fundamental rights, with responses from Pant and Khaliquzzaman, 28 August 1947, *CWSVP* 12, 178–80.

95. Speech, 13 November 1947, ibid., 236.

not a coming together of differences in a single 'bouquet' as it was for Nehru in his famous formulation of Indian nationality as 'unity in diversity'. Nehru's view took India's pluralism as the basis of nationality, in a categorical departure from European nationalism. For Patel, by contrast, the unique principle of nationality was unity, and unity was quintessentially about unitary sovereignty. His project was founded upon the gathering in of sovereign power and limitation of, if not indeed severance from, its multiple sources. With regard to India's Muslims, however, his speeches betrayed both the desire to incorporate and the anxiety that incorporation might be incomplete or impossible.

In Patel's framework, freedom and nationality were both about sovereign order, and the figure of the Muslim was not simply 'other' to some normative self alone. Rather, the splitting and redistribution of this figure along the brother-foreigner-neighbour axis had rendered the Muslim plural, a figure that had fissured specifically in terms of its political identity, threatening a fragmentation that left it not merely vulnerable, but actually beyond being gathered up and incorporated. The formative split of partition had indeed rendered the Indian Muslim structurally intractable with regard to the establishment of unitary sovereignty. Depleted, dispersed and laid claimed to by two national projects, rendered impotent and exhausted by the partition, the Indian Muslim became the focus of violence and strictures that revealed the anxieties of the new sovereign order.

The emergence of the Muslim as simultaneously brother and neighbour displaced estrangement or separateness from its normative association with the alien or foreigner, or even the neighbour alone, projecting it instead onto the brother at home. While the neighbour might standardly be a distant figure who remains behind boundaries to an extent impenetrable, in a curious reversal it was now, with partition, the Muslim brother in one's midst who became an enigmatic and elusive figure.[96] (By the same token, the intentions or motives of the new neighbour, Pakistan, became utterly transparent—even in its hostility.) The demands made upon Indian Muslims to give proof of loyalty to the new nation were categorical, continuous and excessive, assuming the character of a need that can never be satisfied—an insatiable desire for loyalty betraying the anxieties of the sovereign order that Patel represented. This

96. See Sigmund Freud, *Civilization and Its Discontents*, trans. David McLintock (London: Penguin Books, 2002), and Lacan, *Ethics of Psychoanalysis*, for the clearest discussion on the psychic and political distinction of the neighbour.

constant hectoring of Indian Muslims to demonstrate their allegiance displayed the extent to which they had become perceived as unknowable: enigmatic, opaque, secretive—a displacement onto the brother or minority of the suspicion normally reserved for and associated with the figure of the neighbour. The splitting of the Muslim by partition between the figures of neighbour and brother had thus produced the now commonplace assumption of their equivalence. The type of equation of neighbour with brother that was expressed in Patel's demand for proofs of loyalty from Indian Muslims as hostilities broke out in Kashmir in 1948 immediately became entrenched in the new sovereign order of postcolonial India and is now widespread and instinctive, its most significant feature being that it has smuggled in the sense of separation and estrangement associated with the neighbour and foisted it upon the brother at home.

The intimate nature of hostility between Indian and Pakistan prevented their relations as two nations from becoming normatively distant and foreign; and precisely because Pakistan was not alien or foreign, the Muslim in India was burdened with 'foreignness', as a form of historical displacement. This confusion of category represented by perception of the neighbour as intimate rather than foreign and the brother as foreign and distant is evidenced by a political rhetoric which is now commonplace but was certainly inaugurated by Patel, whereby relations between India and Pakistan are couched in terms of 'brotherhood' and even goodwill. Unlike Gandhi, Patel considered the partition as permanent, stating that '[i]t is neither our business nor intention to force a reunion. We only wish to be left alone so that both can live in peace and prosperity, happiness and harmony.'[97]

The Indian Muslim thus became the focus of special attention and of repeated exhortations to relate to the new sovereign order—as though somehow unrelated to it—through full incorporation, with a repeated demand for demonstration of a loyalty that could never be fully proved or adequate. In a speech in Calcutta early in January 1948, a typical early articulation of the political anxiety occasioned by the new relationship, Patel stated,

> One fact is indisputable. Many Muslims in India have helped for the creation of Pakistan. How can one believe that they can change overnight? The Muslims say that they are loyal citizens. Therefore, why should anybody

---

97. Speech at Rajkot, 12 November 1947 ('Knotty Problems'), in Patel, *For a United India*, 9.

doubt their bonafides? To them I would say: 'Why do you ask us? Search your own conscience!'[98]

Patel's speeches caused disquiet in other leaders, and irked Gandhi especially. Expulsions and the cross-border exchange of minorities had inaugurated the rhetoric that justified the logic of the new sovereign order. Incorporation of the remainder completed it. Meanwhile, Patel articulated a strong equivalence between the two nations of India and Pakistan, not because they were originally one, but rather on the basis that division had made them twins bound in a new form of mutual identification rather than being distanced by separation. His rhetoric in this context, as he berated and issued warnings to Muslims in India, reaffirmed relations between Hindus and Muslims as fraternal, but with the new categorical distinction that Muslims in India had been stripped of their last vestige of political subjectivity.

The displacement of intimacy onto the Muslim neighbour would render invisible his identity as a minority, whilst as a brother Indian the Muslim assumed enigmatic qualities. Pakistan as the new neighbour became entirely exposed, transparent and all too easily understood, even in its hostility, in the manner in which only an intimate can be known. Most significantly, both the brother and the neighbour remain constitutive figures of the family or indeed the nation. While the fraternal completes the family or the nation, the neighbour demarcates its limits. As both the intimate neighbour and the enigmatic minority, it was above all the figure of the Muslim that both configured and completed the new unity of India.

The Amnesty of Assassination

On 30 January 1948, Nathuram Godse, a sometime member of the RSS, assassinated Mahatma Gandhi in Delhi. The violent sequence of civil war came to an end with the assassin's bullet.[99] In September of the same year, Jinnah died in Karachi after a spell of illness. Within days of Jinnah's death, Patel and Nehru sent the Indian army into Hyderabad, the largest Indian princely state, with a

---

98. Speech in Calcutta, 3 January 1948 ('These Evils Must Go'), in Vallabhbhai Patel, *Sardar Patel: In Tune with the Millions*, vol. 1, ed. G. M. Nandurkar (Ahmedabad: Sardar Vallabhbhai Patel Samarak Bhavan, 1975), 18–19.

99. Yasmin Khan, 'Performing Peace: Gandhi's Assassination as a Critical Moment in the Consolidation of the Nehruvian State', *Modern Asian Studies* 45:1 (2011), 57–80.

Muslim princely head who also happened to be the richest man in the world. Hyderabad had resisted the Indian Union. With Jinnah's death, 'Operation Polo', as the military and police action was code-named, became the first deployment of sovereign violence against the very people it laid claim to as the source of the new sovereign order. Those violently resisting incorporation into the Indian Union included actors and organisations representing the spectrum of ideologies from communism to incipient Islamism. Hyderabad encapsulated, in short, the tied history of incorporation and popular sovereignty as it was shot through with questions relating to Hindus and Muslims, the princely order and the incipient reign of the people. In his highly original revisionist account, Sunil Purushotham places the incorporation of Hyderabad in the context of partition violence and reconstructs historically the dramatic forging of India as sovereign.[100] The control and absorption, but also dispersal and deployment, of violence in the two short years from 1946 to 1948 consummated India's sovereignty as a departure and break from its British imperial moorings. Gandhi's assassination brought about the cessation of civil war, and Hyderabad's accession became the violent end point of the interval between the regimes of imperial servitude and popular sovereignty.

On 4 February 1948, the RSS was briefly banned: for a year. The RSS, as discussed in an earlier chapter, had forged a new fraternity that was shrouded in secrecy.[101] With Gandhi's assassination, a new and intimate duality within the body politic was also brought to the fore that had hitherto remained unacknowledged, if not indeed wilfully ignored. In January 1948, a couple of weeks prior to Gandhi's assassination, in his infamous speech in Lucknow in which he had issued a warning to Indian Muslims, Patel had also invited the RSS and its political affiliate the Hindu Mahasabha to 'join the Congress' and play its part in the 'reconstruction of India'. This 'reconstruction' referred to transitioning from violence and its conversion into sovereign order. Making the internal duality clear, Patel stated that the votaries of Hindutva were 'not the only custodians of Hinduism' and that 'there was more tolerance in Hinduism' than was evident in the RSS. At the same time, however, he cautioned his political peers in the Congress that their 'power and authority' will not be 'able to crush the R.S.S.' The use of the *danda* (stick/punishment), he asserted, would prove

100. Purushotham, *From Raj to Republic*.

101. See Walter K. Andersen and Shridhar D. Damle, *The RSS: A View to the Inside* (New Delhi: Penguin Random House India, 2018) for an account of the RSS in independent India.

ineffectual against the RSS, as its men were not 'thieves or dacoits', but 'patriots' who needed to be 'won over' with 'love'.[102]

Patel's 'invitation' to the RSS was, in short, an attempt to incorporate and bind together what was fundamentally divided and antagonistic within the nascent nation. It was also an admission that the adversaries of, and aspects of the hostility that existed towards, a unitary sovereign power in the name of the people were neither simple in nature nor singular in number. Above all, this was a new kind of intimate enmity that was not amenable to expulsion and externalisation. Patel identified and isolated those activities of the RSS that he took to be a threat to or subversive of the sovereign order, and sought to restrict culpability for Gandhi's assassination to certain of its individual members.[103] Nehru, by contrast, not only held the RSS as an organisation to be guilty, but understood it as an entity that was susceptible to the easy temptations of violence and that needed to be severely disciplined and dismantled.[104] Patel's invitation sought to defang and depoliticise the secret fraternity of the RSS by seeking its amalgamation into the Congress. With Gandhi's assassination, however, not only did the internal breach between leaders become briefly visible, but any potential suturing, let alone amalgamation of the partisan brotherhoods into the mainstream, became impossible. New lineaments of hostility, both latent and explicit, thus anointed the era of the people.

The violence of the civil war had made the people manifest. The inauguration of India as a republic in 1950 was a declaration of the mastery of the people. As symbol, sign and source of a new sovereign order, 'the people' became a political category precisely at the moment that the violence of its founding was expelled from the historical and political matrix. The assimilation of the people coincided with and conditioned the forgetting of the catastrophic fratricide: a forgetting that constituted an unspoken political duty of the new people. The civil war of 1947 remains to this day unmarked by official memorials and gestures of forgiveness and reconciliation. In a critical sense, this is apt, as 'the peoples' of the nations of India and Pakistan are themselves its living memorial.

102. Speech at Lucknow, 6 January 1948.

103. Patel to Syama Prasad Mookherjee, 18 July 1948, in Vallabhbhai Patel, *Select Correspondence of Sardar Patel, 1945–50*, vol. 2, ed. V. Shankar 2 (Ahmedabad: Navajivan Publishing House, 1976), 277–78; on Nehru–Patel differences from 1947 to 1950, ranging from official appointments to the question of violence and its management and above all the RSS, see ibid., 161–311.

104. Patel to Nehru, 28 March 1950, in Patel, *Select Correspondence*, 217–26.

Gandhi's assassination acted on the civil war as a form of amnesty. Equally, the parricide exhausted the public expression of guilt and culpability for the fratricide and the violent historical interval between empire and nation. Gandhi's death announced a new violent fraternity, one that was not simply shrouded by its own secrecy, but that found a familial cover in the intimacy of its own people.

Epilogue

IN 2016, a little over a century after its memorable identification with the case of Tilak, the law of sedition was weaponised anew in India.[1] It was not that individuals or groups had not been prosecuted for sedition over the long intervening period: in the decades following Tilak's trial and right up to the eve of independence, Indians such as Gandhi and Maulana Azad, among several others, were tried and imprisoned for the offence. As the independence struggle became highly mobilised, the Empire armed itself by amplifying its battery of legislation, from the Defence of India Act to the infamous Rowlatt Acts and a host of other emergency laws. The notion of sedition, involving defiance of emperor and empire alike, remained at the centre of these laws, forming a distinct domain of politics. Independent India is, among other things, an outcome of sedition.

The invocation of sedition today, then, points not simply to the lingering presence of an archaic law belonging to the dead colonial past. That is one aspect of the matter; but the persistence and now repeated deployment of the concept reflects the crucial and ongoing issue of defining and drawing the political domain. The potency of the notion of sedition is more than merely legal: it lies in the fact that it concerns fundamentally the ordering of the norms of the political in relation to sovereign power. For Tilak, in the opening sequence of what is termed here the Indian Age, the issue of sedition and the law more generally became the salient point of departure in the production of a powerful political vocabulary: an anti-statist political subject was powerfully and consequentially presented as the bearer of sovereignty, and questions of life and death in its sovereign dimensions thereby wrested away from the law or 'state' and deposited with the individual.

1. BBC report on 'sedition' charges against students in 2016, https://www.bbc.co.uk/news/world-asia-india-35576855.

The revival of the charge of sedition in our own times points, above all, to a violent redefinition of the national in relation to popular sovereignty. In 2016, it was the charge used to prosecute protesters and critics of the government of the day, whose form of dissent, ominously and tellingly, was declared 'anti-national'. A century after Tilak, sedition still stands as a test of loyalty, but with the one crucial difference that in Tilak's time, loyalty to the sovereign undeniably meant loyalty to the British monarch. The change over the century from empire to nation, though vastly significant, is not in itself the end of the matter: the issue of sovereignty is paramount.

Independent India broke away from imperial forms of legal and substantive sovereignty. The Indian constitution does not recognise any sovereign. In doing away with the British monarch and declaring India's freedom as a republic, founding figures categorically deposited sovereign power with 'the people'. This was the premise and substance of India's constitution. At the time of independence, this allowed Patel to rid the country of nearly six hundred petty and not-so-petty monarchs in the form of the Indian princes since, as he forcefully argued, they derived their sovereignty from the British monarch. Neither God nor what in other traditions is quaintly called the 'divine legislator', nor indeed any monarch, nourished, oversaw or legitimised the sovereignty of free India.[2] Sovereignty now began and ended with the people.

'The people' was anointed in the constitution as the sacred political subject and object of independent India at the inaugural session of the Constituent Assembly. Nehru's famous opening speech on the Objectives Resolution was, in a sense, the originating revolutionary moment of republicanism in India. Yet the discovery of 'the people' as both means and end of sovereignty was in fact rooted in and grew from the intimate hostilities and violence of civil war. The fratricide of 1947 transformed the orientation of the political from a preoccupation with fraternity to the pursuit and elevation to predominance of popular and unitary sovereignty.

Depositing of sovereignty with the people and ensuring that it did not rest with any outside power—be it a king or a god—made it internal to and immanent in the social and national order, as the Constitution became its sole guarantor. Popular sovereignty was strongly equated with the republic and

---

2. Both God and Gandhi as the 'Father of the Nation' were initially considered as invocatory spirits for the Indian Constitution, but were dismissed, 'the people' remaining its sole basis and spirit: 17 October 1949, https://www.constitutionofindia.net/constitution_assembly_debates/volume/10/1949-10-17.

democracy. As Nehru put it in his Resolution in the Constituent Assembly cited above, 'we thought it is obvious that the word "republic" contains . . . [the word] "democratic".[3] Republicanism enshrined popular sovereignty as one and indivisible. Democracy, on the other hand, ensured competition between and diversity of views among the people. Making 'the people' sovereign is what has allowed democracy to become synonymous with the experience of freedom in India. Republicanism, it could be argued, trumped every other political 'ism' and ideology in independent India, with democracy as its mandated expression.

There is an extensive literature on the Indian constitution as the primary political document of democracy. This book, by contrast, has focused instead on rarely discussed fraternal and sovereign dimensions of violence in laying down the political foundations of modern India. In light of the book's arguments, the retention and even subsequent amplification of sedition as a crime in the statutes of India is not perhaps unremarkable, but telling nevertheless. The evidence is that, far from sedition merely being a colonial leftover that the founders of the nation were too distracted to get rid of, the issue was fiercely debated. The Hindu nationalist leader K. M. Munshi moved an (unsuccessful) amendment to drop sedition from free India's constitution, precisely because he thought the statute redolent of a colonial *ancien régime*;[4] strikingly perhaps, it was Ambedkar who advanced arguments for its retention.

In fact, it is entirely unsurprising that Ambedkar, recast in this book as a thinker of sovereignty, should have argued for the retention of sedition, on the basis of upholding order. In dismissing calls for its abrogation, he had responded to a suite of objections relating to the restriction of freedom, including of right to bear arms, in one form or another. While recognising that the revocation of sedition and the right to bear arms were indeed issues of anti-colonialism, he endorsed the primacy of unitary sovereignty as order over the concession of freedoms. He stated, indeed, that it was precisely because the government was no longer 'alien' that 'regulations' or restrictions were essential to the new sovereign order.[5] To this extent, Ambedkar and Patel were complicit in framing India's new legal order in absolute and unitary terms. In

---

3. Nehru, Resolution.

4. K. M. Munshi in the Constituent Assembly of India, 1 December 1948, https://www.constitutionofindia.net/constitution_assembly_debates/volume/7/1948-12-01, 7.64.154ff.

5. B. K Ambedkar, ibid., 2 December 1948, https://www.constitutionofindia.net/constitution_assembly_debates/volume/7/1948-12-02, 7.65.171ff.

retaining the crime of sedition, the founding figures in their role as constitution drafters displayed a profound suspicion of the political, a suspicion that was expressed in legislation as they sought to curb and tame the temptation to violence. Both Ambedkar and Patel understood very well the seductive potential of the political realm lying beyond the legal and ordained norms that had conditioned India's transition from servitude to sovereignty.

An account of the Indian Age focusing upon the intimacies of hostility, the potential for peace and the agonies of agonism stands in distinction from one oriented by and towards the liberal language and moorings of Indian constitutionalism; and this indeed is of the essence of the approach adopted here. While works on India's constitution (making up an extensive list) tend to be celebratory, the political, this book has argued, cannot be exhausted by the law. Far from it: the law remained the outside limit for the radical laying of a new, profound and enduring set of political foundations for India. The transformation of fraternity into popular sovereignty was concerned with the redirection of political violence, and whether the concern was the antagonism of an intimate fraternity or the zealous pursuit of its conversion to agonism, or even separation, the political foundations of India were imagined and related to fundamental questions of ethics and the political subject, invoking questions of time and history.

Fraternity, violence and sovereignty comprised the fundamental categories of an Indian Age that was resolutely future-oriented and involved a global thinking of the political. The grounding of major political figures, from Tilak and Gandhi to Iqbal and Savarkar, each one of whom foregrounded the subject rather than the state as the site of sovereignty and thus violence as much as brotherhood, was anti-liberal: this was a politics defined in terms not of contract, but of violent fraternity. Irreducible to anarchism, however, this subject-centred politics enabled a new kind of thinking about the nature of freedom, the character of the state and the meaning of fraternity, all in conditions of extraordinary social diversity.

The main contribution of the various Indian political leaders considered here rather as thinkers was to redefine Indian political subjectivity and to move it away from the purview of the state, mainly by relocating violence in the individual, thus embedding it in the spaces of intimacy and fraternity rather than those of law, policing or legal citizenship. This allowed the mobilisation of a set of aspirations and subjectivities that removed the political from the hands of the state.

The book opened with Tilak, as he founded a new political theology by shrouding political concepts in theological language and circumventing the state in favour of the subject, in order to think about sovereignty under colonial rule. In this realm of unequal strength, terrorism—what Tilak called 'the bomb'—enabled the democratisation of violence, and so of sovereignty. Unlike in Europe, then, in India the bomb was not a feature of a narrative of class conflict, but rather heightened the objectives of subject and sovereign as it bound them together beyond the limits of the state. Tilak created a breach between violence and the state from which emerged a new political subject whose immanent sovereignty stood against that, abstract and invisible, of the colonial state. His monumental commentary on the *Gita* expounded on the question of enmity as distinctly intimate and fraternal. It can thus be seen that, while the battle against the Empire certainly provided the context for the Indian Age, its principals, starting with Tilak, took their eventual victory as given, and were more interested in the kind of political horizon to be produced for a post-colonial future.

The anti-statist political subject immediately became a mobile and global figure that called into question the strongest principles of both empire and nation, in the process leaving a large if disjointed trace on the twentieth century. The pointillistic action of the Ghadar's militant subject, defined by no single ideology but instead by practices of sacrifice, secrecy and mobility, unsettled imperial attempts as the Ghadar provided a counter-geography to imperial expanse. While it deterritorialised the idea of India, however, the Ghadar reterritorialised Islam by locating India, rather than Arabia, at the centre of an alternative Muslim imperium, flanked by Afghanistan and Turkey.

The secrecy that was central to the Ghadar was powerfully redirected in the articulation and propagation of Hindutva by Savarkar, who was arrested and forced back from the global theatre of anti-imperialism into India. In the inter-war period, after his release from the penal colony of the Andaman Islands, Savarkar redirected the prevailing categories of sacrifice, secrecy and fraternity, to say nothing of violence, all meant to bridge the gap between Hinduism and politics. The cobbled-together history invoked by Hindutva was meant to provide it not with a past, so much as a future: a prognostic operation that sought to read into the past a future in which India was not identified by land, blood or history, but had to be produced by war. Hindutva, as expounded by Savarkar, the book argues, is a theory of violence rather than a history of identity.

Gandhi's politics of truth, by contrast, provided the most visible political grammar. Truth, for the Mahatma, was the oppositional arm against violence. It was a matter not of speech or moral injunction, but of the revelation and recognition of politics as world-making, and its visibility was made possible through the body: not the heavily armed corporeality that embodied the differing ideals of imperialism, fascism and communism, but one defined by sacrifice in the form of fasting, silence and dying. A subjectivity so impossible to institutionalise, however, ran the risk of becoming so excessive as to destroy state and society both. The most intimate of enmities was that between Gandhi and Savarkar, or Hindutva more generally, even as they traversed the same terrain of religion and abstinence, and there remains an irreducible gap between Hindutva and Gandhi's politics of truth—a politics that was not extinguished by his assassination and cannot be sublimated by, let alone incorporated into, Hindu nationalism.

The legacy of the anti-statist thrust of the Indian Age and the new political foundations that the book has elaborated goes well beyond any simple or facile opposition to the 'state'. The anti-statism that has been reactivated, redirected and redistributed in subsequent decades, its potency in independent India evident in movements ranging from environmentalism to Maoism, not to mention lynch mobs, defies attempts to identify in it any single ideological coherence or fidelity. This book does not offer any simplistic genealogy or pre-history of Indian democracy. As a historical reconstruction and interpretation of foundational thinking, the legacy of the Indian Age for Indian democracy is obvious. The conceptual history of Indian democracy, however, though related to these foundations, remains distinct both as belonging to a historical epoch and as a set of political languages. Teleological connections, though easily made, have therefore been resisted here. The emergence of popular sovereignty, the bedrock of democracy has, nevertheless, been a central concern of the book.

Ambedkar assiduously dismantled anti-statism and sought to set sovereignty on a popular and republican course: he emerges, indeed, as a key thinker of sovereignty, as distinct from the prevailing reception of him as primarily concerned with issues of justice and the caste question. Grappling, as a proponent of agonism, with questions of 'majority' and 'minority', he determined that the will of the majority should not automatically be equated with popular sovereignty: that is, that the Hindu should not be the default subject of emergent Indian republicanism. Annexed to the formation of Pakistan, the caste question was made immanent in that of popular sovereignty.

It was a central concern of both Ambedkar and Patel to steer the political subject produced in the early decades of the twentieth century towards popular sovereignty. The anti-statist subject had been constructed in the nexus of fraternity, intimacy and violence, and both Ambedkar and Patel directed it to the radically different, republican idea of the political subjectivity of the category of 'the people', a category which is national, territorial and grounded in the unified and unitary qualities of the nation-state. Though jointly thinkers and executors of Indian republicanism, Patel was focused in particular upon the (figurative) decapitation of the Indian princes, and equally upon the issue of sovereign violence and power. Ambedkar, on the other hand, revealed the Brahmin as the violent, albeit dispersed, locus of historic sovereign power in India. His juxtapositioning of the internal antagonism of caste against the fraternal hostility between Hindus and Muslims had consequences for his thinking on partition as well as the designing of Indian republicanism as an agonistic formation of castes.

In the social realm whence Gandhi derived his politics, Ambedkar saw only an anti-social field of relations which was nevertheless so powerful as to obstruct the emergence of the political. The problem with India's anti-social society, in Ambedkar's view, was that it had digested and pluralised sovereignty in the figure of the Brahmin instead of the king. Unlike in Europe, where regicide led to the making of the sovereign people in a revolution, the Brahmin destruction of kingship in India was counter-revolutionary and prevented the emergence of either the social or political realms, and so of the state. A fraternal society therefore had to be created as the basis for the state and its politics, and this could only be done by institutionalising enmity as agonism through the state. This was to be achieved by caste representation within the state on the one hand, and by the religious partition of colonial India into two separate states on the other. By resolving the antagonisms of India's anti-social society institutionally, making enemies into adversaries, Ambedkar rejected his predecessors' focus on the extra- or anti-statist sovereign subject in favour of a general will created through and by the state.

Republicanism was also uncovered as the true spirit of Islam, in the deft and original remaking of foundational concepts by Muhammad Iqbal. How were Indian Muslims to constitute themselves as a religious community with a political life? For Iqbal, such an enterprise entailed forsaking old-fashioned Muslim narratives of imperial history, civilisational nostalgia and mystical renunciation. More importantly, he rejected the Caliphate which had constituted the grand subject of Muslim mobilisation early in the twentieth century and turned instead to its successor in the Turkish republic. Unlike Pan-Islamism, which Iqbal saw as a sign of Muslim powerlessness, the Turkish republic represented Islam's renewed link with power, as well as a salutary reconsideration of values that made it modern in a Nietzschean way.

Iqbal grounded republicanism in Muhammad, the finality of whose prophecy proscribed any king or priest from claiming sovereignty, instituting instead the reign of Muslim fraternity. But the Prophet's sole possession of sovereignty also meant that it could never be manifested in any state without becoming blasphemous, and in this way the political realm was separated from Islam's universality deposited in the arena of the social. Iqbal bears comparison with both Tilak and Gandhi in different ways, and his focus on sacrifice as the sovereign act by which Muslims could reconstitute themselves socially as well as politically merges him into the mainstream of Indian political thought as one of its central figures, rather than as a purely Islamic thinker linked primarily to the 'Muslim world' and only accidentally to India. Strikingly, hostility and antagonism on his part were directed specifically at his co-religionists, thus marking out the limits of fraternity as also the sovereign boundaries of Islam.

The partition of India has been conceptualised here in a revised form as a civil war, and explored via the activity and rhetoric of Patel as he sought to convert the new nation into a unitary sovereign entity. Hitherto, the political dimension of partition has been obscured by a dominant understanding that either focuses on the equivalence of Hindu, Muslim and Sikh victimisation, or analyses the politics of partition only in crass instrumental rather than conceptual terms. The account of partition as a civil war makes a single powerful point: that it is in partition violence that 'the people' came into being, by actions that exceeded institutions. The sovereignty of the people, in other words, became evident not in a confrontation with the monarch, and certainly not the colonial state, but in a civil war in which brotherhood was both lost and found. The emergence of the Indian republic, then, was achieved not with the transfer of power, but in the surmounting of a fratricide whose iconic moment came with Gandhi's assassination, seen as the sovereign subject's sacrifice making possible a general will.

As a theorist of republican sovereignty, Pakistan and agonism, Ambedkar was clear that the general will or popular sovereignty was not to be equated with the 'majority'. He admitted that the recognition of a 'minority' had by default, and ironically, led to the existence of a 'statutory majority';[6] but he was quick to point out that the conversion of such a statutory majority into a genuine political unity would be impossible, even if there were those who considered its ascendancy desirable. Such a desire was associated above all, he noted, with the Hindu Mahasabha and its affiliate the RSS. In a prescient

6. Ambedkar, *Pakistan*, 117–38.

judgement, he declared that with the formation of Pakistan, the Mahasabha would vanish from the political horizon, losing, as it were, its existential *raison*. Indeed, for Ambedkar, the Muslim League and the Hindu Mahasabha were two sides of the same coin.

Today, does the decisive Modi mandate herald the political arrival of such a majority? For the first time in India's democracy, the electoral majority coincides with the party that overtly and stridently represents Hindu nationalism. Ambedkar's project was based on the principle that numerical majorities were not equivalent to political majorities and that, as experts on democracy remind us, a gap exists between the social and the political.[7] His interventions and innovations were in the cause of forging a precise relationship between the social and political, in a context in which the dominance of the numerical majority was overwhelming. At that point, to be sure, this was not the floating arithmetic of electoral democracy, but referred to the stark and rigid totals enshrined in the census. Ambedkar took the division and antagonism of the social—that deriving from caste—as primary, and as requiring recognition within the realm of the political. The political recognition of the Dalits (the 'untouchables') ensured the pluralisation of the minority form along religious lines that disrupted any claims to or fantasies of cohesion and unity within the religious majority. Thus the Hindu majority could not be equated with or understood to represent 'the people'.[8]

The test of popular sovereignty is not, therefore, a matter of loyalty or sedition, as there is no supreme power above 'the people'. Instead, the test of popular sovereignty is democracy. Democracy enshrines 'majority rule' as its touchstone. In making 'the people' sacred, Indian republicanism categorically disallowed the equation of 'the people' with any partisan group, majority or religion. Popular rule could change hands, but popular sovereignty had to remain constant. Any redefinition of popular sovereignty that splits it such as to identify it with loyalty to any pre-established majority—be that a hereditary majority or simply the government of the day—can now only be successful by imperilling democracy itself. This is the institutionalised logic of popular sovereignty in India today.

7. Rosanvallon, *Democracy*, 243.

8. 'The people', or the subject of democracy, as Rosanvallon insightfully argues, is at once central yet absent, marked repeatedly by excess that militates against its equivalence with any given identity: ibid., 203.

From Mill to Rawls, through a genealogy that includes many of the most
prominent of political thinkers, liberalism, with rights, contract and liberty at
the centre of its conceptual repertoire, has remained the dominant approach to
modern politics. Here, an alternative genealogy is proposed, from Tilak to Patel,
that approaches the political as entailing violence, sovereignty and fraternity,
and in terms of a new canon of thinkers, who positioned India as a futurity.

The Indian Age bequeathed a legacy that is still far from being exhausted,
or even fully accounted for, let alone ossified. The innovation and imagination
that characterised it transformed world history as political visions directed
India into the democratic fold. Today, the political ideas of the Indian Age not
only remain a powerful inheritance but constitute a course of instruction in
the global condition of political violence.

The era of the world's largest democracy was preceded by a deadly civil war
that only came to an end with an assassin's bullet fired at the 'Father' of the
new sovereign nation. Gandhi's assassination had deep and far-reaching effects. In its immediate aftermath, an amnesty was effectively declared in the
raging civil war. At a deeper level the parricide—assassination guaranteeing
Gandhi's status as the Father—inaugurated a new age: a new era of a new
fraternity. And it laid bare the new psychic and political division or antagonism
that would haunt and inform India's democracy.

Gandhi's victory in his lifetime over Ambedkar was pyrrhic; his subject-
oriented political project was overwhelmed by Ambedkar's agonism. The Republic's constitutional architecture, and the trumping by sovereignty of the
concern with fraternity, makes Ambedkar's ideological longevity and final victory all too obvious. While the repeated return, in contemporary Indian political
discourse, to these two figures testifies to their shared foundational and inexhaustible role, contemporary contestations over their relative reputations and
receptions nevertheless reveal the lineaments of new partisan hostilities and
identifications, and the dramatic change in their respective reputations suggests
an initial set of landmarks whereby to trace changes in political languages under
democracy. The search for a new 'father' to compensate for or replace Gandhi
demonstrates that such a figure, in this time of no kings, retains its potency in
the direction of India's political life and future.

Apprehended as political thinkers, founding political actors are far from
dead or frozen in the deep archives of history. As they haunt and animate politics in India today, they remain the objects of passionate identification. Their
living role is not merely to service partisan views of the past, though it may
also be that. Ambedkar is resurrected anew by the young and by a wide

coalition of popular Indian politics today, while Patel is pirated for the pantheon of Hindutva; shifing allegiances and renewed attachments to these figures offer an initial insight into dramatic changes in Indian democracy and its underpinning fraternity. The names of these iconic figurations function as invocations and labels: as a powerful shorthand that distils as it conveys the transformative power of political ideas.

ACKNOWLEDGEMENTS

THE SINGLE MOTIVATION behind this work has been to take the power of political ideas seriously. Deceptively simple, this task was primarily informed by the nature of historical scholarship, be it Indian history, or intellectual history and political thought or theory in general. I am deeply indebted to David Armitage, who first saw the potential of Indian and global political thought more than a decade ago when I first met him in Boston and who unstintingly supported my collaborative efforts in writing histories of Indian and global political thought. Chris Bayly crucially recognised the importance of understanding India's political and intellectual originality and ingenuity—the appreciation of which is an innovation that has remained marginal at best, or more generally scoffed at. In the summer of 2013, Richard Drayton alerted me, on a typical rainy English summer's day in Cambridge, to the fact that a book was shouting at me while I was wilfully neglecting its call. The insights, care and example of Darian Leader were central in helping to sift and understand ideas, emotions, histories and politics; and without Faisal Devji's daily indulgence in conversation this book would either not have been written at all or written a long time ago! It would certainly not be in front of you without either of them, and it is my good fortune to be indebted to both.

This book was started in earnest at the end of 2012, on the back of ongoing teaching at Cambridge, in particular of two graduate courses: 'Global Intellectual History' and 'Violence and Non-Violence in Twentieth-Century South Asia'. I am grateful to the large number of students whose engagement invigorated these courses, which constituted an invitation to think anew about politics, place and ideas. Cambridge has been a most insightful and productive perch for such an undertaking, as political thought, Indian history, world history and British imperial history have all been central to its research life. This book is an outcome of teaching, research seminars and public talks rather than any big grant or significant time spent away from teaching.

The book was written too with the companionship of an excellent cohort of PhD students, all of whom have gone on to impressive writing and teaching careers. Sunil Purushotham was the first to put his faith in me, before I had even started at Cambridge, and he was soon joined by Faridah Zaman, Jesús Cháirez-Garza, Chris Moffat, Vikram Visana and Ammar Ali Jan, who have now explored aspects of twentieth-century political thinking in their own highly original works. Adeel Hussain, Alistair McClure and Saumya Saxena's focus on law was crucial to my own thinking on the rise of Indian sovereignty, especially given their counter-intuitive and revisionist understanding of the work of law; while the recently completed dissertations of Luna Sabastian and Joseph Francombe, along with Salmoli Choudhuri's, Jessica Sequeira's and Arvin Alaigh's ongoing doctoral work, are pushing me to think once more about the global dimensions of political ideas in the last century. My primary debt is to them, for intellectual comradeship, and for their ethical courage in thinking from new perspectives.

I have been enormously fortunate in being able to share my work and research in the form of lectures and conference and workshop papers at a large number of universities and at scholarly, public and even policy-making institutions and venues across the world; these cannot all be named here individually, but my debt of gratitude remains strong to every gracious host for every invitation and opportunity for critical engagement. I thank these hosts for their generosity and kindness, and those who have engaged with my work over the years for their productive comments. It is particularly gratifying to be able to thank both Dilip Menon, who hosted my first talk on the intellectual history of India, at Delhi University a lifetime ago, and Simona Sawhney, also in Delhi (at the Indian Institute of Technology), for hosting my last before going to press.

Arjun Appadurai, David Arnold, Neeladri Bhattacharya, Akeel Bilgrami, Dipesh Chakrabarty, Mary Jacobus, Ayesha Jalal, Ruth Harris, Javed Majeed, Pankaj Mishra, Samuel Moyn, Bhikhu Parekh, Christopher Pinney, Jennifer Pitts, Gyan Prakash, Ajay Skaria, Majid Siddiqi and Romila Thapar have informed and encouraged this work, in conversations past, present or in ongoing dialogue, but above all with their own works. Special thanks go to Cornel West, who during a visit to Cambridge some years ago pointed out incisively the crucial role of political ideas and encouraged this project enormously. None of these is in any way responsible for this book's shortcomings, and I remain indebted to their indulgence and engagement. Pratap Bhanu Mehta, Thomas Blom Hansen and Uday Singh Mehta were extremely generous in sharing their new work and ideas in various workshops on Indian political thought that they led at Cambridge with sparkling insights that, like their scholarship in general have remained with and stimulated this book.

My colleagues in the Cambridge History Faculty have been important interlocutors in enabling this book, and I am especially grateful to Richard Bourke, Chris Clark and Alexandra Walsham for brilliant insights that came with large dollops of humour and plain speaking. Andrew Arsan, Eugenio Biagini, Annabel Brett, Chris Briggs, Lucy Delap, Saul Dubow, Richard Evans, Tim Harper, Mary Laven, Helen Pfeifer, John Robertson, Ulinka Rublack, Magnus Ryan, Sujit Sivasundaram, Andrew Spencer, Gareth Stedman Jones and Sylvana Tomaselli have been wonderfully supportive colleagues. Elizabeth Haresnape's, Rachel McGlone's, Liz Partridge's and Joanne Pearson's guidance and help with administration has been crucial. Beyond the History Faculty, conversations with Ash Amin, Christopher Brooke, John Dunn, Sarah Franklin, the late John Forrester, Lawrence Hamilton, Duncan Kelly, Banu Turnagulo and the late David Washbrook were always clarifying, and I thank Ash especially for recommending that the book be shorter than its initial eleven chapters! Alison Bashford and Megan Vaughan were kind mentors of my academic life in Cambridge.

Corpus Christi College has been a home like no other and the fellowship and staff have been peerless. I am enormously and eternally thankful to Christopher Kelly, Shawn Donnelley, Marina Frasca-Spada, Simon Godsill, Keith Seffen, Alison Smith, Emma Spary, James Warren, Emma Wilson and Patrick Zutshi for their warm support.

The terrific trio of Kevin Greenbank, Barbara Roe and Rachel Rowe at the Centre of South Asian Studies in Cambridge were most helpful in the chasing of books and papers that makes up so much of research activity. The Centre's library and the Nehru Memorial Museum and Library in Delhi were pivotal to this research, and their staff have been peerless.

Without Princeton University Press this book would have remained an unpublished document on my computer, and I am indebted to Ben Tate and Fred Appel for their enthusiastic encouragement. Jill Harris's and Josh Drake's patience and care with the production have been exemplary. I am also grateful to Samuel Garrett Zeitlin for reading and giving excellent comments on the manuscript at a critical stage.

A shorter version of Chapter 5 entitled 'Ambedkar's Agonism' was published in *Comparative Studies of South Asia, Africa and the Middle East* 39:1 (2019), 184–95, and I am grateful to Duke University Press for their permission to republish it.

The long if fitful years of the companionship of the manuscript itself were made all the more enjoyable and stimulating by the presence of a brilliant and motley crew that luck has favoured me with. Manica and Anshul Avijit, Chandrahas Chaudhury, Achim Edelman, Patrick French, Saroj Giri, Rhiannon Harries, Tristram Hunt, Charu Jagat, Leher Kala, Marc Michael, Usha Mishra Hayes, Nayanika Mookherjee, Elinor Payne, Hussein Omar, Vita Peacock, Bunny and Raghu Rao, Nasreen Rehman, John David Rhodes, Martin Ruehl, Kranti Saran, Arghya Sengupta, Christina Skott and Daniel Steinmetz-Jenkins indulged my flights of fancy and intense introspection with the necessary circumspection and humour, not only making them fantastic friends but showing them to be good human beings. Countless conversations with friends in Indian politics and media (they know who they are!) helped to distinguish the past from the present. Arjun Bhagat and Petal Dhillon's stunning home in Uttarakhand allowed for this book to be concluded with the inspiration that only the majestic Himalayas could bestow.

My sister Kriti and my brother Ashish have had the greatest influence on my life, and I can only acknowledge their immeasurable love and support that has given me both a place in the world and a way of being in it. My mother, Madhur Kapila, a novelist in Hindi, has always loved writing not as a ritual practice or vanity project but as an ethereal purpose, and I can only apologise to her for my dogged resistance to producing a full, single-authored book until now. Without my mother, quite literally nothing would be possible, but even more importantly, imaginable. Her love, presence and words animate and nourish me anew every day.

This book is dedicated to my father, Ramesh Kapila, for whose sudden death I was entirely unprepared, and who alone taught me to love ideas, to recognise their power and to find solace and hope in all but the most difficult conditions. His passing exhorted me to put pen to paper to both record and honour our several conversations. This book is a small token of my gratitude and is dedicated to his enduring love and memory.

BIBLIOGRAPHY

Private Papers and Unpublished Primary Sources

British Library, London, India Office Records (IOR)

Kuwait Political Agency Records (R series, 15/5)
Military Proceedings (L/MIL series) 1915–20
Political and Secret Proceedings (L/PS series) 1904–30
Proscribed Publications Microfilms
Public and Judicial Proceedings (L/PJ series) 1929–47

British Library, London, Manuscripts

Peter Wells Papers

Nehru Memorial Museum and Library, Delhi

V.V.S. Aiyar Papers
Pandurang Khankhoje Papers
B. S. Moonje Papers
Sardar Patel Papers (microfilm)

University of Pennsylvania, Philadelphia, USA

Van Wyck Brooks Collection

Published Primary Sources and Collections

A Hindu Nationalist, *Gandhi-Muslim Conspiracy* (Poona: R. D. Ganekar, 1941)
Ambedkar, B. R., 'Annihilation of Caste' [1936], in *BAWS* 1, 23–96
———, 'Castes in India' [1916], in *BAWS* 1, 3–22
———, *Dr Babasaheb Ambedkar: Writings and Speeches*, ed. Vasant Moon (17 vols; Bombay: Government of Maharashtra, 1991) [*BAWS*]
———, 'Frustration', in *BAWS* 12.6 ('Miscellaneous Notes'), 733–35
———, 'India and the Prerequisites of Communism' [n.d., published posthumously] = *BAWS* 3.2

———, 'Manu and the Shudras' in *BAWS* 12.6 ('Miscellaneous Notes'), 719–25

———, *Pakistan or the Partition of India: The Indian Political What's What!* [1946 edn] = *BAWS* 8

———, 'Philosophy of Hinduism' = *BAWS* 3.1

———, 'Revolution and Counter-Revolution' = *BAWS* 3.3

———, *The Untouchables: Who Were They and Why They Became Untouchables?* [1948 edn], in *BAWS* 7, 233–382

———, *What Congress and Gandhi Have Done to the Untouchables* [1945] = *BAWS* 9.1

———, *Who Were the Shudras?* [2nd edn 1947], in *BAWS* 7, 11–227

Anon., *10th May 1911* (n.p., n.d.)

———, *Aankhon ki Gawaahi* (An eyewitness account) (n.p., n.d.)

———, 'Constitution of the Hindustan Republican Association', in Shiv Varma (ed.), *Selected Writings of Shaheed Bhagat Singh* (Kanpur: Samajwadi Sahitya Sadan, 1996), 140–43

———, 'Home Rule is "SVARAJYA"', *The Indian Sociologist* 3:3 (March 1907)

———, 'Pieces of Hate' *Time*, 27 January 1947, 14–17

Barkatullah, Mohammad, *The Khilafat* reprinted (Dacca: Society for Pakistan Studies, 1970)

BAWS = Ambedkar, *Dr Babasaheb Ambedkar: Writings and Speeches*, ed. Moon

Buchan, John, *Greenmantle* (London: Penguin Books, 2008 [1910])

Carter, Lionel (ed.), *Punjab Politics, 3 March–31 May 1947: At the Abyss: Governors' Fortnightly Reports and Other Key Documents* (New Delhi: Manohar, 2007)

———, *Punjab Politics, 1 June 1947–14 August 1947: Tragedy: Governors' Fortnightly Reports and Other Key Documents* (New Delhi: Manohar, 2007)

Chirol, Valentine, *Indian Unrest* (London: Macmillan & Co., 1910)

CWMG = Gandhi, *Collected Works of Mahatma Gandhi*

CWSVP = Patel, *Collected Works of Sardar Vallabhbhai Patel*, ed. Chopra and Chopra

Dharmavira (ed.), *Letters of Lala Har Dayal* (Ambala: Indian Book Agency, 1970)

Divekar, V. D., *Lokmanya Tilak in England, 1918–19, Diary and Documents* (Pune: Tilak Samarak Trust, 1997)

Donogh, Walter Russell, *A Treatise on the Law of Sedition and Cognate Offences in British India, Penal and Preventive, with an Excerpt of the Acts in Force Relating to the Press, the Stage, and Public Meetings* (Calcutta: Thacker and Spink, 1911)

Gandhi, M. K., 'A Dialogue on the Compromise', in *CWMG* 8, 136–47

———, *All Men Are Brothers: Life and Thoughts of Mahatma Gandhi*, ed. Krishna Kripalani (Ahmedabad: Navajivan Publishing House, 1960)

———, 'Curzon Wyllie's Assassination', in *CWMG* 9, 302–3

———, *Hind Swaraj*, ed. Anthony J. Parel (Cambridge: Cambridge University Press, 2005 [1909]) [*HS*]

———, *Hindu Dharma* (Ahmedabad: Navajivan Publishing House, 1950)

———, 'Indian Economics', *Young India*, 8 December 1921, in *CWMG* 25, 213–16.

———, 'Interview to the Press', 20 September 1932, in *CWMG* 57, 94–98

———, 'Johannesburg Letter', in *CWMG* 8, 80–88

———, 'Letter to Jawaharlal Nehru', in *CWMG* 88, 94–95

———, 'One Year's Time-Limit', in *CWMG* 25, 227–30

———, *Satyagraha in South Africa*, trans. Valji Govindji Desai (Madras: S. Ganesan, 1928)

———, 'Speech at Madras', *The Hindu*, 15 September 1921, in *CWMG* 24, 238–46

———, 'Speech at the Minorities Committee Meeting', London, 13 November 1931, in *CWMG* 48, 293–98

———, 'Statement to the Press', 16 September 1932, in *CWMG* 57, 39–42

———, 'Statement to the Press', 23 September 1932, in *CWMG* 57, 109–10

———, 'Talk with Visitors', in *CWMG* 88, 116–17

———, *The Collected Works of Mahatma Gandhi*, www.gandhiserve.net/about-mahatma -gandhi/collected-works-of-mahatma-gandhi (100 vols; New Delhi: Government of India, 1960–94) [*CWMG*]

———, *To the Hindus and Muslims*, ed. Anand T. Hingorani (Allahabad: Allahabad Law Journal Press, 1942)

Godse, Gopal, *Gandhiji's Murder and After*, trans. S. T. Godbole (Delhi: Surya Prakashan, 1989)

Godse, Nathuram, *Why I Assassinated Mahatma Gandhi* (Delhi: Surya Bharti Parkashan, 2003)

Golwalkar, M. S., *Shri Guruji Samagrh: Prabodhan* (Collected works of M. S. Golwalkar, in Hindi] (3 vols; Noida: Suruchi Prakashan, n.d.)

Har Dayal, Lala, *Amrit Mein Vish . . .* (Calcutta: Vanik Press, 1922; in Hindi)

———, *Forty-Four Months in Germany and Turkey, February 1915 to October 1918: A Record of Personal Impressions* (London: P. S. King & Sons, 1920)

———, 'Some Aspects of Zionism', *The People*, 28 March 1926

———, *Hints for Self-Culture* (London: Watts & Co., 1934)

———, 'Marx a Modern Rishi', in Joshi and Damodaran (eds.), *Marx Comes to India*

———, *Our Educational Problem* (Madras: Tata Printing Works, 1922)

———, *The 10th of May*, (n.p., n.d.)

———, *The Yugantar Circular*, IOR Proscribed Publications Microfilms

———, *Writings of Har Dayal* (Benares: Swaraj Publishing House, 1922)

Iqbal, Muhammad, 'A Letter to *The Statesman*', [10 June 1935], in Iqbal, *Speeches, Writings*, 208–11

———, *Bang-i-Dara: The Call of the Marching Bell* [1924], in V. G. Kiernan (trans.), *Poems from Iqbal* (London: John Murray, 1955)

———, 'Divine Right to Rule' [1928], in Iqbal, *Speeches, Writings*, 163–67

———. 'Islam and Ahmadism' [1936], in Iqbal, *Speeches, Writings*, 214–40

———, 'Islam as a Moral and Political Ideal', in Iqbal, *Speeches, Writings*, 97–117

———, *Javid-Nama* [1932], trans. Arthur J. Arberry (London: George Allen & Unwin, 1966)

———, 'Jewish Integrity under Roman Rule' [1935], in Iqbal, *Speeches, Writings*, 211–14

———, *Letters and Writings of Iqbal*, ed. B. A. Dar (Karachi: Iqbal Academy, 1967)

———, *Letters of Iqbal to Jinnah with a Foreword by M. A. Jinnah* (Lahore: Ashraf Press, 1974 [1942])

———, 'Political Thought in Islam', in Iqbal, *Speeches, Writings*, 138–54

———, Presidential Address to the All-India Muslim League, Allahabad, 29 December 1930, in Pirzada (ed.), *Foundations of Pakistan*, 153–71

———, 'Qadianism and Orthodox Muslims' [1935], in Iqbal, *Speeches, Writings*, 197–203

———, *Shikwa and Jawab-i-Shikwa (Complaint and Answer): Iqbal's Dialogue with Allah*, trans. Khushwant Singh (Delhi: Oxford University Press, 1981)

———, *Speeches, Writings and Statements of Iqbal*, ed. Latif Ahmed Sherwani, revised 2nd edn (New Delhi: Adam Publishers, 2006 [1977; 1st edn 1944])

————, 'Statement on Islam and Nationalism in Reply to a Statement of Maulana Husain Ahmad', 9 March 1938, in Iqbal, *Speeches, Writings*, 300–313

————, 'Statement . . . regarding Pan-Islamism', 19 September 1933, in Iqbal, *Speeches, Writings*, 283–84

————, *Stray Reflections* [1910]: *The Private Notebook of Muhammad Iqbal*, ed. Javid Iqbal, 3rd edn (Lahore: Iqbal Academy, 2006)

————, 'The Muslim Community: A Sociological Study' [1910], in Iqbal, *Speeches, Writings*, 118–37

————, *The Mysteries of Selflessness: A Philosophical Poem*, trans. A. J. Arberry (London: John Murray, 1953)

————, *The Reconstruction of Religious Thought in Islam* (Lahore: Hafeez Press, 1977 [1931])

————, *The Secrets of the Self: Asrár-i Khudí*, trans. Reynold Nicholson (London: Macmillan & Co., 1920)

Isemonger F. C. and J. Slattery, *An Account of the Ghadar Conspiracy 1913–1915* (Archana Publications, Meerut, 2007 [Lahore, 1919])

Jinnah, Mohammad Ali, *The Collected Works of Quaid-e-Azam Mohammad Ali Jinnah*, vol. 1: *1906–1921*, ed. S. S. Pirzada (Karachi: East and West Publishing Co., 1984)

Kane, P. V., *History of the Dharmashastra* (3 vols; Poona: Bhandarkar Oriental Research Institute, 1930)

Kapur, J. L., *Report of the Commission of Enquiry into the Conspiracy to Murder Mahatma Gandhi* (New Delhi: Government of India, 1970)

Kelkar, N. C., *Trial of Tilak* (New Delhi: Publications Division, Ministry of Information and Broadcasting, Government of India, 1986 [1908])

Khan, Syed Ahmed, *The Causes of the Indian Revolt*, trans. G. Graham and A. Colvin (Karachi: Oxford University Press, 2000 [1873])

Kiernan, V. G., *Poems from Iqbal* (London: John Murray, 1955)

Lal, Gobind Behari, 'Detailed Account of the Ghadr Movement', in T. R. Sareen (ed.), *Select Documents of the Ghadr Party* (Delhi: Mountbo Publishing House, 1994)

Lenin, V. I., *The National Liberation Movement in the East*, trans. M. Levin (Moscow: Foreign Languages Publishing House, 1962)

MacMunn, G. F., *The Underworld of India* (London: Jarrolds, 1933)

Mansergh, Nicholas and Penderel Moon (eds.), *The Transfer of Power 1942–7: Constitutional Relations between Britain and India*, vol. 11: *The Mountbatten Viceroyalty: Announcement and Reception of the 3 June Plan, 31 May–7 July 1947* (London: HMSO, 1982)

Miyan Deobandi, Muhammad, *Silken Letters Movement: Accounts of 'Silken Handkerchief Letters Conspiracy Case' from British Records*, trans. Muhammadullah Qasmi (New Delhi: Shaikhul Hind Academy/Manak Publications, 2013)

Moonje, B. S., 'Militarisation', speech in Nasik, 12 July 1945, B. S. Moonje Papers, NMML

Nehru, Jawaharlal, Resolution in the Constituent Assembly of India, 13 December 1946, https://www.constitutionofindia.net/constitution_assembly_debates/volume/1/1946-12-13

————, *The Discovery of India* (New Delhi: Asia Publishing House, 1961 [1945])

————, 'The Solidarity of Islam', *Modern Review* 58:5 (1935), 504–7

O'Dwyer, Michael, *India as I Knew It: 1885–1925* (London: Constable & Co., 1926)

Pal, Bipin Chandra, *The Soul of India: A Constructive Study of Indian Thoughts and Ideals* (Calcutta: Choudhury & Choudhury, 1911)

Parmanand, Bhai, *Aapbiti: Kale Pani ki Karawas Kahani* (New Delhi: Prabhat Prakashan, 2007 [1934])

——, 'Pt. Madan Mohan Malaviya', *Hindu Outlook*, 22 July 1941

Patel, Vallabhbhai, *For a United India: Speeches of Sardar Patel, 1947–1950*, 3rd edn (Delhi: Publications Division, Government of India, 1967 [1st edn 1949])

——, *Sardar Patel: In Tune with the Millions*, vol. 1, ed. G. M. Nandurkar (Ahmedabad, Sardar Vallabhbhai Patel Samarak Bhavan, 1975)

——, *Select Correspondence of Sardar Patel, 1945–50*, vol. 2, ed. V. Shankar (Ahmedabad: Navajivan Publishing House, 1976)

——, *The Collected Works of Sardar Vallabhbhai Patel*, ed. P. N. Chopra and Prabha Chopra (15 vols; New Delhi: Konark Publishers, 1990–98) [*CWSVP*]

Pirzada, S. S. (ed.), *Foundations of Pakistan: All-India Muslim League Documents*, vol. 2: *1906–1947* (New Delhi: Metropolitan Book Co., 1982)

Prakash, Indra, *Where We Differ: The Congress and the Hindu Mahasabha* (Delhi: Federal Trade Press, 1942)

Pratap, Raja Mahendra, *My Life Story*, expanded edn, ed. Vir Singh (Delhi: Originals Publishers, 2004 [1943])

——, *Reflections of an Exile* (Lahore: Indian Book Company, 1946)

Pyarelal, *The Epic Fast* (New Delhi: Akhil Bharat Anusuchit Jati Parishad, 1984 [1932])

Rai, Lala Lajpat, *Young India: The Nationalist Movement* (New York: B. W. Huebesch, 1916)

Rowlatt, S.A.T. (committee president), *Sedition Committee Report, 1918* (Calcutta: New Age Publishers, 1973 [1918])

Roy, G. K., *Law Relating to Press and Sedition* (Simla, 1915)

Roy, M. N., *Memoirs* (Delhi: Ajanta Press, 1984)

Sarkar, Sumit (ed.), *Towards Freedom: Documents on the Movement for Independence in India, 1946* (New Delhi: Indian Council for Historical Research, and Oxford University Press, 2007–9)

Savarkar, S. S. and G. M. Joshi (eds.), *Historic Statements of V. D. Savarkar* (Bombay: Popular Prakashan, 1967)

Savarkar, V. D., *Essentials of Hindutva* (Delhi: Hindi Sahitya Sadan, 2005 [1923])

——, *Hindu-Pad-Padshahi, or, A Review of the Hindu Empire of Maharashtra* (New Delhi: Hindi Sahitya Sadan, 2003 [1925])

——, *Oath of Abhinav Bharat* (n.p, n.d.), IOR Proscribed Publications Microfilms

——, *Six Glorious Epochs of Indian History*, in V. D. Savarkar, *Selected Works of Veer Savarkar* (4 vols; Chandigarh: Abhishek Publications, 2007), vol. 3

——, *The Indian War of Independence: 1857* (Bombay: Phoenix Publications, 1947 [1909 (banned)])

——, *The Story of My Transportation for Life: A Biography of Black Days at Andamans* (Bombay: Sadbhakti Publications, 1950)

Sindhi, Ubaidullah, *Dhati Diary* (Lahore, 1946; in Urdu)

——, *Kabul Mein Sat Sal* (Lahore, 1955; in Urdu)

——, *Khulasat al-Quran* (Hyderabad, n.d.; in Urdu)

——, *Qurani Jang-e-Inqlab* (n.p. n.d.; in Urdu)

——, *Shah Walli Allah aur Unki Siyasi Tahrik* (Lahore, 1952; in Urdu)

——, *The Constitution of the Federated Republics of India* (Istanbul, 1926), trans. Zafar Hasan

Smith, W. C., *Modern Islam in India* (Lahore: Ashraf Press, 1963 [1943])

Sykes, Percy, *A History of Persia* (Oxford: Oxford University Press, 1922)

Tilak, B. G., *Bal Gangadhar Tilak: His Writings and Speeches* [with] *Appreciation by Babu Aurobindo Ghose*, 3rd edn (Madras: Ganesh & Co., 1922)

———, *Gita Rahasya or Karma Yoga Sastra*, trans. Bhalachandra Sitaram Suthankar (Poona: Vaibhav Press, 1935 [1915])

———, 'Home Rule Speech at Ahmednagar', 31 May 1916, in Tilak, *Bal Gangadhar Tilak*, 138–62

———, 'Home Rule Speech at Belgaum', 1 May 1916, in Tilak, *Bal Gangadhar Tilak*, 104–37

———, 'Is Shivaji Not a National Hero', in Tilak, *Bal Gangadhar Tilak*, 48–51

———, 'Our Gain at the Congress', speech in Calcutta, 2 January 1907, in Tilak, *Tilak's Speeches*

———, *Selected Documents of Lokmanya Tilak, 1880–1920*, ed. Ravindra Kumar (4 vols; New Delhi: Anmol Publications, 1992)

———, 'Tenets of the New Party', speech at Calcutta, 2 January 1907, in Tilak, *Bal Gangadhar Tilak*, 55–67

———, 'The Bharata Dharma Mahamandala', speech at Benares, 3 January 1906, in Tilak, *Bal Gangadhar Tilak*, 35–41

———, 'The Bomb Outrage and Its Lessons', *The Mahratta*, 10 May 1908

———, 'The Secret of the Bomb' ('Bambgolyaa chaa Kharaa Anth'), *Kesari*, 26 May 1908, in Kelkar, *Trial*, 351

———, 'These Remedies Are Not Lasting' ('Ha Upaay Tikau Naahint'), *Kesari*, 9 June 1908, in Kelkar, *Trial*, 319–24

———, *Tilak's Speeches* published by Raghunath Bhagvat (Poona: Sharda Press, 1908)

Waraich, Malwinder Jit Singh and Kuldip Puri, *Tryst with Martyrdom: Trial of Madan Lal Dhingra* (Chandigarh: Unistar, 2003)

Waraich, Malwinder Singh and Harinder Singh (eds.), *Ghadar Movement Original Documents*, vol 1: *Lahore Conspiracy Cases I and II* (Chandigarh: Unistar, 2008)

Newspapers and Magazines

Hindu Outlook
Hindustan Review
Islamic Fraternity
Modern Review
The Indian Sociologist
The Mahratta
The People
Time

Web Resources (Primary)

https://www.constitutionofindia.net/constitution_assembly_debates/
https://www.etymonline.com/
www.gandhiserve.net/about-mahatma-gandhi/
https://www.oldbaileyonline.org/index.jsp

Secondary Works Cited

Agamben, Giorgio, *Stasis: Civil War as a Political Paradigm*, trans. Nicholas Heron (Edinburgh: Edinburgh University Press, 2015)

Anderson, Benedict, *Under Three Flags: Anarchism and the Anti-Colonial Imagination* (London: Verso, 2005)

Anderson, Perry, *The Indian Ideology* (Delhi: Three Essays Collective, 2012)

Anderson, Walter, 'The Rashtriya Swayam Sangh', *Economic and Political Weekly* 7:11 (1972), 589–97

Anderson, Walter K. and Shridhar D. Damle, *The Brotherhood in Saffron: The Rashtriya Swayamsevak Sangh and Hindu Revivalism* (Boulder: Westview Press, 1987)

———, *The RSS: A View to the Inside* (New Delhi: Penguin Random House India, 2018)

Anghie, Anthony, *Imperialism, Sovereignty and the Making of International Law* (Cambridge: Cambridge University Press, 2007)

Ansari, Humayun, 'Maulana Barkatullah Bhopali's Transnationalism: Pan-Islamism, Colonialism and Radical Politics', in Gotz Nordbruch and Umar Ryad (eds.), *Transnational Islam in Interwar Europe* (New York: Palgrave Macmillan, 2014), 181–209

Appadurai, Arjun, 'Full Attachment', *Public Culture* 10:2 (1998), 443–49

———, 'Introduction', special issue on 'Failure', *Social Research* 83:3 (2016), xix–xxv

———, 'Number in the Colonial Imagination', in Carol Breckenridge and Peter van der Veer (eds.), *Orientalism and the Postcolonial Predicament* (Philadelphia: University of Pennsylvania Press, 1993), 314–39

Arendt, Hannah, *Crises of the Republic* (New York: Harvest Books, 1969)

———, *On Violence* (Orlando: Harcourt Publishing Co., 1970)

———, *On Revolution* (New York: Penguin Books, 2006 [1963])

Armitage, David, *Civil Wars: A History in Ideas* (New Haven, CT: Yale University Press, 2017)

Aydin, Cemil, *The Politics of Anti-Westernism in Asia: Visions of World Order in Pan-Islamic and Pan-Asian Thought* (New York: Columbia University Press, 2007)

Badiou, Alain, *Conditions*, trans. Steven Cochran (London: Continuum, 2008)

———, *Metapolitics*, trans. Jason Barker (London: Verso, 2011)

———, *Saint Paul: The Foundation of Universalism*, trans. Ray Brassier (Stanford: Stanford University Press, 2003)

———, *The Century*, trans. Alberto Toscano (Cambridge: Polity Press, 2007)

———et al., *What Is a People?* (New York: Columbia University Press, 2016)

Bailey, F. M. and Peter Hopkirk, *Mission to Tashkent* (Oxford: Oxford University Press, 2002)

Bajpai, Rochana, *Debating Difference: Group Rights and Liberal Democracy in India* (Oxford: Oxford University Press, 2011)

Bakhle, Janaki, 'Country First? Vinayak Damodar Savarkar (1883–1966) and the Writing of *Essentials of Hindutva*', *Public Culture* 22:1, 149–86

Balibar, Étienne, *Violence and Civility: On the Limits of Political Philosophy*, trans. G. M. Goshgarian (New York: Columbia University Press, 2015)

Banaji, Jairus (ed.), *Fascism: Essays on Europe and India* (New Delhi: Three Essays Collective, 2013)

Banerjee, Milinda, *The Mortal God: Imagining the Sovereign in Colonial India* (Cambridge: Cambridge University Press, 2017)

Banerjee, Partha, *In the Belly of the Beast: The Hindu Supremacist RSS and BJP of India: An Insider's Story* (Delhi: Ajanta Books, 1998)

Barrier, N. G., *Banned: Controversial Literature and Political Control in British India, 1907–1947* (Columbia: University of Missouri Press, 1974)

Barooah, Nirode K., *Chatto: The Life and Times of an Indian Anti-Imperialist in Europe* (Delhi: Oxford University Press, 2004)

———, *India and the Official Germany, 1886–1914* (Frankfurt: Peter Lang, 1977)

Basu, Tapan et al., *Khaki Shorts, Saffron Flags: A Critique of the Hindu Right* (New Delhi: Orient Longman, 1993)

Bayly, C. A., *Empire and Information: Intelligence Gathering and Social Communication in India* (Cambridge: Cambridge University Press, 1996)

———, *Origins of Nationality: Patriotism and Ethical Government in the Making of Modern India* (Oxford: Oxford University Press, 2001)

———, *Recovering Liberties: Indian Thought in the Age of Liberalism and Empire* (Cambridge: Cambridge University Press, 2011)

———, *Remaking the Modern World 1900–2015: Global Connections and Comparisons* (Hoboken, NJ: Wiley Blackwell, 2018)

Benton, Lauren, *A Search for Sovereignty: Law and Geography in European Empires* (Cambridge: Cambridge University Press, 2010)

Bhargava, Rajeev (ed.), *Secularism and Its Critics* (Delhi: Oxford University Press, 1998)

Bilgrami, Akeel, 'Gandhi the Philosopher', *Economic and Political Weekly* 27 (2003), 4159–65

Blom Hansen, Thomas, 'The Political Theology of Violence in India', *South Asia Multidisciplinary Academic Journal* special issue 2, http://samaj.revues.org/1872.html

———, *The Saffron Wave: Democracy and Hindu Nationalism in Modern India* (Princeton, NJ: Princeton University Press, 1999)

———, *Wages of Violence: Naming and Identity in Postcolonial Bombay* (Princeton, NJ: Princeton University Press, 2001)

Blom Hansen, Thomas, and Finn Stepputat, 'Sovereignty Revisited', *Annual Review of Anthropology* 35 (2006), 295–315

Bose, A. C., *Indian Revolutionaries Abroad* (Delhi: Northern Book Centre, 2002)

Brown, Emily C., *Har Dayal, Hindu Revolutionary and Rationalist* (Tucson: University of Arizona Press, 1975)

Butalia, Urvashi, *The Other Side of Silence: Voices from the Partition of India* (London: Hurst & Co., 2000)

Butler, Judith, *The Psychic Life of Power: Theories in Subjection* (Stanford: Stanford University Press, 1997)

Cartledge, Paul et al., 'Special Issue: David Armitage's *Civil Wars: A History in Ideas*', *Global Intellectual History* 3 (2018)

Cashman, Richard I., *The Myth of Lokmanya: Tilak and Mass Politics in Maharashtra* (Berkeley: University of California Press, 1975)

Casolari, Marzia, 'Hindutva's Foreign Tie-up in the 1930s: Archival Evidence', *Economic and Political Weekly* 35:4 (2000), 218–28

Catanach, Ian, 'Plague and the Tensions of Empire: India, 1896–1918', in David Arnold (ed.), *Imperial Medicine and Indigenous Societies* (Manchester: Manchester University Press, 1995), 149–71

Cháirez-Garza, Jesús, 'Nationalizing Untouchability: The Political Thought of B. R. Ambedkar, ca. 1917–56' (unpublished doctoral dissertation, University of Cambridge, 2014)

Chakrabarty, Dipesh, *The Calling of History: Sir Jadunath Sarkar and His Empire of Truth* (Chicago: University of Chicago Press, 2015)

Chandavarkar, Rajnarayan, *Imperial Power and Popular Politics: Class, Resistance and the State in India, 1880–1950* (Cambridge: Cambridge University Press, 1998)

Chandra, Bipan, *The Rise and Growth of Economic Nationalism in India* (New Delhi: People's Publishing House, 1966)

Chatterjee, Partha, *Nationalist Thought and the Colonial World: A Derivative Discourse* (London: Zed Books, 1993)

———, *The Nation and Its Fragments: Colonial and Post-Colonial Histories* (Princeton, NJ: Princeton University Press, 1993)

Chatterji, Joya, *Bengal Divided: Hindu Communalism and Partition 1932–1947* (Cambridge: Cambridge University Press, 1994)

Chaturvedi, Vinayak, 'Rethinking Knowledge with Action: V. D. Savarkar, the *Bhagavad Gita* and Histories of Warfare', in Kapila and Devji (eds.), *Political Thought in Action*

Clark, Christopher, *Time and Power: Visions of History in German Politics from the Thirty Years' War to the Third Reich* (Princeton, NJ: Princeton University Press, 2019)

———. 'Time of the Nazis', in Alexander C. T. Geppert and Till Kossler (eds.), *Obsession der Gegenwart* (Bristol, CT: Vandenhoeck & Ruprecht, 2015), 156–87

Copeman, Jacob, 'The Art of Bleeding: Memory, Martyrdom and Portraits in Blood', *Journal of the Royal Anthropological Institute* 19:1 (2013), 149–71

Copland, Ian, *The Princes of India in the Endgame of Empire, 1917–1947* (Cambridge: Cambridge University Press, 1997)

Das, Veena and Ashis Nandy, 'Violence, Victimhood and the Language of Silence', *Contributions to Indian Sociology* 19:1 (1985), 177–95

Dasgupta, Swapan, *Awakening Bharat Mata: The Political Beliefs of the Indian Right* (New Delhi: Penguin Books, 2019)

de Vries, Hent and Lawrence E. Sullivan (eds.), *Political Theologies: Public Religions in a Post-Secular World* (New York: Fordham University Press, 2006)

Devji, Faisal, 'Gandhi, Hinduism and Humanity', in Gavin Flood (ed.), *Hindu Practice: The Oxford History of Hinduism* (Oxford: Oxford University Press, 2020), 375–97

———, *Landscapes of the Jihad: Militancy, Morality, Modernity* (London: Hurst & Co., 2005)

———, *Muslim Zion: Pakistan as a Political Idea* (London: Hurst & Co., 2013)

———, *The Impossible Indian: Gandhi and the Temptations of Violence* (London: Hurst & Co., 2012)

———, *The Terrorist in Search of Humanity: Militant Islam and Global Politics* (London: Hurst & Co., 2008)

Dharamvir, *Lala Har Dayal: Prassidh Deshbkta . . .* (Delhi: Rajpal & Sons, 1970; in Hindi)

Dharamvira, *I Threw the Bomb: The Revolutionary Life of Rash Behari Bose* (Delhi: Orient Paperbacks, 1979)

Dhulipala, Venkat, *The New Medina: State Power, Islam and the Quest for Pakistan in Late Colonial North India* (Cambridge: Cambridge University Press, 2015)

Dmitriev, G., *Indian Revolutionaries in Central Asia* (Gurgaon: Hope India Publications, 2002)

Dzelzainis, Martin, 'Managing the Later Stuart Press 1662–1696', in Lorna Hutson (ed.), *The Oxford Handbook of English Law and Literature* (Oxford: Oxford University Press, 2017), 530–45

Edney, Matthew, *Mapping an Empire: The Geographical Construction of India* (Chicago: London, University of Chicago Press, 1997)

Elam, Daniel J., 'The Anticolonial Ethics of Lala Har Dayal's *Hints for Self-Culture*', NMML Occasional Paper 9 (New Delhi: Nehru Memorial Museum and Library, 2013)

Elenjimittam, Anthony, *Philosophy and Action of the RSS for the Hind Swaraj* (Bombay: Laxmi Publications, 1951)

Fischer-Tiné, Harald, *Shyamji Krishnavarma: Sanskrit, Sociology and Anti-Imperialism* (Delhi: Routledge India, 2014)

Foucault, Michel, *Hermeneutics of the Subject*, trans. Graham Burchell (New York: Picador, 2005)

Frazer, Michael L., 'Strauss and Esotericism Ancient and Modern: Strauss and Contra Straussianism on the Art of Political-Philosophical Writing', *Political Theory* 34:1 (2006), 33–61

Freitag, Sandra B., *Collective Action and Community: Public Arenas and the Emergence of Communalism in North India* (Berkeley: University of California Press, 1989)

Freud, Sigmund, *Civilization and Its Discontents* [1930], trans. David McLintock (Penguin Books, 2002)

———, *Mass Psychology* [1921] *and Other Writings*, trans. J. A. Underwood (London: Penguin Books, 2014)

———, *The Origins of Religion: 'Totem and Taboo'* [1913], *'Moses and Monotheism'* [1939] *and Other Works* (The Pelican Freud Library, trans. gen. ed. James Strachey, vol. 13, ed. Albert Dickson) (Harmondsworth: Penguin Books, 1985)

———, 'Why War?' [1933] in Sigmund Freud, *On Murder, Mourning and Melancholia: The New Penguin Freud*, trans. Shaun Whiteside (The New Penguin Freud, ed. Adam Phillips) (London: Penguin Books, 2005)

Gallagher, John, *The Decline, Revival and Fall of the British Empire: The Ford Lectures and Other Essays* (Cambridge: Cambridge University Press, 1982)

Gandhi, Rajmohan, *Patel: A Life* (Ahmedabad: Navajivan Press, 1991)

Ganeri, Jonardon, *The Concealed Art of the Soul: Theories of Self and Practices of Truth in Indian Ethics and Epistemology* (Oxford: Oxford University Press, 2007)

Gassem-Fachandi, P., 'Ahimsa, Identification and Sacrifice', *Social Anthropology* 18:2 (2010), 155–75

Geppert, Alexander C. T. and Till Kossler (eds.), *Obsession der Gegenwart* (Bristol, CT: Vandenhoeck & Ruprecht, 2015)

Ghosh, Durba, *Gentlemanly Terrorists: Political Violence and the Colonial State in India, 1919–1947* (Cambridge: Cambridge University Press, 2017)

Girard, René, *Violence and the Sacred*, trans. Patrick Gregory (London: Bloomsbury Press, 2013 [1977])

Gould, William, 'Hindu Militarism and Partition in 1940s Uttar Pradesh: Rethinking the Politics of Violence and Scale', *South Asia* 42:1 (2019), 134–51

Grewal, J. S., Harish K. Puri and Indu Banga (eds.), *The Ghadar Movement: Background, Ideology, Actions and Legacies* (Patiala: Patiala University Publication Bureau, 2013)

Gupta, Charu, *Sexuality, Obscenity, Community: Women, Muslims and the Hindu Public in Colonial India* (London: Palgrave, 2001)

Hardiman, David, *Gandhi in His Time and Ours: The Global Legacy of His Ideas* (New York: Columbia University Press, 2004)

Harper, R.W.E. and Henry Miller, *Singapore Mutiny* (Singapore: Oxford University Press, 1984)

Harper, Tim, 'Singapore, 1915 and the Birth of the Asian Underground', *Modern Asian Studies* 47:6 (2013), 1782–1811

Hartog, François, *Regimes of Historicity: Presentism and the Experience of Time*, trans. Saskia Brown (New York: Columbia University Press, 2015)

Herdt, Gilbert, *Secrecy and Cultural Reality: Utopian Ideologies of the New Guinea's Men's House* (Ann Arbor: University of Michigan Press, 2003)

Hofmeyer, Isabel, *Gandhi's Printing Press: Experiments in Slow Reading* (Cambridge, MA: Harvard University Press, 2013)

Honig, Bonnie, *Democracy and the Foreigner* (Princeton, NJ: Princeton University Press, 2003)

Hussain, Adeel, 'Legal Antagonism and the Making of Muslim Political Thought in India' (unpublished doctoral dissertation, University of Cambridge, 2017)

Ibbetson, David, 'Edward Coke, Roman Law and the Law of Libel', in Lorna Hutson (ed.), *The Oxford Handbook of English Law and Literature* (Oxford: Oxford University Press, 2017), 487–506

Inden, Ronald, 'Paradise on Earth: The Deccan Sultanates', in Daud Ali and Emma J. Flatt (eds.), *Gardens and Landscape Practices in Precolonial India: Histories from the Deccan* (London: Routledge, 2011), ch. 4

Inqalabi, Kirat Singh (ed.), *Gadhri Yodha Shaheed Kartar Singh Sarabha* (Delhi: Delhi Book Shop, 2014)

Irfan, M., *Maulana Barkatullah Bhopali* (Bhopal: n.p, 1969)

Jafferlot, Christophe, *The Hindu Nationalist Movement in India* (New York: Columbia University Press, 1996)

Jalal, Ayesha, 'Striking a Just Balance: Maulana Azad as a Theorist of Trans-National *Jihad*, *Modern Intellectual History* 4:1 (2007), 95–107

——, *The Sole Spokesman: Jinnah, the Muslim League and the Demand for Pakistan* (Cambridge: Cambridge University Press, 1985)

Jan, Ammar Ali, 'A Study of Communist Thought in India, 1919–1951' (unpublished doctoral dissertation, University of Cambridge, 2017)

Jay, Martin, *Songs of Experience: Modern American and European Versions of a Universal Theme* (Berkeley: University of California Press, 2005)

Jones, Kenneth, *Socio-Religious Reform Movements in British India* (Cambridge: Cambridge University Press, 1989)

Joshi, P. C. and K. Damodaran (eds.), *Marx Comes to India: Earliest Indian Biographies* (Delhi: Manohar Book Service, 1975)

Kahn, Paul W., *Out of Eden: Adam and Eve and the Problem of Evil* (Princeton, NJ: Princeton University Press, 2007)

——. *Putting Liberalism in Its Place* (Princeton, NJ: Princeton University Press, 2008)

——. *Sacred Violence: Torture, Terror and Sovereignty* (Ann Arbor: University of Michigan Press, 2008)

Kantorowicz, Ernst, *The King's Two Bodies: A Study of Medieval Theology* (Princeton, NJ: Princeton University Press, 1957)

Kapila, Shruti, 'A History of Violence', *Modern Intellectual History* 7:2 (2010), 437–57

——, 'Ambedkar's Agonism: Sovereign Violence and Pakistan as Peace', *Comparative Studies in Study of South Asia, Africa and the Middle East* 39:1 (2019), 183–95

——, 'Gandhi before Mahatma: The Foundations of Political Truth', *Public Culture* 23:2 (2011), 431–48

——, 'Global Intellectual History and the Indian Political', in Darrin McMahon and Samuel Moyn (eds.), *Rethinking Modern European Intellectual History* (New York: Oxford University Press, 2014), 253–74

——, 'Self, Spencer and Swaraj: Nationalist Thought and Critiques of Liberalism 1890–1920', *Modern Intellectual History* 4:1 (2007), 109–27

——, 'The Majority of Democracy', *Social Text* (Periscope digital issue on 'Politics under Modi'), 27 February 2015, https://socialtextjournal.org/periscope_article/the-majority-of-democracy/

——, 'The Time of Global Politics', in John Robertson (ed.), *Political Thought, Time and History* (Cambridge: Cambridge University Press, forthcoming)

Kapila, Shruti and Faisal Devji, 'The *Bhagavad Gita* and Modern Thought: Introduction', *Modern Intellectual History* 7:2 (2010), 269–73

Kapila, Shruti and Faisal Devji (eds.), *Political Thought in Action: The* Bhagavad Gita *and Modern India* (Cambridge: Cambridge University Press, 2013)

Kaur, Raminder and William Mazzeralla (eds.), *Censorship in South Asia: Cultural Regulation from Sedition to Seduction* (Bloomington: Indiana University Press, 2009)

Kaviraj, Sudipta, *Imaginary Institution of India: Politics and Ideas* (New York: Columbia University Press, 2010)

Keddie, Nikki R., *An Islamic Response to Imperialism: Political and Religious Writings of Sayyid Jamal al Din 'al-Afghani'* (Berkeley: University of California Press, 1968)

Keer, Dhananjay, *Lokmanya Tilak: Father of Our Freedom Struggle* (Bombay: S. B. Kangutkar, 1959)

——, *Savarkar and His Times* (Bombay: A. V. Keer, 1950)

Khan, Yasmin, 'Performing Peace: Gandhi's Assassination as a Critical Moment on the Consolidation of the Nehruvian State', *Modern Asian Studies* 45:1 (2011), 57–80

Khosla, G. D., *The Murder of the Mahatma and Other Cases from a Judge's Notebook* (London: Chatto and Windus, 1963)

Koselleck, Reinhart, *The Practice of Conceptual History: Timing, History, Spacing Concepts*, trans. Todd Samuel Presner et al. (Stanford: Stanford University Press, 2002)

Kumar, Aishwary, *Radical Equality: Ambedkar, Gandhi and the Risk of Democracy* (Stanford: Stanford University Press, 2015)

Kumarasingham, Harshan, *A Political Legacy of the British Empire: Power and Parliamentary System in Postcolonial India and Sri Lanka* (London: I. B. Tauris, 2013)

Kuwajima, Sho, *Mutiny in Singapore: War, Anti-War and the War for India's Independence* (Delhi: Rainbow Publishers, 2006)

Lacan, Jacques, *On the Names-of-the-Father*, trans. Bruce Fink (Cambridge: Polity Press, 2013)

————, *The Four Fundamentals of Psychoanalysis*, trans. Alan Sheridan (London: Penguin Books, 1984)

————, *The Seminar of Jacques Lacan, Book VII: The Ethics of Psychoanalysis*, trans. Jacques-Alain Miller (London: Routledge, 2008 [1992]) / https://www.lacan.com/symptom/extimity.html

Lahiri, Nayanjot, *Ashoka in Ancient India* (Cambridge, MA: Harvard University Press, 2015)

Le Bon, Gustave, *The Crowd: A Study of the Popular Mind* (Createspace Independent Publishing Platform, 2018 [1895])

Leader, Darian, 'The Real, the Symbolic and the Imaginary' CFAR Lecture Series, London, 2015–16 (unpublished)

Lipping, Jüri, 'Sovereignty beyond the State', in Hent Kalmo and Quentin Skinner (eds.), *Sovereignty in Fragments: The Past, Present and Future of a Contested Concept* (Cambridge: Cambridge University Press, 2013), 186–204

Lukes, Steven, *Power: A Radical View* (London: Palgrave, 2005, [1974])

Majeed, Javed, *Autobiography, Travel and Postnational Identity: Gandhi, Nehru and Iqbal* (London: Palgrave, 2007)

————, *Muhammad Iqbal: Islam, Aesthetics and Postcolonialism* (Delhi: Routledge India, 2009)

Malgaonkar, Manohar, *The Men Who Killed the Mahatma* (Delhi: Macmillan, 1978)

Manjapra, Kris, *Age of Entanglement: German and Indian Intellectuals across Empire* (Cambridge, MA: Harvard University Press, 2014)

Masselos, Jim, 'Social Segregation and Crowd Cohesion: Reflections around Some Preliminary Data from 19th Century Bombay City', *Contributions to Indian Sociology* 13:2 (1979), 145–67

Matilal, Bimal Krishna, *The Collected Essays of Bimal Krishna Matilal*, ed. Jonardon Ganeri, vol. 2: *Ethics and Epics* (Delhi: Oxford University Press, 2017)

Mazower, Mark, 'Violence and the State in the Twentieth Century', *American Historical Review*, 2002 107: 4, 1158–78

McClure, Alastair, 'Violence, Sovereignty and the Making of Colonial Criminal Law in India, 1857–1914' (unpublished doctoral dissertation, University of Cambridge, 2017)

McMeeken, Sean, *The Berlin–Baghdad Express: The Ottoman Empire and Germany's Bid for World Power, 1898–1918* (London: Allen Lane, 2010)

McQuade, Joseph, 'Terrorism, Law and Sovereignty in India and the League of Nations, 1897–1945' (unpublished doctoral dissertation, University of Cambridge, 2017)

Mehta, Uday Singh, 'Gandhi on Democracy, Politics and the Ethics of Everyday Life', in Kapila and Devji (eds.), *Political Thought in Action*, 88–106

————, *Liberalism and Empire: A Study in Nineteenth- Century British Liberal Thought* (Chicago: University of Chicago Press, 1999)

————, 'Patience, Inwardness, and Self-Knowledge in Gandhi's *Hind Swaraj*', *Public Culture* 23:2 (2011), 417–30

————, 'The Social Question and the Absolutism of Politics', *Seminar* 615 (November 2010), https://www.india-seminar.com/2010/615/615_uday_s_mehta.htm

Menon, V. P., *Integration of the Indian States* (London: Longmans, 1956)

————, *The Transfer of Power in India* (London: Longmans, 1957)

Metcalf, Barbara D., *Islamic Revival in British India: Deoband, 1860–1900* (Princeton, NJ: Princeton University Press, 1982)

Miller, John, *Egotopia: Narcissism and the New American Landscape* (Tuscaloosa: University of Alabama Press, 1997)

Mishra, Pankaj, *From the Ruins of Empire: The Intellectuals Who Remade Asia* (London: Allen Lane, 2012)

——, 'Gandhi for the Post-Truth Age', *The New Yorker*, 22 October 2018

Moffat, Chris, *India's Revolutionary Inheritance: Politics and the Promise of Bhagat Singh* (Cambridge: Cambridge University Press, 2019)

Moon, Penderel, *Divide and Quit* (London: Chatto & Windus, 1961)

Motadel, David (ed.), *Islam in European Empires* (Oxford: Oxford University Press, 2014)

Mouffe, Chantal, *Agonistics: Thinking the World Politically* (London: Verso, 2013)

——, *Democratic Paradox* (London: Verso, 2005)

——, *On the Political (Thinking in Action)* (Abingdon: Routledge, 2005)

Mukherjee, Janam, *Hungry Bengal: War, Famine, Riots and the End of Empire* (London: Hurst & Co., 2015)

Mukherjee, Mithi, *India in the Shadows of Empire: A Legal and Political History, 1774–1950* (Oxford: Oxford University Press, 2010)

Nagaraj, D. R., *The Flaming Feet and Other Essays: The Dalit Movement in India* (Ranikhet: Permanent Black, 2010)

Nandy, Ashis, 'An Anti-Secularist Manifesto', *India International Centre Quarterly* 22:1 (1995), 35–64

——, 'Final Encounter: The Politics of Assassination of Gandhi', in Ashis Nandy, *At the Edge of Psychology: Essays in Politics and Culture* (Delhi: Oxford University Press, 1999), 7–98.

——, *The Intimate Enemy: Loss and Recovery of Self under Colonialism* (Oxford: Oxford University Press, 1983)

Nasr, S.V.R., *Mawdudi and the Making of Islamic Revivalism* (Oxford: Oxford University Press, 2001)

Negri, Antonio, 'Sovereignty between Government, Exception and Governance', in Hent Kalmo and Quentin Skinner (eds.), *Sovereignty in Fragments: The Past, Present and Future of a Contested Concept* (Cambridge: Cambridge University Press, 2013), 205–21

Noorani, A. G., *Savarkar and Hindutva: The Godse Connection* (New Delhi: Leftworld Books, 2002)

Nussbaum, Martha, *The Clash Within: Democracy, Religious Violence and India's Future* (Cambridge, MA: Harvard University Press, 2007)

Pandey, Gyanendra, *Remembering Partition: Violence, Nationalism and History in India* (Cambridge: Cambridge University Press, 2001)

——, *The Construction of Communalism in Colonial North India* (Delhi: Oxford University Press, 1990)

——(ed.), *Hindus and Others: The Question of Identity in India Today* (New Delhi: Viking,1993)

Pinney, Christopher, 'Iatrogenic Religion and Politics', in Kaur and Mazzeralla (eds.), *Censorship in South Asia*

————, *Photos of the Gods: The Printed Image and Political Struggle in India* (London: Reaktion Books, 2004)

Pitts, Jennifer, *A Turn to Empire: The Rise of Imperial Liberalism in Britain and France* (Princeton, NJ: Princeton University Press, 2005)

Poplewell, Richard J., *Intelligence and Imperial Defence: British Intelligence and the Defence of the Indian Empire* (London: Routledge, 1995)

Prakash, Gyan, *Another Reason: Science and Reason in the Imagination of Modern India* (Princeton, NJ: Princeton University Press, 1999)

Puri, Harish K., *Ghadar Movement: Ideology, Organisation and Strategy* (Amritsar: Guru Nanak Dev University Press, 1983)

Purushotham, Sunil, *From Raj to Republic: Sovereignty, Violence, and Democracy in India* (Stanford: Stanford University Press, 2021)

Ram, Kanshi, *The Chamcha Age: An Era of Stooges* (New Delhi: Vedic Mudranalaya, 1982)

Ramaswamy, Sumathi, *The Goddess and the Nation: Mapping Mother India* (Durham, NC: Duke University Press, 2010)

Ramnath, Maia, *Haj to Utopia: How the Ghadar Movement Charted Global Radicalism and Attempted to Overthrow the British Empire* (Berkeley: University of California Press, 2011)

Rosanvallon, Pierre, *Democracy Past and Future*, trans. Samuel Moyn (New York: Columbia University Press, 2006)

Roy, Arundhati (ed.), *The Annihilation of Caste: The Doctor and the Saint* (London: Verso, 2014)

Rudolph, Lloyd I. and Susanne Hoeber Rudolph, *The Postmodern Gandhi and Other Essays: Gandhi in the World and at Home* (Chicago: University of Chicago Press, 2006)

Ruehl, Martin A., '"In This Time of No Emperors": The Politics of Ernst Kantorowicz's *Kaiser Friedrich der Zweite* Reconsidered', *Journal of the Warburg and Courtauld Institutes* 63 (2000), 187–242

Ruprecht, Adrian P., 'De-Centering Humanitarianism: The Red Cross and India, c. 1877–1939' (unpublished doctoral dissertation, University of Cambridge, 2017)

Rust, Jennifer, 'Political Theologies of the *Corpus Mysticum*: Schmitt, Kantorowicz and de Lubac', in Graham Hammill and Julia Reinhard Lupton (eds.), *Political Theology and Early Modernity* (Chicago: University of Chicago Press, 2012), 102–23

Sabastian, Luna, 'Indian Political Thought and Germany's Fascism, ca. 1918–1950' (unpublished doctoral dissertation, University of Cambridge, 2020)

Sarkar, Sumit, *The Swadeshi Movement in Bengal, 1903–1908* (New Delhi: People's Publishing House, 1973)

Sawhney, Savitri, *I Shall Never Ask for Pardon: A Memoir of Pandurang Khankhoje* (Delhi: Penguin Books, 2008)

Saxena, Shyam Sundar, *Barkatullah Bhopali* (Bhopal: Swaraj Sansathan Sanchalya, Government of Madhya Pradesh, 2004; in Hindi)

Schmitt, Carl, *Political Theology: Four Chapters on the Concept of Sovereignty* [1922], trans. George Schwab (Cambridge, MA: MIT Press, 1986)

————, *Roman Catholicism and Political Form* [1923], trans. G. L. Ulmen (Westport, CT: Greenwood Press, 1996)

————, *The Concept of the Political* [1932], trans. George Schwab (Chicago: University of Chicago Press, 1996)

———, *Theory of the Partisan: Intermediate Commentary on the Concept of the Political* [1963], trans. G. L. Ulmen (New York: Telos Press, 2007)

Sen, Satadru: 'Fascism without Fascists? A Comparative Look at Hindutva and Zionism', *South Asia* 38:4 (2015), 690–711

Sengupta, Hindol, *The Man Who Saved India: Sardar Patel and His Idea of India* (New Delhi: Penguin Random House India, 2018)

Seshadri, H. V. (ed.), *Dr Hedgewar, The Epoch Maker: A Biography* (Bangalore: Sahitya Sindhu, 1981)

———, *RSS: A Vision in Action* (Bangalore: Sahitya Sindhu Prakshana, 2000)

Sevea, Iqbal Singh, *The Political Philosophy of Muhammad Iqbal: Islam and Nationalism in Late Colonial India* (Cambridge: Cambridge University Press, 2012)

Shaikh, Muhammad Hajjan, *Maulana Ubaid Allah Sindhi: A Revolutionary Scholar* (Islamabad: National Institute of Historical and Cultural Research, 1986)

Simmel, George, 'The Sociology of Secrecy and of Secret Societies', *American Journal of Sociology* 11:4 (1906), 441–98

Singh, Guracharan, *Vir Nayak Kartar Singh Sarabha* (Patiala: Punjabi University, Publications Bureau, 1994)

Singh, Iqbal, *The Ardent Pilgrim: An Introduction to the Life and Work of Muhammad Iqbal* (Delhi: Oxford University Press, 1997 [1951])

Sinha, Mrinalani (ed.), *Selections from 'Mother India' by Katherine Mayo* (New Delhi: Kali for Women, 1998)

Skaria, Ajay, 'Gandhi's Politics: Liberalism and the Question of the Ashram', *South Atlantic Quarterly* 101:4 (Fall 2002), 955–86

———, 'Gandhi's Radical Conservatism', *Seminar*, https://www.india-seminar.com/2014/662/662_ajay_skaria.htm

———, *Unconditional Equality: Gandhi's Religion of Resistance* (Minneapolis: University of Minnesota Press, 2016)

Skinner, Quentin, *Hobbes and Republican Liberty* (Cambridge: Cambridge University Press, 2008)

———, 'Hobbes on Sovereignty: An Unknown Discussion', *Political Studies* 13:2 (1965), 213–18

———, *Visions of Politics*, vol. 1: *Regarding Method* (Cambridge: Cambridge University Press, 2002)

Strauss, Leo, *Persecution and the Art of Writing* (Chicago: University of Chicago Press, 1988)

———, *The Political Philosophy of Hobbes: Its Basis and Genesis* (Chicago: University of Chicago Press, 1952)

Taheri, Alireza, 'Of Fathers and Sons: From the Name/No Name of the Father to the Paradoxes of Paternity', *Journal of the Centre for Freudian Analysis and Research* 27 (2016), 65–89

Tambiah, Stanley, *Leveling Crowds: Ethnonationalist Conflicts and Collective Violence in South Asia* (Berkeley: University of California Press, 1996)

Tan, Tai Yong and Gyanesh Kudaisya, *The Aftermath of Partition in South Asia* (London: Routledge, 2000)

Taylor, Charles, *A Secular Age* (Cambridge, MA: Harvard University Press, 2007)

Thapar, Romila, *Asoka and the Decline of the Mauryas* (Delhi: Oxford University Press, 1997)

Troll, C. W., *Sayyid Ahmad Khan: A Reinterpretation of Muslim Theology* (Delhi: Oxford University Press, 1978)

Tuck, Richard, *The Sleeping Sovereign: The Invention of Modern Democracy* (Cambridge: Cambridge University Press, 2016)

Tully, James, *Public Philosophy in a New Key* (Cambridge: Cambridge University Press, 2008)

———, *Strange Multiplicity: Constitutionalism in the Age of Diversity* (Cambridge: Cambridge University Press, 1995)

Visana, Vikram, 'Liberalism, Imperial Citizenship and Indian Self-Government in the Political Thought of Dadabhai Naoroji' (unpublished doctoral dissertation, University of Cambridge, 2016)

Vogelsang, Willem, *The Afghans* (Oxford: Blackwell, 2002)

Wagner, Kim A., *Jallianwala Bagh: An Empire of Fear and the Making of the Amritsar Massacre* (Delhi: Penguin Random House India, 2019)

Wolpert, Stanley, *Tilak and Gokhale: Revolution and Reform in the Making of Modern India* (Berkeley: University of California Press, 1962)

Yajnik, Indulal K., *Gandhi as I Know Him*, rev. enlarged edn (Delhi: Danish Mahal, 1943)

———, *Shyamji Krishnavarma: Life and Times of an Indian Revolutionary* (Bombay: Lakshmi Publications, 1950)

Zaman, Faridah, 'Futurity and the Political Thought of North Indian Muslims' (unpublished doctoral dissertation, University of Cambridge, 2014)

———, 'Revolutionary History and the Post-Colonial Muslim: Re-Writing the "Silk Letters Conspiracy" of 1916', *Journal of Asian Studies* 39:3 (2016), 626–43

Žižek, Slavoj, *How to Read Lacan* (London: Granta Books, 2006)

———, 'The Big Other Doesn't Exist', *Journal of European Psychoanalysis* (Spring/Fall, 1997), www.lacan.com/zizekother.com

———, *The Sublime Object of Ideology* (London: Verso Books, 1989)

———, *Violence: Six Sideways Reflections* (London: Profile Books, 2008)

Web Sources (Secondary)

www.bbc.co.uk

https://www.lacan.com/

https://www.india-seminar.com

https://socialtextjournal.org/periscope/

https://journals.openedition.org/samaj/

INDEX

Nandy, Ashis, 8, 126

Naoroji, Dadabhai, 102, 138

nationalism, 5, 12–13, 19, 57–58, 67, 75, 87, 104, 118, 130, 134, 149, 186, 224, 266

nationality, 182–83, 205, 226

Nazism, 1, 104, 113, 168, 173, 178. *See also* fascism

Nehru, Jawaharlal, 5, 11, 106–9, 179, 186, 209, 224, 229, 233–34, 241–44, 247–50, 254, 256, 265–68, 274

Nehru, Motilal, 201

neo-Hinduism, 102. *See also* Hinduism

Nietzsche, 42, 44n84, 67–68, 86, 165, 174, 178, 278

Non-Cooperation campaign, 148

Non-Cooperation movement, 201

non-violence, 3–4, 44–45, 109, 131, 131n5, 147–48, 164, 177, 250, 252–53. *See also* Gandhi, Mohandas; violence

O'Dwyer, Michael, 57

Open Conspiracy, The, 86

Pakistan: compared to Israel, 185; formation of, 3, 5, 9, 127, 181, 198, 215, 234, 251, 257, 261, 264–65, 280; hostility with India, 267; idea of, 163, 165–66, 180–81, 184, 188, 192, 194–95, 228, 236; loyalty to, 263; and migration, 230, 251; and Muslim nationality, 191; and possibility of peace, 188; recognition of, 183, 189, 191. *See also* India; partition

Pakistan or the Partition of India (Ambedkar), 180

Pan-Asianism, 80

Pan-Islamism, 7, 20, 58, 76–79, 82, 116, 205–6, 278. *See also* Islam

Pant, G. B., 264

Parmanand, Bhai, 124

partition: as civil war, 237; effects of, 3, 52, 262; interpretations of, 181; perceptions of, 191, 236, 240, 248, 254–55, 257, 264, 267, 279; proposal of, 246–47, 254, 258; simultaneity with independence, 234; violence of, 10, 230, 238. *See also* borders; India; Indian civil war; Pakistan

Pasha, Enver, 75

Patel, Sardar: and the British Empire, 243; influence of, 2, 10–12, 247, 249–50, 254, 257, 261–62, 268, 275; political thought of, 260, 278; reputation of, 229–30, 236–37, 246, 254, 262, 265–66; and widespread violence, 242

people (political category): as basic unit, 164; danger of, 262; formation of, 10, 115, 192, 230, 279; and social life, 170; and sovereignty, 183, 235, 273–74; unity of, 259–61; and violence, 232, 270

Pinney, Christopher, 23, 30

political parties, 120, 242, 244, 256

political subjects, 6–7, 38, 42, 59, 65, 67, 70, 74, 87, 95, 108, 142, 198

political theology, 16–17, 23–24, 28, 34, 50, 275–76

politics: and enmity, 44–45, 132; and ethics, 67, 135n12; perceptions of, 8; and religion, 207, 212, 217, 265

politics of truth, 131–33, 137, 161, 250, 276

Poona Pact, 158–59, 163–64, 181, 185, 220. *See also* Ambedkar, B. R.; Gandhi, Mohandas

Pratap, Mahendra, 75, 78, 80–81

privation, 114–15

Provisional Government of India, 78, 81–83

psychoanalysis, 1, 93–94, 126–27, 151

Purushotham, Sunil, 269

Pushyamita, King, 176

race, 86, 104, 113, 141, 171, 175, 175n41, 205. *See also* miscegenation

Rai, Lajpat, 122

Rana, Sardar, 66

Rand, Walter Charles, 25–26, 55–56, 74

realpolitik, 3, 12–13, 231–32

Reconstruction of Religious Thought in Islam, The (Iqbal), 203

refugees, 247n50

religion: distinctions of, 165; and enmity, 106; and politics, 16–17, 23–24, 207, 212, 217, 265; and territoriality, 111. *See also* atheism; Buddhism; divinity; Hinduism; Islam

GPSR Authorized Representative: Easy Access System Europe - Mustamäe tee
50, 10621 Tallinn, Estonia, gpsr.requests@easproject.com

www.ingramcontent.com/pod-product-compliance
Lightning Source LLC
Chambersburg PA
CBHW020824270326
41928CB00006B/437